I0868657

The Roman Impact on the Economy of the Lower Germanic Limes Region

Impact of Empire

ROMAN EMPIRE, C. 200 B.C.–A.D. 476

Edited by

Olivier Hekster
(*Radboud University, Nijmegen, The Netherlands*)

Editorial Board

Stéphane Benoist
Lien Foubert
Marietta Horster
Anne Kolb
Luuk de Ligt
Elio Lo Cascio
Bernhard Palme
Michael Peachin
Francisco Pina Polo
Rubina Raja
Christian Witschel
Greg Woolf

VOLUME 48

The titles published in this series are listed at *brill.com/imem*

The Roman Impact on the Economy of the Lower Germanic Limes Region

By

Erik Timmerman

BRILL

LEIDEN | BOSTON

Cover illustration: A depiction of the *vallus* on a second century AD bas-relief found at Buzenol.
Image courtesy of the Musée Gaumais

The Library of Congress Cataloging-in-Publication Data is available online at https://catalog.loc.gov
LC record available at https://lccn.loc.gov/2023034016

Typeface for the Latin, Greek, and Cyrillic scripts: "Brill". See and download: brill.com/brill-typeface.

ISSN 1572-0500
ISBN 978-90-04-68220-7 (hardback)
ISBN 978-90-04-68221-4 (e-book)

Copyright 2024 by Erik Timmerman. Published by Koninklijke Brill NV, Leiden, The Netherlands.
Koninklijke Brill NV incorporates the imprints Brill, Brill Nijhoff, Brill Schöningh, Brill Fink, Brill mentis, Brill Wageningen Academic, Vandenhoeck & Ruprecht, Böhlau and V&R unipress.
Koninklijke Brill NV reserves the right to protect this publication against unauthorized use. Requests for re-use and/or translations must be addressed to Koninklijke Brill NV via brill.com or copyright.com.

This book is printed on acid-free paper and produced in a sustainable manner.

To the memory of my grandparents,
Hendrik and Bouwina Havinga

Contents

Acknowledgements XI
List of Figures and Tables XIII

1 **Introduction** 1
1.1 The Debate about Roman Economic Growth 3
1.2 This Book's Contribution 16

2 **Setting the Stage** 22
2.1 The Natural Landscape 22
2.2 The Pre-Roman Economy 28
2.3 Conclusions 31

3 **The Roman Impact** 33
3.1 The Roman Army 33
3.2 Urbanisation 39
3.3 Population Growth 43
3.4 Roman Institutions 50
3.4.1 *Taxation* 50
3.4.2 *Monetisation* 52
3.4.3 *Standardisation* 60
3.5 Infrastructure 62
3.6 Conclusions 69

4 **Agricultural Production** 72
4.1 Long-Term Developments 75
4.2 The Villa Landscape 77
4.2.1 *Arable Farming* 78
4.2.2 *Animal Husbandry* 80
4.2.3 *Surplus Production* 82
4.3 The Non-villa Landscapes 86
4.3.1 *Arable Farming* 87
4.3.2 *Animal Husbandry* 87
4.3.3 *Surplus Production* 94
4.4 Conclusions 97

5 Non-agricultural Production 102
5.1 Extractive Industries 107
5.1.1 *Wood* 108
5.1.2 *Stone* 115
5.1.3 *Metal* 123
5.1.4 *Conclusions* 129
5.2 Manufacturing 130
5.2.1 *Ceramics* 132
5.2.1.1 Military Production 134
5.2.1.2 Civilian Production 136
5.2.1.3 Ceramic Building Material 147
5.2.2 *Glass* 151
5.2.3 *Metal* 157
5.2.4 *Conclusions* 161

6 Trade 164
6.1 Amphorae 167
6.2 Terra sigillata 183
6.3 Trade with Other Regions 193
6.4 The Traders 196
6.5 Conclusions 200

7 Living Standards 204
7.1 Housebuilding 207
7.2 Portable Material Culture 214
7.2.1 *Metal Objects* 214
7.2.2 *Pottery* 222
7.3 Conclusions 227

8 Final Conclusions 230
8.1 Synthesis 230
8.2 Interpretation 235
8.3 Future Research 238

Appendix 1 241
Appendix 2 255
Appendix 3 260

Sources and Bibliography 263
Shapefiles 263
Websites 263
Literary sources 263
Epigraphic sources 264
Bibliography 265
Index of Geographical Names 315
Index of Subjects 317

Acknowledgements

This book is an improved version of the PhD thesis I defended at the Faculty of Arts and Humanities of the University of Cologne in June 2021. I look back on my time in Cologne with much fondness and good memories, and I am thankful for the many friendly and inspiring people that I have met along the way. It is therefore a pleasure for me to thank some of them here.

First of all, my *Doktorvater*, Peter Franz Mittag. He always stood ready to discuss my work with him, but he also knew how to keep me on my toes with his critical questions. I also greatly appreciate the encouragement he gave me when I was struggling with my research at times. This has kept me on the right track. My thanks also go to my second supervisor, Eckhard Deschler-Erb. From him, I learned a lot about provincial Roman archaeology, and my work has greatly benefited from the friendly discussions that I had with him. I am also very grateful to Wim Jongman. He introduced me to Roman economic history during my studies in Groningen and has inspired me with his great enthusiasm for the topic. He taught me a lot and gave me the confidence to start doing research. He has also been a great help in formulating the research questions for this book.

I consider myself very fortunate to have been a member of the *DFG Graduiertenkolleg 1878. Archäologie vormoderner Wirtschaftsräume*. My time in the 'Grako' has been a great and valuable experience. I have gained many new insights, and my work has certainly profited from the many good discussions and lectures that we had. At the same time, the social aspect was of great importance. Whether it was a plenum, an international workshop, or just an evening of drinks, we always had lots of fun. I would therefore like to thank everyone who was involved in the Grako. More specifically, I would like to thank Ina Borkenstein, who was the coordinator of the Grako. She always made sure that everything was taken care of, which has made our lives much easier. A word of thanks also goes to Tymon de Haas, who was the leader of our research line. The discussions I had with him have really helped me better plan and structure my research. Of course, I would also like to thank my colleagues in the office, Dean Peeters, Cathalin Recko, and Ella Hetzel, for the many good conversations and the sociability.

A very big thank you also goes to David Brough. Not only was he a great drinking buddy at the Limes Congress in Serbia, but he also proofread the whole manuscript for me. I would also like to thank Caroline van Toor, who has checked the Latin in this work for me.

I am also thankful to the editors of Impact of Empire for accepting my book in this series and to the people at Brill for their fine cooperation and good guidance during the publication process. The anonymous reviewer also made an important contribution to this work by providing useful feedback.

Furthermore, there are several people who I would like to thank for a variety of things, such as helping with my research proposal, sharing (unpublished) work and data, allowing me to reproduce figures, or providing useful literature and bibliographies: Barbara Borgers, Bert Groenewoudt, Gijs Tol, Julia Hoffmann-Salz, Maaike Groot, Marion Brüggler, Paul Beliën, Peter Attema, Philip Verhagen, Rahel Otte, Sebastian Held, Stijn Heeren, Thomas Frank, Tyler Franconi, and Vince Van Thienen.

Finally, I want to thank my parents for the love, support, and opportunities they have always given me. And last, but certainly not least, my sweet girlfriend Franziska. Her love, support, and patience helped me a lot in writing this book.

Erik Timmerman

Figures and Tables

Figures

1 The Lower Germanic Limes region with the main locations and features mentioned in the text 23
2 Central places (military and civilian) that were in existence in the Lower Germanic Limes region in the Roman period 34
3 The total number of soldiers stationed along the Lower Germanic Limes 36
4 The development of the number of urban settlements in the Lower Germanic Limes region 42
5 Estimated population densities in the German Rhineland per km^2 44
6 Estimated population densities in the Dutch part of the MDS region per km^2 45
7 The chronological development of rural settlements in the six subregions of the Lower Germanic Limes region 47
8 The number of stray coin finds in the Roman Netherlands 54
9 The locations where the coins from Figure 8 were found 55
10 Important features of the Roman infrastructure network in the Lower Germanic Limes region 65
11 Dated wood remains from western Germany in absolute numbers 110
12 The percentage distribution of dated finding spots of wooden archaeological objects 111
13 Dated wood finds from the Dutch River Area and Dutch coastal area 113
14 Estimated number of yearly produced millstones in the Eifel quarries near Mayen 118
15 The number of dated pottery kilns that have been found in the Lower Germanic Limes region 136
16 Distribution of settlements where pottery kilns have been documented 138
17 Sites where Roman period glass production has been documented 153
18 Sites where Roman period metal production has been documented 159
19 The distribution of the dated terra sigillata stamps that have been found in the Lower Germanic Limes region 185
20 The total number of dated terra sigillata stamps per 25-year period, divided by region of origin 186
21 The total number of dated terra sigillata stamps from military contexts per 25-year period, divided by region of origin 190
22 The total number of dated terra sigillata stamps from civilian contexts per 25-year period, divided by region of origin 191

23 The total number of dated metal objects that have been collected in the PAN-database in 50-year periods 215
24 The distribution of the metal objects collected in the PAN-database and dated within the Roman period 217
25 The development of the number of metal objects in specific rural settlements 219
26 The development of average proportions of handmade and wheel-thrown pottery in 10 rural settlements 224
27 The sites that were used for Figure 26 and Table 15 225

Tables

1 Available space for surpluses in rural granaries 84
2 The relative proportions of animal species in rural settlements from the western Dutch river delta 88
3 The relative proportions of animal species in rural settlements from the Dutch River Area 89
4 The relative proportions of animal species in Tiel-Passewaaij 92
5 Amphorae from the Hunerberg (19–12 BC), MNI (n=31) 171
6 Amphorae from the Kops Plateau (12 BC–AD 69), MNI (n=654) 172
7 Amphorae from Neuss, fortifications 1–4 (16 BC–AD 16), sherds (n=936) 173
8 Amphorae from Neuss, fortifications 5–6 (AD 16–43), sherds (n=1608) 173
9 Amphorae from Xanten Ostmauer (Augustus–AD 50), sherds (n=2498) 177
10 Amphorae from Xanten Hafengrabung (Nero–second century AD), sherds (n=420) 178
11 Amphorae from Xanten Insula 15 (late first–second centuries AD), sherds (n=746) 178
12 Amphorae from Xanten Insula 39 (Trajan–mid third century AD), sherds (n=3794) 178
13 Amphorae from Bonn (second–third centuries AD), sherds (n=4075) 180
14 Amphorae from Braives (first–fourth centuries AD), MNI (n=146) 182
15 The percentages of handmade vessels in pottery assemblages from 10 different rural settlements 226

CHAPTER 1

Introduction

> The most recent and greatest of the confrontations between Rome and the Gauls is the campaign under the command of Gaius Caesar. For, in the ten years of his command, Roman armies fought against more than four million fierce opponents (if you count them all together), captured a million of them, and killed another million in battle. They subjected four hundred tribes and more than eight hundred towns, some of which had revolted from us, others were new acquisitions.[1]

∵

Julius Caesar's Gallic Wars (58–50 BC) must have been traumatic for many of the native inhabitants of Gaul. The negative consequences for tribes that were willing to cooperate with the Roman overlord may have been more limited, but the tribes that stood in his way really felt the sting of Roman imperialism. In his *Commentarii de Bello Gallico*, Caesar boasts how he annihilated or enslaved several native tribes, such as the Eburones and the Atuatuci.[2] Although we should be cautious in taking literary sources at face value, recent archaeological studies seem to confirm that the Roman conquest, indeed, had 'profound negative effects on the lives of tens of thousands of people'.[3] But was Rome's expansion into North-West Europe just an undesirable and harmful event for the inhabitants of the region? Or did the Roman domination, in the long run, perhaps also bring about more positive changes?

From an economic perspective, the conquest and occupation of the lands up to the Rhine River are believed to have had major consequences for the development of this region. The Rhine attained its role as the northernmost frontier of the Roman Empire as a result of general Varus's disastrous loss of three Roman legions to a coalition of Germanic tribes in the famous Battle of the Teutoburg Forest in AD 9. This event, one of Rome's greatest defeats,

1 App. Hist. Rom. 4, 2, 6.
2 Caes. Gall. 2, 33; 6, 34.
3 Roymans and Fernández-Götz, 2015, p. 71.

© ERIK TIMMERMAN, 2024 | DOI:10.1163/9789004682214_002

halted the Roman imperial expansion into the lands north-east of the Rhine.[4] Henceforth, the river would designate the border between Rome's continental empire and the lands of the free Germanic tribes.[5] Accordingly, a substantial part of the Roman army was stationed here, and, in addition to this, the Lower Germanic Limes was constructed, an impressive line of defensive structures stretching several hundred kilometres.[6] This militarisation of the frontier has traditionally been viewed as the main driver of economic development in this part of the Roman world.[7] It is believed that the Roman army stimulated economic life and transformed the region from a marginal border area, into one of the core areas of Europe.[8]

This transformation will take centre stage in this book, as I will investigate the impact of the Roman occupation (*c.*50 BC–AD 450) on the economy of the Lower Germanic Limes region.[9] This is already an interesting topic in itself. The Roman epoch forms an important chapter in the history of North-western Europe, and the story of its economic development is essential in comprehending its many facets and its long-lasting legacy. Furthermore, it is interesting since such an investigation may have the potential to contribute to the more general debate about the Roman economy. This is an important debate because we want to know how well the Roman economy fared in comparison to the economies of other historical societies, and why. This larger debate about the Roman economy, and its placement within the framework of the economic history of the world already has a long tradition, going back to the late nineteenth century. To clarify the positioning of this work in relation to other research undertaken to date, and in order to justify the theoretical approach that will be used in this study, a few words must first be said about this general debate.[10]

---

4 Although several Roman campaigns ensued in the following years.

5 An exception were the *agri decumates*, a region between the Rhine, Danube, and Main rivers that was conquered from AD 74 onwards.

6 The Upper German-Raetian Limes has been listed as a UNESCO World Heritage Site since 2005. The Lower German Limes followed in 2021.

7 Wierschowski, 1984.

8 Strobel, 2007.

9 Since I focus mainly on the transition from the pre-Roman Iron Age to the Roman period, the late Roman period (*c.* AD 300–450) will be less central. A more detailed demarcation of the research area will be given in section 2.1.

10 For more comprehensive overviews, see Morris, 1999; Polfer, 2001; Drexhage, Konen and Ruffing, 2002a; Morris, Saller and Scheidel, 2007; Scheidel, 2012; Lo Cascio, 2017a.

1.1 The Debate about Roman Economic Growth

Well into the last two decades of the twentieth century, the main consensus among scholars was that the Roman economy did not perform particularly well in comparison to other preindustrial economies. It was believed that the Roman economy was poorly developed, and that society had been highly unequal. Trade and manufacturing played a minimal role in the economy, and the vast majority of the population was involved in agriculture. Peasants aimed at self-sufficiency and produced almost exclusively for their own needs. Life for these peasants was characterised by severe poverty, and the wealth that existed was concentrated in the hands of a small landowning elite. The members of this elite were not profit-oriented. They frowned upon commerce and manufacturing and instead invested their capital in things that brought them social recognition, such as landownership and conspicuous consumption. Because of this mentality, market exchange remained a marginal affair. Cities were centres of consumption, not of production, and, as a result of all this, the economy did not grow. The Roman world, or even the whole ancient world, for that matter, was one of underdevelopment and stagnation, and only in the late medieval and early modern periods had expanding commercial markets allowed economic history to set course on an upward trend.

The architect of this conception of the ancient economic world was Moses Finley, who had elaborately put forth his ideas in his seminal work *The Ancient Economy*.[11] In this work, Finley pointed to the fact that the ancients left us without any satisfactory works of economic analysis, or any reliable statistics. He concluded that this was not merely an accidental, intellectual failure of ancient writers but, instead, a consequence of the actual structure of ancient society. Influenced by the substantivism of Karl Polanyi and the sociology of Max Weber, Finley believed that the economy of the ancient world had been structured along radically different lines than that of our modern world.[12] Ancient economic life was 'embedded' within its socio-political culture, and, unlike in the modern world, there had not been an 'enormous conglomeration of interdependent markets'.[13] Accordingly, he argued that modern economic theory, which is exclusively designed for the study of the modern era, is an inappropriate and wholly anachronistic tool for the study of the ancient economy.[14]

11 Finley, 1999.
12 Morris, 1999.
13 Finley, 1999, p. 22.
14 Finley, 1999, pp. 22–23.

The lasting significance of Finley's work lies in the fact that he laid bare the fundamental differences in structure between the ancient economy and the economies of later periods. Before Finley, so-called primitivists and modernists had debated the performance of the ancient economy with profoundly opposing opinions.[15] The primitivists downplayed the performance of the economy, arguing that the ancient world had been characterised by closed autarkic households that were only to a limited extent involved in trade. The modernists, on the other hand, rejected this characterisation and claimed that the ancient economy had known a well-developed market system that performed similarly to that of early-modern Europe. Both parties in this debate, however, could not conceive of any form of economic exchange other than that of a market economy.[16] It was precisely because of this that Michael Rostovtzeff had been able to secure an initial modernist victory, in the first half of the twentieth century.[17] Within the rigid interpretative framework of the day, his assemblage of widespread archaeological evidence for long-distance movements of goods made any primitivist interpretation of the ancient economy untenable.[18] However, as Finley made clear that non-market types of exchange, such as reciprocity and state redistribution, may have played a prominent role in the ancient world, the modernist victory was annulled, and the terms of the debate were completely redefined.

In the following years, many scholars followed Finley's lead and concerned themselves primarily with discussing the structural aspects of the ancient economy. As a result of this focus on structure, questions about the performance of the economy remained very much in the background. For Finley, it was simple, the embeddedness of the ancient economy inhibited economic growth, and investigating the performance of this stagnant economy was therefore not really relevant. Because of this lack of attention to economic performance, the debate about the ancient economy was essentially conducted in 'culturalist' terms.[19] This had the consequence that ancient economic history became largely dissociated from the larger debates in general economic history, where questions about performance remained very much at the fore. Although unfortunate, this lack of attention to performance is perfectly

15 This debate started in the late nineteenth century with the so-called Bücher-Meyer controversy. Finley, 1979; Schneider, 1990.

16 Even though this point had already been stressed by Weber (in his later work). However, ancient historians, with the exception of Johannes Hasebroek, did not read Weber's more sociological works. Love, 1991, pp. 39–53; Morris, 1999, p. xvi.

17 Rostovtzeff, 1926; 1941.

18 Rostovtzeff was among the first who combined literary and archaeological evidence and thereby broke through the conventional barriers of classical scholarship. Bowersock, 1974.

19 Morley, 2004, p. 41.

understandable considering the extent and nature of research at the time. In contrast to scholars studying later periods, ancient historians had no useful statistical source material at their disposal, as Finley had rightly pointed out. In the light of this paucity of data, how was it then possible to say anything sensible about the performance of the economy?

Things began to change when Keith Hopkins put forth his 'taxes and trade' model of the Roman economy in two publications in the early 1980s.[20] Hopkins presented his model as an 'elaboration of the Finley model' but effectively challenged his former teacher's work on fundamental grounds.[21] Even though Hopkins concurred with the basic primitivism of Finley's characterisation of the ancient economy, he disputed its stasis. Hopkins argued that the Roman economy was dynamic and had witnessed a period of 'modest economic growth and subsequent decline'.[22] The main driver of this growth was the imposition of taxes in money by the Roman government, which forced producers to increase their production and led to an increase in empire-wide trade. Hopkins claimed that, on a macro-level, tax money flowed from so-called tax-exporting provinces (the wealthy core-provinces of Spain, southern Gaul, northern Africa, Asia Minor, Syria, and Egypt) to Italy and the frontier provinces, where the money was spent.[23] To make up for their deficits, the tax-exporting provinces had to increase their exports, thereby stimulating production and inter-regional trade throughout the empire. This increased production and exchange, combined with the spread of several technological and social innovations, led Hopkins to the conclusion that the Roman economy had experienced a certain degree of per capita economic growth.[24] Nonetheless, he believed that the extent of this development should not be overestimated, and he described the growth as 'a thin veneer of sophistication, spread over and tied to the subsistence economy.'[25]

---

20 Hopkins, 1980; 1983.

21 Hopkins, 1983, p. xiv.

22 Hopkins, 1983, p. xiv.

23 Hopkins, 1980, p. 1.

24 When talking about economic growth, it is important to distinguish conceptually between aggregate and per capita economic growth. Aggregate economic growth indicates an increase in the total output of an economy, irrespective of changes in the size of the population. Thus, this type of growth can simply be the result of population growth, since more labourers equals more production. Per capita growth, on the other hand, designates an increase in total economic production measured according to the size of the population. This growth must therefore be the result of an increase in the productivity of the labour force. Of course, both kinds of economic growth can, and often do, occur together, which makes it difficult, but not impossible, to distinguish one from the other. Saller, 2002, pp. 257–258; Ruffing, 2015, p. 14.

25 Hopkins, 1980, p. 104.

But Hopkins did not just challenge the static character of the Roman economy. He also broke with Finley on a conceptual level, as he used concepts derived from modern economic theory in his analysis. He believed that Finley's rejection of these analytical constructs was erroneous and stated that '[t]he achievements of the Roman world need to be interpreted with empathic understanding of what the Romans themselves thought and with concepts we ourselves use.'[26] Hopkins' argument was primarily theoretically structured, consisting of a set of mutually reinforcing propositions.[27] However, in order to support his argumentation, he utilised archaeological source material in a novel way. To prove his proposition that trade in the Roman Empire had increased, he used a quantifiable dataset of dated ancient shipwrecks that indicated that the Mediterranean Sea had, indeed, experienced increased inter-regional trade in the period between 200 BC and AD 200.[28] Similarly, in order to show that the money supply in the Roman Empire had grown, he presented a dataset of Roman coin dies that suggested that the number of silver coins in circulation had gradually increased between 157 and 50 BC.[29]

Hopkins' model of the Roman economy has received some fierce criticism.[30] Largely echoing Finley's arguments about self-sufficient peasants, lack of trade, and the absence of an economic rationality, scholars such as Peter Garnsey, Richard Saller, and Richard Duncan-Jones criticised Hopkins for offering a too optimistic characterisation of Roman economic growth.[31] They did, nonetheless, agree with him that questions about the performance of the Roman economy were crucial to ask. Hopkins' work thus put these questions back on the academic agenda, where they have remained ever since. Moreover, his theoretical approach paved the way for the reintroduction of modern economic theory into the debate. Combined with his pioneering use of quantifiable proxy datasets, which provided a way to actually measure economic performance, Hopkins truly initiated a paradigm shift in ancient economic history.

---

26 Hopkins, 1978, p. ix.

27 Hopkins described this kind of reasoning as the 'wigwam argument': 'There are several pieces of evidence, each insufficient or untrustworthy in itself, which seem collectively to confirm it. I call this the wigwam argument: each pole would fall down by itself, but together the poles stand up, by leaning on each other; they point roughly in the same direction, and circumscribe "truth".' Hopkins, 1978, pp. 19–20.

28 Hopkins, 1980, p. 106.

29 Hopkins, 1980, p. 109.

30 He responded to his critics in Hopkins, 2002.

31 Garnsey and Saller, 1987; Duncan-Jones, 1990.

As is common in scholarship, it would take a while for this new approach to the ancient economy to come to fuller fruition. Throughout the rest of the 1980s, 1990s, and early 2000s, Finley's minimalist and static interpretation of the ancient economy came under increasing scrutiny. An important conceptual counter-argument came from Henri Pleket, who emphasised that Finley's model had been primarily a statement of what the ancient economy *was not*.[32] Finley had gone at length to demonstrate that the ancient world had not seen the emergence of a commercial bourgeoisie or large-scale trade in inter-regional markets. Although Pleket did not completely agree with Finley on this point, his more fundamental criticism concerned Finley's belief in the uniqueness of the ancient economy. Because of his expertise in comparative history, Pleket was able to show that the ancient economy had not been so different from most of the economies of later pre-industrial societies.[33] He demonstrated that many of the economies of the medieval and early modern periods were not at all as developed as Finley had assumed. This cast considerable doubt on Finley's assumption that the ancient economy had been underdeveloped.

In the same period, the variety and amount of source material that came to be used in the discussion of the Roman economy increased significantly.[34] Papyrological evidence, for example, provided insights into prices, wages, and rents in Roman Egypt.[35] Even more significantly, though, was the large increase in archaeological material that has been brought into the debate. An early and influential work in this respect is Kevin Greene's general synthesis of the archaeology of the Roman economy.[36] However, many other important, often more specific, investigations into archaeological material (sometimes with inscriptions) as an economic indicator have also appeared.[37] Altogether, in the light of this vast upsurge in new empirical evidence, Finley's pessimistic interpretation of the ancient economy has become untenable.[38]

32 Pleket, 1990, p. 27.
33 Pleket, 1990, pp. 143–145.
34 For a convenient overview, see Ruffing, 2015.
35 Rathbone, 1991; Drexhage, 1991.
36 Greene, 1986.
37 E.g. Peacock and Williams, 1986; Tchernia, 1986; Martin-Kilcher, 1987; Harris, 1993b; Remesal Rodríguez, 1997; Strobel, 2000; Brun, 2003; Polfer, 2005.
38 An extensive overview of much of the new material can be found in Drexhage, Konen and Ruffing, 2002b.

This paradigm shift culminated in 2007 with the publication of the *Cambridge Economic History of the Greco-Roman World* (CEHGRW), in which the leading scholars within the field take stock of the debate.[39] In the introduction to this monumental volume, the editors set out their aims and their theoretical approach. They state that they take it as their task to explain the structure and performance of the Greco-Roman economy through time and, in doing so, explicitly affiliate themselves with the New Institutional Economics (NIE) of Douglass North.[40]

North has developed his analytical framework in reaction to the substantivism of Polanyi and his followers.[41] In his work, he stresses the significance of institutions in the determination of transaction costs. It should be realised that a perfectly functioning market economy only exists in economics textbooks. In real world economies, wealth maximisation, the central behavioural assumption of the neoclassical paradigm, is always to a certain extent restricted by the additional costs that accompany economic transactions. These so-called transaction costs, which are the costs 'associated with defining, protecting, and exchanging property rights', arise because economic actors have imperfect access to information.[42] They must devote time, energy, and resources to locate and vet potential partners, negotiate contracts with these partners, and enforce the terms of agreement. Institutions, then, are 'the humanly devised constraints that structure political, economic and social interaction'.[43] They define the 'rules of the game', the framework in which economies develop.[44] Institutions that are successful in lowering transaction costs are conducive to economic growth, while institutions that contribute to higher transaction costs inhibit it.[45] Institutions thus matter, and recognizing their influence on economic decision-making provides a viable solution to the problem of embeddedness that led scholars like Finley to the complete rejection of modern economic concepts. By arguing that within the institutional framework of a society, the logic of modern economic theory applies, North found a way to preserve proper economic analysis from substantivist reductionism.

39 Scheidel, Morris and Saller, 2007.
40 Morris, Saller and Scheidel, 2007, pp. 11–12.
41 North explicitly mentions Finley as a prime example of such a follower. North, 1977, p. 703.
42 Lo Cascio, 2006, pp. 218–219.
43 North, 1990, p. 97.
44 North, 1991, p. 98.
45 Cf. Acemoglu and Robinson, 2012.

Although the use of NIE for the study of the Roman economy is not undisputed, many scholars have recognised its value.[46] It is therefore fair to say that today, NIE has become the dominant conceptual approach within the field. However, in assent with the suggestion of the editors of the *CEHGRW* to 'continue Finley's and Hopkins' engagement with the social sciences',[47] scholars have also been exploring theoretical concepts from other disciplines, such as Development Economics, Human Capital Theory, Economic Sociology, and Behavioural Economics, to give only a few examples.[48] Moreover, on a methodological level, scholars have now really begun to explore the possibilities that the statistical analysis of quantifiable (archaeological) proxy datasets can provide.[49] Even though scholars, in this respect, are still just scratching the surface, much progress has already been made. As a result, the study of the Roman economy has changed from one characterised by a paucity of data, to one of an abundance that demands completely new research strategies. In recent years, the debate about the Roman economy has thus become increasingly sophisticated on both the theoretical and methodological level. As a result of this, Roman economic history is also finding its way back into the larger debates in general economic history.

One of the main questions for economic historians, who live in a time in which modern economic growth has led to increasing levels of prosperity for a large proportion of the world's population, is how can it be explained that this modern economic growth is only a fairly recent phenomenon?[50] The traditional explanation, first advocated by scholars writing around the middle of the nineteenth century, is that the Industrial Revolution was, indeed, a revolutionary break with the past.[51] Through the utilisation of modern technology, powered by fossil fuels, and combined with a rational organisation of production, economic growth was able to skyrocket in the modern age. Thus, the revolutionary nature of industrialisation was accepted as a given fact. Only a few scholars initially considered the possibility that modern economic growth

46 For criticism and discussion about the use of NIE, see Bang, 2009; Hobson, 2014; Verboven, 2015; Ruffing, 2016.

47 Morris, Saller and Scheidel, 2007, p. 7.

48 E.g. Morris and Manning, 2005; Scheidel, 2006; Saller, 2012; Verboven, 2015.

49 Bowman and Wilson, 2009b.

50 Modern economic growth can be defined as sustained per capita economic growth combined with population growth. Neal, 2014.

51 Morley, 2004, pp. 33–34.

might have had its roots in the gradual development of increasingly efficient commercial markets, which, driven by an economically innovative bourgeoisie, eventually culminated in the complex economies of the modern industrialised world.[52]

Within the traditional narrative, pre-industrial economies have been characterised as being essentially governed by Malthusian forces.[53] The central thesis of Malthusian theory, in Thomas Malthus' own words, is that 'the power of population is indefinitely greater than the power in the earth to produce subsistence for man'.[54] The logic of the Malthusian model, thus, lies in the interplay between the population and the productive capacity of an economic system. It assumes that the population, as long as it is not somehow restrained, always increases at an exponential rate.[55] However, the productive capacity never increases at such a rate (at least before the Industrial Revolution) because there are diminishing marginal returns on all factors of production (land, labour, and capital). This means that adding more units of one factor of production, under the condition that the others remain the same, will at some point lead to lower returns measured per unit of input. This is, for example, the case when additional labourers are added to a plot of land that has previously been worked by a single farmer. When a second labourer is added, the total production might still increase considerably (but not double); there is enough to do for two farmers on this hypothetical plot of land. Yet if a third or even a fourth labourer is added, the total output increases less and, as a result, the total productivity of the land measured per labourer has decreased. This means that economies can only expand without reducing per capita production for as long as the relative input of capital and land is able to keep up with the population growth. In reality, however, this cannot continue for very long because the amount of land in the world (or in a specific region) is finite: when all the land is being used, it is impossible to get more land (at least without modern technologies).[56]

52 Jongman, 2014b, p. 27.
53 Clark, 2007; Galor, 2011.
54 Malthus, 1966, p. 13.
55 According to Malthus, the population doubled itself every twenty-five years. Galor, 2011, p. 12.
56 In fact, the reduction in productivity already sets in before all the available land has been used. Because the productive potential of land varies, diminishing marginal returns on land occur as soon as all the best quality land is being used.

The Malthusian theorem therefore paints a rather bleak picture of economic life in the pre-industrial world. It describes a situation in which the vast majority of the population is caught in a so-called low-level equilibrium trap.[57] This means that any small increase in per capita incomes that this population experiences remains unsustainable.[58] Although these increases, in the short term, might have allowed people to enjoy higher living standards, in the course of a few generations they would be 'eaten away' by population growth. This demographic expansion would then continue until the point was reached where the growing population, because of reduced per capita production, was unable to sustain itself. At this point, so-called Malthusian checks, such as famine, plague, or warfare, would decimate the population, and the cycle would start all over again. Within the Malthusian worldview, the history of pre-industrial economic development is thus reduced to a story of stagnation, with only insignificant periods of expansion and subsequent decline and without any real technical progress (defined as an increase in the efficiency of the production process).[59] An escape from this era of stasis came only with the onset of the Industrial Revolution, when production was finally able to keep up with, and even outstrip, population growth.

The strong economic logic that underlies the Malthusian model has made it the dominant explanatory framework for pre-industrial economic development. However, despite its persuasive nature, the model has also been criticised. An important point of criticism has been put forth by Ester Boserup, who challenged the central assumption of the Malthusian model that agricultural production is necessarily outstripped by population growth.[60] She argues that agricultural production, under certain circumstances, is able to keep up with the demographic expansion because population pressure can stimulate innovation, which might lead to an intensification of production. On the basis of investigations into contemporary rural societies, she shows that population pressure forced these societies to shift to more labour-intensive forms of agriculture. Such intensification of agricultural production can substantially increase the productivity per unit of land, thereby removing the initial restraint

57 It is well conceivable that only ordinary people and not the elite were subject to Malthusian constraints. Cf. Temin, 2013, p. 215.

58 Scheidel, 2007b, pp. 55–56.

59 Technical progress refers to an increase in output that does not result from changes in the input of the factors of production. It is not restricted to technological changes but includes any change that can make the production process more efficient. In economics, this is called 'Total Factor Productivity'. Jongman, 2014b, p. 31.

60 Boserup, 1965.

formed by the limited amount of available land. Nevertheless, this intensification of agricultural production comes at a price: the increased productivity of the land requires a significant increase in labour input. This does not, however, mean that labour productivity itself declines. The additional labour that was originally largely going to waste because of diminishing marginal returns on labour can now be put to better use. Boserup's work thus demonstrates that population growth does not necessarily act as a brake on economic development but that it can, instead, be a driver of technical progress. This is an important insight, but it does not completely invalidate the Malthusian model. Although a shift to more intensive agriculture leads to an extension of the carrying capacity of the land, within the boundaries of this new situation, the Malthusian logic of population growth constraining per capita growth might still apply.[61]

Elaborating on Boserup's argument, Jan de Vries and Ad van der Woude provided another challenge to the Malthusian model.[62] In their research into the early-modern Dutch economy, they identify a long period where population growth went hand in hand with sustained increases in per capita incomes. They explain that this apparent contradiction to Malthusian theory was rooted in productivity growth that was not just the result of the Dutch Republic's intercontinental commercial expansion. An equally important development for the increase in productivity had been the specialisation and commercialisation of the economy. This process was not just confined to the urban sector but equally applied to the rural economy. In fact, it was essentially progressive and productive agriculture and its integration with the other economic sectors that laid the foundation for the success of the economy.[63] By bringing sufficient agricultural surplus to the market, the rural population provided the non-rural population with the opportunity to specialise in other sectors. As such, this rural-urban specialisation made possible a high degree of division of labour and its beneficial economies of scale.[64] Materialising within an institutional framework conducive to economic growth, this allowed the Dutch economy to develop into what the authors, probably somewhat optimistically, term the 'First Modern Economy'.[65]

61 For the compatibility of Boserupian and Malthusian theory, see Lee, 1986; Wood, 1998.

62 de Vries and van der Woude, 1997.

63 de Vries, 1974.

64 Economies of scale are the cost advantages that arise because of an increase in production output. Economic growth that derives from such an increased division of labour is called 'Smithian growth'.

65 Although their analysis of the Dutch economy is generally admired, their claim that it was comparable to a modern economy remains very controversial. Unger, 2000; van Zanden, 2002.

The evidence from this specific historical context already suggests that Malthus' 'iron law of population' is perhaps not as hard as it was once thought to be. In addition to the work of de Vries and van der Woude, other economic historians have begun to identify times and places where pre-industrial societies experienced periods of rising population combined with increasing per capita incomes. Indications of such 'Malthusian singularities' can, for instance, be found in medieval northern Europe and Italy in the centuries prior to the Black Death, or in Abbasid Iraq from the eight to the eleventh centuries.[66] But scholars have also found evidence of periods of such efflorescence in China under the Song and Qing dynasties and among pre-Columbian societies in Latin America.[67] The earliest examples, however, can be traced as far back as the ancient world, where ancient Egypt, Mesopotamia, Classical Greece, and, indeed, the Roman Empire experienced periods of great prosperity.[68] Although none of these historical economies have been able to actually break the so-called Malthusian ceiling and take off on a trajectory of modern economic growth, these examples at least suggest that there was much more to pre-industrial economic growth than just the natural ebb and flow of population and declining marginal productivity.

Investigations into the economic history of the pre-industrial world have thus become increasingly relevant, and within this larger debate, the Roman Empire is one of the civilisations that attracts particular attention.[69] But did the Roman Empire really witness a period where the economy, for a prolonged period of time, was able to stay ahead of Malthusian constraints? Ancient historians and classical archaeologists are divided amongst themselves on this matter. They all accept that the Roman Empire experienced a significant degree of economic growth as it came to dominate large parts of the ancient world. Their interpretation of this economic growth, though, diverges greatly.

Generally speaking, there are two opposing camps in this debate. Some scholars adhere to a Malthusian growth scenario.[70] They argue that we should not make too much of the growth of the Roman economy, as it can primarily be characterised as aggregate economic growth. As such, the growth essentially represents an increase in scale, caused by territorial expansion and population growth. It is being recognised that the integration of new regions into the Roman economic system initially might have led to some per capita growth,

66 Goldstone, 2002; Pezzolo, 2014; Pamuk, 2014.

67 Goldstone, 2002; Salvucci, 2014; Ortman *et al.*, 2016.

68 Morris, 2004; Neal, 2014; Jursa, 2014; Jongman, 2014a.

69 The contributors to *The Cambridge History of Capitalism*, for instance, make it their aim to discern indications of such technical progress in the source material from a wide range of historical societies. Neal, 2014, pp. 6–16.

70 E.g. Frier, 2001; Bang, 2008; Scheidel, 2009.

as it relaxed existing restraints on land and created conditions in which production and trade could flourish.[71] Still, this growth, as Malthusian theory predicts, would only have stimulated further population growth. After Rome's expansions had finished, the availability of land would soon become a limiting factor. Population growth now started to depress per capita incomes as the productivity of labour decreased. Any increase in per capita incomes would thus, in the long run, remain unsustainable. Accordingly, the vast majority of the Roman population lived at, or just above, subsistence level, and there was no real escape from this stasis.

Other scholars are more optimistic about the performance of the Roman economy.[72] They argue that the economic growth was more than just aggregate growth and some temporary per capita increases. They admit that the growth of the Roman economy was largely an increase of scale. At the same time, however, they claim that the increase in total economic output went together with per capita economic growth, made possible by an increase in the productivity of the workforce. In conflict with the Malthusian scenario, the increase in incomes that derived from this per capita growth could also be sustained for longer periods of time and would have allowed part of the population, in a certain period of time, to experience living standards well above subsistence. For example, Willem Jongman claims that 'Rome could not only maintain an unprecedented population, but it could also provide that population with a standard of living which may well have been at the top of what an advanced organic economy could achieve'.[73]

An important point that must be stressed concerning this last aspect is that the relationship between a rise in per capita incomes and higher living standards is not as straightforward as it might seem at first sight.[74] Although a rise in per capita production is, ceteris paribus, always necessary to raise the standard of living for *anyone*, a rise in per capita production does not always raise the standard of living for *everyone*. This is the case because the benefits of per capita growth are never equally distributed among all layers of a society. For instance, it is very well possible that a small section of the population reaps all the profits, thereby increasing average living standards, while the standard of living of the majority of the population remains unchanged. We should, therefore, be careful to infer higher living standards directly from a rise in per capita production, as it is very well possible that it just resulted in increased

71 Scheidel, 2009, pp. 46–47.
72 E.g. Wilson, 2002; Jongman, 2007b; Temin, 2013; Erdkamp, 2016; Ruffing, 2018.
73 Jongman, 2006, p. 252.
74 Holleran and Pudsey, 2011, p. 6.

inequality.[75] Furthermore, it is important to point out that the concept of living standards is not to be confused with the concept of quality of life. Living standards (or wealth) can be defined as 'the total of desirable goods, both social and material, possessed by someone or existing in a community'.[76] Quality of life, on the other hand, 'is a broader concept than economic production and living standards. It includes the full range of factors that influences what we value in living, reaching beyond its material side.'[77]

The current debate about economic growth in the Roman world is primarily conducted on an empire-wide scale. This has the disadvantage that much of the archaeological source material, which carries the most potential for advancing the debate, is not necessarily available at that scale but rather at a more regional and local level.[78] Moreover, such an overarching perspective cannot sufficiently account for the high degree of inter-regional variability that existed in an empire of such a vast extent. As a result, insights into the conditions that did (or did not) induce growth might be obscured. Then, at the other end of the spectrum, there exists an abundance of locally and regionally oriented archaeological studies that do not directly relate their findings to larger questions about the Roman economy and thereby fail to validate their research to a fuller extent. Synthesising studies, that use existing and newly available archaeological material from the different regions of the Roman Empire are therefore vital in fleshing out the general picture of economic growth in the Roman Empire.[79] Because of their regional focus, such studies are better able to account for inter-regional variability and are, at the same time, capable of linking the many locally oriented studies to the general discussions about the Roman economy.[80]

Investigations into the economic development of the Roman provinces are particularly interesting because the provinces have traditionally been viewed as being exploited for the benefit of the Italian core.[81] Especially during the phases of conquest but also during the subsequent period of occupation, vast amounts of provincial wealth, whether in the form of booty, tribute, or rents,

75 Cf. Milanovic, Lindert and Williamson, 2007; Piketty, 2014; Scheidel, 2017.

76 Smith, 2019b, p. 489.

77 Stiglitz, Sen and Fitoussi, 2010, p. 61.

78 This does, of course, not mean that these empire-wide syntheses are not of crucial importance. They are indispensable in advancing the debate at the macro-scale and in linking the debate about the Roman economy to the general debate about pre-industrial growth in economic history.

79 Remesal Rodríguez, 2001, p. 238.

80 E.g. Millet, 1990; Alcock, 1993; Alston, 1995; Woolf, 1998; Pollard, 2000; Haley, 2003; Hoffmann-Salz, 2011; Hobson, 2012; Franconi, 2014.

81 Hopkins, 1980.

were transferred to Roman Italy.[82] This surely had a positive effect on the Italian economy, but what impact did it have on the provinces? Did the Roman occupation only deplete their wealth or did it, perhaps, also have a beneficial effect on the provincial economies? Of course, we cannot expect all, or even any two, provinces to have followed the same development trajectory. Many factors could determine the way in which regions adapted to the Roman occupation, or, indeed, how the Romans approached the regional government in the first place. The ecological features of Roman Egypt, for instance, were very different from those in Britain, while the initial level of economic development in Asia Minor, in terms of urbanisation and monetisation, differed greatly from that in Gaul, as did the more peripheral regions at the frontiers of the empire, which in many cases were faced with a significant military presence. However, despite the obvious variability of individual contexts, there might be general trends to be observed. Thus, if we want to gauge and explain the performance of the Roman economy as a whole, we need to know how well individual regions fared under Roman domination and why.[83]

1.2 This Book's Contribution

It is one of the main aims of this work to comply with the need for regional synthesis studies by providing a synthesis of the Roman impact on the economy of the Lower Germanic Limes region. Of course, it should be clear that this study does not pretend to be exhaustive in the sense that it integrates all the literature and sources that exist regarding the economy of the research area. Instead, I have attempted to include at least the most important studies and data that are relevant for the answering of this study's main questions. There is no doubt, that I have overlooked some important publications and sources of information. Nevertheless, I am confident that this book will provide the reader with a well-founded overview of current scholarship on the economic development of the research area during the Roman period. However, as the discussion above should have made clear, such a synthesis is of limited academic value if it does not also attempt to find answers to questions that are relevant to the larger debate on economic growth in the Roman Empire.

In accordance with this general debate, I will therefore try to find out to what extent the Roman conquest and occupation led to economic growth in the Lower Germanic Limes region and how we can characterise this growth.

82 Scheidel, 2007a.
83 Jongman, 2014a, pp. 86–87.

Was there only aggregate economic growth, defined as an increase in a region's total economic production without taking its population into account? Or was there also per capita economic growth, which designates an increase in a region's total economic production relative to its population? And if there was per capita growth, who profited from it? Were the benefits of the growth confined to a tiny elite, only leading to increased inequality, or did larger segments of society get a share? Moreover, it is crucial to know what role the Roman army played in this. The military presence must have stimulated the civilian economy in the region, but to what extent should part of the growth be attributed exclusively to the economic activities of the soldiers? Also, it is interesting to know whether the extent and character of the growth was roughly the same everywhere, or if we find a large degree of local variation between or even within sub-regions. And lastly, how can we explain all this?

In order to find answers to these questions, it is good to first briefly summarise the ways economic growth can come about. Theoretically, the total output of an economy is the result of the inputs of the three factors of production (land, labour, and capital). If the input of one or more of these factors of production increases, then output also increases. However, it is important to realise that the output almost never increases at the same rate as the input because there are diminishing marginal returns on all factors of production. This means that adding more units of one factor of production, under the condition that the others remain the same, will at some point lead to lower returns measured per unit of input. This is especially the case because the supply of factors of production is limited and the input cannot always be increased according to the most optimal ratio. For example, once the best land is under cultivation, only the less attractive land remains. If this land is also worked, its productivity will be lower. Alternatively, economic growth can also result from improvements in the productivity of the factors of production. In this case, the same quantitative input leads to a higher output. This is, for example, the case if farmers get hold of better technological equipment, such as an iron plough, with which they can significantly increase the productivity of their labour. Or if they learn of new rotation systems in agriculture that can lead to higher land productivity.

Both quantitative increases in the input of the factors of production and increases in their productivity lead to aggregate economic growth. Indeed, to qualify for this type of growth, it does not matter how the increase in output came about. This is different for per capita economic growth because this growth is measured relative to the size of the population. This means that if an increase in total economic output is due to an increase in labour input, per capita output is likely to have fallen. An exception to this is a situation where the increase in labour is not due to population growth but to the fact that the same population has started to work harder. Of course, per capita growth can also be the result of quantitative increases in the input of land or capital, since these increases do not alter the size of the population. More interesting, however, is the per capita growth that is the result of increases in the productivity of the factors of production.

Saller has provided a good overview of the five main drivers of per capita economic growth that are commonly identified by economic historians.[84] The first of these is trade. The logic behind this is that trade can lead to the division of labour, so that producers can specialise in specific types of production and thus profit from economies of scale. The second cause of per capita economic growth is the intensification of capital investment. This is the quantitative increase in the input of capital that I already addressed above. It means that workers get access to more tools of production and are therefore able to increase their productivity. Of course, as with all quantitative increases in inputs, diminishing marginal returns lurk. This is different for the third driver, which is not about *more* tools of production but about *better* ones. Through improved technology, the productivity of the capital goods themselves increases. The fourth cause is investments in human capital, whose impact is twofold. On the one hand, it educates and trains the workforce to make use of the new technologies, thus increasing their productivity. On the other hand, this education and training also stimulate people to come up with new technological improvements. Lastly, Saller mentions the significance of the institutional framework of an economy. If these institutions are successful in lowering transaction costs and encouraging innovation, this can be an important driver of economic growth. Perhaps climate change should also be added to the list of drivers of per capita economic growth. Since climate has a large impact on crop growth, an improvement in climate (for the sake of arable farming) will lead to higher land productivity.

Thus, there are various ways in which the output of an economy can increase. But how do we know what to look for in the ancient evidence? Aggregate economic growth is relatively easy to identify. Indications of a simple increase in economic output or population are often already enough. It is, however, much more difficult to discern per capita economic growth in the ancient sources. The problem is that our estimates of population growth and increases in economic output are often so imprecise that it is very difficult to determine to what extent these variables have changed relative to each other. Therefore, aggregate economic growth can simply be the result of an increase

84 Saller, 2002, pp. 261–262.

in population, while average economic production measured per person in this population remains the same, or even decreases.

While it is difficult to do so, it is not impossible to find indications of per capita economic growth in the sources. Alan Bowman and Andrew Wilson list two different ways in which we can attempt to discern such indications.[85] The first one is to look for evidence of the potential drivers of per capita growth in the ancient source material. We can look for evidence of trade, improved technology, intensification of capital investment, increased division of labour, education of the workforce, and institutional attitudes and stimuli. The other way to discern per capita growth is to look for indicators that may suggest that this growth did indeed occur, such as urbanisation, import replacement, increased consumption, and higher standards of living. Of course, the identification of one or more of these indications does not automatically mean that we can conclude that per capita growth took place. Much depends on the extent to which these indications can be observed in the sources, and how they compare to our rough estimates of changes in population size. If we can find widespread evidence for multiple of these indicators and population growth does not seem to be the main explanation for this, we can reasonably assume that a certain degree of per capita growth did occur.

As I will demonstrate in this study, there cannot be any doubt that the Lower Germanic Limes region experienced a significant amount of aggregate economic growth during the Roman period. However, as the above should already have made clear, the same cannot be said regarding per capita growth. Nevertheless, I will argue that there are indications that suggest that the regional economy, in addition to aggregate growth, also experienced a certain degree of per capita growth, which possibly even raised the standard of living for large parts of the population.

To develop this argument, the second chapter outlines the initial situation against which the impact of the Roman occupation is to be understood. The chapter gives an overview of the historical geography of the region in the pre-Roman Iron Age. This includes a discussion of the most important features of the natural landscape, but also makes clear how the native population interacted with this landscape and how they, and their economy, can be characterised.

In the third chapter, the most important general aspects of the Roman impact are discussed. These aspects include: the large-scale presence of the Roman army, urbanisation, population growth, the Roman institutional framework, and the development of the regional infrastructure. As I will

85 Bowman and Wilson, 2009a, pp. 12–13.

argue, these developments made a large impact since they turned the largely subsistence-oriented regional economy into an economic system in which market-oriented exchange played an increasingly large role. Thereby, this chapter lays the basis for the more detailed analysis of the economic developments in the different sectors of the economy in the following chapters.

This analysis commences in the fourth chapter, in which the main developments regarding agricultural production are discussed. This discussion focuses on the question of whether the agricultural population was able to produce enough food to feed themselves and the non-agricultural population, and if this was the case, how they could have achieved the necessary increase in agricultural productivity. The answer that I propose is that there are good indications that they were, indeed, largely successful in this and that they achieved the necessary increase in productivity through a combination of more intensive and more efficient cultivation of the existing agricultural land, which was largely made possible by reliable possibilities for market exchange.

The fifth chapter, which is a diptych of two subchapters, deals with non-agricultural production. It investigates to what extent economic growth took place regarding the exploitation of raw materials and manufacturing and how we should interpret this growth. The first sub-chapter makes clear that there was a very significant increase in the total production of raw materials, such as wood, stone, and metal, during the Roman period. Furthermore, it seems that this increase was not just the result of an increase in labour input but that it was also driven by increased specialisation and technological development, in which Roman military specialists played a key role. In the second sub-chapter, I demonstrate that the scale of manufacturing also expanded considerably as a result of the Roman occupation. Throughout the core regions of the research area, specialised manufacturers set up their businesses. Initially, they produced mainly for the army, but over time, a noticeable proportion of production appears to have been destined for consumers in civilian settlements and even in the rural hinterland. This was an important development because it made possible relative specialisation between the agricultural and non-agricultural sectors.

In the sixth chapter, the role of trade is discussed. Since local trade has not left many traces and will already have been dealt with in the third chapter and in the context of the discussions on production in the fourth and fifth chapters, this chapter mainly deals with long-distance trade. It demonstrates that a large-scale and well-organised system of long-distance trade existed, which connected the region with the rest of the Roman Empire and beyond. Moreover, I argue that the role of the state in this was probably rather limited. Instead, trade appears to have been in the hands of highly specialised groups of professional traders and was guided mainly by the free market.

The seventh chapter deals with the question of to what extent we can find indications of an increase in the standard of living of the general population. In the light of the debate about the possibilities for per capita growth, this is a very important question. However, at the same time, it is very difficult to find an answer to this question since the evidence for it is scarce and can be interpreted in various ways. Nevertheless, I argue, very tentatively, that this evidence is suggestive of an increase in the material welfare of a significant portion of the inhabitants of the research area.

Lastly, in the eighth chapter, things are wrapped up and I return to the book's main question: to what extent did the Roman conquest and occupation lead to economic growth in the Lower Germanic Limes region and how can we characterise and explain this growth? After a synthesis of the main conclusions of the preceding chapters, I make a case for an interpretation of the economic growth in the research area as a combination of aggregate and per capita growth. Finally, I end the study with a few recommendations for future research that I believe deserve particular attention.

CHAPTER 2

Setting the Stage

Before commencing with the analysis of the Roman impact on the economic development of the Lower Germanic Limes region, it is first necessary to understand what this region looked like before the arrival of the Romans. In order to do so, this chapter will provide an overview of the historical geography of the research area in the pre-Roman Iron Age.

The geographic characteristics of a landscape consist of both physical and human characteristics.[1] Physical characteristics are the elements that together form the natural environment of a landscape. They include physical features, such as landforms and bodies of water, soil types, climate, natural resources, and the region's flora and fauna. Human characteristics are the properties that make up the cultural environment of a landscape. They are the result of the human interactions within and with an area and include aspects such as modifications to the land (buildings, infrastructure, and cultivation), population distribution, political organisation, economic activities, and socio-cultural aspects of life (e.g. language and belief systems). In this chapter, I therefore discuss the main geographic characteristics of the historical landscape of the region that are required to provide a solid starting point for my later analysis.

2.1 The Natural Landscape

The research area is in the east and the north, largely demarcated by the Rhine and its distributaries, and in the north-west by the North Sea (Figure 1). The western border is less clear but roughly runs from the Scheldt Estuary southward towards the Belgium-France border. In the south, the boundary is formed by the Ardennes and Eifel. Although the southernmost parts of these mountainous lands fall outside of the research area, the majority of their acreage lies within it. Accordingly, the region essentially corresponds to the Roman province of Germania Inferior as it was established in the late first century AD under emperor Domitian. It should, however, be noted that in the south-east, the borders are more flexible, in order to include some of the resource-rich areas to the east of the Rhine and south of the Ahr. The region, as such, includes

1 However, it should be noted that human and natural characteristics mutually influence each other. Castree, Demeritt and Liverman, 2009.

© ERIK TIMMERMAN, 2024 | DOI:10.1163/9789004682214_003

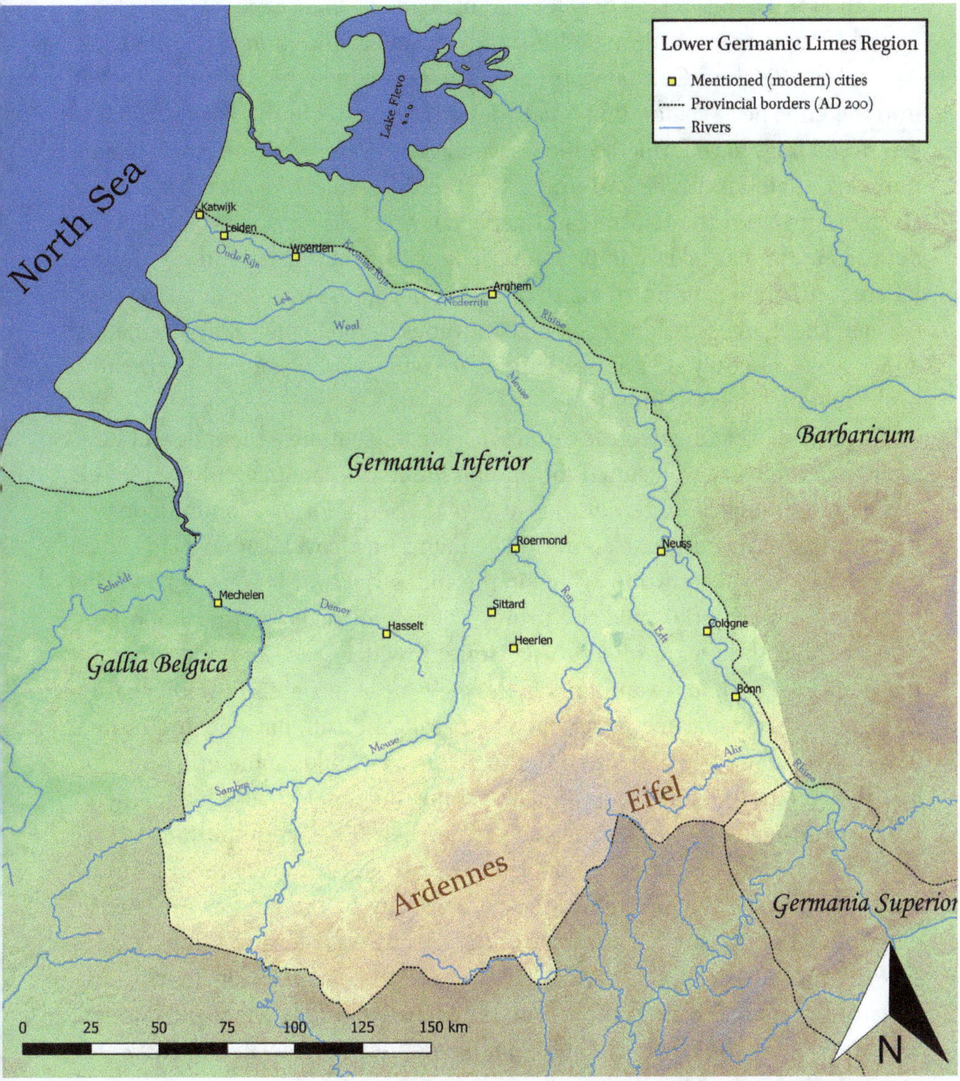

FIGURE 1 The Lower Germanic Limes region with the main locations and features mentioned in the text
Note: The non-shaded part is the research area.

a very diverse natural landscape, which to a large degree has influenced the way in which humans have lived in the region throughout (pre)history.

Geographically, the research area can be divided into several sub-regions with distinctive physical characteristics. In the south lie the rugged lands of the Ardennes and Eifel. The relief of these mountain ranges lies between 400 and 750 meters above sea level, and the rocky grounds, consisting primarily of slate and sandstone, are not very fertile.[2] Instead, the landscape is largely dominated by forests, even though grasslands occur on the more level plateaus. Around the Belgium-Germany border, in the area where the Ardennes go over into the Eifel, lies a region that is called the High Fens.[3] In this region, numerous raised bogs have formed, which have made the area very unfavourable for human settlement. In the eastern part of the Eifel, volcanic activity has left a strong imprint on the natural landscape.[4] In this area, various volcanic rock deposits and maar lakes can be found. The soils resulting from these deposits are much richer in nutrients than those in the rest of the Eifel. However, because these areas are located at high altitudes (often higher than 500 meters above sea level), they are not well suited for arable farming and, like in the rest of the region, forests predominate.[5]

The overall roughness of the terrain has meant that the Ardennes and Eifel are not particularly well suited for human habitation and agriculture. At the same time, though, the terrain has always carried a lot of economic potential because of its natural resources. The high forest coverage has made it an important reservoir of wood, which in pre-industrial times formed one of the main building materials and the primary source of fuel. Another important resource that the region offered was stone. A widely used building stone in the Roman period, for example, was the greywacke, which is omnipresent in the region. Also, volcanic rocks, such as basalt and tuff, have been quarried in the area since early times, in order to be used as building materials and for other purposes. In addition to wood and stone, the region is also rich in metal ores. In particular, the High Fens and the northern Eifel are important in this respect and feature reserves of iron, lead, copper, and zinc.[6] For the transportability of these heavy resources, the connectivity of the area to the Meuse and Rhine, the two main waterways of the region, was of crucial importance. The river Rur, for instance, springs from the High Fens and runs northwards towards Roermond, where it flows into the Meuse. Similarly, the rivers Erft and Ahr both rise in the northern Eifel from where they flow north and eastward, respectively, towards the Rhine.

Towards the north of these mountainous lands, the landscape gradually changes into a less rough and much more fertile area. From the Cologne Bay in the east, a long belt predominated by loess soils stretches westwards through the southernmost tip of the Netherlands and central Belgium into Northern

2 Graafen, 2006, p. 40; Beyaert *et al.*, 2006, pp. 114–117.
3 Beyaert *et al.*, 2006, pp. 100–103.
4 Meschede, 2015, pp. 194–200.
5 Graafen, 2006.
6 Rothenhöfer, 2005a, p. 22.

France.[7] Loess is an aeolian deposit and is very well suited for arable farming. It is relatively rich in nutrients, sufficiently drainable, and easy to cultivate. Although the soil is susceptible to erosion, this is primarily a factor in sloped areas. The part of the loess belt that lies east of the Meuse extends roughly northwards from Sittard to Neuss and southwards from Heerlen to Bonn. This eastern part is divided into three parts by the rivers Erft and Rur. The so-called Jülicher and Zülpicher Börde are mostly flat, while the Limburger Börde has somewhat more relief and, thus, reduced loess coverage. West of the Meuse, the loess zone roughly follows the line Hasselt-Mechelen as its northern border and the Sambre and Meuse rivers as its southern limit. This Belgian loess zone also has some areas with a more distinct relief, which go together with erosion and reduced agricultural potential.[8] In general, however, the entire above-described loess belt clearly formed the region with the most productive potential for arable farming in the research area.

The productive potential of the arable landscape was markedly lower in the regions that lie directly to the north of the loess areas. The part to the west of the Meuse is known as the Meuse-Demer-Scheldt (MDS) region, which derives its name from the three rivers that together constitute the main outlines of its geographical borders. The landscape of this region is generally flat and is primarily covered by mineralogical poor sandy soils, which provide limited natural fertility.[9] This area contains numerous small streams, and because the drainage in certain parts of the area is poor, this has sometimes led to marshy conditions and peat formation. This is especially the case in the north-west of the region, where the marshland continues up to the Dutch coast, and in the east of the region. In general, the MDS region can thus be characterised as an area that is not particularly suitable for crop growing, and animal husbandry might therefore have been more important here.

The region that lies to the east of the Meuse is slightly different from that of the MDS region. This region is called the Lower Rhine Plain, and it encompasses the area between the Rhine and Meuse and extends from Neuss in the south to the Germany-Netherlands border in the north. The flat landscape here is very diverse.[10] It consists of cover sand soils with poor natural fertility, but it also has a significant proportion of highly fertile loess soils. Furthermore, it

7 Bakels, 2009, pp. 2–4.

8 This is, for example, the case in the Condroz region. Beyaert *et al.*, 2006, pp. 96–99; De Brue *et al.*, 2017, pp. 154–156.

9 Gerritsen, 2003; De Clercq, Creemers and Hiddink, 2015.

10 Brüggler *et al.*, 2017, pp. 74–79.

has a large share of alluvial deposits. Although these clayey, loamy, and sandy soils are very rich in nutrients, they were not very suitable for arable farming because of their wetness. Instead, they were more often used as meadows and pasturelands. In sum, the Lower Rhine Plain is better suited for arable farming than the MDS region, but its potential does not come close to that of the more southerly loess region. Instead, the varied composition of the landscape provides good opportunities for both arable farming and animal husbandry.

Following the course of the Rhine and Meuse further westwards into the northernmost part of the research area, the landscape turns into a river delta.[11] Here, the Rhine branches off into the Waal.[12] The Waal follows a westward trajectory towards the North Sea and joins with the Meuse and Lek in the estuary near Naaldwijk which, in Roman times, was known as the *Helinium*.[13] The Rhine itself continues a little bit further north and eventually reaches the North Sea at Katwijk. This northern track formed the edge of the Roman Empire, and it also forms the border of the current research area.

The eastern part of this river delta, roughly the area lying to the east of Woerden, is known as the Dutch River Area.[14] This was a dynamic region where the interaction between land and water to a large extent shaped the natural landscape. Although all the land was prone to flooding, especially the lower lying flood basins, human habitation was relatively safe at the somewhat higher located levees and stream ridges. Because of the regular flooding, the alluvial soils, consisting of sand, silt, and clay, belonged to the most nutrient rich lands of the research area. The risk of flooding and the general wetness of the land, however, meant that the suitability of the area for arable farming remained largely limited to the higher situated parts. The lower and wetter parts of the region, then, were more suited for pasture and hay meadows.

In the western part of the river delta, in the area between Leiden and Woerden, stretched an extensive peat-forming wetland area.[15] This marshland consisted primarily of swamps, fens, and raised bogs, and the rivers that flowed through them formed the only corridors of access in this largely

---

11 The landscape of this river delta has (to a larger extent than the rest of the research area) changed considerably throughout the ages as a result of the impact of the rivers and the sea. I have based my description of the landscape on the supposed situation at the beginning of the first century AD, as presented in Polak and Kooistra, 2013, pp. 386–389; Kooistra *et al.*, 2013.

12 Cf. Tac. Ann. 2, 6; Caes. Gall. 4, 10.

13 Plin. Nat. 4.101.

14 Groot and Kooistra, 2009.

15 Kooistra *et al.*, 2013, pp. 7–10; Polak and Kooistra, 2013, pp. 367–373.

impassable landscape. The narrow ridges of these rivers were the only places where human habitation and agricultural exploitation were possible, as these riverbanks provided similar conditions to those in the Dutch River Area.

Along the Dutch North Sea coast, a thin strip of sandy beach barriers separated the peat area from the North Sea.[16] Even though these high standing dunes were suitable for habitation, their sandy soils were not very fertile. Along the estuaries, where the rivers cut through the coastline into the sea, the ridges with their sandy and clayey soil were better suited for arable farming. Moreover, on the somewhat lower lying parts of the riverbanks, lay brackish reed and sedge marshes that provided good grazing grounds.

Apart from the terrain, the (agricultural) economic potential of a landscape is to a large extent influenced by its climate.[17] In general, the climatic conditions in the research area have not changed radically in the last 2,200 years.[18] Like today, the region fell within the temperate oceanic climate zone. This means that it had mild winters and moderately warm summers, which formed an ideal backdrop for crop growing. Nevertheless, the climate has experienced various important fluctuations throughout the centuries, as is evidenced by several natural-scientific proxy datasets that have been compiled in recent years.[19] These paleoclimatic indicators suggest that many regions in central Europe in the period between circa 100 BC and 200 AD experienced exceptionally stable, warm and wet climatic conditions. This so-called Roman Warm Period is believed to have been a very favourable time for agricultural production and has, therefore, often been viewed as one of the main drivers of the Roman Empire's economic growth in this period. After circa AD 200, the climatic circumstances seem to have worsened. The third century AD was a very dry period, and from around AD 280 onwards, the temperature also dropped significantly. Although the fourth and fifth centuries AD were again somewhat wetter, temperatures remained low. In general, the period after AD 200 can, thus, be characterised as an unstable period with more unfavourable conditions for agriculture. Better climatic conditions returned in the Early Middle Ages, as temperatures and precipitation levels began to increase from around AD 650 onwards.

---

16 Kooistra *et al.*, 2013, pp. 7–10; Polak and Kooistra, 2013, pp. 367–373.

17 Strabo describes the climate in the region as rainy, foggy, and without much sun. Strab. 4, 5, 2.

18 We are still living in the so-called Sub-Atlantic stage.

19 These proxies vary from tree rings and ice cores to speleothems and lake sedimentation. The climatic developments presented here are primarily based on Klostermann, 2001; Schmidt and Gruhle, 2003a; 2003b; Büntgen *et al.*, 2011; McCormick *et al.*, 2012.

2.2 The Pre-Roman Economy

By the time that the Romans first set foot in the above-described area, they found a landscape that had already been inhabited by man for thousands of years. Even though the image of a largely undisturbed natural landscape covered by primeval forests still holds sway over the general imagination, archaeo-botanical studies have shown that this image does not correspond well with reality.[20] Pollen diagrams from various parts of the Lower Germanic Limes region show that the proportion of woodland to agricultural land had already been considerably reduced long before the Roman period.[21] Thus, at the time of the Romans' arrival, much of the landscape was already opened up and being cultivated by its inhabitants.

On the eve of the Roman conquest, in the period that is called the Late Iron Age (or Late La Tène period), the region was inhabited by various native tribes.[22] Since these tribes had no written tradition themselves, our primary source of information about them is Caesar's account of the Gallic War. Still, even though Caesar deals extensively with the (supposed) ethnicity and military actions of the various tribes, his description of their (economic) way of life is limited and probably not very accurate.[23] For instance, he describes the Germanic people as hunters who did not practice agriculture and lived mainly off milk, cheese, and meat.[24] Archaeological research, on the other hand, is probably a more reliable source of information in this regard and has significantly increased our knowledge of these tribes in recent decades.

In modern research, these tribes are generally characterised as segmentary warrior societies, whose rural economies were aimed at local self-sufficiency and the spread of risk.[25] Almost the entire population was involved in agriculture and practiced a mixed agricultural strategy, consisting of a combination of arable and livestock farming. The most important cultivated crops were cereals, such as barley, millet, and wheat (primarily emmer and spelt), but the

---

20 The image probably owes much to Tacitus, who famously stated that, in general, the landscape of *Germania*: 'either bristles with woods or festers with swamps.' Tac. Germ. 5.

21 E.g. Kalis and Meurers-Balke, 2007; Kalis *et al.*, 2008; Kooistra, 2008; van den Bos *et al.*, 2014.

22 In general, this period refers to the second and first centuries BC. Sometimes, the second half of the third century BC is also included.

23 A better description can perhaps be found in Tacitus' *Germania*. However, it should be noted that his work deals with the Germanic peoples outside the borders of the Roman Empire and covers a somewhat later period. Nevertheless, many of his observations might also apply to the tribes that lived in the research area in the pre-Roman period.

24 Caes. Gall. 6, 21–22.

25 van Heeringen, 1989, pp. 241–244; Roymans, 1996, pp. 44–51; Jansen, 2021, pp. 9–11.

crop spectrum also included pulses, such as beans, peas, and lentils, as well as some oil-rich and fibrous plants, such as flax and gold-of-pleasure.[26] The most important animal species that were bred were cattle, pigs, sheep, and goats, often supplemented by small-scale breeding of horses, which were primarily utilised for prestige or for military purposes.[27] Non-agricultural goods such as ceramics, textiles, and wooden or metal tools were produced at the household level without much technological sophistication. Specialised craft workers were few, and the extent of trade was limited.[28] Exchange of goods, whether agricultural products or prestige items, did occur, but often in the context of the reproduction of social networks or in the ritualistic sphere.[29] Coinage was not unknown among these tribes. It is known that already in the second century BC, imported gold coins circulated among them and that they minted gold, silver, and bronze coins in the second half of the first century BC.[30] It does seem, however, that these coins were not always used in a monetary sense (i.e. as a medium of impersonal exchange) but that their use was often embedded in social and religious structures, being used in the context of gift-exchanges and rituals.[31] Furthermore, bartering still may have played an important role.[32]

The social structure of these societies is believed to have been essentially egalitarian.[33] This is, for example, suggested by the structure of the settlement landscape, which was dotted with small, unfortified rural settlements and single farmsteads. A hierarchy between these settlements did not exist, and larger settlements that functioned as central places were practically non-existent.[34] With the exception of the Belgian part of the loess zone, settlement areas were generally not enclosed by ditches or other enclosures, which seems to indicate that the land and the herds of these communities were being shared as common property.[35] The people inhabiting these rural settlements and farmsteads lived in houses that were constructed entirely from wood and other organic materials. Within the research area, a broad dichotomy in housebuilding traditions can be observed between the north and the south.[36] In the northern part,

26 Roymans, 1990, pp. 103–105; Kooistra, 2009a, p. 223.
27 Roymans, 1996, p. 49.
28 Heimberg, 2011, p. 19.
29 Cf. Tac. Germ. 15.
30 Roymans and Aarts, 2009, pp. 19–21.
31 Roymans and Aarts, 2009, p. 20; Komnick, 2018, pp. 57–59; Otte, 2022, pp. 165–166.
32 Cf. Tac. Germ. 5.
33 Caes. Gall. 6,22; Roymans, 1990, pp. 43–45; Heimberg, 2003, pp. 59–62; Jansen, 2021, p. 480.
34 Cf. Tac. Germ. 16,1.
35 Cf. Tac. Germ. 26; Heimberg, 2011, p. 19; Habermehl, 2013, p. 38.
36 Joachim, 2007b.

which comprises the lands to the north of the loess zone, the typical house type was the byre house (*Wohnstallhaus*), a type of house where the inhabitants shared a roof with their livestock.[37] This housebuilding tradition apparently coincided with the agricultural regime of the areas, where livestock farming held a prominent place. In the southern loess area, where the economy was more oriented towards arable farming, this housebuilding tradition was largely absent, and houses appear to have been constructed as separate structures and set apart from secondary buildings such as stables and granaries.[38] There are no clear indications of differences in the wealth or social status of their inhabitants between the houses in the research area. The same goes for their burials, which are characterised by their simplicity.[39] Although people might have expressed their status through other forms of personal belongings, the social differentiation in this region would probably not have been too great.

The situation in the research area stood in stark contrast with the more southerly region of central Gaul, where the so-called *oppida* zone found its heartland.[40] Here the settlement landscape also consisted of small, scattered rural settlements and farms, but these units were mostly enclosed, which suggests a more pronounced system of landed property and seems to point to a more hierarchical social structure.[41] Of particular interest, in this respect, are the *Viereckschanzen*, which are farmsteads enclosed by a rectangular palisaded rampart and ditch. The buildings and precious objects that have been found within these enclosures, suggest that they were the farmsteads of the nobility.[42] In addition to these smaller settlements, the region also contained many larger fortified settlements, which Caesar called *oppida*. Although much variety existed between *oppida*, many of them played an important role in political, social, economic, and religious life. They were the ruling elite's seats of power, and they had a differentiated social system. Additionally, they were often centres of industry and trade. They housed specialist craft workers and traders, who, like the elite and their military entourages, did not produce their own food. The required food came from the rural hinterlands of the *oppida*, where farmers produced agricultural surpluses, which made possible

37 Well excavated examples have been found in Wijk bij Duurstede-De Horden, Tiel-Passewaaij, and Geldermalsen-Hondsgemet. Boreel and van Renswoude, 2014.

38 Well-known examples have been excavated in Jüchen-Neuholz, Pulheim-Braunweiler, and Niederzier-Hambach. Frank and Keller, 2007; Joachim, 2007a; 2016.

39 Bechert, 2001, p. 3.

40 There is some discussion about the precise definition of this term and about the extent to which they might be characterised as (proto-)urban. Woolf, 1993; Fernández-Götz, 2014.

41 Heimberg, 2000, pp. 190–193.

42 Sievers, 2020, p. 12.

an increased division of labour. Through this blooming economic life, some *oppida*, for example, the Titelberg in southern Luxembourg, could develop into hubs of inter-regional trade.[43] Other *oppida*, such as the Martberg near Pommern, were centres of religious activity and owed their importance to the presence of a temple or sanctuary.[44]

It should be noted that recent research has begun to cast some doubt on the rigid disparity between the 'Celtic' *oppida* zone and the 'Germanic' lands that lay north of them. Nico Roymans argues that the societies that inhabited the northern regions may have been more complex than traditionally assumed.[45] He challenges the apparent lack of larger central places by drawing attention to temple complexes that were found in the Dutch River Area. These complexes, located in Empel, Elst, and Kessel, are believed to have been religious centres of supra-local importance. Moreover, the significance of Kessel might even have extended beyond the religious sphere. Even though the evidence is very scanty, there are some indications that the site was also an important socio-political and economic centre. According to Roymans, the existence of these central places, as well as the issuing of gold and silver coins in the region, indicates that the power of local elite warbands (so-called *comitatus*) must have been greater than previously believed.[46] This research thus suggests that our traditional view might require a slight revision, although additional archaeological research is required to solidify many of the claims. In any case, it seems that the stark contrast with central Gaul, where the settlement structure and social relations were clearly more developed, does hold up.

2.3 Conclusions

The Lower Germanic Limes region consisted of various sub-regions with different economic potential. The rough area in the outermost south was not very suitable for agriculture but was rich in important natural resources, such as wood, stone, and metal. Directly to the north of these rugged lands lay a long strip of loess soil that formed the most fertile region of the research area. This region had the greatest potential for arable farming. This was different from the more northerly areas. The sandy soils of the so-called MDS region were not very suitable for agriculture but offered opportunities for animal husbandry.

43 Metzler, 1995, p. 154.
44 Wegner, 2007, pp. 68–71.
45 Roymans, 2004, pp. 9–16.
46 Roymans, 2004, pp. 18–22.

For the areas in the far north and north-east of the research area, the agricultural potential was largely determined by the influence of the Rhine and its tributaries. Here, certain areas were well-suited for arable farming, others for stock raising, but there were also parts where no agricultural production was feasible.

In the pre-Roman Late Iron Age, this natural landscape had already been largely cultivated by the several native tribes that inhabited the area. The rural economies of these warrior tribes were largely geared towards self-sufficiency and the spread of risk. These subsistence farmers lived primarily off a combination of arable and livestock farming. In this respect, the emphasis was probably more on arable farming in the southern loess zone and more on animal husbandry in the northern areas. The farmers mainly produced their non-agricultural products themselves, without much technological sophistication at the household level. Accordingly, specialised craft workers were few, and the extent of trade was limited. Moreover, when the exchange of goods did take place, there was often a social or ritualistic component to it. The focus on subsistence is also reflected in the settlement landscape, which was almost entirely made up of small rural settlements, while central places were extremely scarce.

CHAPTER 3

The Roman Impact

The arrival of the Romans initiated dramatic changes in many aspects of life in the above-described research area. As is the case with practically every violent conquest, the initial consequences of the Roman presence can be characterised as destructive and disruptive. However, after things began to normalize, the inhabitants of the region could recover and began to adapt to the new situation. But what did this new situation encompass, and to what extent did the Roman domination bring change to the societies that had lived in the region in the Late Iron Age?

In this chapter, I begin to provide an answer to these questions by discussing the most important general developments that made an impact on the regional economy. These developments include the large-scale militarisation of the Rhine frontier, increased urbanisation, (rural) population growth, the introduction of Roman institutions in the region, and the development of the regional infrastructure.[1] As a combined result of these developments, the subsistence economy that had existed in the Late Iron Age was gradually transformed into an economic system, in which market-oriented exchange played an increasingly important role. As such, the discussion in this chapter provides a general background for the more detailed analysis of the developments in the different sectors of the economy in the following chapters.

3.1 The Roman Army

One of the most important and striking aspects of the Roman occupation in the Lower Germanic Limes region was the large-scale presence of the Roman army (Figure 2). The earliest military fortifications along the Lower Rhine served mainly to provide operating bases for the campaigns in the lands east of the Rhine.[2] However, after Rome's expansionist ambitions in Germania Magna had come to an end in the early first century AD, the Roman military presence

1 There was, of course, overlap and mutual dependence between these developments. This broad categorisation, however, is chosen for conceptual reasons.

2 Gechter, 2007, pp. 91–92; Hanel, 2007, p. 398.

© ERIK TIMMERMAN, 2024 | DOI:10.1163/9789004682214_004

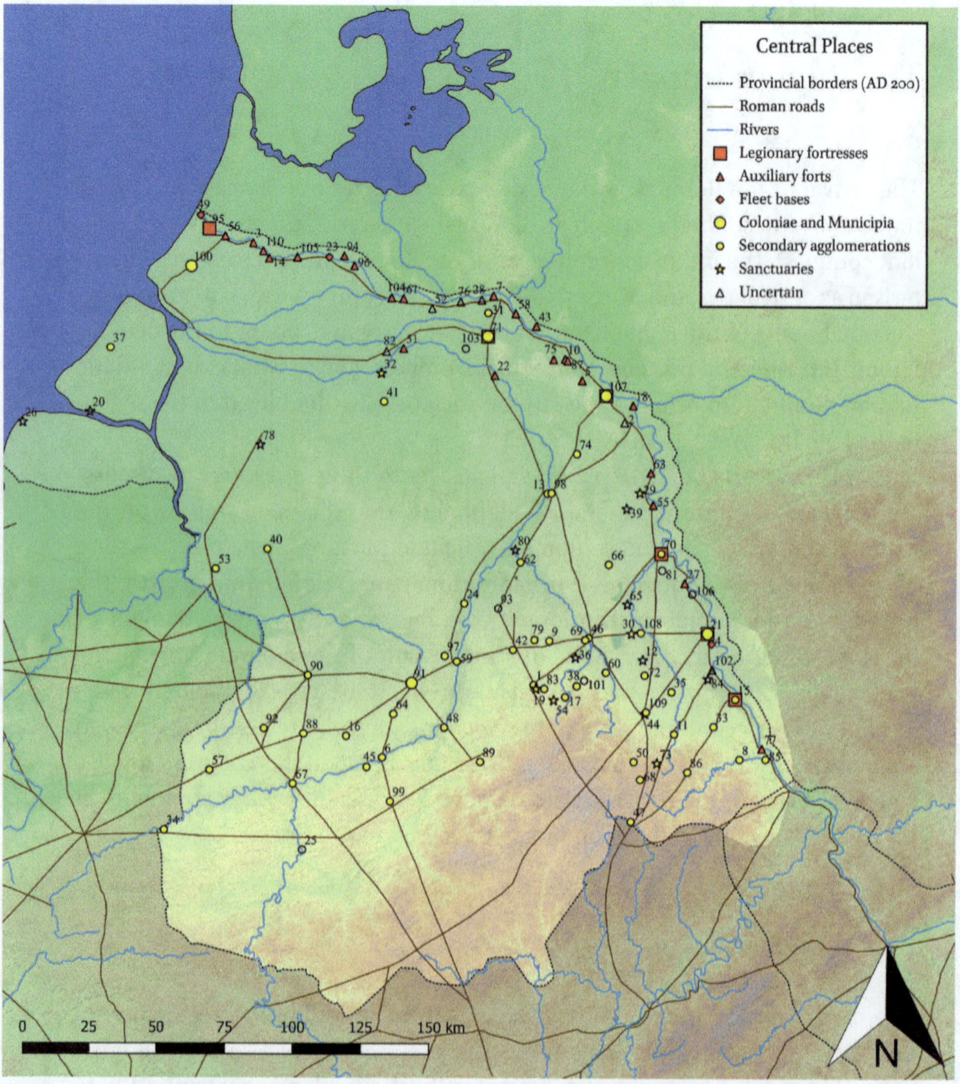

FIGURE 2 Central places (military and civilian) that were in existence in the Lower Germanic Limes region in the Roman period
Note: Data in Appendix 1.

attained a more permanent and defensive oriented character.[3] By the end of the first century AD, the fortification of the Lower Germanic Limes had reached its greatest extent and Roman fortresses and forts could now be found all along the Rhine from Remagen in the south-east to Katwijk in the

3 Fischer, 2012, pp. 303–304.

north-west.[4] This state of affairs would remain largely unchanged until the Germanic invasions of the late third century AD.

Nonetheless, the number of soldiers stationed within the military bases varied considerably throughout the Roman period (Figure 3). The military presence was greatest in the first century AD. It is unclear how many troops were present in the Augustan period, but calculations suggest that in the period between the reign of Tiberius and that of Nero around 42,000 soldiers had been active in the region. Of these soldiers, 22,000 were legionaries, while the rest were auxiliaries (20,000). After the Batavian Revolt, Vespasian dissolved or replaced the auxiliary troops, so that their number was reduced to circa 15,500.[5] This trend continued under Domitian, until at the end of his reign, the auxiliaries were reduced to 13,000. Meanwhile, the number of legionaries had remained stable. The largest reduction of troops in the region took place under Trajan, who must have needed the manpower for his Dacian Wars.[6] The number of legionaries was now reduced to 11,000, which, combined with 10,000 auxiliaries, made a total force of 21,000 soldiers. Except for the momentary increase in the number of legionaries to 16,500, which led to a total of 26,500 soldiers under Hadrian, the total number of soldiers would now remain around 21,000 until the third century AD.[7] Even though the military presence from the second century AD onwards was less substantial than it had been before, the region remained one of the most densely militarised provinces of the empire. Considering that estimates of the total size of the Roman army assume a total of 300,000 soldiers under Augustus and 400,000 soldiers at the end of the reign of Septimius Severus, the stationing of between 42,000 and 21,000 soldiers along the circa 320 kilometres long Lower-Rhine frontier was very significant.[8]

It is difficult to overstate the economic impact that the large-scale presence of the Roman army had on the research area. As a safeguard against both external and internal threats, the military was, most of the time, successful in keeping the peace in the region and, thus, created circumstances that were beneficial for investments and trade. This period of peace in the region was largely part of the empire-wide *Pax Romana*, which denotes the relatively peaceful conditions that the Roman Empire experienced in the period from the reign of Augustus to the reign of Marcus Aurelius. This 'Roman Peace' ensured that the

4 I will use the terms fortress and fort to denote legionary and auxiliary fortifications, respectively.

5 Fischer, 2012, p. 304.

6 Polak, 2009, p. 950.

7 Although not much is known about the army in Late Antiquity, we can assume that the manpower declined even further. Brulet, 2017, p. 40.

8 Garnsey and Saller, 1987, p. 114.

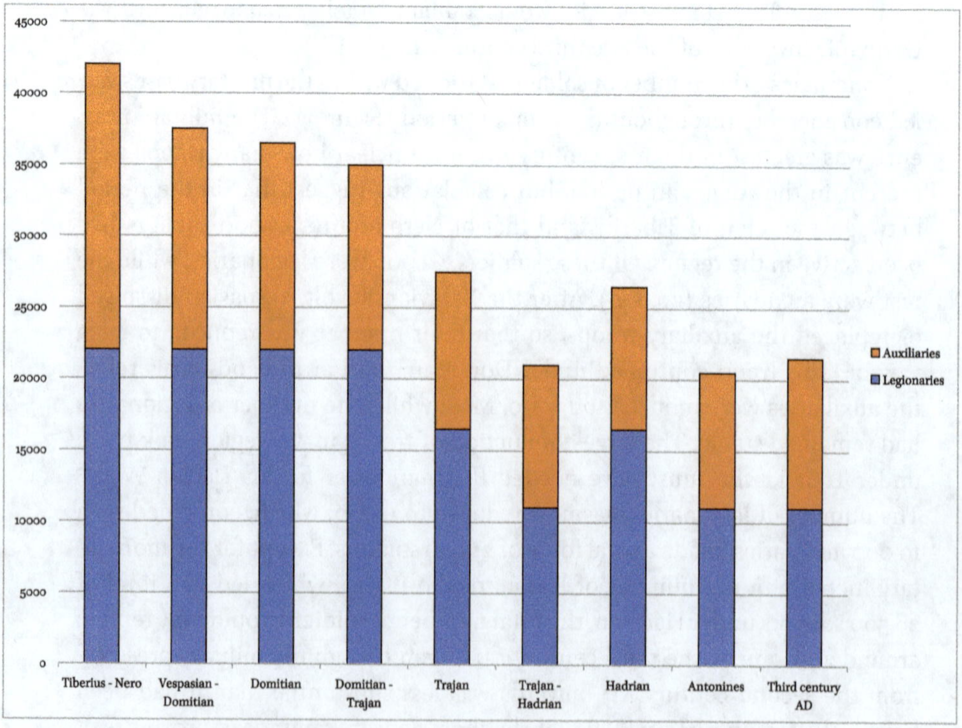

FIGURE 3 The total number of soldiers stationed along the Lower Germanic Limes
Note: Kunow, 1987, p. 55.

financial risks that came with economic transactions and investments were significantly reduced. Tribal wars, civilian unrest, piracy, and banditry could all disrupt economic life and therefore acted as a brake on economic development. The presence of the Roman army and the peace that it defended made sure that these risks were reduced to a minimum. Consequently, economic production, and transportation became more secure, which stimulated producers and traders to invest their money in the regional economy, as the risk of loss of these investments through disruptions had become more limited.

However, the impact of the thorough militarisation of the Lower Germanic Limes region was not restricted to the creation of a safe economic climate. The sudden concentration of manpower in the fortresses and forts along the Rhine also created a large demand for regionally and extra-regionally produced goods and services because the army needed to be supplied with various resources. The most important things for the soldiers' wellbeing were, of course, food and drink. In addition to these nutritional requirements, the soldiers needed clothing and equipment, such as armour, weaponry, and tools; stone, timber, and metal for building; firewood; animals such as horses and mules (which also had to be fed); and leather for the tents and a range of other purposes.[9]

The army had several ways to gain access to these resources.[10] Since the costs of transport were high in the ancient world, the army would ideally look to the surrounding environment for supplies. They could exploit resources themselves, or gain them through interactions with local civilians, whether by way of taxation, requisition, or, if they wanted relations to remain more peaceful, by trading. It is very unlikely that the regional economy, which after all, was largely a subsistence economy, could have produced sufficient surpluses to cover the large military demand in the initial phase of Roman occupation. In this period, a vast share of the resources therefore must have been imported from further away, which was a far more expensive option. Over time, though, the possibilities that military demand afforded, stimulated regional producers to increase their production (see chapters 4 and 5). As the producers gradually adapted to the new situation, and especially after the reduction of the troops in the second century AD, the regional economy appears to have been able to cover a significant part of the army's demand. However, some goods, such as wine and oil, still had to come from elsewhere, as they could not be produced in the research area because of specific climatic requirements.

Besides the army's demand for these essential military supplies, individual Roman soldiers also constituted a large consumer market for non-essential goods and services. They would, for example, crave a better meal or a quality wine, or desire a more expensive set of tableware. Since military pay is believed to have been relatively high compared to civilian incomes, the aggregate purchasing power of soldiers must have been great.[11] The sources indicate that the *stipendium* (i.e. the annual pay) of a legionary was 900 *sestertii* at the beginning of the Principate and was raised to 1,200 *sestertii* during the reign of Domitian.[12] The annual pay of an auxiliary soldier was slightly lower, being estimated at 750 and 1,000 *sestertii*, respectively.[13] The soldiers' wages were not paid out in their entirety; deductions were made for the provisions that the army supplied to them. These provisions included supplies such as their military rations, animal fodder, footwear, clothing, and equipment but

9 Kehne, 2007; Herz, 2010.

10 Carreras, 2002, pp. 71–83.

11 Speidel, 2000.

12 Fischer, 2012, p. 20.

13 The *stipendium* increased even more significantly around the end of the second and in the third century AD. It is, however, unlikely that this corresponded to an actual increase in purchasing power as it coincided with a debasement of the coinage. Cleary, 2013, pp. 20–21.

also for ceremonies or feasts. Altogether, the deductions probably amounted to about a half to three quarters of the total wage of low-ranking soldiers.[14] This would thus leave auxiliaries and legionaries in the time of Domitian with a sum between 250 and 600 *sestertii* to spend yearly on non-essentials. The soldiers that reached their retirement also received a bonus, the *praemium militiae*, which under Augustus was fixed at 12,000 *sestertii*.[15] If we compare these amounts to the estimated yearly subsistence costs of an average Roman in late first century AD Italy, which was somewhere between 235 and 350 *sestertii* a year, it becomes evident that the soldiers were relatively wealthy.[16]

Apart from stimulating intra- and extra-regional production and exchange of goods and services, the large-scale military presence was also a crucial factor in the increased monetisation of the region (see section 3.4.2). As the wages of the Roman soldiers were largely paid out in coin, vast amounts of money flowed into the area. We can be confident that a large amount of the military pay was actually spent and invested in this same area, especially since it seems that many of the soldiers upon retiring settled in the same region in which they had served.[17] Because about half of the soldiers consisted of locally recruited auxiliary troops, at least before the Batavian Revolt, Roman coins were rapidly diffused among the native societies, so that exchange in the region gradually attained a more monetised character.[18]

The military demand and the great purchasing power of the Roman soldiers also led to the development of civilian settlements close to the military fortifications. These extramural settlements, not only provided the soldiers with public buildings, such as temples, fora, amphitheatres, and public baths, but also housed a variety of people who all had close links with the army.[19] There were, for example, smiths who produced and repaired military equipment,

14 The deductions seem to have been reduced after Domitian's reign, allowing the soldiers to acquire their supplies through alternative, perhaps cheaper, channels. Around the middle of the second century AD, emperors began to provide soldiers with food, free of charge. Speidel, 2000, pp. 76–79.

15 There is no evidence that the *praemium militae* was paid after AD 68, nor that auxiliary troops received this payment. Still, this does not necessarily mean that these payments did not take place. Hopkins, 1980; Alston, 1995. Instead of (a part of) this monetary payment, veterans sometimes also received a plot of land. Rathbone, 1996, pp. 309–323.

16 de Ligt, 2012, p. 197. Admittedly, prices between Roman Italy and the frontier regions would not have been the same. However, in comparison, Italian prices were probably more on the high side than on the low.

17 Lo Cascio, 2007.

18 Roymans, 1996, p. 59; Aarts, 2005, pp. 11–12.

19 These extramural settlements can be divided into *canabae* (*legionis*) and so-called military *vici*, with the former indicating settlements near legionary fortresses and the latter settlements near auxiliary forts. Sommer, 1984, pp. 1–5; Hanel, 2007, p. 410.

specialised craftsmen manufacturing various items, merchants providing food and other commodities, but also shop owners, innkeepers, and prostitutes, who provided all kinds of leisure and entertainment. Furthermore, the settlements accommodated the wives and children of the soldiers, as well as veterans that had decided to settle close to the fortresses and forts.[20] In the course of time, many of the extramural settlements developed into blooming economic centres that often became much bigger than the military bases to which they belonged.[21] Accordingly, the population that inhabited many of these extramural settlements is believed to have been larger than that of the fortress or fort itself. Scholars who calculated Roman population densities in the German Rhineland assume a factor of 1.5, which leads to an average population of 1,125 people per settlement.[22] When considering the impact of the Roman army on the regional economy, it should thus be realised that this impact not only comprised the large number of soldiers that came to the region, but their many followers as well. Illustrative of the independent economic impact that went out from these civilian settlements is the fact that some of them, such as the extramural settlements in Moers-Asberg and Cuijk, continued to prosper as civilian urban settlements even after the military garrison had moved away.[23]

3.2 Urbanisation

In addition to these extramural settlements, which were intrinsically linked to the fortresses and forts, the region also witnessed the rise of multiple civilian urban settlements with a more independent character, so that the research area became increasingly urbanised (Figure 2).[24] This was an important development because urbanisation is believed to have been a main driver of per capita economic growth.[25] Like the military fortifications, the urban settlements created a large demand for regionally and extra-regionally produced goods and services, which stimulated production and trade in the research

20 Wierschowski, 2002, pp. 284–288.

21 E.g. the *canabae* of the legionary fortress of Nijmegen is believed to have been at least 100 hectares large. Franzen, 2009.

22 Wendt and Zimmermann, 2009, p. 55. However, it needs to be stressed that this estimate concerns the second century AD. In the first century AD, the factor would have been different as the military population was larger and the civilian population was probably smaller.

23 van Enckevort and Thijssen, 2002; Ulbert, 2013, pp. 14–15.

24 However, this does not mean that these settlements did not have a military connection at all.

25 For discussion of the role of urbanisation for the Roman economy, see Hanson, 2016, pp. 10–18.

area and beyond. Moreover, it provided the opportunity for increasing specialisation and division of labour in and between the urban settlements and their rural hinterlands.[26]

When discussing urban settlements, it is important to clarify how such a settlement is to be defined. However, finding an unambiguous definition of an urban settlement that is valid for all periods and regions is impossible. To arrive at a suitable definition, scholars look at different aspects of 'urban-ness'.[27] My own definition of an urban settlement is largely 'functional'. This means that non-military (and non-agricultural) central place settlements that fulfilled certain social, economic, or cultural functions for their own population and their hinterlands, will be considered as urban.[28] Indeed, I believe that such a definition is appropriate in a work in which the economic relations between different settlements are most important. At the same time, many of the settlements that I define as urban will be left out according to other definitions, for example, definitions based on population size or juridical status.

The so-defined civilian urban settlements in the region varied largely in size and character. The most important were Cologne and Xanten, the two *coloniae* of the region.[29] These were large and populous urban centres that provided regional producers with many opportunities for the exchange of goods and services. Furthermore, the region counted three *municipia*: Nijmegen, Tongeren, and Voorburg.[30] Although smaller than the two *coloniae*, these settlements were still sufficiently large to act as important central markets of supply and demand for their hinterlands. In addition to these *coloniae* and *municipia*, there existed a large number of secondary agglomerations that in the literature have often been called *vici*.[31] These secondary agglomerations can be defined as settlements with a non-agricultural character, in which the economic basis is most often grounded in artisanal or industrial production or in trade. This does not mean, however, that the inhabitants of these settlements were not involved in agriculture at all. It is evident that part of their population worked as farmers, and it is also clear that even larger percentages of inhabitants will

26 I will discuss these developments in more detail in the following two chapters.

27 For discussion, see de Ligt and Bintliff, 2020, pp. 10–15; Zuiderhoek, 2017, pp. 4–12.

28 Cf. Erdkamp, 2012, pp. 245–246; Pellegrino, 2018, pp. 5–21.

29 Cologne was elevated to the status of a *colonia* in AD 50 and Xanten around AD 100.

30 All three settlements received their legal status in the second century AD.

31 Kunow, 1988; Heimberg, 2000; Magerman, 2006; Ulbert, 2013. I myself, however, refrain from using the word *vicus* for these settlements. The reason for this is that it remains unclear what the precise meaning of this word was in Roman times. Instead, I will use the term secondary agglomeration for these settlements. For similar reasons, I will also not speak of military *vici* but of extramural settlements (the use of the word *canabae* is not problematic). For discussion, see Tarpin, 2002; Pellegrino, 2018, pp. 8–10.

have worked the land as seasonal labourers when demand for agricultural labour was highest (i.e. during the harvest). For the majority of the inhabitants, though, agriculture was not their primary occupation.[32]

If we look at the geographic spread of the secondary agglomerations throughout the research area, there are a few observations that can be made. The majority of the settlements are located in the loess region in the south. It is thus highly probable that their presence is related to the fertile soil of this region, which was very well-suited for agricultural exploitation. Moreover, the secondary agglomerations in this region (but also elsewhere) were clearly located along the important transport routes (cf. section 3.5). This seems to confirm their role as central nodes between their rural hinterlands and larger exchange networks. For some other settlements , especially those in the mountainous lands of the Ardennes and Eifel, the presence of natural resources and mineral deposits was decisive; they developed close to sources of metal, stone, clay, or sand.[33] In the northern river area and the MDS region, the number of secondary agglomerations is remarkably low. In the river area, this was probably the result of the large military presence. The fortresses and forts, along with their extramural settlements, must have served as central places here.[34] For the MDS region, the explanation for the lack of secondary agglomerations must be sought in a combination of mineralogically poor soils and a relatively poorly developed infrastructure, which made this region a more marginal area.[35] Lastly, there existed a few secondary agglomerations for which considerations for settlement were not necessarily economically driven: they grew around a sanctuary or a spa.[36]

Thus, in the course of the Roman period, an increasing number of people agglomerated in these urban settlements. Figure 4 gives an impression of how the total number of these settlements developed through time.[37] The first settlements, including Cologne, Xanten, Nijmegen, and Tongeren, already came into being during the early Augustan period. However, in the first century AD, the region witnessed the largest increase in settlements, reaching a total of 49 settlements.[38] In the second century AD, the highest number of settlements was reached: a total of 53 settlements were at the same time in existence in the first half of the second century AD. A first decline can already be observed in

32 Hanel, 2020, p. 110.
33 Ulbert, 2013, p. 10.
34 Heimberg, 2000, p. 200.
35 Roymans and Derks, 2015.
36 Ulbert, 2013, pp. 10–11.
37 The graph is based on the data in Appendix 1.
38 At least in the dataset on which this graph is based.

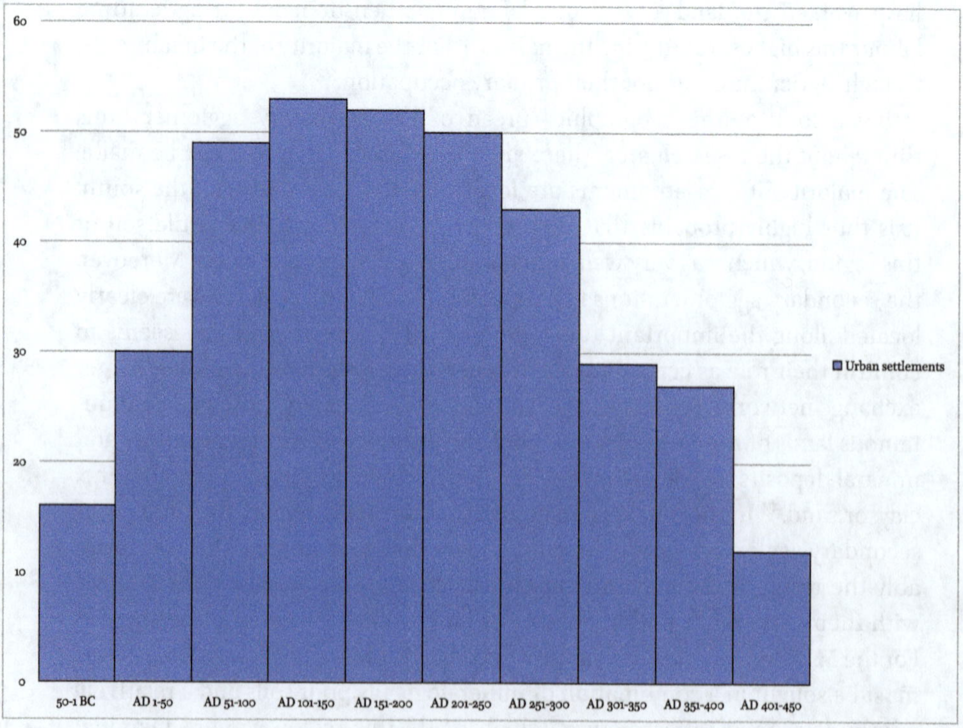

FIGURE 4 The development of the number of urban settlements in the Lower Germanic Limes region

the second half of the third century AD, when settlement numbers dropped to 43. A more substantial decline, though, is observable in the first half of the fourth century AD. This decline is probably related to the Germanic invasions that became more frequent from the late third century AD onwards. At the end of the fourth century AD, the number of settlements was reduced to 27. Finally, the abandonment of settlements carries on into the fifth century AD, when only a few settlements are still in existence. Importantly, the general trend that can be observed in the graph must roughly reflect the total number of people that were living in these urban settlements during the Roman period.[39] It therefore appears that the region experienced a considerable

39 I admit that the graph only shows the total number of settlements that were in existence at a certain moment in time and does not take into account things such as the size or population of the settlements. I believe, however, that although the inclusion of (estimates of) such variables would probably refine the graph to a certain extent, it would not significantly alter the general observed trend.

urban population increase in the first two centuries AD, followed by a just as significant decline from the second half of the third century AD onwards.

3.3 Population Growth

The increase in the urban population in the Lower Germanic Limes region was not an isolated phenomenon. It is clear that the area also experienced a significant increase in total population during the Roman period. This was an important development because population growth led to an increase in the scale of the regional economy. Thus, an increase in the population meant increased demand for various products (including food), but also an increase in the available labour force, which in turn enlarged the total regional economic output. Of course, given the debates about the nature of economic growth (see chapter 1), it is important to realise that such growth may have been essentially aggregate economic growth and that per capita production did not necessarily increase as a result. Theoretically, it is even more likely that per capita output may have fallen, as land may have become more of a constraining factor. Yet, as I will argue in more detail later in this book, this was probably not what happened in the research area. In any case, population growth is one of the most important variables for a proper understanding of the scale and nature of economic growth in the region.

We can get a good impression of the region's population dynamics in the very long run, from a research project that reconstructed population densities in the German Rhineland (Figure 5).[40] The authors of this demographic study estimate the population density in Roman times (during the second half of the second century AD) at between 10.8 and 17.9 people per square kilometre, which was around ten times as high as in the pre-Roman Iron Age (between 1.2 and 2.3 per km^2) or in the post-Roman Merovingian period (between 0.8 and 1 per km^2). Although this study is based on detailed and high-quality archaeological research, its conclusions might only be representative of the easternmost part of the research area (the Cologne Bay). To see if the findings from this particularly fertile region stand on their own, or whether they are part of a regional trend, they need to be compared with findings from other parts of the research area. An interesting area for comparison is the Dutch part of the sandy MDS region, for which long-term population dynamics have been

40 Zimmermann, Hilpert and Wendt, 2009.

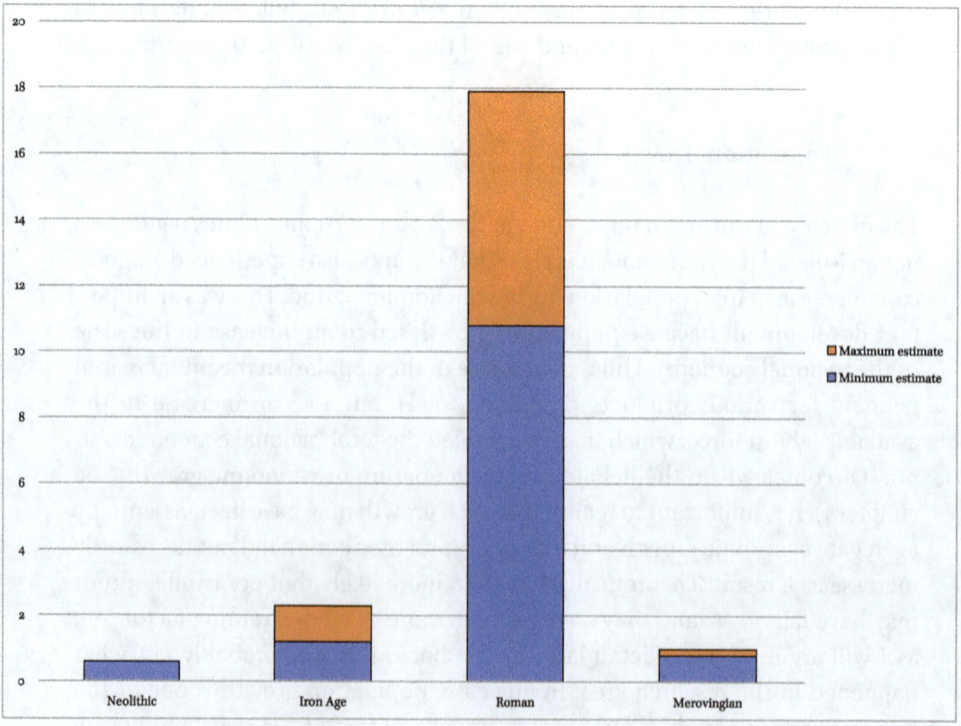

FIGURE 5 Estimated population densities in the German Rhineland per km^2
Note: Zimmermann, Hilpert and Wendt, 2009, p. 377; Jongman, 2014a, p. 80.

reconstructed in a recent article (Figure 6).[41] The results from this study are largely similar to the data from the Rhineland. The population density for the Roman period is estimated at 4.9 per km^2, which is around four times as high as that from the Iron Age (1.2 per km^2) and almost ten times as high as that from the Merovingian period (0.5 per km^2). In addition to the estimate for the 'regular' Iron Age (800 BC), the study also includes an estimate for the Late Iron Age (125 BC, 2.5 per km^2), which indicates that the population increase from the Iron Age to the Roman period was not as radical as it would seem at first sight. In the Late Iron Age, the population density had already doubled compared to the 'regular' Iron Age before it would double again in the Roman period. It should, however, be emphasised that the increase in the Roman period happened in a much shorter span of time.

The main conclusion that can be drawn from these two *longue durée* studies is clear: there were significantly more people living in the research area during the Roman period than before or after (at least before the beginning

41 Groenewoudt and van Lanen, 2018, p. 198.

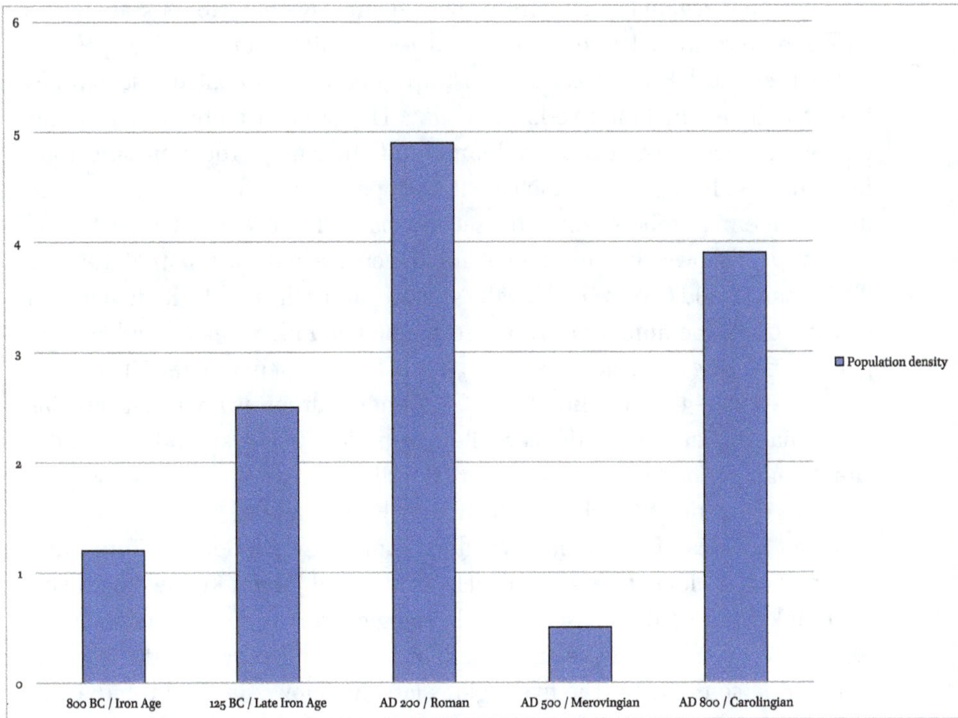

FIGURE 6 Estimated population densities in the Dutch part of the MDS region per km^2

of the second millennium AD). Even though we should not make too much of these calculations, as they include a large margin of error, it is convincing to see that the Iron Age and Merovingian densities from both regions are roughly in the same range. The difference between the estimated densities for the Roman period in the Rhineland and the MDS region can perhaps be explained by the higher natural fertility of the landscape and by the importance that Cologne and its hinterland attained in the Roman period. The estimate of the Late Iron Age from the MDS region, furthermore, cautions us not to overstate the increase from the Iron Age to the Roman period; an important degree of population growth already seems to have been underway before the arrival of the Romans. The decline in the post-Roman Merovingian period, though, was probably radical: population densities fell even below Iron Age levels.

The broad temporal scope of these estimates of population densities is important in highlighting the large differences between the Roman and the pre- and post-Roman periods. At the same time, however, this broad scope obscures the more detailed population dynamics within the Roman period itself. Moreover, the estimates from two of the region's sub-regions are not automatically representative of the research area as a whole. To add more temporal and regional precision to these figures, we have to look at studies with a more restricted chronological and geographical scope (Figure 7).[42]

For the Dutch River Area, the most up-to-date and detailed research has been conducted by Philip Verhagen *et al.*[43] This study used the Dutch Archis database to reconstruct the development of the rural settlement landscape from the Late Iron Age until the Late Roman period.[44] It shows a first increase in settlement numbers from the second part of the early Roman period (AD 25–70), followed by a more substantial increase in the first part of the middle Roman period (AD 70–150). By the second part of the middle Roman period (AD 150–270), the number of rural settlements had more than doubled compared to the Late Iron Age (250–12 BC) levels. In the first part of the late Roman period (AD 270–350), the number of settlements drops again, but it remains somewhat higher than in the early Roman period. In the second part of the late Roman period (AD 350–450), there is a slight recovery, but the settlement numbers come nowhere close to the middle Roman levels.[45]

To get an idea of the population development in the German Rhineland, the somewhat older study by Michael Gechter and Jürgen Kunow might still be useful.[46] The study is based on archaeological survey data from five different micro-regions.[47] Even though there are slight differences in the number of reported settlements, the five regions largely follow a general trend. Until AD 50, the regions were practically empty, with only a very few settlements being reported. This begins to change in the second half of the first century AD, when the number of settlements increases significantly. However, it seems that in the second century AD, nothing short of a settlement explosion occurred in the regions. Compared to the first half of the first century AD, the average number of settlements in the second half of the second century AD has increased almost fifty-fold. In the following centuries, a downward trend sets in. Although this decline is not as rapid as the increase, by the fifth century AD, the number of identified settlements is again close to zero.

---

42 Scholars have also estimated population numbers in parts of the research area at static moments in time. Although such estimates are valuable, I am here only concerned with development through time. For examples of such studies, see Wendt and Zimmermann, 2010; Hiddink, 2015; van Lanen *et al.*, 2018.

43 Verhagen *et al.*, 2016.

44 The Archis database aims to collect all registered archaeological finds on Dutch soil. *Archis*, no date.

45 This recovery was probably the result of the settlement of Germanic immigrants. Heeren, 2017.

46 Kunow and Gechter, 1986.

47 These micro-regions are: the Köln-Bonner Niederterrasse, the Rheinbacher Lößplatte, the Erfttal, the Hürtgener Hochfläche, and the Kempener Lehmplatte.

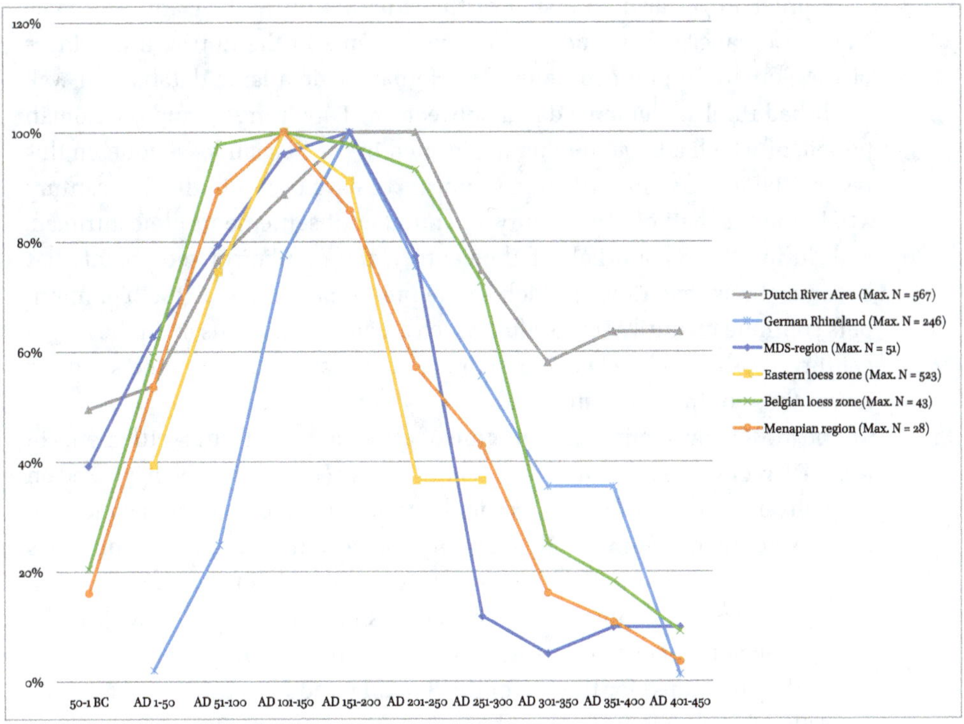

FIGURE 7 The chronological development of rural settlements in the six subregions of the Lower Germanic Limes region
Note: The original studies on which this graph is based use various kinds of periodisation and have largely different numbers of total settlements. In order to make the data comparable, it has first been divided into 50-year periods. Thereafter, the number of settlements in each 50-year period has been given a percentage relative to the period with the maximum number of settlements. The 50-year period with the highest number of settlements is thus 100%. The same method is used in Deru, 2017, p. 225.

More recently, Karen Jeneson has conducted research into the rural landscape in the loess zone between Cologne and Tongeren (eastern loess zone).[48] For this work, she has constructed a detailed geo-database from a variety of sources, including the national databases for archaeological heritage from three different countries (Belgium, the Netherlands, and Germany). Even though the chronological precision of the data is limited, it does allow an interesting observation. In the middle Roman period (*c.* AD 71–192), the number of dated settlements is more than two and a half times higher than in the early and late Roman periods (*c.* AD 0–70 and 193–300, respectively).

48 Jeneson, 2013.

In order to get an impression of the situation in the Belgian loess zone, Diederick Habermehl's study of villa settlements in the northern provinces of the Roman Empire can be used.[49] He has made a large database of well published rural settlements dated between the Late Iron Age and the Roman period, of which a large number are located in the Belgian loess zone. In this region, the increase in settlements appears to have begun in the first century AD. In the first half of this century, the number of settlements almost tripled, and during the second half of the century, the number of settlements has become almost five times as high as the pre-Roman levels. These high numbers continue up until AD 250, after which a slight decline sets in. In the fourth century AD, this decline becomes more rapid and settlement numbers drop as low as those of the first century BC.

The most convenient representation of the evolution of rural settlements in the MDS region has been made by Niels Janssens.[50] His study, which is based on a significant number of published rural settlements, shows a gradual increase in the settlements from the first century AD onwards. This trend continues until the maximum number of settlements is reached in the period between AD 125 and 200. After this phase, decline sets in, essentially after AD 225. By AD 250, the number of settlements had even fallen far below pre-Roman levels, where they remained for the rest of the Roman period.

Lastly, Wim de Clercq's research into the Menapian region might be interesting to include.[51] Although this neighbouring region does not belong to the research area, its proximity and well researched rural settlement landscape make it a good area for comparison. The dataset, which is constructed on the basis of excavation data, indicates that the number of settlements increased rapidly during the first century AD. After the first half of this century, the number of settlements has already increased threefold compared to the pre-Roman period. In the second half of this same century, the number of settlements reaches its maximum after being doubled again.[52] These high levels are essentially retained until the end of the second century AD, after which the number of settlements is reduced at an equally rapid pace to reach levels similar to the pre-Roman period.

It is tempting to view the results from these studies as objective reflections of the rural population dynamics in the individual sub-regions; the assumption that settlement numbers reflect actual population numbers does, after all,

---

49 Habermehl, 2013.

50 Janssens, 2015.

51 De Clercq, 2009.

52 In Figure 7, the maximum lies in the next 50-year period. This is the result of taking an average of the two 25-year periods, of which the original data consists.

make sense.[53] It should, however, be realised that the evidence is, to a certain extent, biased towards the period in which the use of durable material culture was highest. This is especially the case with the studies that are (partly) based on surface finds. A settlement in which stone or ceramic building materials and solid Roman pottery were used, is much more likely to be identified during a survey than a settlement consisting of organic building materials and easily crumbled handmade pottery. Consequently, the low numbers of settlements in the Late Iron Age and early and late Roman periods are not necessarily the result of fewer settlements but more of lower archaeological visibility.[54] This bias is probably much less in the studies that are (partly) based on excavations. Excavation research allows a much more careful and detailed interpretation of settlements, and it is, therefore, not as likely that a less visible period might be overlooked. Nevertheless, the decision to start an excavation in the first place is, at least sometimes, also subject to a similar bias, as very visible sites are most likely to draw the archaeologist's attention.[55]

Despite these problematic biases, we should not throw the baby out with the bathwater. As long as we are aware that these reconstructions are not very precise and only give us a rough indication of the development of the number of settlements, they can be a valuable source for understanding the region's population dynamics. It is, in any case, interesting to see that all sub-regions, irrespective of the different research approaches, show a largely similar trend. Around the start of the first century AD, the number of settlements increased significantly until a maximum was reached in the second century AD. Then, in the third century AD, the number of settlements starts to decline again and is largely reduced to pre-Roman levels in the fourth century AD. Accordingly, we can be quite confident that the research area's countryside experienced substantial population growth during the first and second centuries AD, followed by a just as significant decline from the third century AD onwards. It should be realised, though, that it is very unlikely that this considerable population growth was solely the result of an increase in natural fertility.[56] Therefore, we must assume that it was also due to immigration from other parts of the empire (or perhaps from across the Rhine).[57]

---

53 Even though the number of people living in these settlements will have varied.

54 This might be part of the explanation for the settlement explosion observed in the study by Gechter and Kunow.

55 For this reason, rural settlement research in the loess zone has long been biased towards the larger and more visible villa sites.

56 Reddé, 2018, p. 133.

57 Kakoschke, 2002; Heimberg, 2003, pp. 71–77.

3.4 Roman Institutions

The large inflow of soldiers and civilians was not the only aspect of the Roman occupation that made a large impact on the regional economy. Being part of the Roman Empire also brought about several other changes that had important consequences for economic life in conquered provinces. It seems that the Roman conquest, in addition to the army, also introduced other institutions that stimulated and facilitated production and commercial exchange in the Lower Germanic Limes region. These institutions include the Roman system of taxation, the advent of a single currency, a common language, a common metrological system, and Roman law. Taken together, these institutions created an institutional framework that was much more conducive to economic growth than that of the pre-Roman Iron Age.

The aims of the Roman state regarding the governance of its provinces were quite straightforward: keep the peace, administer justice, and collect taxes. In order to accomplish these aims in an empire of such extensive scope, the Romans combined a well-organised and strategically placed army with a political structure that was organised in a very minimalistic way.[58] The central government left the administration of the provinces in the hands of regional and local administrators. These administrators, who consisted of (local) aristocrats and large landowners, were supposed to maintain peace and order and bring in taxes and tribute from the provinces. In return for their efforts, they were allowed to pocket parts of this revenue.[59] By way of this decentralised political organisation, the Roman government could run its empire in an effective way and was, at the same time, able to keep the costs of its bureaucracy relatively low. Calculations suggest that only around 15 percent of the imperial budget was spent on administration, which was far less than the 60 to 65 percent that was spent on military personnel.[60]

3.4.1 *Taxation*

Even though this 'government without bureaucracy' did not control its provinces with a large and intrusive administration, Roman rule surely had an impact on economic life in the region.[61] The part of this impact that the

58 Galsterer, 2000.

59 Garnsey and Saller, 1987, p. 53.

60 In Han China, which was the other world empire of the time, governmental spending on civilian administrators was probably more than twice, and perhaps even three times, as high as in the Roman Empire. The estimated 10,000 paid officials in the Roman Empire, however, pale in comparison to the 130,000 to 153,000 in Han China. Scheidel, 2015, pp. 165–174.

61 This term is used by Garnsey and Saller, 1987, p. 35.

provincial population undoubtedly felt most clearly was the fact that they now had to pay taxes. According to Hopkins, the main economic consequence of the Roman system of taxation was that taxation forced producers to increase their production and to sell their surpluses for money, so that they were able to meet their tax requirements.[62] This would imply that, previously, the productive capacity of these producers had not been fully employed, that they had consumed their surpluses themselves, or a combination of the two. If not, the taxation would have driven them to ruin, something that might have happened to those producers that were already struggling to make a living prior to the Roman conquest. The vast majority of the producers, however, had probably been able to cope with the tax burden, which, according to scholarly consensus, was quite low.[63]

Even though Hopkins' proposition that the imposition of taxes stimulated market-oriented production and exchange makes perfect sense, his claim that these taxes were primarily paid in money is more controversial.[64] For the current research area, for example, an important part of the taxes seems to have been levied in kind, instead of in money, at least during the pre-Flavian period. A famous example of such taxation in kind is the case of the Batavians, who, according to Tacitus, were exempt from regular taxation but supplied the army with manpower.[65] Although the Batavians were not the only tribe in the region that supplied manpower, the sheer size of their contribution was exceptional.[66] It is believed that a total of 5,000 to 5,500 Batavian soldiers were simultaneously active in this period, which, according to demographic calculations, would mean that the average Batavian family had at least one son in the army.[67] Taxation in kind could also be provided in the form of agricultural or animal products. We know, again from Tacitus, that the *Frisii*, until their revolt in AD 28, had paid part of their taxes in cowhides. These examples already indicate that the system of Roman taxation in the research area was more flexible than Hopkins' model suggests. Following Roymans, it seems more logical to assume that tax collectors took the needs of the frontier army as well as the productive potential of local economies into account when they drafted the tax requirements.[68] In his view, the regions that had a stronger emphasis on

62 Hopkins, 1980, p. 101.

63 E.g. Hopkins, 1980, p. 120; Duncan-Jones, 1990, p. 198; Roymans, 1996. However, see Bowman, 2018, pp. 27–52.

64 For general criticism, see Duncan-Jones, 1990. Hopkins reacted to this criticism in Hopkins, 2002.

65 Tac. Hist. 4, 14.

66 For the contribution of tribal units to the army, see Roymans, 1996, pp. 22–23.

67 Nicolay, 2007, p. 7.

68 Roymans, 1996, p. 85.

animal husbandry (see section 2.2) would have paid the majority of their taxes through the supply of manpower, animals, and animal products, while the regions with a stronger emphasis on arable farming would have paid the majority of their taxes by supplying a combination of manpower and agricultural products (primarily cereals).

Although taxation in kind in the research area was probably more important than Hopkins' model suggests, this does not necessarily invalidate the assumption that taxation stimulated market-oriented production.[69] Taking the large amounts of goods that the army required into account, combined with the low degree of monetisation of the native economies, it may just have been the most practical solution to exact the taxes in kind in this region.[70] Moreover, taxes levied in kind did just as well to stimulate tax payers to produce surpluses as monetary taxes would do, and, in case these produced surpluses exceeded the tax-requirement, the extra surplus could, because of the large regional demand, be sold to the new military and civilian markets. Therefore, even if taxation was in the initial phase of Roman occupation primarily exacted in kind, it was still an important driving force behind the increased monetisation and market-oriented exchange in the region. Furthermore, from the Flavian period onwards, this process must have accelerated because the majority of taxes were now levied in money, requiring producers to convert their surpluses into cash in the monetised markets.[71]

3.4.2 *Monetisation*

The large-scale influx of Roman coins via military pay, combined with the introduction of the Roman system of taxation, had the result that economic life in the Lower Germanic Limes region became increasingly monetised.[72] The tri-metallic Roman coinage provided transacting parties with a single currency that could cover all levels of exchange.[73] It allowed people to conduct small-scale, everyday transactions, such as buying a loaf of bread or a jar of wine, but it also enabled people to make larger investments, such as the building of a house or the purchase of a slave. This was an important development because a smooth-functioning monetary system can significantly reduce the transaction costs that are involved in commercial exchange. In this way, monetisation facilitates and stimulates trade and is often seen as an important

69 As Hopkins argues himself. Hopkins, 2002.

70 Aarts, 2000, p. 15.

71 Aarts, 2015b, p. 226.

72 I use the term 'monetisation' to describe the process in which the use of money for market exchange increases through time and space relative to its non-commercial uses. For definition and discussion, see Aarts, 2005; Bursche, 2008; Howgego, 2013; Komnick, 2018.

73 Aarts, 2015b, p. 208.

driver of economic growth. Still, we should beware of viewing this development as a simple binary opposition between an un-monetised Late Iron Age period and a completely monetised Roman period.[74] Late Iron Age coins were not exclusively used for the reproduction of the social and religious order but were also used in market exchange.[75] Coin use in the Roman period was, at the same time, not entirely free from social and cultural embeddedness and coins were, in this period, also used outside of the commercial domain.[76] Coin use in both periods, thus, encompassed monetary as well as non-monetary functions. What is clear, however, is that the monetary functions of coins became increasingly important in the course of the Roman period.

Clear evidence for this development has been provided by an article that looked at the distribution of coin finds in the Netherlands.[77] The empirical core of this research is formed by the NUMIS-database, which collects all the coin finds that have been made on Dutch soil.[78] In the study, the distribution of coin finds from the pre-Roman, the Roman, and the post-Roman periods has been analysed, focusing on the density and the precious metal content of these finds. The authors start from the premise that small denomination coins (i.e. coins with a low fraction of precious metal) were probably used for small-scale, local transactions, while coins with a larger denomination were more likely to be used for larger-scale transactions or as a way to accumulate wealth.[79] On the basis of the low density of total coin finds and the relatively low proportion of small denomination coins in finds from the pre-Roman period, they argue that the regional economy in this period cannot be considered a market economy. In the Roman period, though, they note a higher density of total coin finds as well as a higher percentage of coins with small denominations. This pattern is particularly evident in the areas that belonged to the Roman Empire, while the finds from the areas north of the Rhine show a much lower density and a higher proportion of coins with larger denominations. This evidence, thus, suggests that the economy of the region that fell within the borders of the Roman Empire can indeed be characterised as a lively, largely monetised market economy. In the post-Roman period (AD 500–700), this would change again. The low density of coin finds and the high precious metal content of

74 Aarts, 2005.

75 Howgego, 2013, pp. 26–44.

76 van Heesch, 2008.

77 Buringh, van Zanden and Bosker, 2012. Some coin finds from outside of the Netherlands have also been included.

78 The dataset consists of 59,691 coins and is publicly available. *NUMIS*, no date.

79 Nonetheless, because people were more careful with these coins, they are less frequently recovered in stray finds. Buringh, van Zanden and Bosker, 2012, pp. 7–17.

these coins suggest that the extent of local market exchange was reduced significantly after the Romans had left.[80]

In order to graphically illustrate the development observed by this study and to verify its results, I have made a rough analysis of (a part of) the NUMIS-database. Figure 8 shows the number of dated stray coin finds in the Roman part of the Netherlands, distributed over 50-year periods between 250 BC and AD 750.[81] It shows that the total number of coin finds from the Roman period (50 BC–AD 450) is significantly higher than that from the pre-Roman Iron Age or from the post-Roman early medieval period. This already indicates that coin

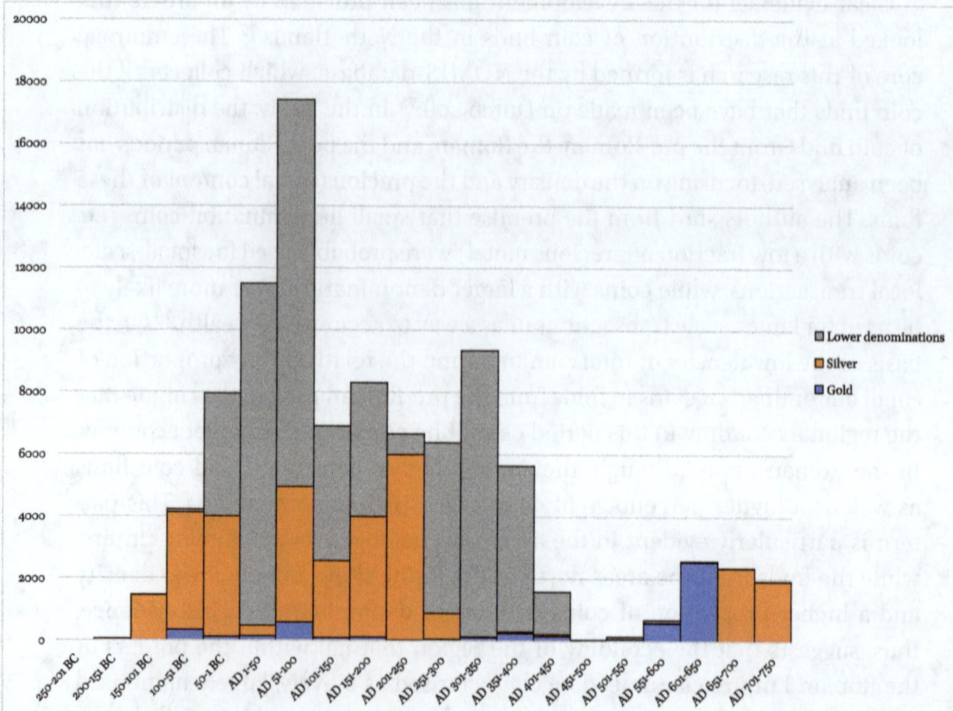

FIGURE 8 The number of stray coin finds in the Roman Netherlands

80 Buringh, van Zanden and Bosker, 2012, pp. 11–17.
81 The NUMIS-database also includes hoard finds. The problem with hoard finds is that they tend to cluster in periods of political instability and that they are biased towards coins of higher value. Like Buringh, van Zanden and Bosker, I have therefore decided to focus exclusively on 'stray finds' as they are generally believed to be a better representation of the coins in circulation. The disadvantage of stray finds, however, is that coins of lower value are overrepresented. For discussion of the coin evidence with the inclusion of hoards, see Aarts, 2015a; 2015b.

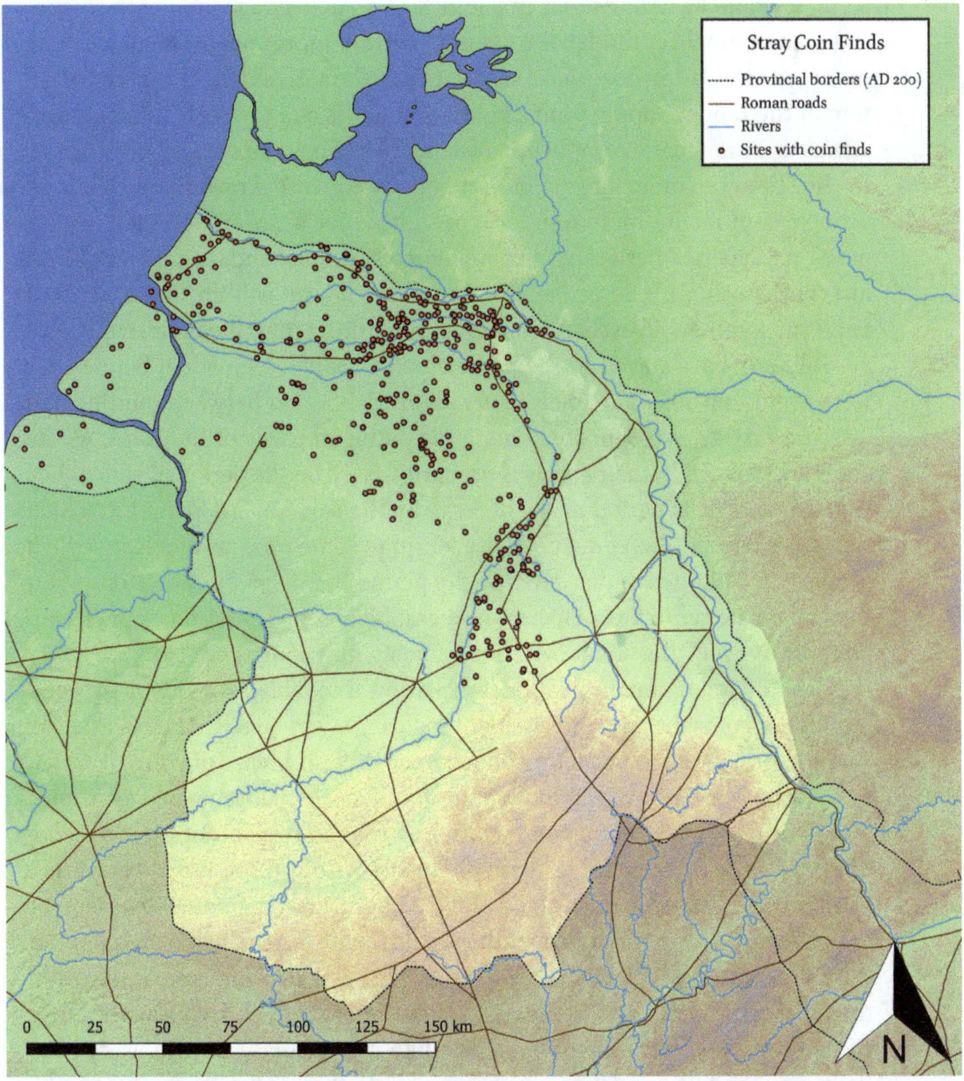

FIGURE 9 The locations where the coins from Figure 8 were found
Note: The finds are aggregated by toponym.

use increased dramatically during the Roman period. We should, however, realise that this can, at least partly, be attributed to population growth (see section 3.3). Furthermore, the graph clearly demonstrates the increase in small change during Roman times: almost all coins in the pre- and post-Roman periods were of a high denomination (i.e. gold or silver), whereas in the Roman period, the vast majority of coins were of lower denominations (primarily of copper or a copper alloy).

Yet it would be wrong to see in Figure 8 an objective reflection of the historical money supply. Although the assumption that more coin finds equals more money in circulation does make sense, it has to be stressed that the reconstruction of the money supply from single coin finds is a notoriously difficult exercise as there are many complicating factors.[82] As I have already stressed above, the line between monetary and non-monetary coin use is not always clear, and a single coin might, moreover, have been used for a variety of different purposes in the period between the moment it was minted and the moment it was lost (or deposited).[83] Some of the coins in the dataset will thus have changed hands in commercial exchanges many times during their life cycle, while others will only have stayed in the possession of a single individual before they were eventually lost. The uncertainty about the period between minting and loss also raises a problem concerning the dating of many of the coins. As the coins are stray finds, their dating is primarily based on the period in which they were minted. This period is not necessarily the same as the period in which they were used. Coins could be in use for quite some time, as the relative high proportion of Roman coins dated to the period before 50 BC makes clear.[84] It thus seems better to view Figure 8 as a graphical representation of the *terminus post quem* of the coins. Without knowing how long these coins were, on average, in circulation, it is impossible to give a reliable estimate of the total number of coins that were in circulation during a very precise time period.[85]

Another complicating factor concerns the different types of coins of which the dataset is made up. Even though the graph makes a division between coins of gold, silver, and lower value metals, this rough division does still obscure the large disparities in value that could exist within these broad categories. Within this context, it might be enough to point to the gradual debasement of the *denarius*.[86] In the course of the second century AD, the silver content of the coin had already declined from 90 to 75%. This devaluation continued in the third century AD, and in the period between AD 253 and AD 270, the silver content dropped from 40–45% to less than 5%, so that the coin was essentially reduced to a copper coin.[87] This example shows that we cannot equate

82 Cf. Harl, 1996, pp. 18–20.

83 Wigg-Wolf, 2011, pp. 303–304.

84 Although it is possible that (some of) these coins had already come to the region in the pre-Roman period.

85 Even if an average circulation time were known, this average would probably not be appropriate for each period or every type of coin.

86 The following percentages are found in Corbier, 2005, pp. 338–344.

87 Accordingly, NUMIS classifies many of the *denarii* and *antoninianii* (which is a modern term) that are dated later than the second half of the third century AD as copper coins. The shift from silver to copper *denarii* in the third century AD is also visible in Figure 8.

an increase in coin finds with an increase in money supply; there may have been more coins in circulation, but their individual monetary value may have been much lower.

Furthermore, it should be realised that the increase in coin finds in the Roman period could also just have been the result of population growth. More people also lose more coins. Therefore, the question arises to what extent the increase in coin finds transcended the degree of population growth that the region experienced. Thus, ideally, we would want to compare the coin data against the background of the population increase that the region experienced. The problem with this, however, is that the estimates of both variables are very uncertain. Even though it is my impression that the increase in coin finds in the Roman Netherlands was significantly greater than the demographic increase that was observed for the Dutch River Area and the MDS region (which are the most suitable regions for comparison), this cannot really be substantiated.

Lastly, the question remains whether the increased monetisation in the region was just an urban and military phenomenon or if the process also extended into the rural hinterland. Yet this is not an easy question to answer. The statistical study mentioned above has calculated that the coin find density along the Dutch part of the *limes* was almost eight times as high as in the parts in the south of the Netherlands. This might, at first sight, give the impression that these southern areas were less monetised. Interestingly, though, the proportion of coins of a low denomination is almost twice as high in the south, which suggests that there was relatively more small change in circulation. It should, moreover, be realised that the high density of coin finds in the *limes* area is probably skewed by the exceptionally favourable conditions for the conservation of metal objects in the Dutch River Area.[88] Furthermore, a natural bias towards urban and military settlements can be expected, as these must have been the places where most of the monetary transactions took place. Since the rural population may have come to these central places to trade, the relatively lower density of coin finds in the rural hinterland does not necessarily mean that the inhabitants of these areas were less monetised. Coins are, after all, mostly lost where they are being used. Accordingly, we should not underestimate the degree of monetisation of the rural population during the Roman period.

Still, it is clear that significant regional differences must have existed.[89] In the Batavian area, for example, in which a relatively large part of the population was from early on involved with the Roman army, there was practically no delay between the supply of coins to the military fortifications and the rural

88 Aarts, 2015b, p. 217.
89 Cf. Komnick, 2018, pp. 64–65.

settlements.[90] This may indicate that Batavian soldiers had quickly learned how to use coinage in a monetary way and brought this knowledge with them to their native villages.[91] That the Batavians were dependent on the coin supply of the Roman army is also underscored by the fact that the number of coins decreased significantly after the withdrawal of a large part of the troops in the early second century AD. The Batavian monetary economy probably never really recovered from this setback, and a gradual decline can be observed from this period onwards.

Although the spread of coinage in the MDS region can also be linked to the establishment of the Roman military, the speed and extent of monetisation in this area must have been less than in the more heavily militarised Batavian societies.[92] The region seems to have been supplied with Roman coins from around the beginning of the first century AD, and especially from the Flavian period onwards, the supply of coins increased significantly. This had the effect that not only more people were using coins, but the same people also used more coins.[93] The impact of the withdrawal of the troops in the second century AD was also not very significant in this region: coin supply remained stable until the early third century AD. In the following period, however, the MDS region largely lost its connection to the Roman monetary economy. Only in the areas along the Meuse in the north and east, which had better connections to the Roman infrastructural system, did the coin supply stay intact longer. But after the first half of the fourth century AD, this also came to an end.

Interestingly, in the *civitas Cananefatium* (in the western part of the Dutch river delta), the army does also not seem to have been such an important factor. Instead, coin supply correlates more strongly with the development of civic structures: rural coin finds increase after the establishment of *Forum Hadriani* (Voorburg) and peak during the period of the settlement's greatest prosperity (the late first and second centuries AD).[94] After this period, the number of coin finds decreases again and the coin supply appears to have practically dried up during the fourth century AD.

90 Aarts, 2015a, pp. 401–402.
91 This is not to say that these coins are reflective of market exchange, which did primarily take place in the central places. Most rural coin finds probably reflect ritual depositions or were part of a hoard. Aarts, 2015a, p. 13.
92 Aarts, 2015b.
93 Aarts, 2015b, p. 222.
94 Kemmers, 2008, pp. 98–99.

A somewhat similar development can be observed in the German loess area.[95] Again, the stationing of soldiers along the frontier did provide the initial impetus for monetisation in the area: from the middle of the Augustan period, Roman coinage arrived, via the army, in the secondary agglomerations that had developed throughout the area. During this period, some coins also turn up in rural settlements, but their numbers are still too small to indicate monetisation.[96] However, from the Flavian period onwards, this begins to change and the rural hinterland is increasingly integrated into the monetised economy. A key role in this process was played by the secondary agglomerations, which performed market functions for farmers in their hinterland who wanted to sell their agricultural surpluses (see chapter 4.2).[97] Accordingly, in order to facilitate this intensive local trade, money was needed. Interestingly, this also meant that the monetary economy had a very stable foundation. There is, for example, no noticeable effect of the withdrawal of the troops in the second century AD on the rural money supply. In fact, the supply of coinage and the circulation of money experienced an upswing in the second century AD and remained high until the fourth century AD.

This contrasts sharply with the slightly more northern Lower Rhine Plain.[98] Here, the coin finds indicate that monetary transactions primarily took place in the military and urban settlements. In the rural hinterland, on the other hand, the number of coin finds is very limited. This may be related to the fact that farmers in this area were more subsistence-oriented and did not produce as significant agricultural surpluses as the people in the south (see chapter 4.3). As a result, the need for money was probably less, and it is also conceivable that the rural population in this area to a large extent engaged in bartering.[99]

Thus, it is clear that the process of monetisation among the rural population in the research area was not uniform. The intensity of contact with the Roman army or with urban centres, the agricultural potential of the landscape, and the connection to the Roman infrastructure network could all influence a rural settlement's need for coins and the possibility of obtaining them.

---

95 Otte, 2022.

96 The high denominations of the coins in the rural hinterland suggest that, during this period, the coins were mainly used for saving and not for everyday transactions. Otte, 2022, p. 226.

97 Otte, 2022, pp. 368–369.

98 Komnick, 2018, pp. 63–64.

99 Komnick, 2018, p. 64.

3.4.3 *Standardisation*

In addition to the advent of a single currency, the incorporation of the research area into the Roman Empire is also likely to have led to a higher degree of standardisation in other fields that were of economic significance.[100] Standardisation was important because the Roman Empire was made up of many different communities and cultures that had their own traditions and customs. In order to facilitate trade and other interactions between people with different backgrounds, it was helpful to have a certain degree of uniformity. Accordingly, the Romans had a common metrological system that specified several standard values for the measurement of length, distance, area, weight, volume (dry or fluid), as well as time.[101] This reduced uncertainty, and thus additional costs during commercial exchanges, as it provided transacting parties with clear information on the traded goods. In this manner, a consumer purchasing an amphora wine in Cologne would receive (roughly) the same amount of wine (*c.*26 litres) as he would in Rome.[102] In order to ensure such uniformity and precision, measuring instruments were kept in public places where commercial exchange took place, such as the forum or marketplace.[103] It was the task of local magistrates to control these instruments and to supervise the general quality of the goods that were being traded.[104]

What also helped to counter economic uncertainty and therefore reduced the risks involved in trade and investment was the existence of common legal rules. There is debate about the question of whether the Romans had something like a commercial law, but it is clear that Roman law included certain regulations that, at least, had the potential to reduce transaction costs.[105] The law defined property rights and regulated the transfer of property between Roman citizens.[106] Furthermore, there were laws that inhibited speculative and deceptive behaviour. Although the local magistrates who supervised the markets did not regulate prices, they did aim to guarantee 'fair prices' that largely had to concur with the market value of a good.[107] Moreover, they could also provide

---

100 It does, however, remain impossible to establish the extent to which standardisation has permeated regional societies and what its precise impact has been.

101 Hosch, 2011, pp. 206–208.

102 Besides a unit of liquid volume, an amphora is also the vessel in which such liquids were kept.

103 Agustoni, 2018, pp. 31–39.

104 de Ligt, 2016, p. 665.

105 Lo Cascio, 2017b, pp. 5–26.

106 Epstein, 2016.

107 Lo Cascio, 2017b, p. 5.

legal protection to buyers of slaves or draught animals who believed that they had been wronged by the seller.[108]

Finally, the use of Latin as a common language should be mentioned. The spread of this *lingua franca* throughout the empire not only made communication between people of different cultural backgrounds easier, but it also went hand in hand with increased literacy and the use of writing.[109] This is not to say that the Late Iron Age societies were completely illiterate; there are some indications of the use of writing in the pre-Roman period.[110] However, in the Roman period, writing seems to have permeated society to a much larger extent.[111] The Vindolanda and Vindonissa writing tablets, which have been found in England and Switzerland, respectively, give us a good idea of the important role that writing played in the daily lives of Roman soldiers in the north-western provinces.[112] The tablets include documents connected with the military administration, the supply of goods through both military and civilian channels, contracts between individuals, as well as a wide array of personal letters. Interestingly, the writings appear to belong to soldiers of all ranks, which suggests that literacy was widespread among the Roman military.[113] The most important evidence of writing and literacy in the research area (besides epigraphic material) comes from the findings of bronze seal-boxes.[114] These seal-boxes were used to contain written messages and have primarily been found in military fortifications and extramural settlements along the *limes*. Some seal-boxes have also been recovered in the *civitas* capitals or in secondary agglomerations, but the number of finds in the rural hinterland has, generally, been low. In the Batavian area, however, where the conditions for preservation as well as archaeological practices (i.e. metal detecting) have been favourable, the number of findings in the rural hinterland is exceptionally high. This seems to indicate that the rural inhabitants of this area possessed widespread knowledge of Latin. Whether this was also the case for the rural population in other parts of the research area remains unclear. We should realise that the Batavians, because of their thorough integration into the Roman army, represent a very specific case.

---

108 de Ligt, 2016, pp. 6–7.

109 In addition to writing and reading, numeracy might also be included as an element of literacy. Matijević, 2020, pp. 287–288.

110 Matijević, 2020, pp. 4–5.

111 Hopkins, 2017.

112 Bowman and Thomas, 1994; Speidel, 1996; Strobel, 1999.

113 Bowman and Thomas, 1994, p. 88.

114 Epigraphy is, of course, also important in this respect. However, it does not necessarily reflect everyday writing and literacy. MacMullen, 1982; Derks and Roymans, 2002.

In any case, the increased literacy and use of writing must have had a positive impact on the regional economy.[115] Writing added a whole new dimension to communication, as it enabled writers to reach people who were far removed in space or time. Because of this, information and knowledge could be collected, stored, and shared much more effectively than before, which allowed a rationalisation of economic life. We know from Egypt, where climatic conditions have allowed the conservation of exceptional numbers of documentary sources, that the Roman government kept extensive fiscal and military records and also administered contracts between people in 'private' matters.[116] On the basis of the above-discussed evidence of writing in the north-western provinces, it does not seem too far-fetched to assume that a similar situation existed in this part of the empire. The benefits of writing probably also had an impact on commercial life. We know, for example, that many Roman producers stamped their products (bricks, amphorae, pottery, etc.) with short inscriptions.[117] Although the precise aim of such stamps is not always clear, they did convey important information and are, thus, indicative of a certain degree of development in the organisation of production.[118]

3.5 Infrastructure

The final general development that thoroughly transformed economic life in the Lower Germanic Limes region was the expansion of the regional infrastructure that followed in the wake of the Roman conquest. The Roman state required an efficient traffic system for the proper administration of its provinces. Accordingly, the Romans invested a great deal of effort and resources to provide their empire with an infrastructural system of ports, roads, bridges, and canals. The primary goal of this system was to facilitate the logistics of the Roman army, but this system was, at the same time, beneficial to the economic development of the region. Better infrastructure ensured that goods could be moved faster and cheaper, which reduced the cost of transport. Together with transaction costs, transport costs form the additional costs that

115 Cf. Bowman and Wilson, 2009a; Saller, 2012; Hopkins, 2017.
116 Bowman and Wilson, 2009a, pp. 39–41; Hopkins, 2017, pp. 368–370.
117 Harris, 1993a.
118 Producers might have stamped their products with a signature in order to merchandise their wares, but the inscriptions could also have served as a guarantee of the quality of the products, or to enable (fiscal) accounting. Pucci, 2001, pp. 144–147.

make economic transactions more expensive.[119] As these additional costs are reduced, it becomes more advantageous for economic actors to exchange, and total production and trade are likely to rise. Moreover, in addition to a lowering of transport costs, the Roman infrastructure is likely to have reduced transaction costs in the region, as it allowed a more effective distribution of information. Access to information is crucial for economic actors, as it allows them to find and arrange potential trade opportunities. An efficient communication system, facilitated by an effective infrastructure, greatly contributed to the reduction of information costs in the Roman Empire. Ian Haynes, in this respect, even speaks of an 'Information Revolution' that transformed economic life.[120]

The Romans undoubtedly built on the pre-existing infrastructural system of the research area.[121] Yet the pre-Roman road network is almost completely unknown, and although the rapid advances of Caesar's troops in the Gallic Wars suggest that the region must have had some kind of artificial road network, it does not seem likely that this entailed much beyond simple unpaved roads and, in wetter areas, timber trackways, which are well known from the peatlands in more northerly regions.[122] It is, however, clear that the region was also furnished with an important natural infrastructure in the form of the North Sea and the many rivers that traversed the area. The economic potential of these waterways was great, but we should also be aware of the difficulties involved in utilizing them. Maritime transport was risky, and a good knowledge of shipbuilding was required before any enterprise could safely be attempted. Riverine transport was perhaps safer, but seasonal variability led to low water levels or freezing, which could seriously inhibit the navigability of rivers. This will primarily have been a problem on the smaller rivers, but even parts of the Rhine appear to have been blocked for traffic periodically.[123] Furthermore, it should be realised that it was much more complicated to navigate upstream than it was to go downstream. Instead of just going with the currents, upstream navigation required sailing, rowing, or even towing and, accordingly, took significantly more time and effort.[124] Nevertheless, where and whenever

119 This means that the price of an amphora with Italian wine is likely to have been significantly higher in Cologne than it would have been in Rome.

120 Although Haynes is concerned with Roman Britain, the same will have been the case in the other regions where the Roman infrastructural system was introduced. Haynes, 2002.

121 Rathmann, 2004, p. 23; Kicken and Mols, 2020.

122 Casparie, 1986; Bockius, 2018, pp. 187–194; Andrikopoulou-Strack and Jenter, 2018, p. 201; Burmeister, 2018.

123 Roggenkamp and Herget, 2014; Franconi, 2016.

124 Campbell, 2012.

possible, transport over water was a highly effective alternative to transport over land. It thus seems logical to assume that already in the pre-Roman Iron Age, the inhabitants of the research area would have taken advantage of the waterways.[125] Nonetheless, given the economic structure of the pre-Roman tribal societies (see section 2.2), it does not seem likely that a too intensive exchange system developed on these waters.

In the Roman period, the potential of the waterways must have been exploited to a much larger extent. This increased use of water transportation went together with an improved naval infrastructure. It is difficult to assess how extensive this infrastructure has been because harbours and landing stages, being located at extremely erosion-sensitive locations, have often left behind very few archaeological remains.[126] Nevertheless, several antique harbours and landing stages have been found in the research area, and many more are suspected (Figure 10).[127] Assuming that the identified structures represent only a small part of the whole, it is likely that many more will have existed along the region's main rivers and the coast. In addition to building these harbours, the Romans made several even more impressive alternations to the natural infrastructure.[128] For example, somewhere between 12 and 9 BC, Drusus is believed to have had one or more canals dug, which connected the Rhine, through the *Lacus Flevo* (Lake Flevo), with the Wadden Sea.[129] This would have created a safer route for his ships in the campaign against the *Frisii* and *Chauci*, as it avoided the dangerous North Sea. In the same period, he also constructed a dam at the bifurcation point of the Rhine and Waal, which served to channel more water into the former river to make it better navigable.[130] Furthermore, around AD 50, general Corbulo had his soldiers dig a circa 35-kilometre-long canal in the western part of the Dutch river area.[131] This canal, which ran from the *Helinium* at Naaldwijk, via Voorburg, to the Oude Rijn at Leiden, connected the Meuse to the Rhine. This artificial waterway probably also served as a safer

125 Whether this included navigating the North Sea is doubtful, as the simple boats used in the Late Iron Age were probably not seaworthy. Bockius, 2018, pp. 180–184.

126 Therefore, it is good not to follow a very strict harbour definition. Instead of restricting the identification of a harbour to places where typical harbour structures, such as wharfs and piers, have been identified, it is better to define a harbour as a place where harbour activity took place. Manuela Mirschenz therefore uses the following definition: 'Harbour is where harbour happens'. Mirschenz, 2016a; Bemmann and Mirschenz, 2016a.

127 A recent research project has studied the role of harbours in the German part of the Lower Rhine. Kennecke, 2014a; Bemmann and Mirschenz, 2016b.

128 Suet. Claud. 1, 2; Tac. Ann. 2, 8; 11, 20.

129 Huisman, 1995; Verhagen, Kluiving and Kars, 2022.

130 Verhagen *et al.*, 2017.

131 Tac. Ann. 11, 20; Cass. Dio 61, 30. Parts of the canal have been uncovered in the last decades of the twenty-first century. Waasdorp, 2016, pp. 27–31.

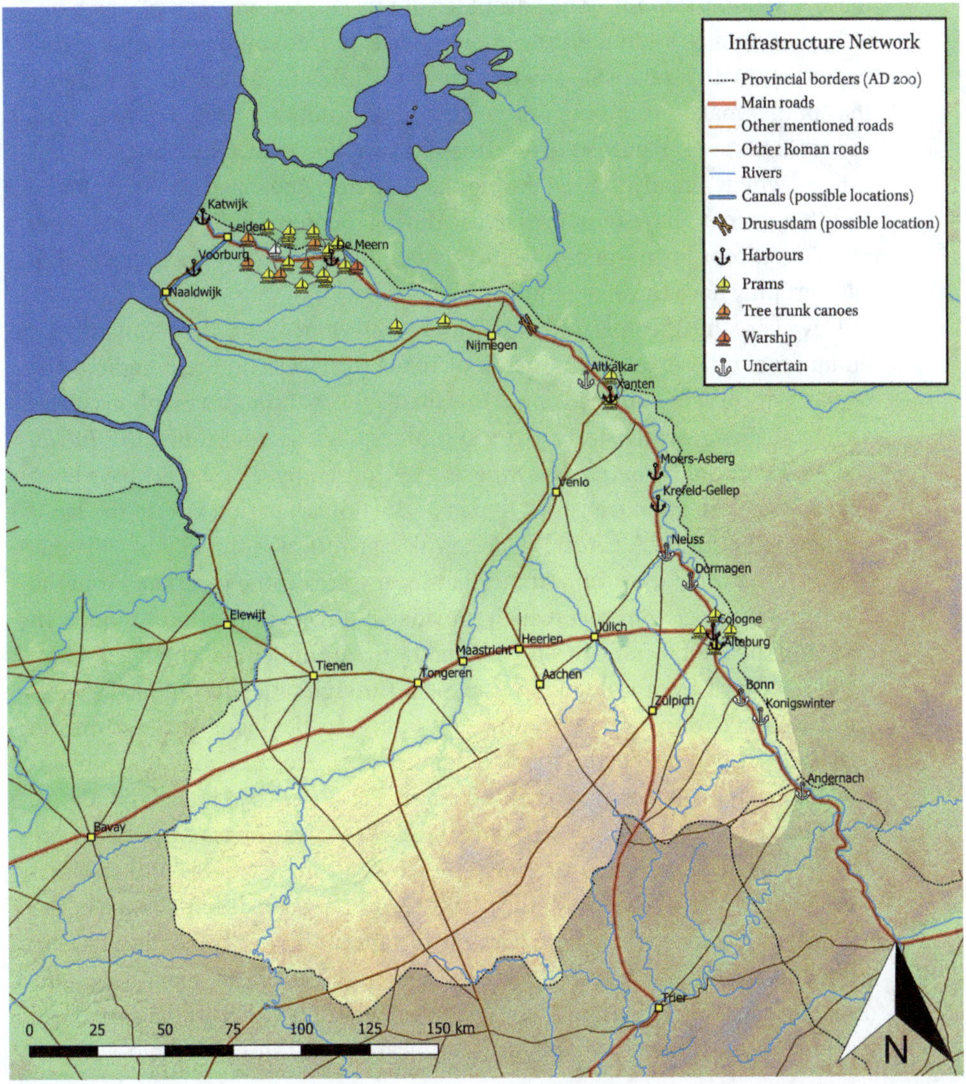

FIGURE 10 Important features of the Roman infrastructure network in the Lower Germanic Limes region

alternative to travel along the North Sea coast, although it can also be seen as an attempt to prevent the flooding of the rivers.[132]

Apart from this improvement of the naval infrastructure, the possibilities for riverine transport must also have been significantly enhanced by Roman shipbuilding. In this respect, the introduction of the pram seems to have

132 de Kort, 2013, pp. 233–234. How long the canal was in use remains unknown. On the Rhine side, the canal seems to have silted up around AD 150. Buijtendorp, 2010, pp. 142–145.

played an important role. The advantage of this flat-bottomed ship, which had either a Celtic or a Mediterranean origin, was that it could carry a large and heavy load with a relatively shallow draught.[133] It is therefore no coincidence that prams make up the majority of the total number of dated wrecks from the research area (Figure 10). Nevertheless, simpler vessels, such as tree trunk canoes, which already existed during the Late Iron Age, have also been found and thus seem to have remained in use during the Roman period. Other types of ships, except for a warship from Vechten, have not been documented but will certainly have traversed the regional waters.[134]

However, the greatest infrastructural achievement of the Romans was undoubtedly the extensive network of roads that were built throughout the region. We are well informed about this road-system through a combination of archaeological research and historical sources, such as milestones, the *Tabula Peutingeriana*, and the *Antonine Itinerary*.[135] Consequently, scholars have been able to trace the main transport routes of the Roman period within the landscape (Figure 10).[136] A central node in this network was the city of Cologne, in which the three most important roads in the area came together. From the south came the *Via Agrippa*, which provided a direct connection to southern Gaul and the Mediterranean via Trier and Lyon. Another road (the *Via Belgica*) went westward from Cologne.[137] It passed through cities in the fertile loess zone, such as Tongeren and Bavay, and ended in Boulogne-sur-Mer on the coast of the Channel. Furthermore, Cologne was crossed by a road that ran parallel to the *limes* on the left side of the Rhine. This *limes* road linked the Alps to the North Sea coast near Katwijk, crossing cities such as Augst, Mainz, Xanten, and Nijmegen. In addition to these three long-distance routes, the research area counted many other roads that made traffic between different parts of the region more convenient. There was, for instance, a route that continued the stretch of the *Via Agrippa* between Cologne and Zülpich in a south-western direction towards Reims and, thus, went through the southernmost part of the research area. Moreover, a road went southward from Xanten to Venlo, where it

---

133 Schmidhuber-Aspöck, 2018, pp. 232–233.

134 Bockius, 2002.

135 The latter two sources are so-called *itineraria*, road maps that schematically describe the main road network. The *Tabula Peutingeriana* is a medieval copy of a (probably) fourth century AD document, while the *Antonine Itinerary* dates to the second or third century AD.

136 Rathmann, 2004; Rogge, 2004; Andrikopoulou-Strack and Jenter, 2018.

137 These are the modern names of the roads; the names that the Romans gave to them are unknown.

split into two different tracks, connecting Xanten with the *Via Belgica* at Jülich and Heerlen (from where a road probably continued towards Aachen). In the Dutch River area, Nijmegen was the most important hub. Not only was the city located on (or at least close to) the *limes* road, but a largely parallel road also ran westward from it, on the southern bank of the Waal, towards the *Helinium*. From there, the road continued north along Voorburg and connected with the *limes* road near Leiden. From the south of Nijmegen, a road followed the west bank of the Meuse to reach the *Via Belgica* near Maastricht, thus creating a more central connection between the northern and south-western parts of the research area. In this south-western part, Tongeren was a major settlement centre. It was located along the *Via Belgica* and, in addition to this, provided an alternative route towards Boulogne-sur-Mer over Tienen and Elewijt, from which it also seems to have branched off towards the north. Additionally, a road towards Arlon, which intersected the road from Zülpich to Reims, connected Tongeren with the southernmost part of the research area.

It is difficult to pinpoint the timeframe in which this road network developed. This is especially the case because the development was a continuous process, with the existing road system being expanded, maintained, and improved over time. Nevertheless, scholars have been able to identify the main phases of road building activity in the region. In the first building phase, which fell within the second consulship of Agrippa, the *Via Agrippa* and *Via Belgica* were constructed.[138] The construction of the *limes* road took place later. Dendrochronological research has shown that the road to the south of Cologne was built in 17 AD.[139] Whether this also applies to the northern part of the *limes* road remains largely unknown. There is, in any case, historical evidence for a next phase of construction during the reign of Claudius (AD 41–54).[140] Furthermore, archaeological research indicates that by the end of the first century AD (perhaps during the provincial reorganisation of Domitian), road construction had taken place along the Dutch part of the *limes*.[141] Work on the regional road network seems to have continued to at least the (early) fourth century AD, after which the roads gradually fell into disuse.[142] Thus, in sum, it appears that all parts of the research area, with the exception of the MDS

138 Rogge, 2004, p. 175.

139 Becker, 2009, p. 940.

140 Rathmann, 2004, p. 6.

141 Vos and Graafstal, 2016; van der Heijden, 2016a.

142 Rathmann, 2004, p. 7; van der Heijden, 2016b, p. 13.

region, were, from around the end of the first century AD onwards, closely integrated into the Roman road network.[143]

Although we are reasonably well informed about the main routes in the Lower Germanic Limes region, it is much more difficult to get a picture of the road network at the local level. The problem with identifying these local roads is that they were not important enough to be mentioned in historical sources and are very difficult to trace archaeologically (to an even greater extent than the more important roads). The best evidence of local roads comes from the large-scale excavations in the lignite mining region to the west of Cologne.[144] The detailed research in the Hambach region has not only uncovered nine kilometres of the *Via Belgica* but has also found parts of three local roads, of which the longest measured more than seven kilometres in length. On the basis of the meandering courses they follow, it seems clear that these local roads connected the rural settlements with each other and with the *Via Belgica*. The findings from this exceptionally well-preserved and studied micro-region probably indicate that a comparable network of secondary roads may have existed elsewhere in the research area. Unfortunately, except for an occasionally identified section of a sand or gravel road, there is no evidence to further substantiate this assumption.[145]

Even if much about secondary roads remains unknown, it is clear that the Roman road network as a whole represented a tremendous boon to traffic in the region. Compared to the simple country roads of the Late Iron Age, the Roman roads were of much better quality. This already made it easier for travellers on foot or horseback, but especially for transport by cart or wagon, solid roads were of crucial importance. Furthermore, in order to overcome the obstacles represented by rivers and streams, the Romans built various bridges as extensions of the road network.[146] Moreover, in addition to the roads and bridges themselves, the Roman road infrastructure included numerous smaller places along the roads, such as the stations of the state-run courier and transportation service (*cursus publicus*), military surveillance posts, inns, and sanctuaries, which made travel safer and more convenient.[147]

143 However, it is possible that the MDS region was connected to the regional road network but that these roads are unknown to us since paved roads were not required on the sandy soils in the MDS region. van der Heijden, 2011, p. 33.

144 Gaitzsch, 2011, pp. 291–293; Andrikopoulou-Strack and Jenter, 2018, pp. 161–162.

145 Vos, 2009, pp. 40–43; Hiddink and Roymans, 2015, pp. 48–50.

146 Eck, 2007, p. 120.

147 Andrikopoulou-Strack and Jenter, 2018, p. 206.

3.6 Conclusions

The Roman conquest and occupation had a major impact on the economy of the Lower Germanic Limes region. In this chapter, the large-scale presence of the Roman army, the increased urbanisation and population growth, the introduction of the Roman institutional framework, and the development of the regional infrastructure, have been identified as the most important general developments that initiated the far-reaching changes that took place in the region. Together, these developments ensured that the regional economy, which had largely been subsistence oriented, expanded significantly and was transformed into an economic system in which market exchange became much more important.

In particular, the large-scale presence of the Roman army played a role that can hardly be overestimated. First, except for the phase of the initial Roman conquest and the final period of Germanic invasions, the army had been able to ensure a long period of mostly peaceful conditions in the area. This was important because it created safe circumstances for investments and trade, so that the regional economy could flourish. Furthermore, the concentration of manpower in the military bases created a large demand for regional and inter-regional produced goods and services. In combination with the relatively wealthy economic situation of the Roman soldiers, who were paid in coin, this meant that the army constituted a very attractive market and thus acted as a central stimulus for economic development in the region. It is therefore not surprising that civilian settlements arose in the immediate vicinity of practically all the fortresses and forts, the main purpose of which was to provide the military market with goods and services.

At the same time, important demographic changes had an impact on the civilian settlement landscape. In addition to the military fortifications and their extramural settlements, the region saw the rise of a multitude of civilian settlements with a more independent character. These urban settlements, which varied considerably in size and character, were central places with a non-agricultural character. They often formed centres of production or trade and acted as central nodes between their rural hinterlands and larger exchange networks. It seems that they were especially widespread in the southern loess region and were mostly located along the main transport routes. Based on the development of the total number of these settlements, we can assume that the region experienced a large urban population increase during the first two centuries AD, followed by a just as significant decline from the middle of the third century AD onwards.

This urbanisation was part of the general population growth that took place during the Roman period. Estimations of population densities in the German Rhineland and the Dutch MDS region indicate that the number of people living in these regions was substantially higher than before or after. A more detailed impression of this development can be gained from several (demographic) studies from different parts of the research area. In general, these studies suggest that the rural population, as indicated by the number of rural settlements, increased during the first century AD and reached its maximum in the second century AD. From the third century AD onwards, decline set in and rural settlement numbers were again reduced to their earlier levels.

Apart from the impact of the Roman army and the civilian demographic transformation, the integration of the research area into the Roman Empire introduced several institutional changes to the region. These changes were important as they stimulated and facilitated market-oriented production and trade. The introduction of the Roman system of taxation, for example, forced taxpayers to produce surpluses with which they could pay their taxes. Furthermore, if the size of the surpluses exceeded the tax requirement, the producers could sell the rest of their surpluses at the new military or civilian markets. Therefore, in combination with the large influx of coinage through the pay of the Roman soldiers, taxation contributed to the increased monetisation of the economy, especially after the taxes had to be paid in coin from the Flavian period onwards.

This increased monetisation was an important development, because a smooth functioning monetary system facilitates and stimulates market exchange. Clear evidence for the monetisation of the research area comes from the distribution of coin finds in the Netherlands. Statistical analysis of these finds indicates that the total number of coins in circulation was much larger during the Roman period than in the Late Iron Age or early medieval periods. This is suggestive of a general increase in the use of money in the Roman period, even though it should be realised that this was partly the result of population growth. Moreover, it is even more interesting that the relative proportion of low-denomination coins increased considerably. Since these coins were probably used mainly for small-scale, local transactions, this development suggests that such transactions were increasingly conducted by way of monetary exchange. It thus seems clear that in Roman times, a lively, largely monetised market economy existed in the region and that even (part of) the rural population participated in this.

In addition to the advent of a single currency, the Roman domination also brought about a higher degree of standardisation in other fields that were of economic significance. The introduction of a common metrological system, common legal rules, and Latin as a common language, helped to provide people with better and more reliable information and reduced the risk and uncertainty that came with commercial exchanges. As a result of this, the transaction costs that came with such exchanges were reduced, and it became more profitable for parties to engage in trade with each other.

Last but not least, the Romans also expanded and improved the regional infrastructure. Although the main aim of this development was to provide a more efficient infrastructure system for the logistics of the army and the administration of the empire, it was also beneficial for the economic development of the region. Good infrastructure not only reduced transportation costs but also led to lower transaction costs, as it allowed a more effective distribution of commercial information. The potential of the waterways was better utilised through the development of improved naval infrastructure and shipbuilding. Moreover, the Romans significantly improved the existing road network by constructing several large long-distance roads, as well as many smaller secondary roads. As a result, practically the entire research area was closely integrated into the empire-wide Roman road network.

CHAPTER 4

Agricultural Production

Now that the most important general developments that had an impact on the regional economy have been discussed, it is time to commence with the more detailed analysis of the development of the economy of the Lower Germanic Limes region. The aim of this analysis is to find out to what extent the integration of this region into the Roman Empire led to economic growth and how we can characterise this growth. Since it is commonly accepted that the majority (around eighty percent) of the population in the ancient world was engaged in agriculture, a discussion of the developments in the agricultural sector seems to be the most convenient starting point for this analysis.[1]

From the discussion in the previous chapter, it should have become clear that the arrival of the Romans presented the agricultural economy with a serious challenge. The strong militarisation and the increasing rate of urbanisation meant that large groups of people who did not produce their own food were now living in the region. The fact that these people were able to sustain themselves implies that they must have had access to sufficient food. Logically, there are two possibilities as to where these people obtained their food: either they acquired the food from within the region itself, or they got it from outside the region. It is very unlikely that the largely subsistence-oriented farmers that inhabited the research area at the beginning of the Roman period could produce sufficient agricultural surpluses to meet this new demand. It is therefore clear that imports from other (probably nearby) regions of the empire will, for an important part, have catered for the needs of these people in this initial phase.[2] Yet as the regional farmers had some more time to adapt to the new situation, they might have been able to account for an increasing share of this regional demand for food.[3]

Still, matters were complicated by the fact that the rural population itself also seems to have grown in the Roman period (see section 3.3). This was problematic because it reduced the land-to-labour ratio. If all else remained the

1 Erdkamp, 2005, p. 12. It should be stressed that agricultural production encompasses more than just food production. Yet since food production was the principal element of this sector of the economy, this will be the main focus of the chapter.

2 In addition, palynological evidence from the Dutch River Area indicates that the Roman soldiers produced their own food in the immediate vicinity of their military bases. Pals, 1997, p. 28.

3 Cf. Reddé, 2018, pp. 158–160.

© ERIK TIMMERMAN, 2024 | DOI:10.1163/9789004682214_005

same, this would have the consequence that labour productivity declined. Thus, although the larger labour force would lead to an increased aggregate agricultural output of the land, this output measured per capita would be lower than before.[4] This implies that it became more difficult for the subsistence farmers that lived in the research area to sustain themselves. How was it then even possible for these farmers to produce sufficient agricultural surpluses to also feed a large non-rural population?

Theoretically, there are three ways in which the growing rural population could have achieved the increase in per capita production that would have been required to produce these surpluses. The first is through an expansion of the total amount of land that was under cultivation (extensification). Just as population growth leads to decreasing per capita production, the extension of land improves the land-to-labour ratio and, accordingly, raises per capita production. However, to counter the negative effects of population growth, the extension of land had to be at least as large as the increase in population. This means, for example, that in order to outstrip a doubling of the population, the total amount of land under cultivation should have more than doubled. This observation is also the reason why it is very unlikely that an expansion of the available agricultural land was the main cause of an increase in per capita production in the research area. As I have already mentioned in section 2.2, palynological research (see also section 4.1) indicates that much of the land in this region had already been under cultivation in the Late Iron Age. This means that although it is possible that the total amount of cultivated land expanded somewhat in the Roman period, it is impossible that such a relatively small expansion would be enough to outweigh the population boom that the region experienced. Furthermore, since farmers prioritize the best agricultural land, it is likely that the only land still available for expansion in Roman times was the more marginal land.

The second way in which a rising rural population can go together with increased per capita production is through the more intensive cultivation of the existing agricultural land. By increasing the input of labour and capital, the productivity of the land can be raised so that the same amount of land provides higher yields. This can, for instance, be accomplished by ploughing, weeding, watering, or manuring the land. The disadvantage of this, however, is that the increase in the input of labour and capital goes together with diminishing marginal returns on both of these factors of production. Accordingly, the increase in agricultural production, as long as it is not disproportionally caused by an

4 Yet it should be noted that labour productivity and per capita production are not synonymous, as the labour input per capita can change itself. See also below.

increase in capital, will coincide with a decrease in labour productivity.[5] This means that in order to achieve an increase in per capita production, the same labour force had to provide a larger input of labour. In other words, agricultural workers had to work harder than they had done before.[6]

From an economic point of view, the extensification and intensification of agricultural land are broadly comparable. In both these situations, the increase in agricultural output is the result of a simple quantitative increase in the factors of production. This means that the increase is only an increase in scale and does not improve the efficiency of the production process itself. This is different from the third possibility, where the increase in agricultural production is due to an improvement in the quality of (one of) the factors of production and thus is reflective of actual technical progress (cf. section 1.1). This implies that the same composition of inputs now produces a higher output than before. The causes of such increases in productivity can be the utilisation of better agricultural equipment or techniques, but they can also result from the rationalisation of production through specialisation or improved management strategies, such as crop rotation. Technically, increases in productivity that result from favourable climatic conditions also fall into this category. However, this is, of course, not something that farmers themselves could influence.

It is difficult to determine exactly which aspects were most important for the increase in agricultural productivity in the research area. This is especially the case since all three developments might have occurred in conjunction with each other. As I have already indicated above, a possible extension of the cultivable land does not seem to have played too important a role.[7] Instead, as I argue below, the increase in productivity was primarily the result of more intensive cultivation of the existing agricultural land. Crucially, the potential for this intensification of agriculture was significantly enhanced by the rationalisation of the production process and even by some technological developments. Possibly, the favourable climatic conditions of the Roman Warm Period (see section 2.1) might also have played a role. Accordingly, the agricultural economy did not just increase in scale but also became more productive.

In order to support this argument empirically, it is necessary to identify indications of extensification, intensification, specialisation, technological improvement, and actual surplus production in the ancient source material. Although the obscurity of the sources often makes unambiguous

---

5 If the input of capital lagged behind that of labour, a correction of that ratio could lead to an increase in labour productivity.

6 This is something that is practically impossible to identify in the sources.

7 Nevertheless, in the areas where agricultural extensification did take place, this will at least have relaxed population pressure somewhat.

interpretations impossible, there are a number of generally accepted methods that can help to identify such indications.[8] Especially when these indications mutually reinforce each other, a reasonably reliable picture of the historical situation can be formed. An increase in the proportion of cereal pollen in a pollen record might, for example, already point to an intensification of arable farming in an area. But the argument becomes much stronger when it coincides with an increase in granary sizes and an increased focus on cattle husbandry (used for traction and manure) in the region.

In the following pages, I thus analyse the source material regarding agricultural change from the various parts of the research area. I begin with an overview of the long-term developments, with palynological evidence taking centre stage. Next, I discuss in more detail the developments in agriculture in the different parts of the research area. Here, I make a broad subdivision between the so-called villa landscape in the south and the so-called non-villa landscapes of the more northern regions. Altogether, this provides a coherent interpretation of the development of the agricultural economy in the Lower Germanic Limes region.

4.1 Long-Term Developments

The favourable climatic conditions in many parts of central Europe in the period between circa 100 BC and AD 200 have already been mentioned in chapter 2. Climate is an important determining factor for the potential productivity of agricultural land. Therefore, it seems likely that these generally beneficial climatic circumstances had a positive effect on the agricultural economy in the research area. Similarly, the worsening of climatic conditions, which started after AD 200, must have had a negative impact on productivity in this sector of the economy. Unfortunately, it is very difficult to establish how significant these effects were. Moreover, it is unclear to what extent the positive effects of the climate optimum, which are believed to have begun prior to the Roman conquest, already contributed to an increase in productivity in the Late Iron Age.

Other broad insights into the long-term dynamics of the agricultural economy can be gained from the pollen evidence that exists in the research area. This evidence indicates that much of the available land in the area was already under cultivation during the Late Iron Age. This is most clear in the pollen

8 For a general introduction of how to identify such indications in the evidence, see Bakels, 1996; Kooistra, 1996, pp. 18–22; Thomas and Stallibrass, 2008; Groot and Lentjes, 2013.

diagrams from the area between Xanten and Nijmegen.[9] Here, the proportion of pollen from cultivated plants, indicative of the anthropogenic influence on the landscape, was essentially the same in the Roman period as it had been in the Late Iron Age. Only from the third century AD onwards, can a change in the use of land be observed, as the proportion of arboreal pollen appears to have increased considerably. A largely comparable picture emerges from a study into the vegetative history of an area close to Breda.[10] In this micro-region, which is located on the sandy soils of the MDS region, there is also no real observable change between the Late Iron Age and the Roman period.

A slightly more dynamic development apparently took place in the German loess zone.[11] In this area, the amount of arable and pastureland seems to have been very close to its maximum already in the second century BC. Then, in the early phase of the Roman domination, probably as a result of the disruptive effects of the Caesarian campaigns, the human pressure on the landscape must have relaxed somewhat; the pollen data suggests a regeneration of the forests around 50 BC. However, from the second half of the first century AD onwards, this trend is reversed, and in the second century AD, the proportion of arboreal pollen reaches a new low, indicating that this was the period of the most significant agricultural cultivation. This increase is most pronounced in the pollen diagram of the Malefinkbachtal near Jülich. Here, the pollen of cultural plants increased steadily from 50 BC onwards and reached a clear peak in the period between 100 and 250 AD. An important part of this upheaval was caused by an increase in cereal pollen, which indicates that the amount of arable land had expanded substantially in this period.[12] This high level of farming seems to have been maintained into the first half of the third century AD, after which a stark decline set in.

Although the transition from the Late Iron Age to the Roman period in most of the research area does not appear to have had too great an impact on the natural landscape, some more significant differences can be observed in a few areas. In the western Volcanic Eifel, for example, the Roman period went hand in hand with increased deforestation.[13] This development seems to be the result of a growing demand for wood combined with an increasing need for agricultural land. An even larger impact can be observed in an area near the Roman fort of Vechten, in the Dutch River Area, which was almost completely

9 Kalis *et al.*, 2008.
10 Kooistra, 2008.
11 Kalis and Meurers-Balke, 2007.
12 Interestingly, pollen data from Porz-Lind suggests that on the right side of the Rhine, the situation did largely remain the same in the Roman period. Bunnik *et al.*, 1995, p. 183.
13 Henrich, 2006, pp. 122–123.

deforested in the Roman period and was transformed into an open landscape of meadows and agricultural fields.[14]

Thus, the total area of agricultural land did not change too considerably in the long run. Nevertheless, the agricultural economy of the research area underwent an important transformation in the course of the Roman period. As I have explained in section 2.2, agriculture in the Late Iron Age was versatile and focused on the production of various crops and animal products. Such diverse crop growing, combined with animal husbandry, is perfectly understandable for farmers that aim at subsistence and need a strategy to deal with risk and uncertainty.[15] However, such a strategy is unlikely to lead to significant surpluses, as most farmers can only successfully produce one or perhaps two types of products.[16] An alternative strategy would therefore be to specialise in one or two specific products, with which sufficient surpluses could be created. This, of course, only pays off when reliable possibilities for market exchange exist, where these surpluses can be sold in order to gain access to other necessities. In this light, it is very interesting to see that, in the Roman period, farmers in various parts of the Lower Germanic Limes region increasingly began to focus more specifically on certain types of products, which would have allowed them to produce agricultural surpluses.

4.2 The Villa Landscape

The region that had the greatest potential for surplus production was undoubtedly the fertile loess zone in the south of the research area. It is therefore not surprising that in Roman times, farmers increasingly took advantage of the opportunities offered by this landscape and transformed it into the most important grain chamber in the region. This flourishing of agriculture, which took place from the second half of the first century AD until the early third century AD, coincided with the spread of villa settlements, which increasingly transformed the region into a villa landscape.[17] Of course, these villa

14 van den Bos *et al.*, 2014.

15 Cf. Halstead and O'Shea, 1989.

16 Bakels, 1996, pp. 330–331.

17 According to Roymans and Ton Derks, a villa landscape can be defined as 'a rural landscape that is dominated by villa settlements, if not in a numerical sense, then at least in terms of how they are perceived by rural populations in the light of their monumental nature and social status.' Villas (or villa settlements) they define in a morphological sense as 'an agrarian settlement with a Roman-style, multi-roomed main house, partly constructed of stone and with a rectangular ground plan, solid floors, a tiled roof, and sometimes a hypocaust and a set of baths.' Roymans and Derks, 2011, pp. 2–4.

settlements did not completely replace the native settlements. It is worth pointing out that the numerical dominance of villa settlements has often been overstated, as archaeological research is more likely to document settlements consisting of more durable materials. This has been confirmed by the large-scale excavations in the lignite mining areas west of Cologne, where very detailed archaeological research has uncovered a remarkably large number of settlements built in native traditions, with organic materials (i.e. primarily wood).[18] Accordingly, this suggests that the number of these traditional settlements was probably also higher in the parts of the loess area where no in-depth investigation has taken place. Nevertheless, it does not seem that such an adjustment would really undo the significance of the villas in the landscape. According to Jeneson, the proportion of stone-built to post-built settlements was, at least in the Hambach mining region, roughly equal.[19]

Even though villas were, in the first place, a reflection of the adoption of Roman-style architecture, they were also linked to the spread of a new economic complexity. Accordingly, villa settlements can be defined as agricultural units of operation that are focused on the production of agricultural goods and the sale of surpluses generated.[20] The spread of the villas in this economic sense thus represented a radical break with the subsistence-oriented rural settlements that had so far determined the pattern of settlement in the region.[21]

4.2.1 *Arable Farming*

One of the clearest indications of agricultural specialisation in this region is an important shift that occurred in the crop spectrum of the villa settlements. In the Late Iron Age, barley was the most common type of cereal that was grown in rural settlements, followed by emmer and spelt.[22] Then, in the Roman period, at least from the second half of the first century AD onwards, the crop spectrum was clearly dominated by a single crop, namely spelt.[23] Spelt was a very suitable crop for surplus production because its husk protected it against insects and fungi, which made it highly suitable for storage and transportation.[24] It also has the advantage that it thrives well in relatively

18 E.g. Gaitzsch, 1986; 2011.

19 Jeneson, 2013, pp. 155–156.

20 Heimberg, 2003, pp. 57–59; Fischer, 2013, pp. 323–326.

21 It is true that villas in this economic sense do not necessarily overlap with the morphological definition.

22 Schamuhn and Zerl, 2009, pp. 241–244. Einkorn, common wheat, and millet have also been found, but they seem to have been of less importance.

23 Kooistra, 1996, pp. 120–122; Schamuhn and Zerl, 2009, pp. 245–248. The increasing dominance of spelt in the region is part of a much larger trend in the north-western provinces of the Roman Empire. Bakels, 2009, p. 167.

24 Wiethold, 1998, p. 531.

cold environments. Correspondingly, Pliny the Elder categorised it as a winter grain.[25] Furthermore, its yields per acre are believed by some scholars to have been about twice as high in weight in comparison to barley and common wheat.[26] The growing predominance of spelt in the crop spectrum appears to be closely related to the Roman presence in the region. Since spelt, because of its stickiness, was very suitable for baking bread, the Romans must have appreciated it.[27] Thus, it can hardly be a coincidence that the predominance of spelt is first noticeable in the vicinity of the early military fortifications.[28]

However, apart from introducing a taste for this particular type of cereal, which might already be indicative of a more market-oriented attitude towards agricultural production, the Roman military presence also seems to have played a crucial role in the expansion of more specialised farming methods. The large number of veterans that settled in the region from the second half of the first century AD onwards formed a vital link in the spread of Roman know-how in a variety of different fields.[29] Although it is very difficult to trace archaeologically, it is generally believed that the Romans introduced better methods of soil improvement, such as the use of manure, fallowing, and crop rotation, which could increase the productivity of the land significantly.[30] In this respect, the ditch and parcelling systems, of which traces have been found in the rural hinterlands of Tongeren and Cologne, might also have played a role, as they are likely to have facilitated the organisation and planning of agriculture.[31] Moreover, the abundance of finds of a wide diversity of iron agricultural tools, such as hoes, scythes, and ploughs at villa sites, indicates a clear improvement in technical equipment compared to the Late Iron Age.[32]

Perhaps the most striking example of technological innovation in agriculture is the introduction of the so-called *vallus* (or *vehiculum per messes*), the Gallic harvesting machine that is described in the works of Pliny the Elder (first century AD) and Palladius (fourth century AD) and is depicted on funerary reliefs from Buzenol, Arlon, Trier, Reims, and Koblenz dating to the second and third centuries AD.[33] Even though it remains unclear whether the *vallus* was also utilised in the Lower Germanic Limes region (and if so, on what scale),

25 Plin. Nat. 18,10.

26 Rothenhöfer, 2005a. However, it should be noted that estimates of the yields of ancient agriculture are controversial. Schubert, 2016; Reddé, 2018.

27 Wiethold, 1998, p. 531.

28 Rothenhöfer, 2005a, pp. 60–61.

29 Greene, 1992, p. 103.

30 Kooistra, 1996, p. 121; Rothenhöfer, 2005a, pp. 61–62.

31 Rothenhöfer, 2005a, pp. 50–52; Bonnie, 2010.

32 Roymans, 1996, p. 65.

33 Plin. Nat. 18,72; Pall. Agric. 7, 2, 2–4; White, 1967, pp. 157–176; Raepsaet, 1995.

this machine, which was driven by draught animals, at least had the potential to significantly reduce the required input of labour for grain cultivation. Also noteworthy in this respect is the interesting connection between the use of the *vallus* and the shift towards spelt cultivation that is made by Julian Wiethold.[34] He refers to an experimental study on the functioning of the machine, which observed that spelt wheat, in comparison with other cereals, was particularly well suited for this harvesting method.

4.2.2 *Animal Husbandry*

In addition to arable farming, animal husbandry formed another central element of the agricultural economy. Unfortunately, our state of knowledge on this topic is somewhat limited by the relatively poor conditions for archaeological preservation in the loess soils. Nonetheless, it is possible to trace several of the main developments that occurred in this sector during the Roman period.

In the Late Iron Age, the proportions of the main domestic animal species (cattle, sheep/goat, pig, and horse) seem to have been varied.[35] Cattle make up circa half of the total number of bones in assemblages from the eastern loess zone from this period, while sheep/goats and pigs together make up the other half.[36] Such a division of animals appears to be representative of an agricultural economy focused on subsistence. Then, in Roman times, farmers increasingly specialised in cattle: the assemblages in this part of the loess zone now consist of about three-quarters of cattle bones.[37] This development was probably part of a much larger trend. Archaeozoological evidence from the western Rhine-Danube provinces shows a similar increase from AD 70 onwards.[38] It is difficult to tell what the main cause of this increase in cattle was. Joris Peters argues that this increase in cattle was primarily the result of the large demand of the Roman army, which would have required great amounts of meat, milk products, and leather.[39] However, in the case of the loess landscape, which, after all, was very well suited for arable farming, it also seems likely that the increase was related to the importance of cattle as a source of traction power and manure.[40]

---

34 Wiethold, 2000; Wiethold and Zech-Matterne, 2009.

35 Sheep and goats are conventionally counted as one animal species by archaeozoologists as the species are very difficult to distinguish on the basis of the bone material.

36 Becker, 2007, p. 136. Horses are not included in this study.

37 Becker, 2007, p. 136.

38 The author does not precisely specify this region, but it probably encompasses Germania Inferior and Superior, Raetia, and perhaps Noricum. Peters, 1994, p. 39.

39 Peters, 1994, p. 39.

40 Eck, 2004, pp. 430–431.

This is also confirmed by archaeozoological research into several settlements in the area around Tongeren.[41] The vast majority of the bone material from these settlements consists of cattle bones, which also underscores the economic importance of this animal in this western part of the region. More detailed analysis of this material has made it clear that the cattle in this region had a double purpose.[42] On the one hand, there is evidence of many young and sub-adult animals, which were clearly bred for their meat. On the other hand, there are numerous adult animals, of which the majority consisted of males. Many of these males were oxen, castrated at an early age, and showed notable pathological indices for traction. These older animals must thus have been kept primarily for their working power. Unfortunately, it still remains unclear whether individual rural settlements specialised in either of these breeding strategies, or if they combined the two.[43]

The need for strong working animals may also have been one of the reasons for an increase in their size. Measurements of animal bones have indicated that the wither heights of cattle and horses increased considerably throughout the north-western provinces in the course of the Roman period, and the loess area was no exception.[44] This process seems to have been a deliberate choice of the Romans, who judged the size of the local animals to be inadequate.[45] The increase in size was probably due to a combination of selective breeding and improved feeding practices. Large male animals from other parts of the empire appear to have been imported to be crossbred with suitable females of the local stock. In combination with the provision of improved animal fodder, in the form of hay or specialised fodder crops such as barley, the average size of the animals was significantly increased in comparison to the pre-Roman period.[46] In the post-Roman period, cattle again decreased in size, while horses remained large. Large and strong draught animals would be useful in the first place for arable farming because it was easier for them to pull heavy tools,

41 This research has recently been synthesised by Fabienne Pigière in a series of publications. Pigière and Lepot, 2013; Pigière, 2015; 2017.

42 Pigière, 2017, pp. 483–484.

43 Such relative specialisation has, for example, been shown in the Dutch River Area (see section 4.3.2).

44 Roymans, 1996, p. 47; Peters, 1998, pp. 276–278; Becker, 2007, pp. 137–139; Pigière, 2017, pp. 484–485.

45 Caes. Gall. 4, 2; Tac. Germ. 5.

46 Peters, 1998, pp. 301–304.

such as ploughs. In the case of the horses, military purposes will also have played a role. For cattle, which were also reared for meat and secondary products, an increase in size would also have meant an increase in yields. This increase, however, has to be set against an increase in food intake, as bigger animals also eat more. In the case of leather, the advantage of larger cattle is that they provide better quality (i.e. larger) hides.

4.2.3 *Surplus Production*

There are thus clear indications of agricultural intensification, specialisation, and technological improvement in the evidence from the loess area. These indications suggest that the farmers in this region were able to produce surpluses on top of what they needed for themselves. Yet it is difficult to find direct evidence for the production of these surpluses. The fact that agricultural surpluses must have been consumed in the nearby urban and military settlements does indicate a rural production surplus. However, the possibility of imports might exclude a relationship with the immediate hinterland. Nevertheless, due to high transport costs, it seems likely that, at least from the second half of the first century AD onwards, a large part of the consumed surpluses in the cities and fortifications came from closely located areas, such as the loess zone.[47]

This also works the other way around. If the rural inhabitants were exchanging their agricultural surpluses with the non-rural population, the rural farmers must have gotten something in return, at least when they were not just supplying in order to meet the demands of the authorities or the elite (exploitation). Evidence of imported material culture in rural settlements may thus be indicative of rural surplus production. Therefore, as I argue in more detail in section 7.1, the widespread investments of the rural population in villa building in this region can probably be viewed as an indication of surplus production.[48]

Still, more direct evidence for surplus production in the loess region comes from evidence of cereal imports from the Dutch River Area. This evidence consists of votive inscriptions from the second century AD, which were found in Nijmegen and Vechten. The inscription from Nijmegen mentions a *neg(otiator)*

47 Kooistra, 2009b, p. 231; 2012, pp. 183–184.

48 Even though it is also possible that the villas were built by wealthy new settlers, such as retiring veterans (see also section 7.1).

frum(entarius) (grain trader) from the territory of the *Nervii* (just to the south-west of the research area), while the inscription from Vechten mentions *nautae* (sailors) from the territory of the *Tungri* (in the western loess zone), which were probably involved in the grain supply of the Roman army.[49] Moreover, the discovery of a well-preserved second century AD grain ship in Woerden, of which weeds found among the cargo traced its origin to the southern loess zone, clearly indicates that such transfers of cereal did take place.[50] Although the ship from Woerden is exceptional in terms of the conservation of archaeobotanical material, finds from other flat-bottomed vessels show that such transports were certainly not exceptional along the Lower Rhine.[51] However, during the late Roman period, these southern surpluses might no longer have been sufficient. Ammianus Marcellinus mentions regular imports from Britannia taking place during Julian's reign.[52]

Another way to identify surplus production is to look at the size of the granaries in rural settlements. The logic behind this method is simple: if the storage capacity of these structures exceeded the demands of the population, they must have been used to store surpluses. Such an approach has, for example, been employed in a recent study into granaries that have been excavated in the Hambach region.[53] This study has compared the surface areas of four of these granaries with estimates of the amount of grain that would be required for the subsistence of the population of their settlements, plus the seed required for the next year. As can be seen in Table 1, large percentages of the total surface areas of these granaries were available for the storage of surplus grain. Nevertheless, there are many matters that complicate such a straight-forward approach. Not only are the demands of the population, because of unknown population numbers, difficult to specify with much precision, but it is also unknown how much grain was actually stored in the granaries. This depends on many factors. Was the grain winnowed before it was stored? Was the building also used for the storage of other products? What proportion of the maximum capacity of the granary was actually used for the storage of grain? Et cetera.[54]

49 CIL XIII 8725; 8815.
50 Pals and Hakbijl, 1992; Haalebos, 1997.
51 Schmidhuber-Aspöck, 2018.
52 Amm. Marc. 18, 2, 3.
53 Schubert, 2016.
54 For discussion, see Martin, 2019a.

TABLE 1 Available space for surpluses in rural granaries[a]

Site	Surface area	Subsistence + seed	Available for surplus	Percentage of total
Hambach 111	37.5 m^2	18.32 m^2	19.18 m^2	51%
Hambach 127	112.5 m^2	31.95 m^2	80.55 m^2	72%
Hambach 130	85.0 m^2	27.75 m^2	57.25 m^2	67%
Hambach 206	58.5 m^2	22.15 m^2	36.35 m^2	62%

a This table is based on a comparison of surface areas and requirements for subsistence and seed. Schubert, 2016, p. 363.

A possible way to circumvent these problems, at least to a certain extent, is to look at developments over time. When the size of the granaries in a settlement increases without clear signs of an increase in population, it can reasonably be assumed that there has been an increase in production.[55] It is therefore interesting to see that Habermehl observes a considerable increase in the size of the granaries in the loess region and beyond.[56] Nevertheless, as he admits, his evidence is rather limited, and the increase in size may also be related to increased central control over the produce, implying that a number of smaller granaries were replaced by a larger one.[57]

The above discussion has thus shown that there are indications that suggest that the farmers in the loess region were able to produce significant surpluses (of primarily cereal) on top of what they needed for themselves. An interesting question is how large this agricultural surplus was. Although it is impossible to determine the extent of this surplus with much precision, some scholars have tried to give at least a rough estimate of the size of this agricultural surplus. Laura Kooistra has, for instance, constructed a detailed quantitative model based on excavated villas in the Dutch and German loess zone. On the basis of the available arable land of these villa estates, she has calculated the possible size of the agricultural surpluses produced by these villas for three different rotation systems (a three-year system, a two-course system, and a three-course system) and for four different sowing/yield ratios (150/750, 150/1,500, 200/1000, and 200/2000).[58]

55 Although it can also just represent a change in storage practices.
56 Habermehl, 2013, pp. 148–155.
57 See also section 4.3.3.
58 Kooistra, 1996, pp. 96–113.

She concludes that fourteen villa estates in the Hambacher Forst, which together comprised an arable area of 686 hectares and housed 210 people, could have fed between 168 and 1,722 additional people with cereal, depending on the rotation system and sowing/yield ratios that are used in the calculation.[59] Moreover, the storage capacity of the granaries of these villas was more than five times larger than what would be required for the villa inhabitants themselves.[60] An even larger surplus could be produced in the Heerlen Basin, where seven larger villa estates, which together comprised an arable area of 1,372 hectares and housed 350 people, were able to provide 700–2,800 extra people with surplus cereal.[61] In this case, the storage capacity of the granaries of the villas exceeded the needs of their inhabitants by a factor of almost four.[62]

A different calculation is made by Werner Eck, who begins with the observation that the total surface area of the Cologne territory consists of at least 400,000 hectares of land.[63] Since part of this land was covered by settlements, infrastructure, and woodlands, or was used for fallowing and pasturing, he assumes that about half of this land (200,000 hectares) was used for the cultivation of cereal. Furthermore, he assumes that the fertile soil of this area could provide yearly yields of between 0.4 and 3.6 tons of cereal per hectare.[64] This means that the Cologne territory would produce between 80,000 and 720,000 tons of cereals per year. To calculate the demand for cereal of the inhabitants of this area, he assumes a population of 150,000 people (including the army), who would each need 1 kilogram of cereal per day. This leads to a total regional demand of almost 55,000 tons of cereal per year.[65] A demand that would allow for a surplus even at the lowest estimate of cereal production, while allowing for massive surpluses at more optimistic estimates. Nevertheless, it should be realised that these calculations rest on a lot of assumptions and that even an alteration of one of the inputs can yield completely different results.[66]

59 Kooistra, 1996, pp. 125–127.
60 Kooistra, 1996, p. 101.
61 Kooistra, 1996, pp. 125–127.
62 Kooistra, 1996, p. 109.
63 For Eck's definition of the Cologne territory, see Eck, 2004, pp. 10–22.
64 He bases these numbers on Rothenhöfer, 2005a, p. 56.
65 Eck, 2004, pp. 427–428.
66 For criticism, see Reddé, 2018, pp. 142–143.

4.3 The Non-villa Landscapes

The transformation of the agricultural economy that took place in the loess area was exceptional. In the rest of the Lower Germanic Limes region, there was no intensification and specialisation in arable farming on a comparable scale. Furthermore, the characteristics of the rural settlement landscape in these regions appear to have changed less dramatically. In spite of the fact that villa settlements have also been found here, for instance in Hoogeloon, Druten, and Rijswijk, their presence was nowhere large enough to characterise the rural countryside as a villa landscape.[67] Instead, in these areas, which have been described as 'non-villa landscapes', rural settlements seem to have held on more to Late Iron Age characteristics and consisted primarily of the native byrehouses.[68]

However, the rigid division between villa and non-villa landscapes perhaps needs to be put into perspective to some extent. According to Harry van Enckevort, this distinction does not take the specific regional conditions of the areas outside of the loess zone sufficiently into account.[69] He believes that too much emphasis is placed on the use of stone for construction, which was simply not as readily available in the northern regions. Accordingly, the settlement landscape in this area, from the end of the first century AD onwards, knew its own specific dynamics and villa forms. The best example of this is the so-called porticushouse, which is essentially a byrehouse to which a colonnade (a porticus) has been added. Although there is still much debate about the interpretation of this building, it is clear that it was influenced by Roman building techniques.[70] This reminds us that there was probably more to the development of the settlements in the north than the simple dichotomous opposition between villa and non-villa landscapes would suggest at first sight.

Moreover, the absence of (stone) villa settlements does not mean that the agricultural economies of the northern regions did not undergo any significant changes at all. Although the characteristics of the natural environments in these areas, as well as their cultural traditions, inhibited the potential for large-scale arable farming, they did provide possibilities for agricultural development in their own specific ways.[71] Thus, in the areas to the north of the loess

---

67 Heeren, 2009, pp. 203–204, 216–218; Hiddink, 2014.

68 Roymans and Derks, 2011, p. 3. Nevertheless, in these regions, certain developments, such as increased stability and durability of settlements, as well as a small increase in the number of houses per settlement, can be observed in some of the areas. Habermehl, 2013.

69 van Enckevort, 2012, pp. 287–288.

70 Vos, 2009, pp. 237–251; Heeren, 2009, pp. 153–160.

71 For the role of cultural traditions, see Roymans, 1999.

area, agricultural economies that were less focused on arable farming but more geared towards the exploitation of livestock developed.[72] The extent to which these areas were successful in raising their production might have varied, and the surpluses obtained were certainly not as large as in the south. Yet they still represent an important break with the situation from the Late Iron Age.

4.3.1 *Arable Farming*

Still, as far as arable farming is concerned, the change was probably not very significant. In fact, it seems that crop growing largely continued in the way it had been practiced in the Late Iron Age. The crop spectrum, for example, retained its Late Iron Age characteristics. The main cereals that were grown were barley, emmer wheat, oats, and sometimes millet. Furthermore, a shift towards the production of spelt, like in the loess region, does not appear to have occurred.[73] Nevertheless, we should not exclude the possibility that arable farming also intensified in these regions and that farmers were able to produce some surpluses of grain (see also section 4.3.3). It is quite possible that the better methods of soil improvement, land division, and technological improvement (with the exception of the *vallus*, which was mainly suitable for spelt harvesting) that spread throughout the loess zone also contributed to an increase in arable yields in these other regions. Yet there is little evidence for this, and it is widely assumed that arable farming in the non-villa landscapes remained primarily subsistence oriented, and that we should not overestimate any potential cereal surpluses.[74]

4.3.2 *Animal Husbandry*

The agricultural economies of the non-villa landscapes were thus more oriented towards animal husbandry. We are relatively well informed about the developments in this sector of the economy, but some variability exists in this respect between the different sub-regions. The area where research is currently most developed is the Dutch River Area. This is largely the result of the exceptionally good conditions for the conservation of organic material (e.g. animal bones) in the wet clayey soils. Because of this, we have a wealth of information on livestock production. Importantly, large synthesising works have made

---

72 I will not discuss the agricultural economies of the mountainous regions in the south of the research area, which were generally less suitable for agriculture.

73 Groot and Kooistra, 2009; Kooistra *et al.*, 2013, p. 18; Ball and van Heeringen, 2016, p. 211; Brüggler *et al.*, 2017, pp. 80–86.

74 The evidence is largely limited to indications of manuring and crop rotating. Kooistra, 1996, pp. 120–121; van Beurden, 2002, pp. 288–301; Ball and van Heeringen, 2016, p. 246.

much of this data understandable.[75] For the western part of the Dutch river delta, the situation is largely comparable, although similar overviews are still lacking. For the MDS region and the Lower Rhine Plain, the mostly sandy soils have not allowed the preservation of much bone material, and unfortunately, the research is less developed.

In any case, it is clear that cattle were already the most important domestic animal in all the regions before the Romans arrived. Joyce van Dijk and Maaike Groot have analysed bone assemblages from the western part of the Dutch river delta and the Dutch River Area.[76] They show that in both areas, cattle bones make up 63% of the total number of bones from the Late Iron Age (Table 2 and Table 3). The second most important animal was sheep/goat with 28 and 21%, respectively. Moreover, the mortality profiles of the cattle bones show that most of these animals reached adulthood.[77] From a strictly economic perspective, this would suggest that cattle were primarily kept for their secondary products and labour, while sheep/goats, which were slaughtered young, were primarily kept for their meat.[78] However, the authors also suggest an alternative explanation for the high percentage of cattle. Following Roymans, they emphasize that cattle also played an important role in the social organisation and cultural world of the societies in north-western Europe during the Late Iron Age (and before).[79] Cattle were thus raised not only for

TABLE 2 The relative proportions of animal species in rural settlements from the western Dutch river delta[a]

	% Cattle	**% Sheep/goat**	**% Pig**	**% Horse**
Late Iron Age	63	28	5	4
Early Roman/ Early Middle Roman	60	29	2	9

a van Dijk and Groot, 2013, p. 192. For the periodisation, see Table 3.

75 Lauwerier, 1988; Groot, 2016.

76 van Dijk and Groot, 2013.

77 In the Dutch River Area, 65–72% of the cattle reached adulthood (> 36 months) in the Late Iron Age. Groot, 2016, p. 82. In the western river delta, 79% of the Late Iron Age cattle were older than 48 months. van Dijk and Groot, 2013, pp. 182–192.

78 Only 14 and 17% of the sheep/goat in the Dutch River Area and the western river delta, respectively, were older than 3.5 years. van Dijk and Groot, 2013, pp. 194–195.

79 Roymans, 1999.

TABLE 3 The relative proportions of animal species in rural settlements from the Dutch River Area[a]

	% Cattle	% Sheep/goat	% Pig	% Horse
Late Iron Age	63	21	8	7
Late Iron Age/ Early Roman	61	23	6	10
Early Roman	49	31	8	12
Early Roman/ Middle Roman	52	23	6	19
Middle Roman	52	16	8	24
Late Roman	61	5	21	12

a Late Iron Age: 250–12 BC Early Roman: 12 BC–AD 70, Middle Roman: AD 70–270, Late Roman: AD 270–350. Data from: Groot, 2016, pp. 82–92.

consumption of their products, but also as a standard of value and a medium of exchange in social and ritual interactions. Accordingly, large herds were a sign of wealth and prestige, and this may therefore explain the dominance of adult cattle in the bone assemblages.

During the Roman period, cattle gradually lost their cultural significance. Although the continuation of the byrehouse building traditions, with humans and animals sharing a roof, can be viewed as a remnant of the high cultural valuation of livestock, the economic role of animal husbandry seems to have become more important. The introduction of coinage must also have played a role in this, as it took over parts of the functions that had previously been fulfilled by the cattle.[80] In addition to this, the increased demand for animal products by the Roman army and the civilian settlements is likely to have initiated a shift towards more market-oriented production. Such a shift required a large degree of adaptation on the part of the farmers, and it is likely that this will have taken some time. However, the fact that farmers already had larger herds for socio-cultural reasons probably made the step to surplus production for an external market somewhat easier for them.[81]

80 Roymans, 1999, p. 295.
81 van Dijk and Groot, 2013, p. 187.

Although cattle remained the most important domestic animal in the Lower Germanic Limes region throughout the Roman period, their exploitation had changed since the Late Iron Age.[82] In the Early Roman period, a larger proportion of the cattle from the Dutch River Area were slaughtered at a young age, which indicates that they were raised primarily for their meat.[83] In the Middle Roman period, especially after AD 150, this proportion dropped again, which suggests that the labour and secondary products of the cattle were becoming more important.[84] However, considering rural settlements as a whole obscures the large variability that existed between individual settlements. In the transition phase of the Early to the Middle and in the Middle Roman period, there seems to have been relative specialisation in either meat production or labour and secondary products in many individual settlements.[85]

The increase in wither heights of cattle that occurred in the north-western provinces at large (see section 4.2.2) has also been documented for the Dutch River Area.[86] In the Late Iron Age, the preference for extensive herds may have inhibited such an increase: numbers of cattle were valued more than their size.[87] In the Roman period, though, larger cattle were preferred for various reasons. First, they might have better satisfied the desire for meat and secondary products. Still, the relatively high proportions of adult cattle, which were probably not kept for dairying, suggest that the main benefit of larger cattle was their working power.[88] It thus appears that, like in the loess area, the main purpose of cattle husbandry lay in the support of arable farming. So, even though indications for intensification and specialisation in arable farming in this area are generally scarce (see section 4.3.1), the archaeo-zoological evidence does seem to provide evidence for this. This is somewhat remarkable because the region has traditionally been viewed as not very suitable for arable farming and primarily oriented towards animal husbandry. Since research also indicates that the importance of arable farming in neighbouring regions is being underplayed (see section 4.3.3.), it is becoming increasingly clear that this traditional image of the agricultural economy in the northern regions might be in need of revision.

---

82 Since Groot's book provides the most elaborate and up-to-date overview of animal husbandry in the Dutch River Area, much of the following is based on it. Groot, 2016.

83 Only 33% of the cattle reach adulthood. Groot, 2016, p. 97.

84 Now 47% of the cattle reached adulthood. This proportion stayed roughly the same, at 45%, in the Late Roman period. Groot, 2016, p. 97.

85 Groot, 2016, pp. 129–130.

86 Groot, 2016, pp. 122–123.

87 Roymans, 1999. Cf. Tac. Germ. 5.

88 There are too few young animals. A cow needs to have calves in order to give milk. Groot, 2016, p. 224.

Nevertheless, apart from cattle husbandry, the exploitation of the other main animal species also underwent important changes in the Roman period. Although there are some indications of an intensification of pig farming in the area around Nijmegen, it seems that the role of pigs within the agricultural economy, at least until the Late Roman period, was not very significant.[89] More important were the transformations that occurred concerning the husbandry of sheep/goats and horses. As can be seen in Table 3, the general trends in the Dutch River Area were an increased focus on sheep/goats in the Early Roman period and a large-scale specialisation in horse breeding in the Middle Roman period. The mortality profiles of the sheep/goats indicate that in the Early Roman period they were primarily kept for their meat, while in the Middle Roman period their exploitation probably shifted more to wool production.[90] The horses were essentially raised as riding animals, even though they were also eaten occasionally.[91] A ready market for horses could be found in the nearby Roman army, which would have required more than one thousand fresh horses every year.[92] In fact, there seems to be a correlation between horse keeping and the houses of veterans, which suggests that returning veterans played an important role in adapting their rural production to the demands of the army.[93] Moreover, just like with cattle, analyses of the wither heights make clear that the size of horses also increased significantly in the Roman period, which would also have fitted better with the requirements of the cavalry.[94] Again, the problem with such general conclusions on animal exploitation in the region as a whole is that they easily overlook local specialisation within individual settlements. As Groot shows, such relative specialisation was, especially in the Middle Roman period, widespread in the Dutch River Area.[95] Besides cattle husbandry, which clearly remained the most important in the region, there were many settlements that increasingly specialised in wool or horse production.

A good example of a settlement that underwent a dynamic development is the well-researched settlement of Tiel-Passewaaij.[96] Here, the proportion of sheep/goat bones from the Late Iron Age was already high, but the relative number of sheep/goats seems to have increased even more after the Roman

89 Groot, 2016, p. 225.
90 Groot, 2016, p. 199.
91 Lauwerier, 1999.
92 This is estimated for the whole army present in Germania Inferior. Groot, 2008b, p. 93.
93 Groot, 2011.
94 Groot, 2016, p. 204.
95 Groot, 2016, pp. 211–217.
96 Groot, 2008a.

TABLE 4 The relative proportions of animal species in Tiel-Passewaaij[a]

	% Cattle	% Sheep/goat	% Pig	% Horse
300–175 BC	49	30	15	6
50 BC–AD 50	40	44	9	7
AD 40–140	39	42	7	12
AD 130–220	47	22	8	23
AD 210–270	40	12	17	31
AD 270–350	47	6	22	25

a There is a slight overlap between the periods, which probably has to do with the uncertainty of the dating of the bones. Groot, 2008a, p. 41.

conquest (Table 4). Initially, many of the sheep/goats were primarily kept for meat and milk, but from around the second half of the first century AD onwards, later slaughtering ages indicate that they were now increasingly kept for their wool. This is also corroborated by findings of ceramic spindle-whorls and loom weights that were used for textile production. Contrary to what might perhaps be expected, the largest quantities of these objects date to the period before the shift towards wool production. However, as Groot explains, this is exactly what we would expect if the settlement specialised in wool production for export. Whereas the farmers in Tiel-Passewaaij had previously produced their textiles at home, in the later period they increasingly exported raw wool to external markets, where, at the same time, they collected their finished textile products.[97]

However, towards the middle of the second century AD, the proportion of sheep decreased, while the percentage of horses went up. In addition, a lower age of slaughtering for sheep suggests that they were no longer primarily held for their wool but increasingly for their meat. In the case of the horses young individuals are overrepresented. This may reflect the sale of young adults, who therefore died in another location. The young animals that have been found in Tiel-Passewaaij can then be explained as the ones that were too weak to be sold.[98] The rise in the proportion of horses certainly indicates specialisation and surplus production: such a high proportion of horses is more than would be expected of a self-sufficient community. Also interesting in this respect is

97 Groot, 2008a, p. 95. A similar development can be observed in several rural settlements in Breda. van Enckevort, 2012, p. 288.

98 Groot *et al.*, 2009, 246–247.

the discovery of a pair of iron pliers in Tiel-Passewaaij. These pliers were initially believed to have been a tool for castration, but modern veterinarians have pointed out that they were in fact a twitch. A twitch is a tool that is put around the upper lip of a horse to keep it calm during treatments.[99] This finding thus demonstrates that the inhabitants of Tiel-Passewaaij possessed far-reaching specialist knowledge with regard to horse husbandry.

Lastly, a remarkable shift in the animal bone spectrum can be observed in the Late Roman period. As Table 3 shows, the proportions of sheep/goats and horses drop greatly in this period, while those of cattle and pigs increase significantly. The increase of these latter animal types, however, does not appear to have been the result of intensification or increased specialisation. Instead, since the bones indicate a larger proportion of male specimens than before, it seems that few young males were exported to external markets. Groot therefore interprets the archaeozoological evidence of the Late Roman period as a reflection of the collapse of the agricultural system as a result of the disturbances of the time, perhaps combined with the influx of new ethnic groups.[100]

Since research in the other parts of the research area is nowhere as developed as in the Dutch River Area, it is very difficult to say whether the developments in this region are part of a larger trend. As Table 2 shows, the differences in animal species between the Late Iron Age and the Roman period are much less dramatic in the western part of the Dutch river delta than they are in the Dutch River Area. However, mortality profiles show that there was some more variation in cattle rearing during the Roman period, with some settlements retaining the Late Iron Age focus on older cattle, while others had larger proportions of younger animals.[101] The sheep/goats in the area were mainly slaughtered young, underlining their role as meat suppliers.[102] Thus, on the whole, it appears that the impact of the Roman conquest on animal husbandry was less profound here than in the Dutch River Area. However, we should beware that the dataset on which this conclusion is based is very small and that more future research might alter it significantly.

It is even more difficult to grasp the development of animal husbandry in the MDS region and the Lower Rhine Plain. It can reasonably be assumed that livestock farming also played an important role here. Yet it is very difficult to know to what extent the situation in the Roman period was different from that

99 Heeren, 2009, pp. 118–120.

100 Groot, 2016, p. 219.

101 Besides indicating an increased focus on meat production, these younger animals might also reflect dairying, but this remains uncertain. van Dijk and Groot, 2013, pp. 181–184.

102 There is, however, one settlement where the sheep/goats were slaughtered at a later age. van Dijk and Groot, 2013, p. 185.

of the Late Iron Age. In any case, the high proportion of cattle bones found in assemblages from the eastern part of the MDS region suggests that cattle were also the most common animal here.[103] Like elsewhere in the research area, cattle might well have played an important supporting role in arable farming. On the poor sandy soils of the MDS region, good fertilisation was of great importance, and there are also indications that many of the byrehouses in this region had a deepened section where manure was collected.[104] Research into the villa settlement at Hoogeloon also seems to confirm the subordinate role of animal husbandry to arable farming. At this site, a large cattle-pond and an enclosure have been found, which, according to Kooistra and Groot, were used to temporarily accommodate large numbers of animals.[105] Accordingly, they argue that Hoogeloon served as a central collection point for animals from rural settlements in the region that were exported to Tongeren. Although this provides evidence for the exploitation of cattle for their meat, most of these animals were probably old drafting and breeding cattle or young bulls that were not required for the reproduction of the herd.[106] According to Marion Brüggler, a similar scenario of animal husbandry might apply to the Lower Rhine Plain, but there is, unfortunately, no data to test this hypothesis.[107]

4.3.3 *Surplus Production*

Indications for the production of agricultural surpluses also exist for the northern parts of the research area. The most direct indication of these surpluses is the imported material culture that has been found in rural settlements throughout the region (see section 7.2). The presence of (primarily portable) material culture that was not produced in the rural settlements themselves indicates that it was probably acquired through market exchange. Since the rural consumers would need to have offered something in return, it seems clear that they were producing agricultural surpluses.[108] The size and composition of these surpluses, though, remain largely unknown.

Traditionally, it was believed that the region had not been able to produce any agricultural surpluses and that food had to be imported from elsewhere.[109] In recent years, however, this traditional image has been increasingly challenged.

103 Ball and Jansen, 2018, pp. 192–193.
104 Ball and Jansen, 2018, pp. 192–193.
105 Kooistra and Groot, 2015, pp. 150–152.
106 Kooistra and Groot, 2015, pp. 159–161.
107 Brüggler, 2018, pp. 295–296.
108 Another possibility is that the material culture was bought or brought back by returning veterans. Although this is something to take into account, I will argue that this does not seem to have been the main driver of these movements of goods.
109 E.g. Willems, 1986; Whittaker, 1994.

Concerning the production of animal products, recent synthesizing work in the Dutch River Area has shown that this region had been able to produce significant surpluses.[110] This is not only suggested by the specialisation in certain types of animals in rural settlements, which, after all, only remains relative. It is also clear from the fact that the animal products consumed in the military and civilian settlements, from around the second half of the first century AD onwards, largely correspond to what was locally produced.[111] Furthermore, in the rural settlements of Wijk bij Duurstede-De Horden and Tiel-Passewaaij, the capacity of excavated stables clearly exceeded the minimum herd size that would be required for the calculated subsistence of the population during the first and second centuries AD.[112] This suggests that parts of the herds, which in reality could even exceed the total stable capacity as not all animals had to be stabled, were raised as surplus animals.

There also appears to be evidence of the existence of cereal surpluses, although this matter remains more controversial. It is clear that the main cereals, spelt and common wheat, had to be imported (from the south) as they were not produced locally. Yet after AD 70, the military and civilian settlements also seem to have acquired a certain amount of barley and emmer from local sources, which would thus indicate rural surplus production.[113] Like in the loess area, there is also an increase in the size of the granaries observable in several rural settlements during the second and third centuries AD, which has been interpreted as a sign of surplus cereal production.[114] However, it should be noted that this interpretation has recently been criticised by Stéphane Martin.[115] First of all, he claims that the storage capacities of many of the granaries have been overestimated and would, accordingly, have allowed much less space for surplus grain. Still, he recognizes the fact that many of the granaries, indeed, became larger in the Roman period. He does, however, argue that this does not necessarily reflect surplus production, as the spread of the larger granaries may also be related to an increased control over production as a result of an increased hierarchisation within the settlements.[116] The larger granaries would, in this scenario, have replaced multiple smaller ones, so that the total storage capacity would not have changed (cf. section 4.2.3). Although

110 This is, to a large extent, the accomplishment of Groot, see above.

111 Groot, 2016, pp. 215–218.

112 Groot *et al.*, 2009, p. 242.

113 Cavallo, Kooistra and Dütting, 2008, pp. 77–78; Kooistra, 2009a, pp. 223–230.

114 Habermehl, 2013, pp. 148–152.

115 Martin, 2019b.

116 He substantiates his argument by pointing to other developments reflective of social distinction that took place at roughly the same time, such as the structuring of the settlements with ditches and enclosures and new house types. Martin, 2019b, pp. 122–126.

this is a plausible explanation for the larger granaries, with the current level of research, it is difficult to tell whether this or actual surplus production was the cause of this. I therefore believe that it is best to at least allow for a certain degree of surplus production, without overestimating its scale.

Since the landscape of the region has often been considered a limiting factor for the possibility of producing significant surpluses, a group of researchers has constructed a detailed quantitative model that compares the carrying capacity of the landscape of the western part of the Dutch river delta with the aggregate demand for food (and wood) of the inhabitants of this region.[117] The model assumes that the total population consisted of 5,750 people in the early Roman period (AD 40–69) and rose to 9,700 people in the middle Roman period (AD 70–140).[118] Of these totals, 4,550 and 7,700 people (both 79%), for the respective periods, were uninvolved in agricultural production since they were either soldiers or inhabitants of the extramural settlements. This means that the remaining 1,200 and 2,000 people, in the respective periods, were involved in agricultural production. Furthermore, it is assumed that the military population (including the inhabitants of the extramural settlements) obtained 50% of its grain requirements through imports from elsewhere. According to the model, the landscape posed no limitation on the production of sufficient surpluses of cereal and meat to feed the total population in both periods, even though the system must have come close to its limits in the middle Roman period.[119] More problematic was probably the availability of a sufficiently large labour force. With regard to grain production, there may have been enough workers, although harvest time could certainly cause problems. However, with regard to meat production, it seems very unlikely that, despite the availability of sufficient pastureland, the relatively small rural population (21% of the total) would have been able to keep sufficiently large herds to provide for the needs of the whole region. According to the model, only 36% of the total demand for meat could be covered in the early Roman period, and in the middle Roman period this was even less, at just 32%.[120]

In another publication, Brüggler used the same model to investigate the potential for surplus production in the Lower Rhine Plain during the first half of the second century AD.[121] The results of her calculations are, to a large degree,

---

117 van Dinter *et al.*, 2014.

118 van Dinter *et al.*, 2014, 14–15. These numbers are the minimal estimated values that are used for the calculations. The authors also discuss the impact of using maximum estimates but conclude that the use of these other values does not alter the main conclusions much. van Dinter *et al.*, 2014, 28–31.

119 van Dinter *et al.*, 2014, p. 18.

120 These percentages are calculated on the basis of data in van Dinter *et al.*, 2014, p. 20.

121 Brüggler *et al.*, 2017, pp. 65–71.

similar to those of the model for the western part of the Dutch river delta. Like in the other model, the landscape does not appear to have been a main factor in limiting agricultural production, as there was sufficient land available to produce both cereal and meat for the whole population (estimated at 44,870 people).[122] Although the 20% of the population that was directly involved in agricultural production, according to the model, could have produced 99% of the required cereal, it would also have had problems providing the area with sufficient meat: it seems that the rural population could only provide 58% of the meat requirements.[123]

Of course, we should realise that such quantification models are hypothetical and rest on a lot of uncertain assumptions. Nevertheless, their conclusions might provide some insights into the factors that played a role in the agricultural production of certain regions. What is interesting to see in the case of the above discussed models and regions is that they both make clear that it was not so much the landscape that posed a limit to the degree of surplus production, as was traditionally believed, but more the non-availability of a sufficiently large rural labour force. Moreover, the models clearly demonstrate that there was sufficient potential in the regions to produce quite significant surpluses. The models suggest that rural producers were primarily successful in providing sufficient cereal, while the regional demand for meat could, most probably, not be met. This is perhaps a somewhat unexpected outcome, as the regions have often been described as being mainly focused on animal husbandry. It therefore seems that the role of cereal production has been underplayed and that it stands in a more balanced relationship with livestock farming. Whether the same conclusions also apply to the Dutch River Area and the MDS region remains unclear. In view of the shortage of meat surplus in the other regions, it is maybe not very far-fetched to assume that these two regions did have a larger focus on animal husbandry with which (part of) the remaining demand of the army and the civilian settlements could be met.[124]

4.4 Conclusions

In this chapter, it has become clear that the agricultural economy in the Lower Germanic Limes region underwent an important transformation during the Roman period. The change was driven by the settlement of large groups of

122 This is the average of the minimum and maximum values used in the text. Brüggler *et al.*, 2017, pp. 66–69.

123 Brüggler *et al.*, 2017, pp. 65–71.

124 Although some imports might also have come from outside of the Roman Empire.

people in the region, many of whom did not produce their own food. This meant that the farmers, who during the Late Iron Age had been producing largely on a subsistence basis, had to increase their productivity significantly in order to meet the increased demand for agricultural products. Theoretically, there are several ways in which such an increase in productivity could have taken place. The increase in production could result from an extension of the total volume of land that was worked, a more intensive cultivation of the existing land, a more efficient working of the land, an improvement of climatic conditions, or a combination of these four possibilities.

Through an investigation of indications of extensification, intensification, specialisation, technological improvement, and surplus production in the ancient evidence, I have argued that it was primarily a combination of more intensive and more efficient cultivation of the existing land that led to an increase in agricultural productivity in the research area. That an extensification of agricultural land did not play much of a role in this is clear from the pollen evidence. In general, most of the land that was cultivated in Roman times already seems to have been in use as early as the Late Iron Age. Regarding climatic change, it is difficult to say what role it played. After all, the beginning of the climate optimum was already in pre-Roman times. However, the deterioration of the climate after AD 200 may have played an important role in the decline of the agricultural economy in the late Roman period.

The indications of an increase in agricultural productivity are most clearly visible in the southern loess zone. The fertile soils in this area were very suitable for arable farming, and it is therefore not surprising that the region became the most important supplier of grain for the research area. A characteristic element of this region was the villa settlement, which was an agricultural unit of operation that focused on the production of agricultural surpluses. An important development that took place in this villa landscape was the increased specialisation in the production of spelt. This was probably a very suitable crop for the production of surpluses and seems to have matched the taste of the Romans. Moreover, the Romans are believed to have introduced better methods of soil improvement, which would allow a more intensive cultivation of the land. There are also some indications of an improvement in the technical equipment. The *vallus*, which appears to have been particularly suitable for the harvesting of spelt, was perhaps also used in this area, although no direct indications of this have been found.

Furthermore, specialisation must have taken place in the field of animal husbandry. Cattle seem to have become increasingly important in Roman times. This can partly be explained by an increasing demand for meat, milk products, and leather. Still, cattle will also have played an important role as a source of traction and manure, which were crucial for the more intensive cultivation of the arable land. The importance of strong working animals may also have been a major cause of the increase in their size. Probably through a combination of selective breeding and improved feeding practices, the wither heights of both cattle and horses appear to have increased significantly. An additional advantage of these larger animals was that they had larger hides, which provided more valuable leather.

Concrete evidence of the actual production of agricultural surpluses is difficult to find. As I will argue in section 7.1, the large investments in villa building made by the rural population can be interpreted as a sign that these people had acquired wealth through the selling of their surpluses. However, more direct evidence comes from votive inscriptions and remains of a grain ship that were found in the Dutch River Area and indicate that surpluses from the loess region were indeed transported along the Rhine. Moreover, the storage capacity of granaries seems to have increased and was much larger than was necessary for their own consumption. This may therefore suggest that grain surpluses were stored, even though it is also possible that this just reflects more centralised control over the product. All in all, there can be little doubt that considerable surpluses were produced in the loess area during Roman times. This is also the conclusion of two different quantitative models that demonstrate that total agricultural production in the region was probably substantially higher than regional demand. Yet it should be realised that such models rest on a lot of uncertain assumptions.

Unlike in the southern area, there are almost no indications of intensification or improvement of the production process in arable farming in the non-villa landscapes of the north (but see below). Although this does not necessarily mean that there were no changes at all in this sector, it seems that crop growing largely continued in the way it had been practiced in the Late Iron Age. In the field of animal husbandry, though, there is evidence that suggests that intensification, specialisation, and surplus production did take place. However, it should be noted that this conclusion is mainly based on evidence from the Dutch River Area and does not necessarily apply equally to the rest of the northern areas.

During the Late Iron Age, cattle were the most important domestic animal. Since relatively many cattle reached adulthood, they might have been kept primarily for their secondary products and working power. Still, it must be realised that cattle also played an important role in the socio-cultural sphere, which can also explain the preference for sizable herds of adult animals. Sheep/goats, which were the second most common type of animal, were generally slaughtered young and thus seem to have been kept primarily for their meat. Horses and pigs do not appear to have played too significant a role in the Late Iron Age.

In the Roman period, animal husbandry became more market-oriented. Even though cattle remained the most common type of animal, they probably lost much of their socio-cultural significance. In the Early Roman period, the majority of the cattle were slaughtered young and were thus kept primarily for their meat. The proportion of sheep/goats, which were still mainly raised as meat providers, also increased during this period. However, especially in the Middle Roman period, important changes seem to have taken place regarding animal husbandry. Most considerably, the proportion of horses increased, which must have been sold primarily to the Roman army. Moreover, in general, the focus of the exploitation of cattle again shifts back to secondary products and labour power, while that of sheep/goats now focuses more on wool production. Yet though these broad trends are interesting, they do not reflect the increased relative specialisation that occurred at the level of the individual settlements. Many settlements focused on specific animals or animal products, such as meat or secondary products. Furthermore, as in the southern areas, an increase in the size of cattle and horses took place during the Roman period. For the horses, the reason for this must have been that larger animals better suited the requirements of the Roman cavalry. For the cattle, the greater working power of larger animals was probably the main cause. It thus appears that during this period, cattle were primarily raised in order to support arable farming. This is remarkable since it may call into question the traditional picture, which assumes that the agricultural economy in the northern regions was more focused on animal husbandry than on arable farming.

As was the case for the southern loess region, it is also difficult to find direct evidence for the production of agricultural surpluses in the northern parts of the research area. Although there are indications in some settlements that the capacity of the stables was greater than what was required for subsistence and that the size of the granaries increased over time, this is not yet overly convincing evidence. Still, the fact that part of the agricultural products that were consumed in the military and civilian settlements, at least from around the second half of the first century AD, largely corresponded to what was locally produced, makes it likely that market exchange between these central places and the rural hinterland took place. This seems to be further confirmed by the fact that imported material culture has been discovered in the rural settlements (see section 7.2). This suggests, therefore, that the rural settlements must have created agricultural surpluses, but it remains unclear how large these surpluses were.

Furthermore, model-based calculations suggest that, at least in the western part of the Dutch river delta and in the Lower Rhine Plain, quite significant agricultural surpluses could have been produced. Moreover, it is interesting that these calculations show that it was not so much the landscape that restricted the production of agricultural surpluses but rather the unavailability of a sufficiently large rural labour force. It is also striking that the calculations show that, in theory, enough cereal surpluses could be produced in the regions, while the production of meat was probably not sufficient. Therefore, these calculations, too, make it clear that the traditional image of the agricultural economy in the northern regions may need to be adjusted.

CHAPTER 5

Non-agricultural Production

In the previous chapter, I argued that the agricultural economy in the Lower Germanic Limes region in the course of the Roman period underwent an important transformation. In the absence of enough new land to bring under cultivation, farmers intensified, specialised, and even technologically improved agricultural production on existing land, so that surpluses could be produced. Although the size of these surpluses remains largely unknown and can only be approached through rough, hypothetical estimations, it is very well possible that they were sufficiently large to sustain a significant part of the non-agricultural population. This was an important achievement because it would have allowed this part of the population to contribute to the development of the non-agricultural sectors of the economy.

In the current and the following chapter, the main questions are to what extent the development of these non-agricultural sectors led to economic growth and how we should interpret this growth. The non-agricultural sectors of the economy can be defined simply as those parts of the economy that are not directly related to agricultural production. As such, they include the exploitation of (non-agricultural) raw materials, the processing of these raw materials into finished products, and the provision of services, of which trade (or exchange) is the most important element. These sectors harbour great potential for (per capita) economic growth. Still, it would be wrong to presume high levels of such growth solely on the basis of the agricultural producers' ability to sustain a significantly large non-agricultural population.[1]

This is the case because there are essentially two alternative scenarios that explain how the exchange relations between the agricultural producers and the non-agricultural consumers could have taken place.[2] In the first, which might be called the 'specialisation scenario', the relationship between both sides is

---

1 For discussion of the role of urbanisation in the generation of economic growth, see Lo Cascio, 2009; Bagnall, 2009; Morley, 2011; Hanson, 2016; Smith, 2019a.

2 In essence, these scenarios correspond to the opposing ideal types in the so-called consumer city debate, which has traditionally played an important role in the debate about the ancient economy. Although the limitations of the terms of this debate have become increasingly clear in recent decades, some of the underlying principles can still serve as a useful conceptual framework to understand exchange relations between agricultural producers and non-agricultural consumers in the ancient world. For the most clear and comprehensive discussion of these concepts, see Erdkamp, 2001. For a theoretical discussion of similar elements from an early modern perspective, see de Vries, 1974, pp. 4–21.

© ERIK TIMMERMAN, 2024 | DOI:10.1163/9789004682214_006

a reciprocal one. In exchange for the agricultural products with which the farmers supply the non-agricultural population, these farmers receive money, goods, or services of roughly equal value. The advantage of this situation is that both transacting parties can specialise in their own production and focus almost exclusively on the production of either agricultural or non-agricultural products or services.[3] This relative specialisation leads to an increase in the productivity of both producers (because of economies of scale), and through their commercial exchanges they can both profit from this. Such specialisation does not have to remain limited to either agricultural or non-agricultural production. Specialisation can go a lot further, with farmers focusing on the production of specific agricultural products and non-agricultural workers specializing in (part of) a specific type of non-agricultural activity.[4] The main importance here is that there is a reliable and well-functioning market system in place that allows people to acquire the things that they need, or desire, from the revenues of their own production. If such a system does not exist, the risk of specializing will be too great, and it would be more sensible to try to produce everything, less effectively, yourself.

However, even if the market system had functioned perfectly, it is still possible that the degree of specialisation would be more limited. In the second scenario, which can be labelled the 'exploitation scenario', the relationship between the agricultural producers and the non-agricultural consumers is a non-reciprocal one. This means that the farmers will provide part of their agricultural produce in order to sustain the non-agricultural population but that they will not receive anything in return. Instead, they are forced to give away part of their products (or sell them to an intermediary) on the basis of social or political entitlements that (part of) the non-agricultural population exercises over them. Such entitlements most often come in the form of rents or taxes, with a landlord or the Roman state exacting a proportion of a farmer's produce, but more direct forms of economic exploitation are also possible.

The potential for (per capita) economic growth is smaller in the exploitation scenario. Whereas in the specialisation scenario, the reciprocal relations allow large-scale specialisation in both the agricultural and non-agricultural sectors,

3 This is not necessarily true if the non-agricultural consumer pays with money and is no economic producer in the strict sense himself, because he is, for example, a soldier. However, since the farmer is likely to spend the received money on the products or services of another person, the final consequences remain effectively the same.

4 Specialisation can be either horizontal or vertical. Horizontal specialisation means that a producer specialises in the production of a specific good. Vertical specialisation is even more focused and means that a producer only specialises in a part of the production process of a specific good, while the rest of the process is done by other specialists. Zuiderhoek, 2017, pp. 134–140.

this is less the case in the exploitation scenario. This does not mean that there is no possibility at all for specialisation and economic growth in these sectors.[5] Even in this scenario, agricultural producers may intensify and specialise (part of) their production in order to produce enough surpluses to pay their rents and taxes. The scope for this is more limited, though, as they also need to dedicate sufficient labour time to the production of the goods in which they are not specializing. The disadvantage of this non-specialised production, then, is that it takes up relatively more labour time than it would if it was done by a dedicated specialist. As a result, agricultural producers miss out on the benefits of the economies of scale that would have arisen if they could rely on the market for these goods and focus their efforts on producing the things that they are best suited for. This situation also lowers the potential for development of the non-agricultural sector. Although there is still scope for non-agricultural producers to expand and specialise their production, the aggregate demand for their products is more limited since agricultural producers are no longer buying their goods. This means that the consumer base of these non-agricultural producers is reduced to the landowning elite, the Roman state (including the army), and their fellow non-agricultural producers. As a result of this more limited demand, the non-agricultural sector is bound to be much smaller than it would be in the specialisation scenario, and, accordingly, economic growth will be more moderate.

It must be stressed that these alternative scenarios are ideal types. This means that we should not expect the historical situation to correspond perfectly with either one of the scenarios. Instead, we can assume that the exchange relations between the agricultural and non-agricultural economies were somewhere at the interface between these two extremes. Yet it remains difficult to determine, with much certainty, whether exchange was characterised more by reciprocal or non-reciprocal relations. This is the case because the distinction between the two scenarios is mainly a question of scale, and this is something that is very hard to determine based on the available source material. We know, for example, that farmers had to use part of their agricultural surpluses to pay the Roman taxes, which clearly supports the exploitation scenario. But we do not know what proportion of their surpluses these taxes encompassed, and thus how much of their surpluses were left for reciprocal exchange (or paying rent).[6] The same problem occurs, for instance, with the interpretation of evidence of imported material culture in rural settlements (see section 7.2). Such evidence lends clear support to the specialisation scenario, but at what point is

5 Zuiderhoek, 2017, pp. 43–49.

6 Even though most scholars believe that Roman taxes were rather low. See section 3.4.1.

there enough material to argue that reciprocal relations were more important than non-reciprocal ones?

Despite these serious difficulties, it is good to keep these scenarios in mind, as they can contribute to a better understanding of the underlying causes of the development of the regional economy. Thus, in the analysis of the economic development of non-agricultural production in the Lower Germanic Limes region, which forms the central theme of the current chapter, the interplay between this sector and its agricultural counterpart is important. A fundamental question, in this respect, is whether non-agricultural producers oriented their production mainly towards the military and urban consumer markets, or if they also produced, on a significant scale, for the rural population in the countryside. As I argue in this chapter, the rural population did, indeed, constitute an important consumer market, at least for urban manufacturers.[7] Accordingly, this indicates that reciprocal exchange relations existed between agricultural and non-agricultural producers, which made possible large-scale specialisation in both these sectors.

However, although questions about the extent of reciprocal or non-reciprocal exchange relations are important, the focus in this chapter is mainly on the identification and characterisation of economic growth, which, after all, is possible in both scenarios. In order to accomplish this, I consider to what extent indications of expansion, specialisation, and technological improvement are observable in the evidence concerning non-agricultural production. The chapter is divided into two sub-chapters, of which the first one deals with the exploitation of raw materials and the second one with the production of manufactured goods. Yet it should be noted that both sectors were part of the same production chain and were thus inextricably linked to each other.

As a conceptual framework for the analyses in both chapters, it is useful to introduce the model that David Peacock designed for the analysis of Roman pottery production.[8] On the basis of anthropological analogies, Peacock has identified several 'modes of production' that correspond to different degrees of specialisation and technological development in this industry.[9] The simplest mode of production is the 'household production' level, in which each household produces only for its own needs. Pottery production is of secondary importance compared to agriculture and only takes place sporadically and on a small scale. The degree of technological sophistication is limited, and

7 This was probably less the case for the extractive industries, as their products were more often sold to manufacturers.

8 Peacock, 1982, pp. 6–11.

9 A largely similar evolutionary scheme is used by Eckhard Deschler-Erb for the analysis of Roman manufacturing in Switzerland. Deschler-Erb, 2012, pp. 13–15.

production consists of simple handmade vessels that were fired in open firings. Production is somewhat more specialised at the level of the 'household industry', where a few skilled professionals are producing beyond the needs of their own households in order to produce a marketable surplus. This 'potting for profit' remains a secondary economic activity, but it serves as a complement to the main agricultural income. The technology used is probably somewhat more developed and, in some cases, potters make use of a turntable and a primitive type of kiln.[10] A higher degree of specialisation is observable at the level of the 'individual workshops'. At this stage, pottery production is the main source of income and other economic activities, such as farming, are subsidiary. The potters aim their production at the most profitable markets and make use of a potter's wheel and a kiln. At the level of the 'nucleated workshops' individual workshops are clustering together to exploit the benefits of a specific location, such as the availability of raw materials, a labour force, or a lucrative market. In these industrial towns, pottery production is the single most important occupation, and other economic activities remain minimal. Because of competition and cooperation among individual workshops, production techniques are often highly efficient, and the product is generally of high quality and standardised. This concentration of production also attracts specialised traders, who can take over the task of bringing the goods to the consumers, so that the potters can concentrate entirely on their production.

Peacock's upward scale continues with the 'manufactory' and the 'factory'. Furthermore, two special categories are included, namely, 'estate production' and 'military and other official production'. Of these four, only the last one is of relevance for our analysis of the research area.[11] If local civilian production was insufficient to account for the needs of the military, the army had to supplement their deficits with their own production (or with imports). This production was likely at its largest immediately following the conquest phase, when the army was consolidating its presence and local civilian production had not yet developed sufficiently. Considering the importance of the army, military production can be expected to have made use of the highest technological

10 I believe that with 'turntable', Peacock means a rudimentary form of the potter's wheel, which was slowly turned by hand or foot. These early wheels are also known as tourneys or slow wheels. Although not as efficient as the real potter's wheel, they were still a clear improvement on earlier shaping techniques.

11 The manufactory is essentially a workshop that operates on a larger scale with a larger input of capital. The factory makes use of machinery driven by mechanical power. As such, the factory played, at best, a very minimal role in the Roman period. Estate production is production that takes place on a rural landholding, such as a villa estate. The scale of this production varies but essentially overlaps with household production, household industry, or individual workshops. As such, it does not add much value to this theoretical discussion.

standards known in the empire and to have been structured very efficiently.[12] Non-military state production also took place and could vary from being closely regulated to being controlled much more loosely, such as by leasing out production to private individuals. Whatever the case, it is likely that non-military state production was of a similar complexity as military production.

Peacock's modes of production have been widely used in ancient history and archaeology. Although Peacock developed his modes of production for the analysis of the pottery industry, his models are also easily applicable to other types of production. This applies both to the production of other types of goods and to the exploitation of raw materials. Nevertheless, Peacock's model has been criticised for offering a too simplistic and generalised image of the Roman pottery industry, which in reality showed much more nuance and variability.[13] However, as long as the modes of production are not used in too rigid a way, they can be a helpful tool for understanding the degree of complexity in the organisation of production.

5.1 Extractive Industries

The exploitation of the raw materials of its provinces was of great strategic and economic importance for the Roman Empire. Therefore, there is no doubt that the Roman state took great care of this exploitation after new provinces had been annexed.[14] Still, the precise extent of the state's involvement remains difficult to pin down. Many of the metal and stone deposits in the Lower Germanic Limes region seem to have been formally owned by the Roman state, as were some of the larger forests.[15] Thus, it can safely be assumed that, at least in the early phases of occupation, the army and other government officials were directly involved in the prospection and exploitation of these resources. But to what extent was there also a civilian component of any importance to this sector of the economy? In line with Rome's grander strategy concerning the administration of its provinces, we can expect the exploitation of raw materials to have increasingly been leased out to private entrepreneurs or corporations (*publicani*).[16] Furthermore, it is important to find out to what extent developments in the exploitation of raw materials contributed to the economic growth in the research area and how we should interpret this growth. Are there

12 Peacock, 1982, p. 11; van Daele, 1999, p. 130.
13 Greene, 2005; Murphy and Poblome, 2011.
14 Rüger, 2000, p. 505.
15 Horn, 1987, p. 154; Nenninger, 2001, pp. 55–59; Bechert, 2001, p. 8.
16 Hirt, 2010, p. 261.

indications of an expansion of total production and, if so, what are the reasons for this expansion? Was the increase in production simply the result of an increased input of labour, or are there indications that production increased because of increased specialisation and technological development?

In this subchapter, I argue that the exploitation of raw materials was a combined effort of state-directed and private initiatives, and that this sector of the economy witnessed significant economic expansion through a combination of increased input of labour, specialisation, and technological development. To pursue this point, I discuss the main developments in the exploitation of wood, stone, and metal. These three materials were, of course, not the only raw materials that were exploited in the region. There is also evidence of the exploitation of other resources, such as sand, clay, salt, and coal.[17] However, I believe that the discussion of wood, stone, and metal will suffice to give a good and concise impression of the exploitation of raw materials in general.[18]

5.1.1 *Wood*

Wood had already been the most important raw material in the research area long before the Romans first set foot in it. In comparison to other natural resources, such as metal or stone, wood has the advantage that it is a renewable resource, is relatively easy to exploit, and is available in practically all types of landscapes.[19] This meant that timber, in the absence of sufficient easily exploitable natural stone, formed one of the main construction materials in the area during the pre-Roman period.[20] Moreover, wood (or charcoal) was the main source of fuel for the inhabitants of this region, who made use of it for a variety of daily activities and for the production of metal and other manufactured products.[21] Lastly, wood was an important base material for a wide variety of objects, which could range from boats and wagons to (parts of) weapons and tools.[22]

---

17 Rothenhöfer, 2005a, pp. 77–117; Stockinger, 2018.

18 Some information about the exploitation of clay and sand will be given in the second part of this chapter in sections 5.2.1 and 5.2.2, respectively.

19 Ehmig, 2012, pp. 165–166.

20 Another important construction material was loam, which was often used in combination with timber. Cf. Tac. Germ. 16.

21 Charcoal is made from wood in a chemical process called pyrolysis, which essentially consists of heating the wood in the absence of oxygen. One of the advantages of charcoal is that it burns at a higher temperature and with much less smoke than wood. This is, for example, important for iron smelting. Schneider, 2007, pp. 151–152. Regular coal was also used, but the scale of exploitation seems to have been limited. Rothenhöfer, 2005a, pp. 101–102.

22 Lange, 2017; Tegtmeier, 2018.

In the Roman period, the demand for wood increased substantially. Although the Romans also introduced stone building traditions to the area (see section 5.1.2), timber remained a very important construction material for the many structures that they built throughout the region. The fortresses, forts, watchtowers, secondary agglomerations, and rural settlements were to a large extent constructed in timber, while wood was also required for the construction and maintenance of the infrastructural system. In addition, the industrial and manufacturing sectors seem to have expanded significantly, which increased the demand for wood as fuel and as a base material.

Some scholars have tried to estimate the demand for wood in (parts of) the Lower Germanic Limes region during the Roman period. Ulrike Ehmig has investigated the total demand for wood in the German Rhineland (which overlaps with a large part of the research area).[23] Her calculations of the demand for construction wood indicate that especially the construction of the civilian settlement landscape (cities, secondary agglomerations, and villas) required vast amounts of wood. In comparison, the requirements for military structures were much lower.[24] However, in her conclusion, she warns that her calculations rest on a multitude of uncertain assumptions, and that much more data will be required before any statements can be made about the demand for wood in the region.[25] Ronald Visser is well aware of this in his carefully calculated estimation of the demand for construction wood in the Dutch part of the *limes*.[26] He concludes that especially the construction and maintenance of the military fortifications required a lot of timber, while the construction and maintenance of the *limes* road and, to an even greater degree, the native rural settlements, were less taxing on the forest resources.[27]

Although Ehmig's concerns about the problematic nature of this type of calculation are certainly valid, I think that the results discussed here at least allow us to confirm the above statement that the demand for wood increased considerably in Roman times. As I have explained in section 2.2, the pre-Roman settlement landscape consisted mainly of indigenous rural settlements, which, according to Visser's figures, required relatively small amounts of wood. In the Roman period, the total number of such settlements, and thus the total amount of wood required, seems to have increased. More importantly, though, is the construction of military and civilian structures and infrastructure, which

23 Ehmig, 2012.
24 Ehmig, 2012, p. 191.
25 Ehmig, 2012, pp. 194–195.
26 Visser, 2006.
27 He did not calculate the requirements for cities, secondary agglomerations, and villas. Visser, 2006, pp. 108–113.

has been calculated to require much larger quantities of timber. So, even without considering the increase in the use of wood as a fuel or for other uses, we can already be sure that the demand for wood in Roman times must have been considerably higher than it was before. It nevertheless remains impossible to quantify the magnitude of this increase with any precision.

Instead of determining the increase in wood use from the demand side, it is also possible to turn the question around and try to find out whether there is evidence for an increase in the actual consumption of wood.[28] A large dataset of dendrochronologically dated wood remains from western Germany shows an interesting trend (Figure 11).[29] After a more or less stable number of wood

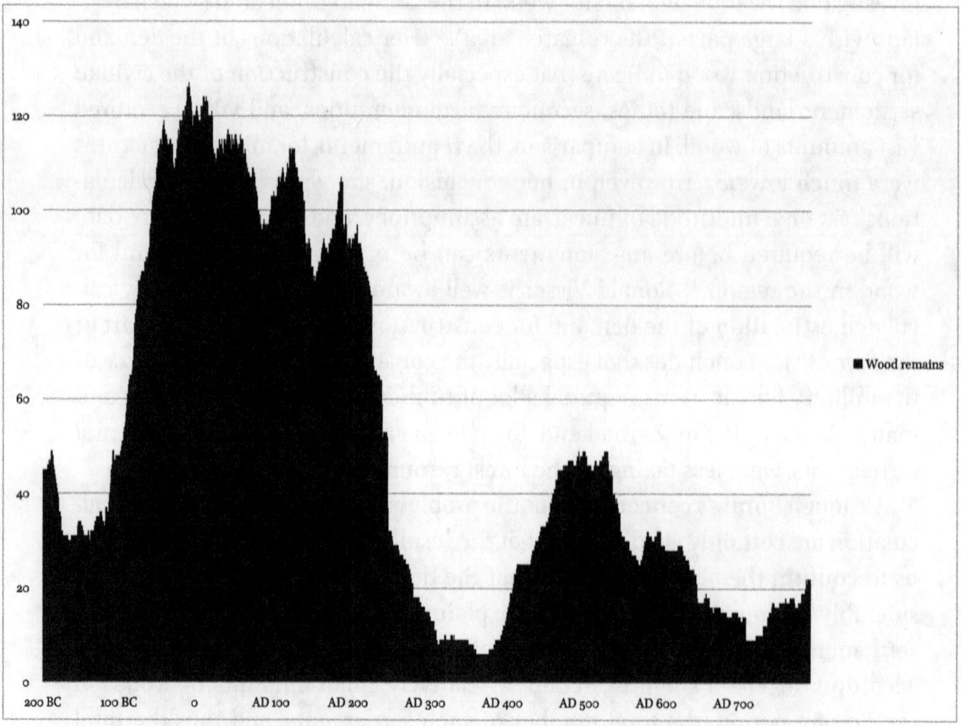

FIGURE 11 Dated wood remains from western Germany in absolute numbers
Note: Jongman, 2007a, p. 190; Schmidt and Gruhle, 2003a, p. 422.

28 The great thing about archaeological wood remains is that they can generally be dated very precisely, often to one specific year, because of their tree-rings. The downside is that wood remains are very scarce in the archaeological record, since they are mainly conserved in wet and oxygen-poor contexts.

29 The original publication is Holstein, 1980. The wood remains come from locations in (south-)western Germany (and beyond). Still, the core of the dataset consists of finds from the German states of Nordrhein-Westfalen, Rheinland-Pfalz, and Hessen. See also Schmidt and Gruhle, 2003a.

finds from the second century BC, the consumption of wood appears to have expanded significantly in the period between the first century BC and the second century AD. The following two centuries see a clear decline in wood finds, followed by a small revival in the fifth and sixth centuries AD. It is, however, somewhat remarkable that the consumption boom already seems to have started around 100 BC and not, as we would perhaps expect, some fifty years later when the Romans had conquered the area. Although it is possible that this trend truly indicates a pre-Roman construction boom, which in the context of the above discussion would be strange, it may also be the case that it is just the result of a distortion in the dataset. This second explanation is supported by the fact that another graph (Figure 12), which (for the most part) seems to have used the same dataset but quantifies the wood finds according to finding spot, shows a picture where the consumption explosion does start around half a century later (and also declines later).[30]

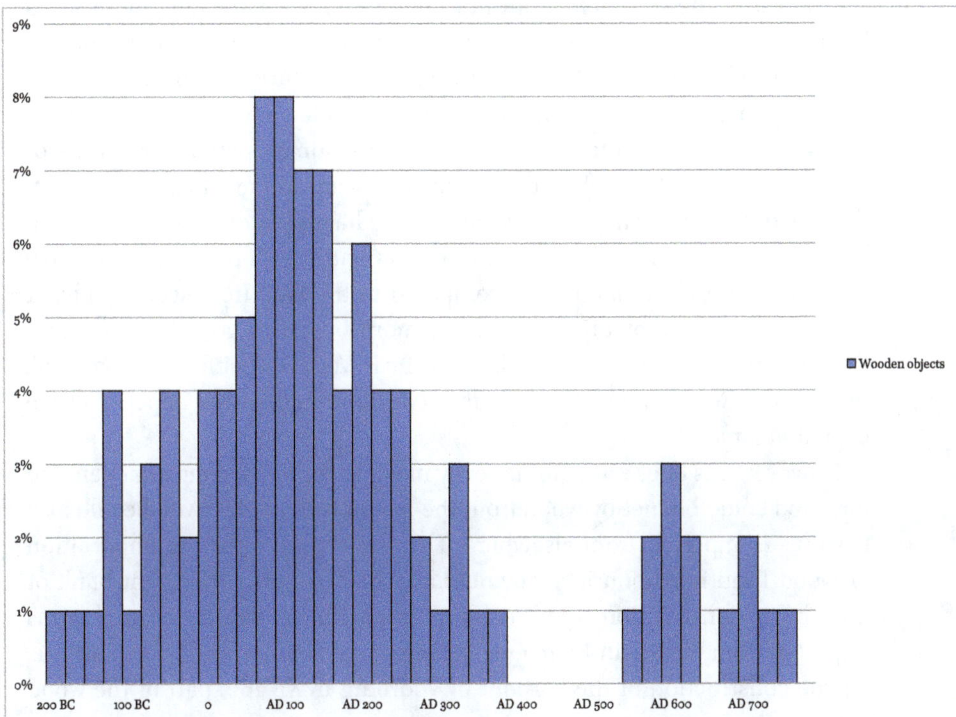

FIGURE 12 The percentage distribution of dated finding spots of wooden archaeological objects
Note: Jongman, 2007a, p. 190; Schmidt and Gruhle, 2003a, p. 422.

30 The reason for the distortion would thus be that Figure 11 is skewed by the inclusion of single sites with an exceptionally high number of wood finds from a specific period. Unfortunately, I have not been able to check whether this is indeed the case, because it

Still, it should be noted that the geographical scope of the discussed dataset is much larger than the research area on which I am focusing. For this reason, it is also useful to discuss two studies that use datasets with quantified wood finds from smaller geographical areas. The first of these is a study that uses dated wood finds from the lignite mining area in the German Rhineland.[31] Although the dataset of this study is much more limited, it is interesting to note that the trend is largely similar to that observed in Figure 12, with the largest number of finds dating to the period between roughly the last quarter of the first century BC and the first quarter of the 3rd century AD. Another study uses a dataset with quantified wood finds from the Dutch River Area and the coastal area.[32] Since this study focuses on changes between the Roman and Medieval periods, it does, unfortunately, not include data for the pre-Roman period. Nevertheless, it clearly shows that the consumption of wood was already substantial in the first half of the first century AD and reached its high point in the second half of the first and the first half of the second century AD (Figure 13). In the second half of the second century AD, the amount of wood began to decline, and in the following centuries, the consumption would not even come close to the high level of the first two centuries of Roman rule.

The Romans' large consumption of wood has led some scholars, at least in a Mediterranean context, to believe that the Roman period was a time of large-scale deforestation.[33] Yet this does not seem to have been the case in the research area. In the previous chapter, we have already seen that the pollen evidence, in general, does not show a dramatic reduction in the available woodlands in the Roman period compared to the Late Iron Age. Significant deforestation undoubtedly occurred on a more local scale, as pollen data from the western Volcanic Eifel and the area near Vechten confirms. In general, though, the Roman impact on the density of forests does not appear to have been that large.

However, this does not automatically mean that the large regional demand for wood could be met by wood from the region itself, as the wood could also have been imported from elsewhere. There is evidence for the importation of wood from neighbouring provinces and from areas on the right bank of the Rhine. Construction wood for the harbour in Xanten, for example, was imported from the Rhein-Main area in the second century AD.[34] Furthermore, for the construction of the harbour of Voorburg in AD 160, part of the wood

remains unclear to me on which data Figure 11 is based and to what extent this data overlaps with the data used for Figure 12.

31 Frank *et al.*, 2013.

32 Groenewoudt and van Lanen, 2018, pp. 208–209.

33 E.g. Hughes, 2011; Harris, 2013. For an alternative view, see Veal, 2017.

34 Bemmann, 2007, p. 99.

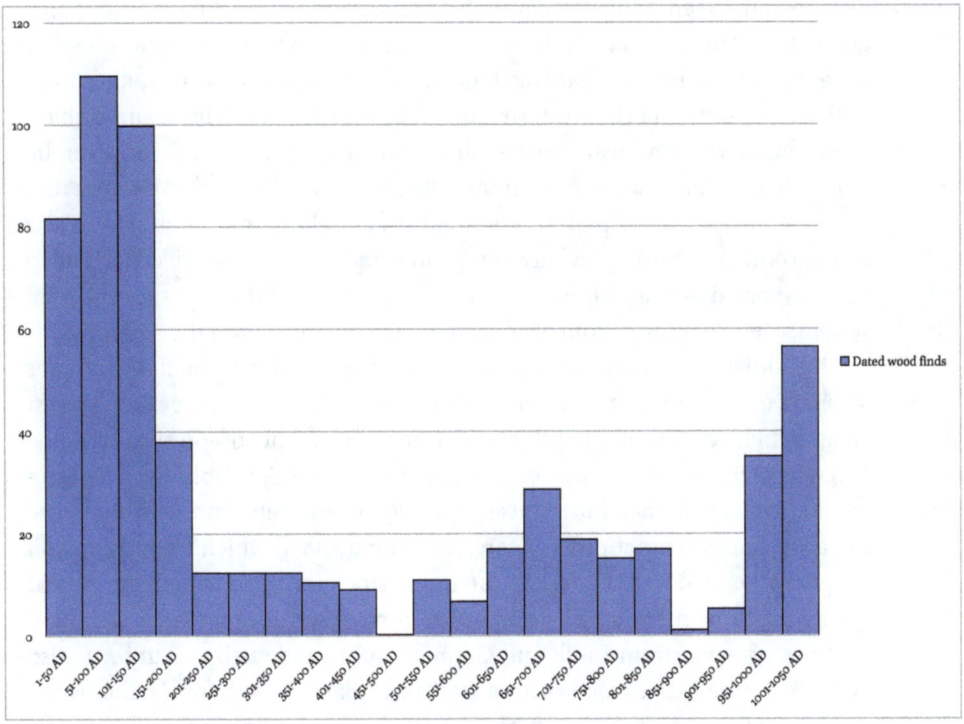

FIGURE 13 Dated wood finds from the Dutch River Area and Dutch coastal area
Note: Groenewoudt and van Lanen, 2018, p. 208.

was imported over a distance of more than 600 kilometres from an area to the east of the Neckar.[35] For the second building phase of this harbour, the wood was obtained from a somewhat closer location, namely the Mosel area, but was still transported over a very long distance.[36]

Even though such imports occurred, they do not seem to have represented a significant portion of the total supply of wood. Visser concludes in his study of the Roman wood supply in the Lower Germanic Limes that only 14% of the wood came from outside the region.[37] Much of this wood was used for the construction of ships, which could also have taken place in the area of origin.[38] Thus, although this specific wood, which had to be of suitable length,

35 Domínguez-Delmás *et al.*, 2014.
36 Domínguez-Delmás *et al.*, 2014.
37 Visser, 2009, pp. 8–9.
38 Three Roman boats that have been found in Utrecht, for example, came from the lower-Scheldt region. Jansma, Haneca and Kosian, 2014, pp. 491–493.

may not have been sufficiently available in the region itself, there was probably enough local or regional wood that could be used for many other purposes. For instance, all the timber that was required for the fortresses, forts, and other military structures in the western part of the Dutch river delta seems to have been obtained from local and regional woodlands.[39] It should, however, be noted that regional supplies were not always easily obtained. We know that for the construction of parts of the road system along the Dutch part of the *limes*, wood from the region between Xanten and Venlo was used, which had to be transported over a distance of circa 100 km.[40] For another part of the road system, the wood came from even further away, namely from the Ardennes.[41]

The Romans are known to have used certain forest management techniques in order to maintain their wood resources.[42] Instead of felling entire forest areas, which severely limited the long-term wood supply of forests, more sustainable silvicultural systems were practiced. There is epigraphic and dendrochronological evidence for the use of a selection system. In this system, the so-called *saltuarii* functioned as foresters who decided which trees could and could not be felled, thus keeping the forest stock intact. Interestingly, one of the inscriptions mentioning a *saltuarius* comes from the research area, and analyses of wood from Cuijk and Gennep, from the fourth century AD, also indicate that selective wood cutting may have taken place there.[43] Other wood management systems that, according to the literary sources, were being practiced are coppicing and pollarding.[44] These systems exploit the capacity of cut trees to produce new shoots from their stumps.[45] Although these systems were generally not very suitable for the supply of larger timbers, they were very suitable for producing smaller timbers and firewood. Within the Lower Germanic Limes region, coppicing has been indicated in the western part of the Dutch river delta and in Aachen, in the period between the first and second centuries AD.[46] Unfortunately, it is impossible to tell how widespread these forest management techniques were. Yet the fact that these techniques were used by the Romans, combined with the fact that the forest resources in the research area

39 Kooistra *et al.*, 2013, pp. 10–12.
40 Visser, 2015.
41 van der Linden *et al.*, 2016.
42 Nenninger, 2001, pp. 59–72; R. M. Visser, 2010.
43 AE 1938, 0032; R. M. Visser, 2010, pp. 15–17.
44 Colum. Rust 4, 33, 1; 4, 21, 2–3; Plin. Nat. 16, 60.
45 In coppicing the trees are cut off near the ground level, while in pollarding the trees are cut off more towards the top.
46 Kooistra *et al.*, 2013, pp. 10–12; Chorus, 2017, pp. 24–25; Tegtmeier, 2018, p. 479.

do not seem to have been depleted to a large extent, might at least suggest that the Romans were somewhat careful with the exploitation of their forests.

It is not entirely clear how the wood trade was organised, but it is likely that the military and the civilian supply were to a certain extent separate from each other.[47] The army largely appears to have taken care of its own needs. For their regular supplies of wood, they sent out simple foraging parties to exploit nearby forests (if available).[48] However, for larger building projects, there seem to have been specialised wood-gathering divisions. These so-called *vexillationes agentium in lignariis* are known from four inscriptions that have been found in the German state of Hessen.[49] It is probable that such divisions were involved in the large-scale exploitation and transport of wood over longer distances, as this required a high degree of planning and organisation. The army's involvement in the wood trade was probably not limited to projects with a direct military connection. Army contributions will also have been important for large civilian construction projects, for example in Cologne.[50] Purely civilian exploitation and trade undoubtedly took place too. For the rural population, the exploitation of local wood resources must have sufficed. The population in the urban centres must have relied to a greater extent on the wood provided by dedicated wood traders, such as the *negotiator lignarius* that is mentioned in an inscription from Cologne.[51]

5.1.2 *Stone*

Another natural resource that became increasingly important in the Roman period was natural stone. Stone was mainly important as a building material, although it was also used for other purposes, such as the production of millstones, statues, or monuments. In comparison to wood or other organic materials, stone has the advantage that it is a much stronger and more durable material. This is important because it allowed the construction of more monumental structures, which, in some cases, still stand to this day. The disadvantage of stone, however, is that its exploitation requires significantly more energy and technological knowledge. Furthermore, since quality stone does not naturally occur in all landscapes, stone often had to be transported over large distances, which caused very high transportation costs.[52] This was

---

47 Visser, 2009, p. 6.

48 Roth, 1999, pp. 123–125.

49 RSO 028; AE 1984, 0699; AE 2010, 1081; CIL XIII 06623; Nenninger, 2001, pp. 175–176.

50 Schäfer, 2014.

51 *Nego/tiato(ri) / lign(ario)*. IKöln[2] 428; Galsterer and Galsterer, 2010, p. 357.

52 Natural stone is especially lacking in the northern regions of the research area.

especially the case for transportation over land, and good connections to the waterways were therefore indispensable.[53]

In the pre-Roman period, buildings were essentially constructed from organic materials, and the use of stone was largely confined to quern stones used for grinding grain into flour (see below). This began to change as the Romans introduced stone building traditions into the research area. The first building in stone that is known from the Lower Germanic Limes region is the so-called Ubiermonument in Cologne, a tower that formed part of the city's wall and was erected around AD 5. This building, marks the beginning of a sequence of state-directed building projects that, especially after the Batavian Revolt, increasingly brought stone architecture to the region.[54] Besides these state-directed initiatives, which seem to have been limited to building projects in the larger urban centres and in the military fortifications, private individuals increasingly began to adopt the 'Roman' way of building. From the beginning of the second century AD onwards, stone building occurred in many of the secondary agglomerations throughout the research area and even in many rural settlements in the southern areas.[55] All in all, we can thus be sure that as the Romans introduced stone building traditions, the overall demand for stone in the region increased significantly.

In most parts of the Lower Germanic Limes region, natural stone was not sufficiently available, and the required stone thus had to come from the mountainous lands in the south of the research area, where large-scale exploitation of stone reserves took place during the Roman period.[56] It seems that this exploitation was sufficiently large to meet the regional demand, although certain specific or luxurious stones, such as Lorraine limestone and (substitute) marbles, had to be imported from neighbouring provinces and the Mediterranean region.[57] We are especially well informed about stone extraction in the Eifel and the neighbouring Siebengebirge. In these areas, evidence exists of a wide variety of volcanic and sedimentary rocks that were exploited by the Romans.[58] For the Ardennes, current research is much less developed. It is known that exploitable rock formations existed in the area, and petrographic

53 Medieval comparisons suggest that transporting a block of stone 19 kilometres over land would cost roughly the same as the purchase of the block at the quarry. Russell, 2017, p. 241.

54 Schaaff, 2018.

55 Heimberg, 2000, pp. 223–224; Habermehl, 2013, pp. 60–65. This is not to say that the development of stone architecture in the larger urban centres was solely the result of state-directed projects. Private initiatives will also have played an important role here.

56 Exceptional in this respect are the two sandstone quarries near Neuss, which are not in the south of the research area. Horn, 1987, pp. 156–157.

57 Horn, 1987, p. 158; Dreesen, De Ceukelaire and Ruppienė, 2018.

58 Horn, 1987, pp. 157–160.

analyses of Roman millstones have indicated that stone from the Ardennes was indeed exploited.[59] Nevertheless, there is not yet sufficient archaeological evidence to say much about the scale of exploitation in this area.[60]

The area about which we are best informed is the Volcanic Eifel region around Mayen, which has been thoroughly researched in recent decades.[61] This region contains vast sources of igneous rock that were exploited on a large scale in Roman times. Since the region was near to the Rhine, to which the stone could be transported relatively easily via smaller waterways, a blooming stone industry of inter-regional importance developed here.[62]

Most significantly, in this respect, was the exploitation of basalt lava, a type of stone that was primarily used for the production of grind- and millstones.[63] The exploitation of basalt already had a long history before the Roman occupation, starting around 5,000 BC with the production of simple grindstones.[64] In the Late Iron Age, the invention of the much more efficient rotary mill led to an important expansion of production.[65] Fritz Mangartz even characterises part of this production as profit oriented, with exported millstones reaching as far as Hessen and the northern Netherlands.[66]

However, in the Roman period, the production of millstones expanded even further. On the basis of archaeological researched extraction volumes, Mangartz has calculated the yearly output of rotary millstones in the Eifel quarries for several historical periods.[67] He comes to the conclusion that in the Roman period, the annual production of rotary millstones peaked and was around three times as high as it had been in the preceding Late Iron Age and about two and a half times as large as the total number in the succeeding early medieval period (Figure 14). In addition to this, the quarries also produced many millstones of the so-called hourglass type that are most commonly known from Pompeii. Since these millstones were much larger than the rotary mills, they required around five times as much stone.[68] Thus, even though the contribution of these larger millstones in absolute numbers might not seem too large, they do represent a significant amount of exploited volume.

---

59 Picavet, 2015; Reniere *et al.*, 2016, p. 408.

60 Brulet, 2008, pp. 204–205.

61 This is primarily the accomplishment of the researchers at the Römisch-Germanisches Zentralmuseum in Mainz.

62 Wenzel, 2014.

63 Although the stone was also, though on a much more limited scale, used as a building material. Mangartz, 2008, p. 131ff.

64 Schaaff, 2010, p. 265.

65 Hunold, 2011, p. 7.

66 Mangartz, 2008, pp. 48–49.

67 Mangartz, 2008, pp. 93–97.

68 Mangartz, 2008, p. 96.

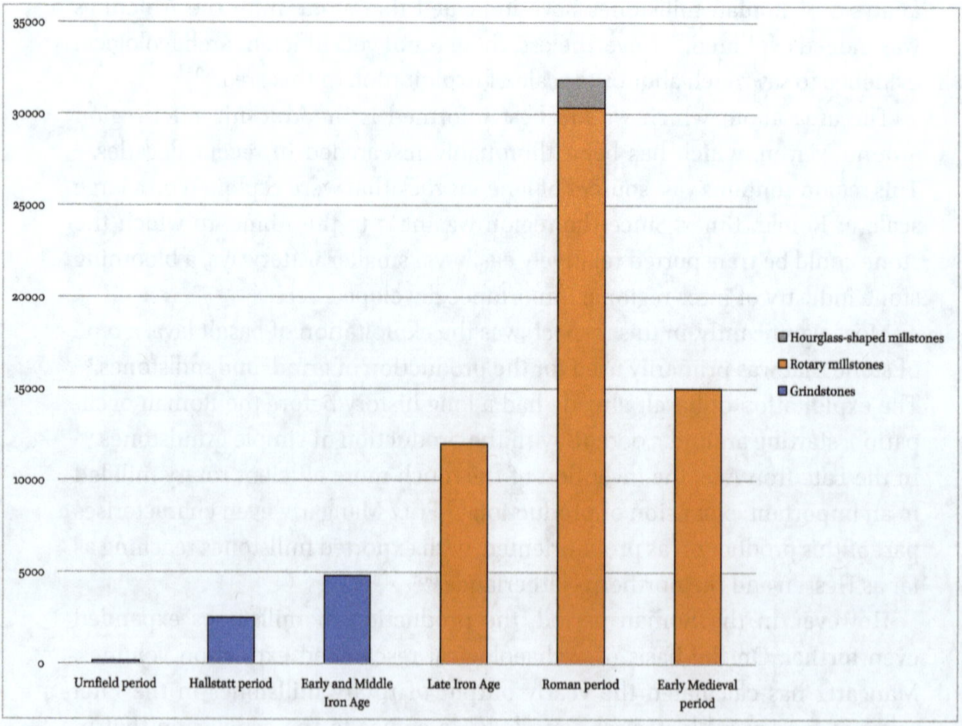

FIGURE 14 Estimated number of yearly produced millstones in the Eifel quarries near Mayen
Note: Mangartz, 2008, p. 96.

The organisation of the basalt industry was probably a combined effort of state-directed and private initiatives. As Mangartz observes, there is no epigraphic evidence for the direct involvement of Roman soldiers in the production process.[69] This is different from the situation in the tuff industry, where such evidence does exist (see below). This does not, however, mean that the Roman state left the industry entirely in the hands of the civilians. Since Eifel millstones were already an important item in the equipment of Roman soldiers during Augustus' Germanic campaigns, it seems that the Roman state took great care to regulate and improve the production process.[70] Military specialists may have played a supervising role, in which they spread their technological knowhow and contributed to a rationalisation of production. There is, for example, clear evidence for a greater division of labour in the Roman period. Whereas in the Late Iron Age the whole production process, from the

69 Mangartz, 2008, p. 92.
70 Hunold, 2011, p. 7.

quarrying of the stone to the finishing of the end product, was done by the same group of people at the same location, this process was now divided among different specialist groups at different locations.[71] Furthermore, the quantity as well as the variety of iron stonemasonry and quarrying tools that are dated to the Roman period are much larger than those of the preceding period.[72]

Because of the good connection between the Eifel quarries and the Rhine, the millstones could be transported relatively cheaply over long distances. Therefore, but also because of the good quality of the stones, the millstones from the Eifel region were distributed all over Central Europe and even to Britain.[73] This large-scale distribution of millstones is of particular interest because it can also be interpreted as a clear sign of technological development in food production. Since grain milling is a very labour-intensive process, the possession of high-quality milling equipment can greatly reduce the total amount of time that is required for this practice, leaving more time for other economic activities. Moreover, the ownership of large millstones, driven by animal or water power, may have allowed specific people to become dedicated grain millers, thus contributing to increased specialisation and division of labour.[74] At the moment, it remains unclear how widespread the use of animal or water powered mills was in the Lower Germanic Limes region. Jean-Pierre Brun has shown that ample evidence of water powered mills exists in Gaul, Britain, and Germania Superior. For Gallia Narbonensis (southern France), he even concludes that almost every villa settlement in this province may have been equipped with a hydraulic mill.[75] In this light, the widespread distribution of Eifel millstones throughout the research area might indicate that water powered mills were also a common feature in settlements in this part of the empire, although more research is needed to confirm this conclusion.

The second type of stone that was exploited on a large scale in the region around Mayen was tuff. Tuff is a light stone that is easy to quarry and to work. Moreover, it is a stable stone, which makes it very suitable for building.[76] Therefore, tuff has been used in practically all cities, fortresses, forts, and other larger settlements along the Rhine.[77] In contrast to basalt, there is no evidence for the use of tuff in the research area during the pre-Roman period. It seems likely that specialists from the Roman army, who must have been familiar with

71 Mangartz, 2008, p. 90.
72 Mangartz, 2008, p. 57.
73 Gluhak and Hofmeister, 2011, pp. 1603–1604.
74 Wilson, 2009b, pp. 79–80.
75 Brun, 2013, p. 474.
76 Schaaff, 2015, pp. 1–2.
77 Hunold, 2011, p. 7.

Italian tuff, were the ones who, soon after the conquest, discovered the stone in this part of the empire.[78] Since there was no pre-Roman tradition of civilian exploitation to build on, the role of the Roman military in the tuff industry appears to have been significantly larger than in the basalt industry. Military inscriptions suggest that soldiers were, at least during the first and second centuries AD, directly involved in quarrying, and it is very well possible that this involvement continued until the second half of the fourth century AD.[79] It seems that the military exploitation of the tuff resources was largely similar to the military exploitation of wood; with temporary divisions (*vexillationes*), supported by specialised stoneworkers, being dedicated to the gathering of stone for large state-directed building projects.

Parallel to the military exploitation, there was civilian involvement in the tuff industry. This may have included civilian workers who contributed to the state-directed exploitation but also exploitation that the state rented out to leaseholders and was meant exclusively for the private sector. There is, for instance, evidence for the use of tuff in the mortuary cult and in private construction in urban and rural (villa) settlements, from the first century AD and especially from the second century AD onwards.[80] This private exploitation must have had a more permanent character than the military, which, as I have already mentioned, was based more on temporary (but much larger) construction projects and continued until at least the middle of the fifth century AD.[81]

Holger Schaaff has estimated the total output of the two most important tuff quarries in the region around Mayen.[82] He concludes that in the Krufter Bachtal, around two million tonnes of stone were exploited in total. In order to make this large number more comprehensible, he has calculated that this volume of tuff was sufficient to construct 45 buildings the size of the Xanten city wall, which was 3.4 kilometres long, 6.6 metres high, and 1.65 metres thick, if constructed entirely of tuff, or 249 such buildings if only the outer sides of the wall were made up of tuff (15 cm each). For the Brohltal he assumes a total production of 300,000–400,000 tonnes of stone, which corresponds to 7 to 9 buildings entirely from tuff, or 37 to 51 buildings with only facings of tuff.

Another building stone that was widely used in the Roman period was trachyte. Trachyte is a hard stone and is thus a solid building material. Moreover, the stone is widely available on the Drachenfels, which is a mountain directly

78 Giljohann, Hunold and Wenzel, 2017, p. 127.
79 Schaaff, 2015, pp. 202–210.
80 Schaaff, 2015, p. 208.
81 Schaaff, 2015, p. 210.
82 Schaaff, 2015, pp. 193–199.

on the right bank of the Rhine near Bonn. This location made transportation of the stone easy, as the blocks could be loaded on ships almost directly after quarrying. The importance of this waterway connection is underscored by the distribution of the trachyte finds: except for the trachyte dedicatory stones from Remagen, all findings have been located downstream in close proximity to the Rhine.[83] Trachyte, has been found as far away as in Vechten, but the main areas of distribution lay in the region around Cologne and Bonn, and to a lesser extent, in the area around Xanten.

Like with tuff, there was no pre-Roman tradition of trachyte exploitation. The Roman military must have discovered the stone in search for good construction materials and exploited it during the first three centuries AD. There are several indications that the exploitation was entirely in the hands of the Roman military.[84] Trachyte has not been traced in private buildings but only in buildings that were public or had military or defensive purposes. Furthermore, all the votive stones from trachyte that have been found in the region have been dedicated by the members of the military. One of the stones, which has been dated to AD 160, is of particular interest as it mentions that a *vexillatio* from the *classis Germanica* (Germanic fleet) went out to get stone for the building of the forum in Xanten.[85] Lastly, the Drachenfels was located outside of the borders of the empire but inside of the military controlled territory, which makes it unlikely that the stone was exploited by any non-military association. Like with the military tuff exploitation, the trachyte industry also seems to have had a temporary character, with large amounts of trachyte being exploited when a large construction project was about to begin. Since the stone was extracted on the surface, a large enough workforce could amass a significant amount of stone in a relatively short amount of time.[86] According to Josef Röder, the total amount of trachyte that was excavated at the Drachenfels in Roman times lay somewhere between 400,000 and 450,000 m^3.[87]

It goes beyond the scope of this chapter to discuss the rest of the stone industry in too much detail.[88] The exploitation of limestone, however, does merit special attention. Even though limestone was used to produce stone monuments and specific architectural elements, its main economic importance lay in the fact that it could be burnt to produce quicklime (also known as burnt lime). Quicklime was used to produce mortar and the famed *opus*

83 Kennecke, 2016, p. 43.
84 Kennecke, 2014b, pp. 100–101.
85 CIL XIII 08036; Kennecke, 2014b, p. 100.
86 Grabowski, 2016, p. 119.
87 Röder, 1974.
88 For such an overview, see Rothenhöfer, 2005a, pp. 106–110.

caementicium (Roman concrete). The gradual solidification of these materials made them of great significance for Roman architecture, and consequently, their use was widespread.[89]

Limestone was extensively available in the northern part of the Eifel. The most important centre of production developed in the area around Bad Münstereifel, where especially the industry of Iversheim was very impressive.[90] Here, several kiln batteries burned vast amounts of lime from the first to fourth centuries AD. According to calculations, one battery of six kilns could reach a monthly output of 200 tonnes of quicklime.[91] On the assumption that around ten such batteries existed in the area, the total monthly output of the Iversheim kilns, with a workforce of 700 to 1,000 people, would amount to 2,000 tonnes of quicklime per month.[92] At this rate of production, it would take only around 2.5 months to produce sufficient quicklime to build a building as large as the Xanten city wall if this building consisted of simple stone masonry.[93] Although this calculation is probably somewhat optimistic, especially since it is unlikely that all these kilns were contemporary and the kilns will certainly not always have functioned at their full capacity, it is, in any case, clear that the productive capacity of the Iversheim industry was enormous.

The exploitation of the Iversheim kilns was to a large extent in the hands of the Roman military. Epigraphic evidence that has been found near several of the kilns makes clear that *vexillationes* from the fortresses in Bonn and Xanten burned lime here.[94] However, the question of whether all of the kilns belonged to the army remains open.[95] It does not seem unlikely that private entrepreneurs were also active in the quicklime industry, and even though their scale of production may have been more limited than that of the army, their joint contribution to the industry must have been significant.[96]

89 Lamprecht, 1987; Schneider, 2007, pp. 162–163.

90 Sölter, 1970; Wagner, 2007. Another important centre was located in the area around Aachen. Rothenhöfer, 2005a, p. 112.

91 Sölter, 1970, p. 40.

92 Wagner, 2007, p. 114.

93 This estimate is based on the calculations in Wagner, 2007. The numbers there have been applied to the proportions of the city wall as mentioned above. It should be noted that these calculations only give an estimate of the amount of quicklime used in the total volume of stone masonry. This means that, in addition to the quicklime, large amounts of other types of stone were needed.

94 CIL XIII 07943; 07944; 07945; 07946; 07947; AE 1977, 0560; Sölter, 1970, pp. 24–28.

95 Rothenhöfer, 2005a, p. 111.

96 Wagner, 2007, p. 114.

5.1.3 *Metal*

Apart from stone deposits, the southern part of the Lower Germanic Limes region also contained rich deposits of various kinds of metal ore. Even though evidence of pre-Roman exploitation of these metal deposits exists, the exploitation clearly intensified significantly in the Roman period.[97] This intensification was primarily driven by the demand for metal from the Roman state and military. Roman expertise in the field of mining probably enabled both the prospecting of new metal deposits and more intensive exploitation of existing sources. The utilisation of more advanced mining techniques must also have played an important role in this respect. In an important article, Wilson argues that the Romans mechanised the whole production process of metal extraction.[98] He states that Roman mining 'saw some of the most advanced and large-scale applications of technology to economical critical work ever to be practised before the European industrial revolution'.[99] Although Wilson's article is primarily concerned with gold and silver mining in the Iberian Peninsula, the same technological knowhow, spread by military specialists, could be applied in the mining districts in other parts of the empire.

The region does not seem to have harboured any important reserves of precious metals.[100] Gold could be panned from certain streams and rivers in the Ardennes, the High Fens, and Eifel, but this would hardly have been worth the effort.[101] The possibilities for obtaining silver might have been somewhat better, since lead, which was plentifully available in the research area, contains a very small proportion of silver, which can be extracted from it in a process called cupellation. There are indications that such silver extraction took place in the region.[102] However, since the silver content of the lead in the research area was generally very low, the extraction of silver probably only played a very limited role. Similarly, the exploitation of other metals, such as copper and zinc, also appears to have been of little importance.[103]

The two types of metal that were exploited on a large scale in this region during Roman times were lead and iron. Lead was of minimal economic and cultural importance for the Late Iron Age societies that inhabited the research

97 Bechert, 2001, 6–7.
98 Wilson, 2002.
99 Wilson, 2002, p. 17.
100 Cf. Tac. Germ. 5.
101 Horn, 1987, p. 155; Dommergue *et al.*, 2006, p. 136.
102 Rothenhöfer, 2005a, p. 95.
103 Rothenhöfer, 2005a, pp. 95–98.

area prior to the Roman arrival.[104] Within the Roman Empire, though, lead was used for a wide range of purposes. Lead has a very low melting point, which makes it one of the easiest metals to extract and process.[105] It was very useful in the building industry, as it could be used to coat the iron brackets and anchors that held large building stones together. It has, for example, been estimated that for the construction of the Porta Nigra in Trier seven tonnes of lead were used in this manner.[106] But lead was also extensively used for many other purposes, such as the piping of aqueducts, and for a range of items for everyday use.[107] It thus seems clear that after the Romans had conquered the area, the regional demand for lead increased substantially.

Within the southern part of the research area and its immediate surroundings, several large reserves of lead could be found. The most important sources that were exploited during the Roman period were located in the northern Eifel, of which those near Mechernich and Stolberg were the most significant.[108] In addition to these Eifel locations, lead was exploited in the High Fens near Verviers and on the right side of the Rhine in Lüderich and Königswinter-Oberpleis.[109] The Romans seem to have begun with lead exploitation almost as soon as they had brought the region under their control. The exploitation in the northern Eifel began in the Augustan period and quickly reached a large output.[110] This production probably continued to at least the fourth century AD.[111] The exploitation on the right side of the Rhine also began in the Augustan period, as the region was then still under direct Roman control. After the Varian disaster, most Roman exploitation on this side of the Rhine ceased, even though lead mining continued in Lüderich during the first two centuries AD.[112] In this context, it is also interesting to mention a mining centre much further to the east in Brilon (Sauerland). Here, evidence for lead production has been found in settlements from the first and second centuries AD. Since Roman control of this area must have ceased after AD 9, this production was in the hands of the native population. This is remarkable as these people generally did not have use of the metal themselves.

104 The metal's softness and not very appealing appearance made it largely unsuited for the production of military equipment, tools, and jewellery. Rothenhöfer and Bode, 2012, p. 345.

105 Boulakia, 1972.

106 Bode, Hauptmann and Mezger, 2009, p. 177.

107 Rothenhöfer, Hanel and Bode, 2013, pp. 68–69.

108 Rothenhöfer and Bode, 2012, pp. 346–347.

109 De Vleeschouwer *et al.*, 2007, pp. 291–292; Rothenhöfer and Bode, 2012, pp. 346–347.

110 Rothenhöfer and Hanel, 2013, p. 278.

111 Rothenhöfer, 2005a, pp. 89–91.

112 Bode, Hauptmann and Mezger, 2009, pp. 183–184.

It thus appears that the short-lived Roman occupation had initiated lead exploitation in this area, which the natives continued in order to sell the lead to Roman merchants.[113]

Although it is impossible to give reliable quantitative estimates of the total output of lead production in the research area, there are some indications that give us an impression of the scale of this industry. A good indication of the vast increase in lead production has been provided by a study that has analysed lead deposits in the sediments of two maar lakes in the western Eifel region.[114] The results of this study show a remarkable peak in these deposits in the first 230 years of the first millennium, which the authors link to intensive mining and metallurgical activities in the north-western Eifel. On the basis of these lead deposits, they have estimated that the average output of lead might have been 450 tonnes per year.[115] Similarly, studies that have looked at metal pollution in a Belgian peat bog in the High Fens also observed remarkable high lead values during the Roman period.[116]

It seems that the large-scale production of lead in the Lower Germanic Limes region (and beyond), at least during the first two centuries AD, could have covered the regional demand for lead rather easily. Isotopic analyses of more than 240 Roman lead objects from several archaeological sites in Germany have shown that over 85% of these objects have been produced from Eifel ore deposits.[117] Moreover, there is evidence that suggests that, apart from supplying the local market, the production centres in the research area were also able to supply inter-regional markets with lead. The finds of two shipwrecks in the Western Mediterranean, for instance, bear witness to the fact that German lead was being exported over long distances.[118] The shipwreck of Saint-Maries-de-la-Mer, which was found in the Rhône estuary (southern France), contained 99 lead ingots, with a total weight of 5.5 tonnes, which were inscribed with the text *Flavi Veruclae plumb(um) Germ(anicum)*. Similarly, a ship that sank off the coast of Sardinia, at Rena Maiore, contained around 50 lead ingots, of which many were inscribed with the text *Augusti Caesaris (plumbum) Germanicum*. Moreover, isotopic analyses of these inscribed ingots

113 Rothenhöfer and Hanel, 2013, pp. 277–278.

114 Schettler and Romer, 1998.

115 Schettler and Romer, 1998, p. 795.

116 De Vleeschouwer *et al.*, 2007, pp. 291–293; Renson *et al.*, 2008.

117 It should be noted that none of the archaeological sites fall within the research area. However, since most of them are located rather close to the northern Eifel, a similar, or even higher, percentage can be expected for sites within the research area. Durali-Müller *et al.*, 2009. A similar conclusion can be found in Mirschenz, 2016b.

118 Rothenhöfer and Bode, 2015.

have confirmed that these ingots were indeed produced in Germany.[119] From the third century AD onwards, the scale of the exports seems to have been reduced. The already mentioned study that analyses German lead objects indicates that an increasing number of objects from this period can be traced to British ore deposits (although the majority were still of Eifel origin).[120]

Apart from providing evidence about their provenance, inscribed lead ingots can also give us information about the organisation of the lead industry.[121] Ingots were inscribed for several reasons. The inscriptions could mention the name of the producer, the owner of the mine, the place of production, the recipient of the ingot, the weight of the ingot, and other relevant information. Based on this epigraphic information, it appears that (most of) the lead mines were imperial possessions, which the Roman state, in some cases, leased out to private individuals or organisations. Clear evidence of direct state production is provided by the ingots from the already mentioned shipwreck of Rena Maiore; here the inscriptions unmistakably suggest that the ingots were the result of state production.[122] The ingots from the shipwreck of Saint-Maries-de-la-Mer, on the other hand, are inscribed with the name of a private individual: Flavius Verucla.[123] What is interesting is that the words *Imp(erator) Caes(ar)* are inscribed on the back of the ingots, indicating that the ingots were the property of the emperor. It therefore seems that this Flavius had leased the exploitation of a lead mine from the emperor and, in return, provided the state with a part of his production. Evidence for the leasing of lead production by private organisations is provided by two ingots from Fos-sur-Mer (southern France) and Basel.[124] The ingot from Fos-sur-Mer is inscribed with the text *sociorum plumb(um) Ger(manicum)*, which suggests that the ingot was produced by an anonymous private organisation. The ingot from Basel mentions a *societat(is) S(exti et) T(iti) Lucreti(orum)* and thus seems to have been produced by the private organisation of two brothers. Furthermore, it is interesting to mention an ingot that has been found in Haltern. This ingot is inscribed with the text *Leg(io)* XIX, which probably indicates the recipient of the ingot.[125] Interestingly, isotopic analysis has traced the production of the ingot to Lüderich. Therefore,

119 The ingots came from the production centres in the Eifel region and/or from the Sauerland. Since the isotopic values of both regions are largely similar, it is impossible to distinguish between both them. Bode, 2008, p. 200; Rothenhöfer and Bode, 2012, pp. 354–56.

120 Durali-Müller *et al.*, 2009, pp. 141–142.

121 Rothenhöfer and Bode, 2012; Raepsaet-Charlier and Raepsaet, 2013.

122 Although the same shipment also contained ingots produced by a certain Pudentis, who may have been a private entrepreneur. Rothenhöfer and Bode, 2012, pp. 355–356.

123 Rothenhöfer, 2013, p. 65.

124 Rothenhöfer and Bode, 2012, pp. 353–354.

125 Rothenhöfer and Bode, 2012, pp. 349–350.

it may be possible that Lüderich was a military exploitation centre that provided lead for the Roman army. This can also explain why production continued in Lüderich after AD 9, as the mine now fell outside of the borders of the empire but remained within the zone of military control.

In comparison to the knowledge that we have on the lead industry, our current understanding of the exploitation of iron is very limited.[126] This is especially the case for the Late Iron Age. There is, for example, no direct evidence for pre-Roman iron mining in the northern Eifel. Nevertheless, there can hardly be any doubt that the inhabitants of this area had already extracted part of the iron reserves before the Romans invaded.[127] Similarly, no evidence of iron exploitation from the Ardennes has yet been dated specifically to the pre-Roman period.[128] Still, some scholars believe that here, in the region between the Sambre and the Meuse, one of the most important iron mining areas of pre-Roman Western Europe existed.[129]

The demand for iron must have increased considerably in the Roman period. Not only did the Roman army require vast amounts of iron to produce their military equipment and for a range of other purposes, but in the course of the first two centuries AD, the growing civilian population also increased the demand for iron products. Since the state of knowledge concerning iron mining in the Roman period is only slightly better than that of the Late Iron Age, it remains very difficult to make accurate statements about the changes that this industry underwent. Nevertheless, there is a broad consensus among scholars that the iron industry in the region expanded during the Roman period, the causes of which are most likely to be found in the spread of Roman technological know-how and more rationally organised production.[130]

Not much is known about Roman exploitation of iron in the Ardennes, but it is likely that the region between the Sambre and the Meuse remained the most important production centre there.[131] We are better informed about iron production in the northern Eifel region, where exploitation seems to have occurred along the whole length of the region from the Rhine to the High Fens. In contrast to the exploitation of lead, the production of iron in this area does

126 This is partly the result of the low intensity of research into this topic. More fundamentally, however, much of the (older) traces of exploitation have been disturbed by exploitation in later historical periods.

127 Rothenhöfer, 2005a, pp. 86–88.

128 Dommergue *et al.*, 2006, p. 139.

129 Denayer, Pacyna and Boulavin, 2011, p. 13.

130 Rothenhöfer, 2005a, pp. 86–88; Dommergue *et al.*, 2006, pp. 139–155; Denayer, Pacyna and Boulavin, 2011, pp. 12–14.

131 However, the importance that scholars have traditionally attributed to this region might be doubted, because it is based on a very limited amount of evidence. Polfer, 2000, pp. 70–71.

not appear to have taken place in large-scale exploitation centres. Instead, the iron industry was characterised much more by small-scale production on small and medium sized villas, or in secondary agglomerations, which were primarily found around Ahrweiler, Lommersdorf-Freilingen, the Hürtgen Forest, and Aachen.[132] This situation is perhaps unexpected and gives the impression that the exploitation of iron was much more left in the hands of civilian producers than was the case with lead or stone. A possible explanation for this may be the fact that iron ore was fairly common within the landscape, which may have made the decentralised exploitation by smaller scale production centres settled close to the sources the most efficient way to extract the iron.[133] Furthermore, such a scenario does not necessarily rule out state involvement altogether. Considering the importance of iron for the army, it is likely that the state still controlled the iron production in order to ensure that a steady supply of iron was available for military purposes.

In the absence of any quantifiable data, estimates of the total scale of the increase in iron production can hardly be made.[134] However, there is discussion about whether the scale of Roman iron production was significant or not. According to Michel Polfer, the scale of iron production in the Ardennes and Eifel can, at least in comparison to central and southern Gaul, be characterised as small.[135] Consequently, he believes that the region had not been able to satisfy the large military and civilian demand for iron and was therefore dependent on imports from other parts of the empire. A more optimistic interpretation of the scale of production is advocated by scholars who argue that Polfer has overlooked the contribution of the many small and medium sized production sites that clustered together near sources of iron in the northern Eifel.[136] Although the individual contributions of these smaller production sites were small, their aggregate production volume must have been substantial.[137] Therefore, Peter Rothenhöfer concludes that while regional production may not have been large enough to produce exports, it was, at least from the second century AD onwards, large enough to meet a significant part of the regional demand for iron.[138] However, until future research provides more clarity on these topics, most of this remains hypothetical.

132 Rothenhöfer, 2005a, pp. 78–85.
133 Rothenhöfer, 2005a, pp. 98–99.
134 For discussion of the possibilities, see Kuhnen, 2012, pp. 207–216.
135 It should be noted that Polfer stresses the provisional nature of his conclusions. Polfer, 1999, pp. 59–60.
136 Ritzdorf, 2003, pp. 114–115; Rothenhöfer, 2005a, p. 87; Kuhnen, 2012, pp. 215–216.
137 Kuhnen, 2012, pp. 214–215.
138 Rothenhöfer, 2005a, p. 87.

5.1.4 *Conclusions*

Now that the main developments in the exploitation of wood, stone, and metal have been discussed, there are several general conclusions to be made. Most importantly, there can be no doubt that the exploitation of raw materials expanded massively in the Roman period. There are good indications that the total output of wood and basalt was, at least during the first three centuries AD, much higher than it had been in the Late Iron Age or would be in the Early Medieval period. For iron, such indications are lacking, even though the increased demand for this material by the Roman army and the rest of the population in the Lower Germanic Limes region suggests that a largely similar increase in output probably occurred. Furthermore, there is evidence for large-scale exploitation of tuff, trachyte, quicklime, and lead during the Roman period. These resources had not been exploited at all before the Roman conquest.

The importance of the Roman state and army for the increase in the output of raw materials in the region can hardly be overstated. The industries that were new in the research area were initiated by the Romans, who had a use for the new materials and had the technological and organisational capacity to exploit them. Moreover, the Romans expanded existing industries and improved their efficiency. The clearest example of this can be found in the basalt industry, where Roman specialists are believed to have increased productivity significantly. Altogether, the evidence concerning state and military exploitation of raw materials largely seems to concur with Peacock's characterisation of this mode of production as being structured very efficiently and making use of the highest technological standards available.

In addition to state and military production, there was also an important civilian component involved in the exploitation of raw materials. In some cases, this civilian component appears to have operated largely independently from the state and military. This is, for example, the case for the wood industry, where civilian exploitation was probably small-scale, with the rural population collecting their own wood and the population in the urban settlements relying more on dedicated wood traders. However, in most cases, the civilian workforce is likely to have been overseen and organised by specialists from the Roman state or military. Sometimes, the production of a mine or quarry was leased out to private individuals. Clear epigraphic evidence for this is known from the lead industry. This leasing out of parts of the production, made sure that raw materials also became available for consumers on the free market. In general, it seems that civilian exploitation of raw materials was organised at a level of complexity close to, or even equal to, that of state and military exploitation. In terms of Peacock's modes of production, most of the stone quarries and lead mines, should probably be considered as 'nucleated workshops' as they appear to have been highly efficient industrial towns in which everything revolved around the exploitation of the material. The iron industry was apparently less complex, as this industry was small-scale and much more decentralised. Therefore, most iron mines can be considered to have been on the level of the 'individual workshop' or even the 'household industry'. The same might be the case for the production of quick lime, although not enough is known about the civilian component of this industry to say anything with certainty. For civilian wood exploitation, we can probably assume a range of complexity from the 'household production' level to that of the 'individual workshop'.

The exploitation of raw materials in the research area was primarily aimed at covering the demand of the region itself. Military and state production were used to supply the army and for large-scale construction projects, while civilian production accounted for the needs of the general population. The only industries of inter-regional importance were the basalt and lead industries. The products of these industries are known to have been distributed over long distances within the Western Roman Empire.

5.2 Manufacturing

Another sector of the economy that expanded significantly during the Roman period was manufacturing. Manufacturing can be defined as the production of consumer goods from agricultural or non-agricultural raw materials for commercial purposes.[139] As such, manufacturing is distinguished from craftwork at the household level, which is primarily aimed at production for personal use. In terms of Peacock's modes of production, manufacturing thus corresponds to the level of the household industry or higher levels of economic complexity. Military manufacturing is a somewhat exceptional form of manufacturing since it lacks a commercial incentive but instead aims to account for the needs of the army. However, as with civilian manufacturing, the degree of organisation and complexity in military manufacturing is, generally, higher than that at the household level.

Following this definition, the scale of manufacturing in the Late Iron Age was very small (see section 2.2). The vast majority of the population in the Lower Germanic Limes region consisted of farmers, who dedicated most of their labour time to agricultural work. Craftworking was practiced as a secondary activity and only served to meet the needs and desires of the household, or

139 This definition is based on definitions in Polfer, 2008, p. 37; Deschler-Erb, 2012, p. 13; Brun, 2016, pp. 80–81.

at best, of a slightly larger community (e.g. a village). Accordingly, the degree of economic complexity in craftworking was low. Things such as clothing, tableware, and tools were produced sporadically and on a small scale. A good example of this is pottery, which in the pre-Roman period was almost completely handmade (see section 7.2.2). This strongly suggests that this pottery was produced at the household level, even though it should be stressed that handmade pottery is not by definition the result of household production.[140]

As I will argue in this second subchapter, the scale of manufacturing expanded substantially as a result of the Roman conquest. The main cause of this was the emergence of a large non-agricultural population in the region, which dramatically increased the demand for manufactured products. Initially, it was primarily the Roman military that constituted a large demand for such goods. In order to satisfy this demand, the army had to import their products from other regions or produce them by themselves, since the regional scale of manufacturing in this early period was largely insufficient to do so. Still, in the course of the Roman period, the civilian population in the urban centres set up their businesses and increasingly took over a large part of the military production, while, at the same time, their own demands for products increased the aggregate demand for manufactured goods in the region even further. Moreover, it seems that the rural population also constituted an important consumer market for manufactured goods, although many farmers undoubtedly still produced part of their needs by themselves.

Epigraphic and archaeological sources from Cologne give an impression of the wide variety of different manufacturers (as well as people with other professions) that worked in the city during the Roman period.[141] Evidence has, for example, been found of millers, potters, fullers, weavers, tanners, shoemakers, woodworkers, and many others. This material suggests that Cologne was an important centre of manufacturing and that the city had a high degree of division of labour and specialisation. The situation in Cologne, being one of the largest urban centres in the research area, is not really representative of the situation in the rest of the urban settlements in the region. However, since most of these settlements have yielded evidence of at least one type of manufacturing activity, it can reasonably be assumed that manufacturing also took place in most of these settlements.[142] This is especially the case since the archaeological record is very fragmentary. In particular, the manufacturing of

140 Nor is it impossible that wheel-thrown pottery was produced at the household level. However, as a general rule, this distinction is probably appropriate. Peacock, 1982, pp. 8–9.

141 For an overview, see Eck, 2004, pp. 433–436.

142 See Appendix 1. See also Rothenhöfer, 2005b, pp. 65–66.

organic materials, such as textiles, leather, or wood, has seldom left any archaeological traces. More durable materials, such as metal, glass, and especially ceramics, are better conserved and are thus our best guesses for finding out to what extent the manufacturing sector played a role of any importance in the Roman period.

In the following pages, I will therefore focus on the manufacturing of ceramics, glass, and metal in order to find out to what extent the development of the manufacturing sector led to economic growth in the region and how we should interpret this growth. As with the previous investigations, the main questions will be whether evidence can be found of an increase in total production, specialisation, and technological development. In the absence of sufficient evidence concerning other categories of manufacturing and to keep the chapter more concise, the discussion of these three material categories will serve as an indication for the manufacturing sector as a whole.

5.2.1 *Ceramics*

The industry that, by far, has left the largest amount of evidence in the archaeological record is the ceramics industry. Ceramics played a central role in Roman life. Not only did the Romans use a wide spectrum of pottery, ranging from luxurious tablewares to simple coarse wares, used for transportation, storage, or food preparation, but they also used other ceramic objects such as lamps and figurines.[143] Furthermore, ceramic building materials, such as bricks and tiles, formed an important addition, or alternative, to the construction materials made from natural stone. This was especially of relevance in the northern regions of the research area, where natural stone was not locally present and had to be imported over long distances. The production of ceramics only required clay, water, firewood, and sometimes a temper (e.g. sand or grog). These natural resources were widely available in the Lower Germanic Limes region, and ceramics could thus be produced practically everywhere, although

143 In the following pages, I will use the very general terms 'fine wares' and 'coarse wares' to describe the main categories of pottery in the research area. Both categories can be divided into many subcategories that correspond to the function and also the specific style of the pottery. However, since this study is not very concerned with such detailed differences but more with the economic complexity of the production of such vessels, this binary distinction between the more luxurious tableware and the more basic everyday pottery will suffice. Nevertheless, where possible and deemed relevant, I will use some of the more detailed subcategories. This is especially the case with the fine wares, which often have a very specific style. Regarding the coarse wares, a distinction will often be made between 'regular' coarse wares and the so-called heavy ceramics (*Schwerkeramik* in German), which include mortaria and storage containers.

certain specific products sometimes required a specific type of clay.[144] The preponderance of ceramics in archaeological evidence reflects its widespread use in Roman society. Moreover, it is the result of the non-recyclable and imperishable nature of the material itself. Combined with the fact that the kilns used for ceramic production were often built partly under the ground level and after their period of usage were simply filled up, this means that we are exceptionally well informed about this particular type of production.[145]

The clear visibility of ceramic remains is not only typical for the Roman period. Ceramics did also play an important role in the lives of the people that inhabited the research area before the Roman conquest and are the most commonly discovered type of material object in archaeological contexts from this period as well. However, the diversity of the products and the scale of production seem to have been more limited in the Late Iron Age. In this period, the production of ceramics was essentially confined to pottery because the Late Iron Age societies did not produce ceramic building materials. This pottery was mainly produced at the household level, and there was little or no specialisation. The products consisted of simple, handmade vessels that were often fired in open fires or pit kilns.[146] In contrast to the much more durable kilns that were used during the Roman period, such firings have not left many archaeological traces.

It should be stressed that the Late Iron Age tradition of pottery production remained in use throughout the research area during the entire Roman period and beyond (see section 7.2.2). The most important change that took place during the Roman period, though, was that an increasing share of the total pottery produced was made in a typical 'Roman' style, being shaped on a potter's wheel and fired in a (Mediterranean style) pottery kiln.[147] Figure 15 gives a rough idea of the general development of the pottery industry during the Roman period. The graph shows the number of dated pottery kilns that have been documented in the region per 50-year period.[148] Kilns have been categorised according to the nature of the settlement in which they were found. These categories include urban settlements (220 kilns), military settlements (62 kilns), and rural settlements (15 kilns). The city of Cologne (91 kilns) has been listed as a separate category because this single city, with almost a quarter of the total number of kilns, has a large impact on the shape of the total graph.

144 E.g. Terra Sigillata, Gallo-Belgic wares, and coloured slip wares. Höpken, 2011, p. 75.

145 Höpken, 1999, p. 759.

146 Ickler, 2007, pp. 100–107; Taayke *et al.*, 2012, pp. 264–265; van den Broeke, 2012, pp. 195–196.

147 Clerbaut, 2010, pp. 3–4.

148 See Appendix 2.

Of course, these kilns represent only a fraction of the total number of kilns that must have been in existence during the Roman period. Moreover, it must be noted that the dating of the kilns is variable, with some of the kilns being dated very precisely within a range of several years or decades, while others are dated only in (part of) a century, or even in several centuries.[149] This variable dating has an effect on the shape of the graph, as kilns with a broad dating are represented in several of the 50-year periods, while the more precisely dated kilns fall only within one or perhaps two of the 50-year periods. However, since 313 of the 388 dated kilns have been dated within a timeframe of 100 years or less and 229 even within a period of 50 years or less, the impact of the variable dating is probably not very significant. Another, more fundamental, consideration is the fact that the graph only shows the number of kilns that may have been in existence during a certain period, which does not equate directly with the output of ceramic products, which certainly varied widely between kilns. Nevertheless, in the absence of other proxy data that might provide insights into such numbers, it does not seem too farfetched to assume that the number of kilns in existence, as shown in Figure 15, at least illustrates the main trends in the development of the pottery industry.

5.2.1.1 Military Production

The changes that occurred regarding pottery production during the Roman period were initiated by the demand for pottery by the Roman army. Roman soldiers desired good quality pottery and had enough purchasing power to buy such pottery. The civilian population of the Lower Germanic Limes region, however, was unable to satisfy the military demand, as it was only accustomed to producing simple handmade vessels primarily meant for their own use. Nevertheless, handmade vessels seem to have covered at least some of the most basic needs for pottery at the early Roman military sites, although it remains unclear whether they were bought from civilians or were produced by the soldiers themselves.[150] To acquire the rest of its pottery, the military was left with two options: they could either import it from other parts of the empire, or they could set up their own production centres. Logistically difficult and expensive imports from Italy and southern Gaul seem to have been the norm in the earliest phase of the Roman occupation.[151] Yet, the army soon began to reduce its dependency on these imports by setting up its own production centres in and

149 The kilns that have just been dated as 'Roman' have been left out of the analysis.

150 In Nijmegen, for example, a quarter of the pottery from the Augustan fortress was handmade. Polak, 2005, p. 243.

151 Liesen, 2018.

near the fortresses and forts along the frontier. Concrete evidence of such early production has been found in Remagen, Bonn, Neuss, Moers-Asberg, Xanten, Altkalkar, and Nijmegen.

It is difficult to say how successful the military production centres were in substituting imports with locally produced products. In Nijmegen, production of simple pottery for everyday use began in the military bases on the Hunerberg and the Kops plateau somewhere in the period between 19 and 15 BC, but the small-scale workshops appear to have been short-lived and largely unsuccessful.[152] Up until the Flavian period, imports are likely to have accounted for the lion's share of the pottery supply in Nijmegen.[153] More fruitful enterprises probably took place in and near the legionary fortresses in Neuss and Bonn, where production also began in the Augustan period but where the industry seems to have expanded in the Tiberian–Claudian period.[154] In the latter period, significant production also took place near the fort in Remagen.[155] Altogether, the fragmentary evidence gives the impression that the early Roman military production will at least have covered the soldiers' demand for simple everyday pottery to a certain extent, even though this will have varied from site to site. Regarding luxurious tableware and amphorae, of which the latter were imported for their contents, the army must have remained dependent on importation (see section 6.1).

Things began to change in the Flavian period. From this period onwards, the regional pottery industry expanded considerably and is likely to have reduced the imports of external materials to a minimum. Military production, however, was not the prime driver of this upsurge in output. In fact, most of the kilns from military contexts in Appendix 2 were no longer in use from around the middle of the first century AD onwards. Although a significant number of these kilns are still visible in the bar for AD 51–100 in Figure 15, it should be realised that only 4 of these 39 kilns have been dated in the period after AD 60. As can be seen in the further course of the graph, military production probably did not play too important a role in the rest of the Roman period either. Yet Nijmegen clearly forms an exception to this. With the stationing of the Tenth Legion in Nijmegen after the Batavian revolt, military pottery production recommenced in the area. Production did not only take place in the *canabae* near the legionary fortress but is also known from De Holdeurn, a site four

152 Stoffels, 2014; Hendriks, 2014.

153 Hendriks, 2014.

154 Filtzinger, 1972; Wirtz, 1998; Frank, 2007.

155 Friedrich, 2014.

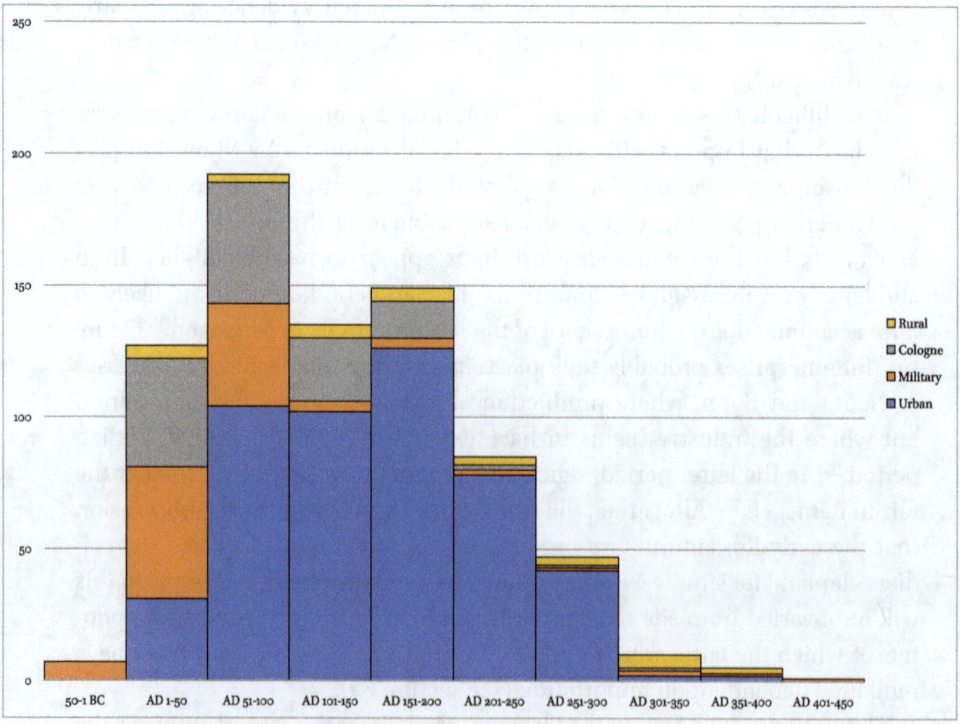

FIGURE 15 The number of dated pottery kilns that have been found in the Lower Germanic Limes region

kilometres to the south-east of the fortress.[156] In these centres, the so-called Nijmegen-Holdeurn ware was produced, which consisted of high-quality fine wares, as well as more basic everyday pottery.[157] At De Holdeurn, production seems to have continued into the third century AD, even though the scale of production was certainly lower than it had been in the second century AD.[158]

5.2.1.2 Civilian Production

The main reason for the large increase in pottery output from the second half of the first century AD onwards, however, was the increase in civilian production centres in many parts of the Lower Germanic Limes region. Civilian pottery production primarily took place in the urban settlements that had spread throughout the region from the early Roman period onwards (see section 3.3). In almost half of the civilian settlements that have been listed in Appendix 1,

156 Hendriks, 2014, pp. 182–183.
157 Kloosterman, 2016.
158 Polak, 2005, p. 244; Weiss-König, 2014, pp. 138–139.

evidence of pottery production has been documented, and even more evidence can be expected to emerge in the future given the sometimes limited current level of research into these settlements. In addition to this, small-scale civilian production did take place in some rural contexts, but the significance of these rural producers was not very large. This is also clearly illustrated by Figure 15 which shows that the vast majority of kilns dated to the period after AD 50, belonged to urban contexts, while only a fraction came from rural contexts.

As can be seen in Figure 16, the civilian industry was largely decentralised. To a large extent, the spread of the production sites is similar to that of the general spread of the urban settlements (see Figure 2). This indicates that proximity to the markets, formed by these settlements and their hinterlands, was one of the primary considerations for the potters who wanted to set up a business. Ceramic production was possible almost everywhere in the research area, and potters were, therefore, not so much restricted to locations with certain natural resources. Instead, good connections to infrastructure and a shorter distance to the market could in many cases outweigh the benefits of more central production because transportation costs could, especially in the case of cheaper products, make up a relatively large proportion of the consumer price of the goods. Accordingly, most production centres produced almost exclusively for local demand. Yet, as the population as well as civilian demand for pottery in the region grew, some production centres managed to expand beyond their local markets.

The civilian site that has yielded the most archaeological evidence for ceramic production, but which at the same time is not the most typical of sites, is the city of Cologne. Pottery production in Cologne began when immigrant potters from Italy and Gaul, who were attracted by the new demand for their products, set up their workshops during the early first century AD.[159] These early workshops were located within the city walls, in quarters in which residential and workshop buildings were mixed.[160] During the first half of the first century AD, almost all Cologne potters produced a standard palette of simple coarse wares and the so-called Gallo-Belgic ware, which was fine tableware that imitated the luxurious terra sigillata but had also incorporated certain Celtic influences. In addition to this, many workshops specialised in specific products, such as the so-called white-red ware, dolia, jugs, lamps, or fine Italian style wares. In doing so, these workshops hardly entered into competition with each other.[161] Perhaps the most remarkable example of this specialisation has

159 Höpken, 2005, p. 42.

160 Höpken, 2005, p. 20.

161 Höpken, 1999, pp. 761–762.

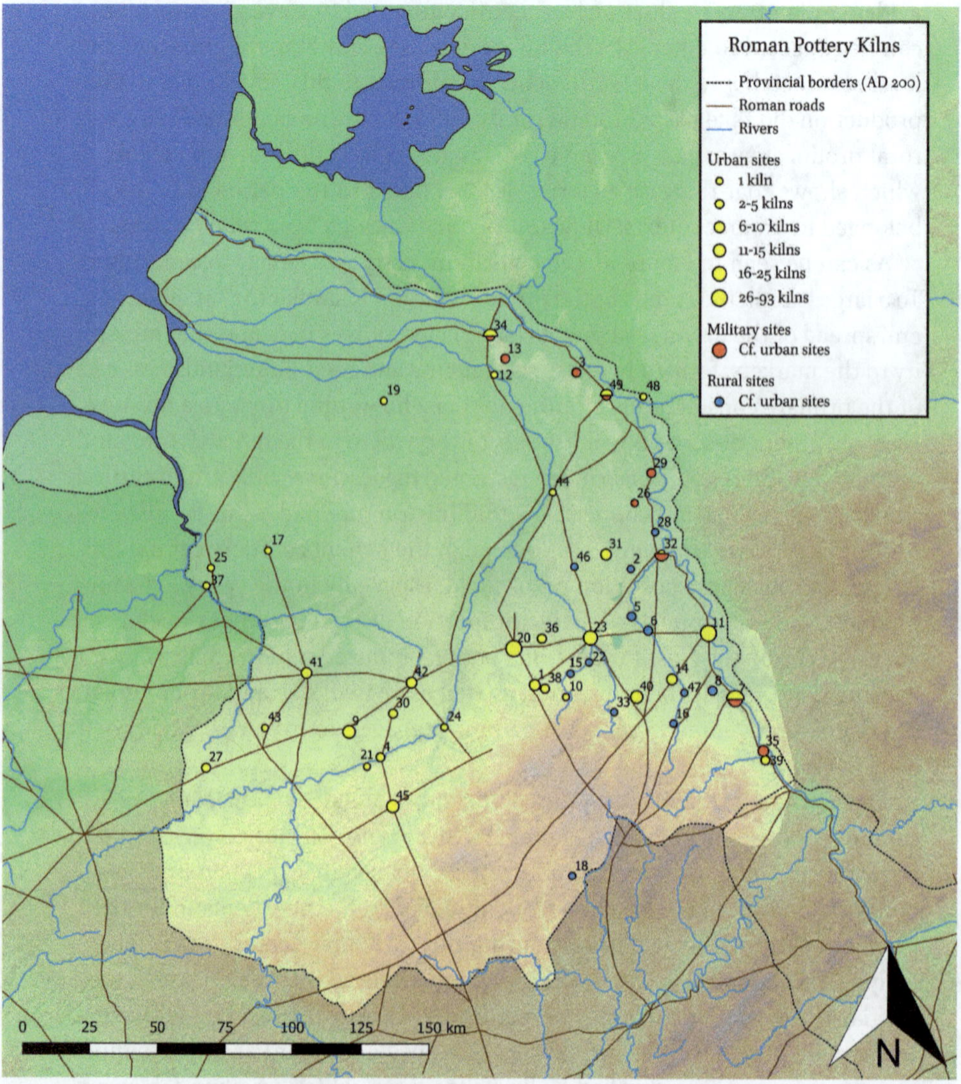

FIGURE 16 Distribution of settlements where pottery kilns have been documented
Note: Data in Appendix 2.

been found in the Lungengasse, where a large pottery workshop with 19 kilns has been found.[162] Some of these kilns were small and were used for the firing of coarse wares, but there were also much larger kilns, which had diameters of circa 2.6 metres, in which large dolia were fired together with mortaria. According to Constanze Höpken, this is the first instance of mass production

162 Carroll, 1998; 2005.

of dolia in Germania Inferior.[163] Already in this early period, Cologne workshops produced beyond the local demand and their products have been found along the Rhine and inland towards Gallia Belgica.[164]

After the middle of the first century AD, the pottery workshops were moved to several different locations outside of the city walls, probably as a result of a reorganisation of the city after its promotion to a Roman colony.[165] By this time, the potters had developed a typical local ('Rhineland') style that combined Italian and Gallo-Roman elements.[166] They also began producing a slipped ware that would gradually replace the Gallo-Belgic ware as the primary produced fine ware in the city.[167]

During the second century AD, the pottery industry of Cologne flourished. Even though Figure 15 shows that most of the discovered pottery kilns in Cologne have been dated to the first century AD, the total number of identified workshops is higher for the second century AD.[168] An important development in this century was that a large number of workshops clustered together in a suburban neighbourhood in the west of the city.[169] The choice of this particular location must have been motivated by the good connection to the *Via Belgica*, which connected the workshops to external markets and supplies of raw materials.[170] Additional advantages of the clustering of the workshops were probably the competition and cooperation between different potters, which may have led to a spread of production techniques, an elevation of the quality of the products, and a reduction of transaction costs.[171] The production range of many of these workshops was diverse, and evidence of clear specialisation in one or two products is scarce. Most workshops produced coarse wares in combination with one or two types of fine wares (mostly slipped ware) and often some form of moulded objects, such as lamps, figurines, or masks.[172] The difficulty involved in the moulding of such terracottas, as well as in the applying of decorations onto the slipped wares, such as the famous '*Kölner Jagdbecher*', testifies to the great technical proficiency that some of these potters must have professed.[173] As a result of this, the pottery industry in Cologne

163 Höpken, 2005, p. 229.
164 Jaschke and Schmitz, 2018, p. 319.
165 Things such as fire hazard, smoke, and odour pollution are likely to have been serious concerns.
166 Höpken, 2015b, p. 125.
167 *Engobierte Ware* in German.
168 Namely, 19 identified workshops for the first century AD and 26 for the second century AD.
169 Höpken, 2005, p. 21.
170 Höpken, 2005, p. 22.
171 Goodman, 2016; Hetzel, 2022.
172 Höpken, 2015b, pp. 125–126.
173 Rothenhöfer, 2005a, p. 145.

became one of the most important in the north-western provinces and many of its mass produced products were exported along the main transport routes to regions as far as Germania Superior, Gallia Belgica, and Britannia.[174]

After the second century AD, the pottery industry in Cologne declined considerably. Only two pottery kilns (from two workshops) are known from the third century AD and only one has been dated to the fourth century AD. Still, more workshops must have been in existence to at least account for the basic needs of the city's inhabitants. The lack of evidence thus appears to be partly the result of the current archaeological record, although it certainly indicates that the importance of the pottery industry of Cologne had been significantly reduced. The exact reason for this decline is not entirely clear, but it seems that increased competition from other production centres played an important role in this. Findings of ceramic imports that originate from Germania Superior indicate that part of the market for ceramics was taken over by producers from this region.[175] Furthermore, it is possible that the potters moved into the hinterland to places such as Aachen and Soller (see below), since the proximity of raw materials may have brought cost benefits there.[176]

Evidence of pottery production has also been found in many settlements in Cologne's hinterland. An early example of such production comes from Erftstadt, where a potter's district produced coarse wares and Gallo-Belgic wares from the second third of the first century AD until the beginning of the second century AD.[177] Most of the production centres, however, commenced in the second half of the first century AD, primarily after the Batavian revolt of AD 69/70. Important centres that started their production in this period are Jülich and Heerlen, which were both located at important junctions of the *Via Belgica*. In Heerlen, an impressive number of 45 pottery kilns have been discovered. This is the second highest of all civilian sites in the research area.[178] These kilns were not all in use contemporaneously but produced more or less continuously from AD 70 until the end of the third century AD.[179] In Jülich, 16 kilns have been found, which in comparison to many of the other sites is also high. Production in Jülich ended earlier than in Heerlen, somewhere around AD 140, after which the production centre in Soller seems to have

174 Höpken, 2005, pp. 52–53; Rothenhöfer, 2005a, p. 146.
175 Eck, 2004, pp. 447–448.
176 Höpken, 2015b, p. 126.
177 Rothenhöfer, 2005a, pp. 127–128.
178 Only Cologne has more (93 kilns).
179 Continuity between AD 230 and the later production is not entirely certain. Van Kerckhove and Boreel, 2014, pp. 269–275.

taken over its market.[180] Production in Heerlen and Jülich consisted primarily of coarsewares and mortaria, although the production range in Heerlen was more varied and also included Gallo-Belgic ware, (black) slipped ware, and dolia.[181] With regard to the style of their pottery, both sites closely resembled each other as well as the typical 'Rhineland' style that was also used by the potters in Cologne.[182] This indicates that there must have been some sort of interaction and knowledge transfer between these potters. The scale of production clearly went beyond local demand, and the potters appear to have operated on a more regional scale.[183] Neutron activation analyses of ceramic findings, for instance, have shown that pottery from Jülich was distributed in a radius of at least 80 kilometres.[184]

Another important site in the region was the large secondary agglomeration of Bonn (80 hectares), which was located only a few kilometres to the south-east of the legionary fortress and its *canabae*.[185] Unfortunately, our knowledge of pottery production in Bonn is more limited than that of Cologne.[186] Nevertheless, the fact that 29 pottery kilns, which have been dated between the late first and the third century AD, have been discovered here, suggests that Bonn had a significant pottery industry. These kilns seem to have produced all of the usual pottery types, such as coarsewares, Gallo-Belgic wares, slipped wares, and heavy ceramics.[187] Moreover, the findings of two utensils that were used for the production of glazed ware indicate that such a fine ware was also produced here during the second and third centuries AD.[188]

Around the turn of the first century AD, potters also began production in Aachen. Several kilns that, until the end of the third century AD, produced the standard palette of Roman table and cooking wares have been discovered in the current city centre and the neighbouring district of Burtscheid.[189] Moreover, around 3.5 kilometres to the east of the city centre, in the suburb of Schönforst, two pottery kilns, dated to the Trajanic period, have been found, of which one is believed to have produced terra sigillata.[190] This sigillata

180 Lenz, Mommsen and Perse, 2007, pp. 120–121.
181 Lenz, Mommsen and Perse, 2007; Van Kerckhove and Boreel, 2014.
182 The Heerlen pottery also incorporated certain elements of the so-called Meuseland style, which was typical of sites in the *civitas Tungrorum*. Hendriks, 2012, p. 64.
183 Hendriks, 2012, p. 64.
184 Perse, 2012, pp. 108–109.
185 Andrikopoulou-Strack, Ulbert and White, 2010.
186 Höpken, Döhner and Fiedler, 2009, p. 139.
187 Höpken, Döhner and Fiedler, 2009, p. 139.
188 Henrich, 2007, p. 89.
189 Schaub, 2013.
190 Kaszab-Olschewski, 2011.

production, however, was not very successful, and the production seems to have ceased after only a few years. According to Tünde Kaszab-Olschewski, the reason for this failed experiment should not so much be sought in a lack of regional demand for the products or the technical proficiency of the potters as in the inadequate quality of the clay.[191]

More successful production of terra sigillata took place in Sinzig. This production commenced around the middle of the second century AD, as potters who most likely came from La Madeleine and Trier set up their workshops here.[192] Although Sinzig, with its favourable location on the Rhine, had great potential to play an important role in the supra-regional terra sigillata market for a prolonged period of time, its production was only of short duration. The cause of the premature abandonment of production, though, is unclear. Poor quality clay, which led to poor quality products, has traditionally been viewed as the main cause of the cessation.[193] Still, in his study of the so-called second Sinziger group, Bernd Liesen has not found a distinction in quality between the products from Sinzig and other types of terra sigillata that were in circulation in the region at the time.[194] Whatever the precise cause may be, during its time of production Sinziger products were successfully distributed over long distances, primarily along the Rhine, from the Wetterau in the east, to the North Sea coast in the west.[195]

Other significant sites that set up their production in Cologne's hinterland during the second century AD were Mönchengladbach, Rimburg, and Soller. At Mönchengladbach, at least 10 kilns, dating from the second third of the second century AD until the middle of the third century AD, have been found.[196] These kilns only produced simple coarsewares, which perhaps indicates that they produced primarily for the local hinterland. In Rimburg, 5 kilns have been discovered, which only produced for a short period around the turn of the second to third century AD.[197] Besides coarsewares, slipped ware was also made, but to what extent these products were produced for supra-local markets is unknown. Of these three sites, Soller was the most important production centre.[198] The 12 kilns that have been found here are dated from the last quarter of the second century AD until the end of the third century AD. The fact that

191 Kaszab-Olschewski, 2011, p. 23.
192 Daszkiewicz, Liesen and Schneider, 2003, p. 29.
193 Rothenhöfer, 2005a, pp. 134–135.
194 Liesen, 2008b.
195 Rothenhöfer, 2005a, p. 132.
196 Hupka, 2011, pp. 87–92.
197 Höpken and Liesen, 2005.
198 Haupt, 1984.

this settlement was not located directly along a major waterway, an important road, or a large population centre suggests that the choice of its location was primarily the result of nearby natural resources.[199] It seems that the settlement owed its existence entirely to the activities of the potters who set up their businesses here. These potters produced an extensive range of products, including coarsewares, slipped ware, glazed ware, mortaria, and storage vessels.[200] These products were primarily distributed in the immediate vicinity of Soller, they reached, for instance, part of the villa landscape north-west of Düren and also parts of the northern Eifel.[201] Furthermore, some specialties were distributed much further and were transported via Cologne over the Rhine to reach destinations as far as Britain.

Around the turn of the second to the third century AD, the production centres in the hinterland of Cologne, appear to have taken over a part of the markets of the province's capital.[202] This most likely also had the result that the Meuse and the main long-distance roads towards Northern Gaul increased somewhat in importance regarding trade in relation to the Rhine. Still, towards the end of the third century AD, the pottery production in this region seems to have ended quite abruptly.

A significant civilian pottery industry also developed in the *civitas Tungrorum*, where the Meuse and Sambre rivers, together with the *Via Belgica* formed the main transport corridors. The earliest traces of pottery production have been found in Momalle, where 2 kilns have been found that produced Gallo-Belgic ware during the first quarter of the first century AD.[203] However, more extensive production seems to have commenced around the middle of the first century AD, when large production centres developed in Braives and Vervoz. In the former, 15 kilns from the second third of the first century AD have been discovered, while in the latter, 14 kilns from the second half of the first century AD have been found (and 1 dating to the end of the second century AD).[204] In both settlements, production appears to have been conducted by experienced potters who maintained a high standard of quality. In Braives, production primarily encompassed Gallo-Belgic ware, which could easily be made available to consumers in the region, given the settlement's

199 Rothenhöfer, 2005a, p. 35.

200 Haupt, 1984, pp. 410–411; Höpken, Döhner and Fiedler, 2009, pp. 141–144.

201 Haupt, 1984, pp. 415–417.

202 The Cologne potters may have moved from the city into the hinterland. Höpken and Liesen, 2005, pp. 62–64.

203 Brulet, 2008, pp. 430–431. However, Borgers *et al.* date the centre in Momalle in the AD 40–70 period. Borgers *et al.*, 2019.

204 Brulet, 2008, pp. 391–393; Borgers, 2015.

convenient location along the *Via Belgica*.[205] The production centre in Vervoz was located on an arterial road of the *Via Belgica* which led southward towards Arlon. The clustered workshops along this road suggest that the potters worked closely together, sharing their technological knowledge, raw materials, and perhaps even their kilns.[206] The workshops specialised in the production of Gallo-Belgic ware, dolia, and amphorae, but did also produce coarse wares. Barbara Borgers has observed that the products of Vervoz are very similar to those from Braives, Bergheim, Mourmelon-le-Petit, and some early workshops from Cologne.[207] She therefore argues that a connection must have existed between the potters from these, sometimes distant, locations and those from Vervoz. Perhaps the potters had emigrated from these settlements to Vervoz or had brought their technological knowledge from there. Borgers even suggests that workshops in different locations might have been sub-divisions of one overarching pottery business, which used its expertise to set up production centres in new market areas.

In the Flavian period, pottery production also commenced at several other sites in the region, of which those of Tienen and Tongeren were probably the most important. In the large secondary agglomeration of Tienen (*c.*60 hectares), situated at an important intersection on a northern parallel road of the *Via Belgica*, successful pottery production took place from the Flavian period to the third century AD.[208] The 7 kilns that have been discovered in the settlement seem to have produced coarseware, fineware, dolia, and amphorae. The potters of Tienen are believed to have been very proficient and to have maintained a very high-quality standard.[209]

The amount of direct evidence for pottery production in the *civitas* capital of Tongeren is quite meagre. This is perhaps somewhat remarkable because Tongeren was the largest urban settlement in the research area (*c.*150 hectares). It should, however, be realised that the amount of research undertaken into this city to date is limited and that only recently the first systematic research into the remnants of several kiln structures has taken place.[210] This research has discovered 4 kilns that date to the Flavian period and 2 kilns that date to the (end of the first and) second and third centuries AD, respectively. Together with 3 less well researched and dated kilns, this brings the

205 Brulet, 1983, p. 33; 2008, pp. 392–393.
206 Borgers, 2015, p. 70.
207 Borgers, 2015, pp. 69–70.
208 Martens, 2012, pp. 303–304.
209 Borgers, Debruyne and Martens, 2014, p. 31.
210 Geerts, Hartoch and Vilvorder, 2014, p. 89.

total number of known kilns in Tongeren to 9.[211] Despite the limited amount of information that can be gained from the kilns, it is generally assumed that the pottery industry in Tongeren continuously produced until its demise in the first quarter of the fourth century AD.[212] Nevertheless, the importance of the pottery industry for the city's economy should perhaps not be overstated, as the distribution of its products was largely confined to rural settlements within a radius of 30 kilometres.[213] The production range in Tongeren included coarse wares, Gallo-Belgic ware, and slipped ware. A clear influence from the pottery traditions of the Rhineland has been observed in the pottery.[214] Yet, from the second century AD, the potters from Tongeren, as well as those in the rest of the *civitas Tungrorum*, developed their own regional style, which made use of a smoked post-firing effect and included typical shapes, such as the *Haspengouwse* flagons and the *Tongerse* beakers.[215]

During the second century AD, some smaller sites also set up their production, but their production was probably not very significant. Except for Liberchies, where 4 kilns were found, only a single kiln is known from each of these sites. During the third century AD, the production in the region apparently began to decline. Kilns from this period are only known from three sites. During the fourth century AD, practically all known sites ceased their production. The only exception is the secondary agglomeration of Huy, where a single kiln has been discovered that produced coarse ware.[216]

In the rest of the Lower Germanic Limes region, evidence for civilian pottery production is rare. Only in the large urban settlements of Xanten and Nijmegen have considerable numbers of civilian pottery kilns been found. In both settlements, the large military presence in the area played a crucial role in the development of the local pottery industry, and the earliest production centres were clearly military in character (see section 5.2.1.1). However, from the second half of the first century AD onwards, civilian production also took place in Xanten and Nijmegen. At Xanten, a total of 11 civilian kilns have been found that together are indicative of more or less continuous pottery production from the Claudian period until at least the beginning of the third century AD. The kilns were spread out inside and outside of the city walls, and pottery production thus seems to have taken place essentially in multiple

211 Vilvorder *et al.*, 2010, p. 242; Veldman and Geerts, 2014, p. 78; De Winter, 2019.

212 Vilvorder *et al.*, 2010, p. 254.

213 Vilvorder *et al.*, 2010, pp. 243–244.

214 Vilvorder *et al.*, 2010, p. 243.

215 Van Kerckhove *et al.*, 2014, p. 174.

216 Brulet, 2008, p. 416.

small workshops.[217] As of yet, only one larger workshop, producing from the second half of the second century AD into the early third century AD, has been identified just outside of the city.[218] The extent of production in Xanten can be regarded as significant.[219] Yet it is unlikely to have come close to the size of the larger production centres in the hinterland of Cologne, and it certainly did not match the production from Cologne itself. The production spectrum included fine ceramics, such as Gallo-Belgic wares and slipped wares, as well as lamps and amphorae.[220] Still, most of the products were simple coarse wares, primarily intended for the local market.[221] Exports of Gallo-Belgic vessels, lamps, and amphorae have been recorded along the Rhine as far as Nijmegen and Hofheim.[222] However, the importance of these exports was probably not great. It is perhaps telling that many ceramics from Cologne have been found in Xanten, while no ceramics from Xanten have been found in Cologne.[223]

In Nijmegen, the situation appears to have been largely similar. Here, 17 kilns have been found that have been dated between the Flavian period and the late second century AD. The vast majority of these kilns operated during the Flavian period and the early second century AD at two locations in the southern part of the city.[224] The kilns were located within the residential area and produced large amounts of coarse wares, as well as fine table wares in the typical 'Rhineland' and 'Gallo-Belgic' traditions.[225] The potters sold their products mainly on the local market, and the fact that hardly any imported pottery was found in the city seems to indicate that they were quite successful in doing so.[226] The kilns that produced during the second half of the second century AD, primarily produced coarse ware that is very similar to the products of the military production centres from the earlier period.[227] At the end of the first half of the third century AD, at the latest, the pottery production in Nijmegen apparently came to an end.[228]

Apart from Xanten and Nijmegen, there is thus no evidence for any other significant production centre for pottery. It seems that these two centres,

217 Liesen, 2006, pp. 190–191.
218 Wirtz, 1998, pp. 302–303; Liesen, 2006, p. 191.
219 Reuter, 2008, pp. 472–473; Liesen, 2018, p. 362.
220 Boelicke, 1995; Reuter, 2008, pp. 472–473.
221 Boelicke, 1995; Liesen, 2001, p. 211.
222 Liesen, 2018, p. 362.
223 Liesen, 2008a, p. 221.
224 Hendriks, 2014.
225 van Enckevort, Haalebos and Thijssen, 2000, pp. 67–71.
226 van Enckevort, Haalebos and Thijssen, 2000, p. 70.
227 Hendriks, 2014, p. 185.
228 van Enckevort, Haalebos and Thijssen, 2000, p. 84.

together with some small-scale production sites, such as those in Cuijk, Venlo, and Halder, were sufficient to cover the regional demand for pottery products.[229] The region was, after all, much less densely settled than, for example, Cologne's hinterland. The only place where the absence of evidence for a pottery industry is perhaps unexpected is in the *civitas* capital of Voorburg. Yet it should be realised that Voorburg, with an estimated maximum size of 14 hectares, was much smaller than the other *civitas* capitals.[230] Furthermore, since the main economic activities in Voorburg were focused on the port, the city must have had little trouble with acquiring its pottery from elsewhere.[231]

5.2.1.3 Ceramic Building Material

The Romans also introduced the use of ceramics as a building material to the research area. Ceramic building material (CBM) was a cheap and versatile alternative to natural stone. The Romans used ceramic tiles, bricks, and pipes to construct walls, floors, roofs, plumbing, and several other structures. Since CBM could be produced almost everywhere in the region and was rather expensive to transport, it was often most economical to produce it close to the place where it was required, or at least close to a major waterway or road.

As was the case with pottery, the production of CBM in the research area was initiated by the Roman army. Since the military producers were accustomed to stamping their products with the mark of their unit or the place of its production, our knowledge of military production is relatively good. Military production was, of course, primarily destined for the army itself, which required vast amounts of material for the construction (and maintenance) of their fortifications and defensive structures. In addition to this, military CBM was used for non-military building projects. For the construction of the bathhouses in Aachen, for instance, military CBM was used, and the same was true for several other public and governmental buildings in Cologne, Xanten, Bonn, Voorburg, and perhaps in Nijmegen.[232] Nonetheless, apart from these buildings, the use of military CBM in non-military contexts was very limited. It thus seems that the army produced almost exclusively for its own needs and several large-scale state-directed building projects and did not produce for the civilian market.[233]

---

229 Hupperetz, 1993; Niemeijer and Thijssen, 2014, p. 278; Borgers, Wijnen-Jackson and Bink, 2017.

230 Buijtendorp, 2010, p. 97.

231 de Bruin, 2017, pp. 178–179.

232 Schmidts, 2018b, pp. 110–111.

233 Schmitz, 2004, p. 252.

Dirk Schmitz has divided the development of the military production of CBM into four phases.[234] In the first phase, which began in the early Claudian period and ended with the Batavian revolt, production has been archaeologically traced in Dormagen, Cologne, and Sinzig and is also believed to have taken place in Xanten and Neuss.[235] In this phase, military production of CBM was exclusively in the hands of specialised divisions of the stationed legions and the *classis Germanica*. They produced mostly for their own needs and only sporadically for the needs of auxiliary units, whose forts were constructed mainly of wood in this early period.[236]

This changed in the second phase, which ran from the Flavian period to the early second century AD.[237] This phase was characterised by an increased demand for CBM as many of the fortifications had been destroyed during the Batavian revolt and were now being rebuilt in stone. Legionary production still accounted for the bulk of the output and took place close to the legionary fortresses in Nijmegen, Xanten, Neuss, and Bonn. However, their production now extended beyond their own demands, and they also supplied several of the auxiliary forts with CBM. Furthermore, some of the auxiliary units, primarily those along the Dutch part of the *limes* also set up their own production centres. These centres mainly produced for the units themselves, but the *cohors XV Voluntariorum*, which was probably stationed in Woerden, also seems to have supplied neighbouring castella.[238] Interesting are also the findings of CBM on which the stamps indicate that they were produced on the right side of the Rhine. The precise location at which these *tegularia transrhenana* were made remains unknown, but it appears likely that at least two sites existed, of which one may have been located in the vicinity of Neuss.[239] Their stamps also indicate that it were temporary *vexillationes* from several legions and auxiliary units that came across the Rhine to produce their CBM.[240] All in all, it seems that the military production of CBM operated smoothly during this phase. The organisation of production was essentially decentralised; with units producing for their own demand either at locations close to, or sometimes further away from, their military bases. If the supply at a certain time or location was

234 Schmitz, 2002, pp. 339–366; 2004, pp. 233–238.
235 Schmitz, 2002, pp. 339–344; 2004, p. 239.
236 Schmitz, 2002, pp. 344–347.
237 Schmitz, 2004, p. 235.
238 Schmitz, 2002, pp. 354–355.
239 Schmidts, 2018b, p. 79.
240 Schmidts, 2018b, p. 79.

insufficient to cover the local demand, supplies could come from sites where production was higher, such as in the legionary production centres.[241]

The third phase ran from the first to the last quarter of the second century AD and has been characterised by Schmitz as a period of transition.[242] In this phase, the regional production of CBM decreased, and the only producers that were left were the legions from Xanten and Bonn and the fleet. Even though the large-scale building activities of the previous period must have satisfied the demand for new buildings (and thus for CBM) in the region to a large extent, the decreased production in this period was not entirely sufficient to cover the regional demand, as the existence of imports from Germania Superior suggests.[243] There is also an interesting inscription from Bonn, mentioning two *immunes figlinarii* (kiln workers), which dates to this period.[244] *Immunes* seem to have been soldiers that were excused from (some of) their general duties in order to work as specialists in their specific fields. Most *immunes* were probably artisans, but there were also *immunes* that worked in administrative functions.[245]

The fourth phase began in the last quarter of the second century AD and ended around the middle of the third century AD.[246] In this period, the increasing threat of Germanic hostilities necessitated the strengthening of the fortifications and in order to facilitate this, the CBM industry was radically reorganised.[247] The decentralised system of production of the previous periods now made way for a largely centralised system that supplied practically the whole *limes* zone from a single site. Apart from some less sizable production that took place in Bonn, Xanten, and Venlo, almost all the regionally produced CBM from this period came from the military production centre at De Holdeurn.[248] At this site, 5 large kilns and 1 smaller kiln that produced CBM have been discovered. The large kilns, including the fire tunnel, measured between 7 and 10 metres in length and between 3.5 and 6.5 metres in width.[249] The massive size of these structures, as well as the fact that CBM from De Holdeurn has been found at almost all of the sites along the *limes*, clearly indicates that the production centre at De Holdeurn must have

241 Schmitz, 2002, p. 358.
242 Schmitz, 2002, p. 358.
243 Schmitz, 2002, p. 359.
244 AE 1930, 0033; Schmitz, 2002, p. 351.
245 Campbell, 2017.
246 Schmitz, 2004, pp. 238–239.
247 van Enckevort, Haalebos and Thijssen, 2000, pp. 54–55.
248 Schmitz, 2002, p. 360.
249 van Diepen and Polak, 2009, p. 13.

produced on an unprecedented, almost industrial, scale within the research area.

After the middle of the third century AD, in the context of the unrest associated with the Germanic invasions, the military production of CBM came to an end.[250] In this period, the military demand must have been satisfied by a combination of the reuse of older material, imports from other provinces, and supplies from civilian producers.

Regarding civilian CBM production, we are not as well informed. This is mainly the result of the fact that civilian producers did not stamp their bricks and tiles as often as military producers.[251] Nonetheless, there can be no doubt that civilian production increased significantly in the course of the Roman period. Buildings in the urban settlements as well as the many villas that were built in the rural hinterland required vast amounts of CBM, which must have come from civilian producers since military producers did normally not supply civilian consumers.[252]

Civilian production began shortly after the middle of the first century AD but became especially important during the second century AD.[253] There are a few examples of civilian production centres that, because of a beneficial location along a waterway, were able to obtain a market position of regional, and perhaps even supra-regional, importance.[254] The majority of civilian producers, however, were small-scale enterprises that only produced for a local market. These producers may have followed the demand for their goods, establishing their businesses in areas where demand was high and then moving to other locations once the demand was met.[255] The aggregate output of this decentralised system of production must have been sufficient to account for the regional civilian demand for CBM. Civilian production declined considerably around the end of the third century AD onwards, even though its decline was probably not as dramatic as that of the military production.[256]

250 Schmitz, 2002, p. 366.
251 Schmidts, 2018a, pp. 150–151.
252 Exceptions are the large-scale projects mentioned above. Furthermore, there are indications of the use of military CBM in civilian settlements in the hinterland of Nijmegen. Rothenhöfer, 2005a, p. 155.
253 Rothenhöfer, 2005a, p. 159; Clerbaut, 2015, p. 87.
254 Schmitz, 2004, p. 288.
255 Rothenhöfer, 2005a, p. 158.
256 Schmitz, 2002, p. 366.

5.2.2 *Glass*

During the period of Roman occupation, the research area also witnessed the development of Roman style glass manufacturing. Glass was not entirely new in the region. The large amounts of glass La Tène bracelets that have been found throughout the region show that the Late Iron Age population had already been using the material as jewellery on a large scale.[257] Although direct evidence of production centres is lacking, the high density of finds of these arm rings in the Dutch River Area, of which several specific types have been found exclusively there, strongly suggests that local production must have taken place here.[258] This local production was probably limited to the processing of raw glass into the final goods and thus did not encompass the production of the raw material itself. Still, this does not make the local production any less remarkable, since it implies long-distance imports from the Eastern Mediterranean, where raw glass was being produced in this period.[259] The use of the bracelets seems to have ended during the Augustan period or earlier, which indicates that there was no continuation in glass production from the Late Iron Age to the Roman period.[260] Instead, the glass industry that was introduced to the research area during the first century AD, was typically Roman in its kind. In addition to using glass to make jewellery, the Romans made a wide range of other items from the material, such as tableware, storage vessels, urns, mosaics, and even window glass.[261] In order to produce such a broad range of glass objects, the Romans also made use of new techniques, such as glassblowing, which is believed to have made the production process much more efficient.[262]

It is unclear to what extent raw glass was produced in the region during the Roman period, or whether the region remained largely dependent on imports of raw glass from the Eastern Mediterranean. The only direct evidence for primary glass production comes from Hambach, where a kiln, dated to the second half of the fourth century AD, seems to have produced raw glass.[263] The main ingredient for the production of raw glass was high-quality silica sand, which together with natron as a flux and with hardening lime as another addition, was produced in a wood-fired oven at approximately 1,300 °C. Chemical analyses suggest that the silica sand used for the glass production in Hambach

257 Roymans *et al.*, 2014, pp. 215–218.
258 Roymans and Verniers, 2010, pp. 205–207.
259 Roymans *et al.*, 2014, pp. 223–225.
260 Roymans and Verniers, 2010, pp. 204–205.
261 Trier and Naumann-Steckner, 2016, pp. 41–52.
262 Still, Prior warns that the impact of glassblowing has often been overstated. Prior, 2015.
263 Gaitzsch *et al.*, 2000, pp. 153–154.

came from the Ruraue, a location which lies circa 15 kilometres to the south.[264] In addition to this source, there were also other ample quantities of suitable sand present in areas just to the west of Cologne, so that the availability of this raw material cannot have been a limitation for the production of raw glass in Cologne's hinterland.[265] However, natron was not locally available and probably had to come from Egypt.[266] Local production could therefore not be entirely independent of distant trade, but importing only natron was at least less costly than importing the raw glass as a whole. Considering the large-scale of glass production in the Roman period, it seems at least likely that a large part of the required raw glass was locally produced since transportation costs would otherwise have raised the price of the products too significantly.[267]

The current level of research regarding the secondary production of glass is better. Still, in comparison to ceramic production, our knowledge of glass production remains much more limited. This is mainly the result of two factors. First, the kilns used for glass production were generally smaller than ceramic kilns and have left few archaeological traces.[268] Secondly, the production process has left very little production waste since almost all the material could be reused.[269] Nevertheless, we know of at least 12 different settlements in the research area where glass production took place during the Roman period (Figure 17).[270]

In the earliest phase of the Roman occupation, the demand for glass objects in the region was accounted for by long-distance imports from Northern Italy.[271] These imports encompassed tableware and (filled) unguentaria that, partly due to their fragility and long transport routes, can be considered expensive luxury items. In order to bypass the high transport costs of such imports and to account for the rising regional demand, glass producers began to set up production centres in the research area during the first century AD. The earliest traces of this industry have been found in Cologne, where glass workshops with multiple kilns have been discovered that date to the second quarter of the first century AD. These workshops produced a variety of blue-green vessels for everyday purposes, such as tableware, storage containers, unguentaria, and

264 Gaitzsch *et al.*, 2000, pp. 153–154.

265 Even though traces of the Roman exploitation of these sources are still lacking. Noelke, 2001.

266 Trier and Naumann-Steckner, 2016, pp. 79–80.

267 Eck, 2004, p. 455.

268 van den Dries, 2007, p. 29.

269 The large pits with more than 2,000 shards of glass found in the *canabae* of Nijmegen are a good example of this type of recycling. Polak, 2005.

270 Grünewald and Hartmann, 2014.

271 Höpken and Schäfer, 2006, p. 53.

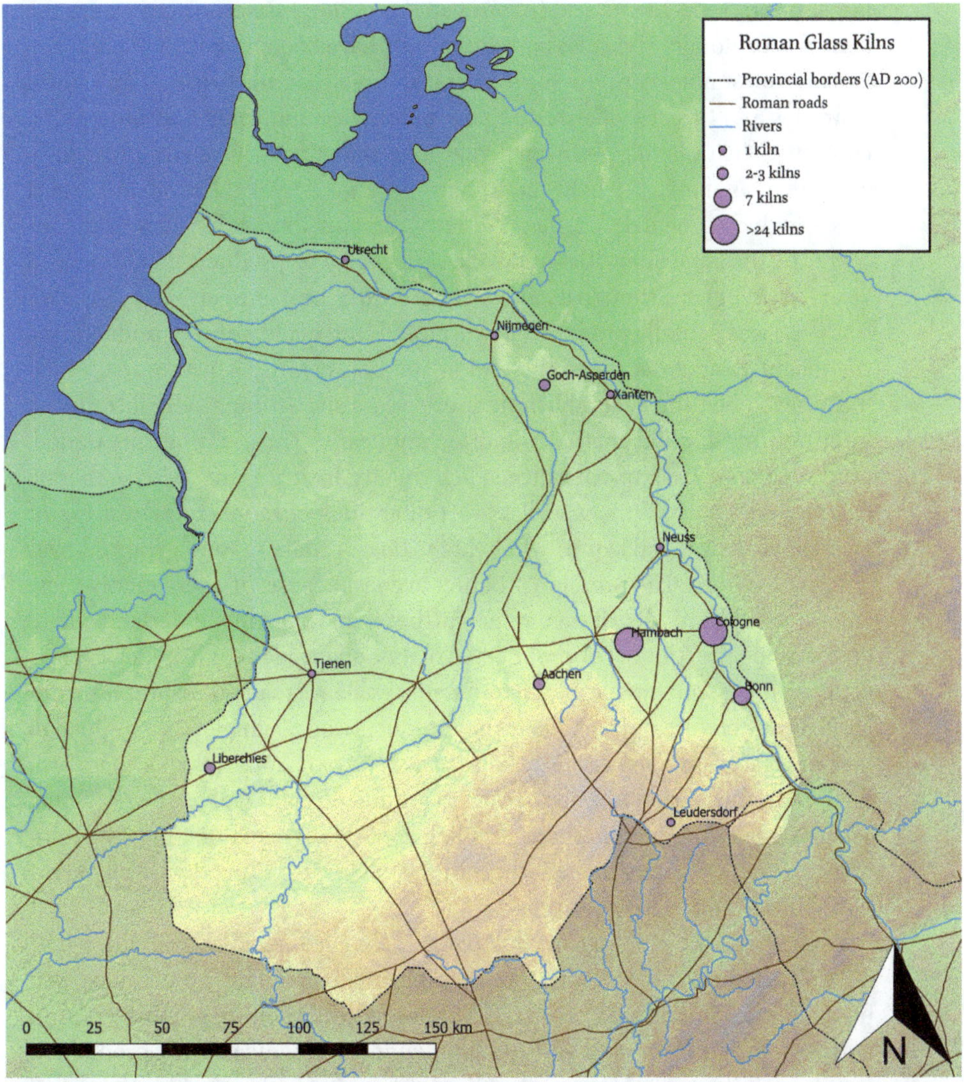

FIGURE 17 Sites where Roman period glass production has been documented

urns.[272] Further evidence for glass production in the first century AD comes from the *canabae* and legionary fortresses of Nijmegen and Bonn, respectively, and possibly from Aachen.[273] Therefore, as far as the fragmented amount of evidence allows us to say, it appears that production only took place in the

272 Höpken and Schäfer, 2006, pp. 53–57; Trier and Naumann-Steckner, 2016, p. 80.
273 Follmann-Schulz, 1991, p. 36; Polak, 2005, p. 249.

larger urban settlements and in, or near, the military bases; places where the demand for Roman style glass products must have been highest.[274]

This does not seem to have changed much in the second and third centuries AD. Direct evidence for glass production indicates that production continued in Cologne.[275] In fact, the glass industry in Cologne must have expanded, as the city is believed to have become one of the most important glass-producing centres of the (Western) Roman Empire.[276] This is underscored by the large quantities and wide variety of glass products that have been found in Cologne, although it cannot be said with complete certainty that all of this glass was actually produced in the city.[277] The quality of the products had significantly increased from the end of the first century AD onwards, which must have been the accomplishment of specialised artisans, who introduced improved production methods and techniques.[278] Thus, during this period, the Cologne workshops produced high-quality luxury wares with elaborate decorations and colours as well as vast quantities of more simple wares, for everyday use. It is unclear to what extent these products were exported over longer distances. The simpler products were, because of their relative low value, probably not distributed much further than Cologne's hinterland and to places along the Rhine. For products of higher quality, longer distance exports could be more worthwhile, but their fragility will have made transportation difficult. It is therefore not very likely that products from Cologne were shipped to faraway places on a significantly large scale.[279] Apart from Cologne, glass production in this period also took place in Xanten, Krefeld-Gellep, Neuss, Bonn, Tienen, Liberchies, and perhaps in Jülich.[280] It thus seems that glass was primarily produced in the main military and civilian sites along the German part of the Rhine and the *Via Belgica*.

After the third century AD, this pattern changed. Even though glass production in the fourth century AD has been documented in Cologne, and possibly also in Aachen and Krefeld-Gellep, evidence of glass production in Goch-Asperden, Hambach, and possibly Leudersdorf indicates that production may have shifted more towards smaller settlements in the rural hinterland.[281] According to Martin Grünewald and Sonngard Hartmann, it was probably the

274 Grünewald and Hartmann, 2014, p. 45.
275 Höpken and Schäfer, 2006, pp. 57–60; Trier and Naumann-Steckner, 2016, pp. 83–87.
276 Carroll, 2001, p. 89; van den Dries, 2007, p. 15.
277 Eck, 2004, pp. 455–457; Trier and Naumann-Steckner, 2016, pp. 91–104.
278 Rothenhöfer, 2005a, pp. 173–174.
279 Eck, 2004, p. 458.
280 Grünewald and Hartmann, 2014, pp. 45–46.
281 Grünewald and Hartmann, 2014, pp. 46–47.

increasing availability of wood, brought about by deteriorating climatic conditions for agriculture, which made such settlements convenient locations for glass production.[282]

At least 37 glass kilns have been excavated in Hambach, which is the most for a single site in the research area, including Cologne.[283] The kilns in Hambach were part of seven different workshops, which seem to have worked closely together.[284] Brüggler assumes that the glass manufacturers sought out different places within the area, produced glass there until the raw materials, mainly wood, were exhausted, and then moved on.[285] However, the remarkably high number of kilns that have been found should be put into perspective because the extensive level of archaeological excavation in the lignite mining area, in which Hambach is located, is exceptional. Nevertheless, there can be no doubt that Hambach was a production centre of considerable importance during the fourth and a large part of the fifth century AD.[286] It is difficult to determine how widely the products from Hambach were distributed, especially because glass recycling makes it difficult to attribute specific products to production centres. Still, the distribution of a specific type of inscribed jug, which is believed to have been produced in Hambach, suggests that the products from Hambach were exported throughout Cologne's hinterland and along the Rhine as far as Krefeld-Gellep and Wolfsheim (near Mainz).[287]

The rise of production in smaller settlements, such as Hambach, may also have had an impact on the significance of the central places where glass production had previously flourished. Although direct evidence of glass production in Cologne during the fourth century AD has been documented, there are indications that the city had lost some of its former importance as a major glass producing centre.[288] Glass objects dating to this century that have been found in Cologne, for example, suggest that the proportion of imports from Italy and from other provinces had increased again.[289] Furthermore, it is clear that glass from Hambach increasingly covered the demand for simple glass vessels in Cologne, but it remains unclear whether it was just the raw glass that

282 Grünewald and Hartmann, 2014, pp. 46–47.
283 Brüggler, 2006, p. 69.
284 Brüggler, 2006, p. 70.
285 Brüggler, 2006, p. 70.
286 Brüggler, 2010, p. 94.
287 Gaitzsch *et al.*, 2000, pp. 119–130.
288 Trier and Naumann-Steckner, 2016, pp. 83–87.
289 Höpken and Schäfer, 2006.

came from Hambach, to be processed further in Cologne itself, or whether the vessels themselves were already produced in Hambach.[290]

Unfortunately, there are not many large-scale quantitative studies that allow us to observe changes in aggregate glass production over time. We can be confident that the total output in Roman times was larger than it had been in the Late Iron Age and that production in the Roman period peaked somewhere during the second or third centuries AD. Yet on the basis of current knowledge, it is hard to specify the main developments of the glass industry with much precision. Dated glass kilns, for instance, may serve as a reliable proxy for glass production, but the number of documented kilns is still too low to be of much significance.

As far as I know, there is only one quantitative study that allows some insights into the dynamics of the glass industry during the Roman period. That study investigated the relative proportions of different categories of glass finds from a variety of settlements and graves in the north-western part of the Roman Empire.[291] Since many of the settlements that are considered in that research are located within Germania Inferior and neighbouring provinces, it can be reasonably assumed that the conclusions of the study are representative for the current research area.[292] The study shows that in the early first century AD, most of the glass findings can be categorised as tableware, which indicates that, in this period, glass products were essentially luxury products.[293] Then, from the late first century AD onwards, a shift towards an increasing proportion of storage vessels seems to have been underway, so that by the middle of the second century AD, about a third of the glass finds belonged to this category. The authors explain that this development may reflect changes in the total output of glass production since glass had apparently become so common that even non-tableware products were now being produced from this material.[294] However, from the late third century AD onwards, the trend seems to have been reversed. In the fourth century AD, the proportion of storage vessels is significantly reduced and luxurious tableware, again, makes up the majority of the glass finds.

290 Höpken and Schäfer, 2006, p. 60.
291 van Lith and Randsborg, 1985.
292 van Lith and Randsborg, 1985, pp. 431–436.
293 van Lith and Randsborg, 1985, pp. 463–464.
294 van Lith and Randsborg, 1985, pp. 463–464.

5.2.3 *Metal*

In section 5.1.3, I have already argued that the exploitation of metals increased substantially in the Roman period. However, before the metal could be used for practical purposes, the raw material had to be manufactured into the desired objects by specialist metalworkers.[295] The Romans used metal to produce military equipment, weapons, tools, building materials, tableware, jewellery, and many other items. From an economic standpoint, metal tools were especially important since they were used in practically all trades, whether it was glass working, leather production, metalworking itself, or agriculture. In these trades, they had the potential to significantly improve the efficiency of the production processes, and the large number and wide variety of Roman tools that have been found by archaeologists are indicative of technological development and increased specialisation in these fields.[296] It is therefore clear, that the manufacturing of metal played a key role in the Roman economy.[297]

Unfortunately, our current knowledge regarding metal manufacturing is very limited. The main reason for this is that metal, just like glass, could be recycled and has thus not left many traces in the form of defective products. Furthermore, just like the glass kilns, the furnaces used for the heating or melting of metal were small and, accordingly, their remains are not very likely to be found. Still, if furnaces, or sufficient concentrations of metal products, raw materials, crucibles, moulds, tools, or slags, are found, it can be assumed that metal manufacturing took place at a site.[298] Yet the identification of a workshop on the basis of slags, which are the most commonly found indicators of metalworking, is problematic. The different phases in the production process of metal, leave different kinds of slags that are hard to distinguish from each other.[299] This makes it, for example, difficult to distinguish between workshops where actual manufacturing took place and smithies where simple repair and maintenance work was carried out. Another problematic issue is the dating of the workshops because the indicators for production do normally not provide much, if any, precision.

295 The production process, from the mining of the ore to the manufacturing of the finished products, included multiple steps. For an overview of this process. Pleiner, 2000; Dungworth, 2016. Since it would be uneconomical to transport the ore over long distances, it can be assumed that the extraction of the metal from the ore occurred close to the source of exploitation. The semi-finished products, in the form of lumps or ingots, would then be transported to blacksmiths and metal workshops to be manufactured into finished products. Horn, 1987, p. 167.

296 Gaitzsch, 1985; Roymans, 1996, p. 65.

297 Horn, 1987, p. 167.

298 Gralfs, 1994, p. 5.

299 Pleiner, 2000, pp. 251–267.

The difficult nature of the archaeological evidence regarding metal manufacturing means that, in most cases, it is not possible to say much more than that production took place at a certain location during a certain (broad) period. This is especially the case with the research on the Late Iron Age, about which there are, as far as I am aware, no synthesizing studies that discuss the organisation of the industry in the research area.[300] Nevertheless, the widespread use of metal objects during this period leaves no doubt that metal manufacturing must already have played an important economic role. Fortunately, research regarding the Roman period is more developed and allows us to gain at least a general insight into how metal manufacturing was organised in the region.

The Roman army seems to have taken care of its own demand for weapons and other military equipment. This production was decentralised and took place in workshops in or near the military bases where the soldiers were stationed.[301] Direct evidence of metal manufacturing has been found in Remagen, Bonn, Alteburg, Neuss, Krefeld-Gellep, Nijmegen, Zwammerdam, and Valkenburg (Figure 18). Moreover, because this production has left relatively few archaeological traces, we can probably conclude that in the proximity of almost all of the fortresses and forts, some degree of military metal production took place. Since weapons and military equipment were of great importance to the army, we can also assume that the quality of the products was high and that production was organised very efficiently.[302] In addition to weapons and military equipment, the military metalworkers also produced other metal objects, but it is also conceivable that the army could rely more on the civilian market for these less essential goods. With the beginning of the Germanic incursions during the latter part of the third century AD, it became increasingly unsafe to rely solely on the decentralised production directly along the *limes*.[303] Therefore, multiple centrally organised weapon and equipment production centres seem to have taken over, at least part of, the military supply. There is no evidence for these large-scale factories from the research area itself. They were probably located somewhat further away from the border. For instance, the *Notitia dignitatum* mentions a weapon factory in Strasbourg and factories for shields and artillery in Trier.[304]

Civilian metal production appears to have taken place primarily in the urban settlements.[305] Indications for some degree of metal manufacturing have been

300 Studies with a larger geographical coverage do discuss the manufacturing of metal during the Late Iron Age. E.g. Pleiner, 2006, pp. 151–160.

301 Hanel, 2006, pp. 20–26.

302 van Daele, 1999, pp. 130–133.

303 van Daele, 1999, p. 134.

304 Not. dign. occ. 9.

305 Rothenhöfer, 2005a, p. 124.

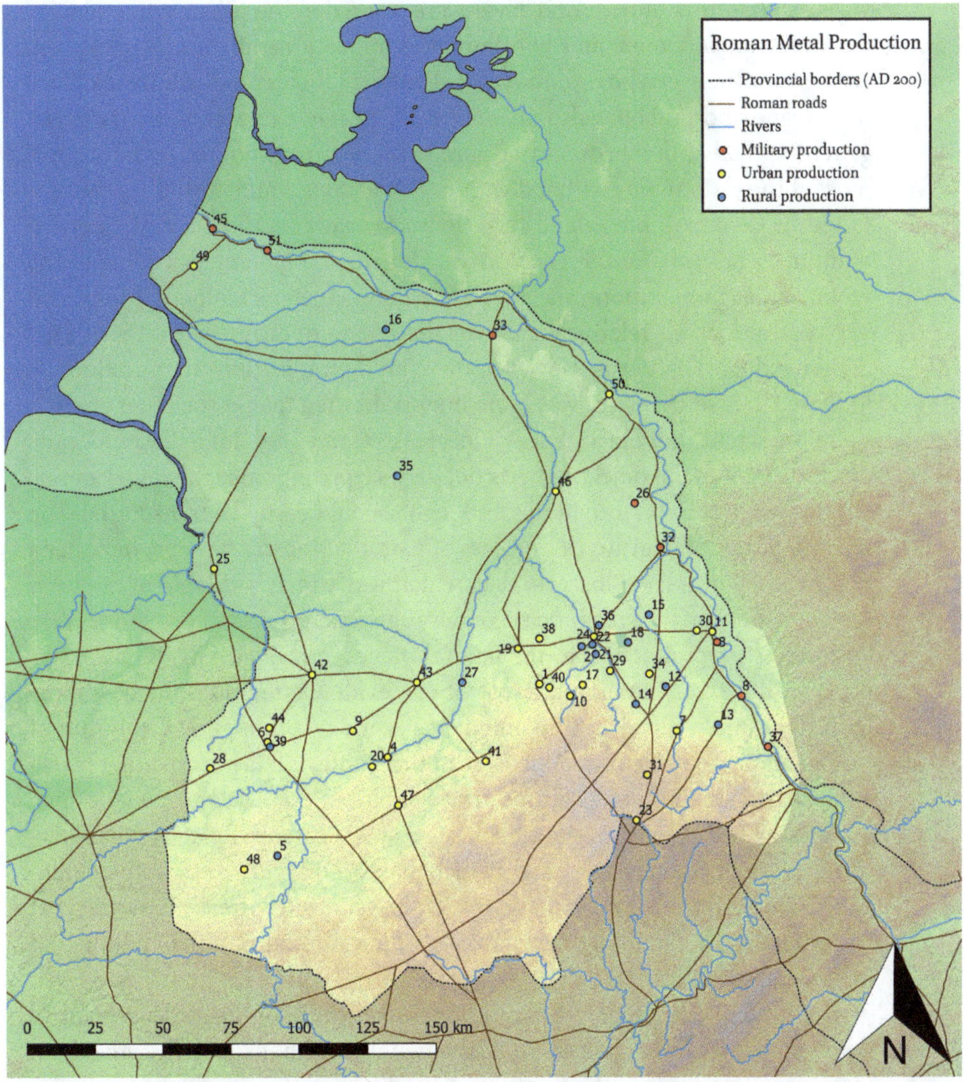

FIGURE 18 Sites where Roman period metal production has been documented
Note: Data in appendix 3.

discovered in all of the *coloniae* and *municipia* and in a large part of the secondary agglomerations. The scale of production and the degree of differentiation were undoubtedly largest in the major centres. For example, in Xanten, evidence has been found for the manufacturing of iron, bronze, lead, tin, and silver.[306] Similarly, evidence from Nijmegen, including multiple small furnaces,

306 Rehren and Hauptman, 1995; Zieling, 1995; Reuter, 2008, pp. 474–475.

suggests that iron, bronze, and silver were worked in the urban settlement.[307] For Cologne, Tongeren, and Voorburg, the indications for metalworking are scarcer, but there can be no doubt that significant metal production took place in Cologne and probably also in Tongeren.[308] Largely in accordance with the general spread of the secondary agglomerations throughout the research area, most of the settlements with indications for metal manufacturing are concentrated in Cologne's hinterland (e.g. Bonn, Mariaweiler, Jülich, and Heerlen) and the *civitas Tungrorum* (e.g. Braives, Tienen, and Liberchies). Some of the secondary agglomerations, such as Nettersheim, Aachen, Stolberg, Theux, and Vervoz, are located relatively close to the ore sources in the northern Eifel region and the High Fens. However, there are no indications that production in these latter settlements, was more important than that in the other areas. It therefore seems that the absence of local ore reserves did not really hinder the production of metal objects. This is not very surprising since the raw material, after it was processed into lumps and ingots, could easily be transported. The most important factor for the success of a production centre must have been the presence of a large local market, which was widely available in the loess region, with its many villas and secondary agglomerations.

Besides the production in the central places, metalworking did also take place in the rural hinterland. Most of the evidence for rural metalworking indicates simple repair and maintenance work and thus provides no proof for the manufacturing of products.[309] In this context, it is possible that blacksmiths with small mobile smithies travelled around an area to provide such services.[310] The number of sites that have yielded evidence for actual manufacturing is, unfortunately, very small, which makes it difficult to assess the significance of rural production. Still, the small number of sites already indicates that rural metal manufacturing must have been far less important than production in the central places.

The limited amount of research undertaken to date makes it difficult to say much about the organisation of the metal workshops. In her study about metal manufacturing in the north-western provinces, Bettine Gralfs concludes that most metal workshops were small to medium-sized and primarily seem to have covered local demands.[311] In the absence of convincing evidence for the existence of workshops that produced and exported on a larger scale in the

307 Polak, 2005, pp. 248–249.

308 Rothenhöfer, 2005a, pp. 119–121; van der Feijst, Langelaar and Kemmers, 2014, p. 266; Stolk, 2014, p. 701.

309 Polfer, 2000, p. 77.

310 van der Feijst, 2011, p. 152; de Bruin, 2017, p. 270.

311 Gralfs, 1994, pp. 73–78.

research area, it is probably best to concur with this general conclusion. It thus appears that metal manufacturing was largely decentralised and took place in small to medium-sized workshops that were spread throughout the region in places where demand for their products was highest.

Furthermore, the imprecise dating of most of the workshops does not allow too many conclusions about the general development of the metal manufacturing industry over time. What is clear, is that production reached its peak during the first three centuries AD, which, considering the general population dynamics in the research area, is hardly surprising.[312] It is, however, interesting to note that a relatively large part of the workshops that are dated into the Late Antique period were located at villas and other rural settlements, while the production in practically all the military and civilian central places had ceased after the third century AD.[313] In analogy to the developments in the ceramics and glass industries, this seems to indicate that metal production also moved to the rural hinterland during the Late Antique period.

5.2.4 *Conclusions*

The discussion in this chapter has made clear that the scale of the manufacturing sector during the Roman period was of a completely different order to that of the Late Iron Age. In the Late Iron Age, the manufacturing sector had been very small since most craft working took place on the 'household production' level. Accordingly, the degree of specialisation and economic complexity in the production of goods during this period was limited. This changed dramatically in the course of the Roman period, as a large-scale and specialised system of manufacturing developed in the main military and civilian settlements of the Lower Germanic Limes region.

The initiation of this development came from the large demand for various manufactured goods by the Roman army. Initially, the army imported these goods, but military manufacturers soon set up their own production centres in, or close to, their bases. Like with the exploitation of raw materials, we can assume that this military production was organised very efficiently and was technologically advanced. Still, for most goods, military production must have been only a temporary necessity, as civilian producers were soon able to meet the army's demand for manufactured goods. The demand for pottery, for example, already appears to have been taken over, to a large extent, by civilian producers during the second half of the first century AD. For some goods, though, this was not the case. For its needs for ceramic building materials, for

312 See Appendix 3.

313 Cf. Polfer, 2000, p. 77.

instance, the army remained completely dependent on its own production up until the Germanic invasions. It also seems very unlikely that the army left the production of other essential goods, such as weapons and military equipment, in the hands of civilians, but the fragmentary nature of research to date makes it impossible to confirm this.

Without discounting the importance of the military producers, civilian production was the main cause for the significant increase in scale of the manufacturing sector during the Roman period. Civilian manufacturing took place in practically all the urban settlements that had spread throughout the region. As such, it seems likely that manufacturing was organised in a largely decentralised way, with most settlements accounting for their own needs and the needs of their immediate hinterlands. This indicates that for most production centres the presence of these local markets was the decisive factor for their foundation. The availability of raw materials was, in most cases, less important, probably because these resources could often be transported quite efficiently. Regarding this last point, good infrastructural connections were important and had already to a large extent determined the foundation of these centres in the first place.

The scale of production and the diversity of manufactured products in a settlement were thus largely dependent on how large the population of the settlement and its hinterland were. Accordingly, large-scale, diverse production is likely to have taken place in major settlements such as Bonn, Cologne, Xanten, Nijmegen, Tongeren, or Tienen. However, production does not seem to have extended much beyond the local scale in all these settlements. In fact, clear evidence for production centres that, on a considerable scale, supplied supra-local markets is scarce. We know that Cologne had a large-scale pottery industry of inter-regional significance during the first two centuries AD and had become one of the most important glass-producing centres of the (Western) Roman Empire during the second and third centuries AD. We also know that the potters from Jülich and Heerlen, conveniently located on the *Via Belgica*, operated on a regional scale. Furthermore, it is clear that the products from pottery workshops from Soller and Sinzig were shipped to faraway markets via the Rhine. Yet for most manufacturers in the research area, the local demand of a central settlement and its hinterland must have sufficed.

In terms of Peacock's modes of production, most manufacturing workshops in the region can probably be considered as 'individual workshops'. This means that these workshops were run by specialised artisans, who had dedicated practically all their labour to their crafts. Regarding pottery production, it is also likely that there were some producers that operated at a lower level of complexity. Since pottery was not the most difficult of activities, it is possible that some people took it up as a secondary activity in order to make some extra money. This can then be categorised as 'household industry' and it may have taken place in the rural settlements where evidence of pottery production has been documented. Nonetheless, the contribution of these less specialised producers to the total output of production will not have been particularly large. It is not very likely that many people will have produced glass or metal as a secondary activity, since glass and metal production was a much more complex process.

There are also some cases where workshops seem to have operated at the level of the 'nucleated workshops', which is the highest level of economic complexity. Production at this level has been documented in the pottery industry, for instance, in Cologne, Soller, and Vervoz. Such a clustering of activity could have significant advantages, such as economies of scale, the spread of technological knowledge, and reduced transaction costs. In the glass industry, clustered workshops may have existed in Cologne and in Hambach. For the metal industry, no indications of considerable concentrations of workshops have been found yet.

Overall, the manufacturing sector experienced substantial economic growth during the Roman period. This growth started in the first century AD and continued until the third century AD, after which a sharp decline set in. The total demand for manufactured goods had increased significantly as a result of the emergence of a large non-agricultural population in the region. We can therefore be confident that the economic growth was partly the result of an increase in labour input. However, at the same time, the sector had become increasingly complex, which meant manufacturing had become much more efficient.

CHAPTER 6

Trade

With the most important aspects of the production side of the economy now having been discussed, it is time to focus our attention on the role of trade for the economy of the Lower Germanic Limes region. Trade is an important part of economic life since it provides a crucial link between producers and consumers.[1] Without trade, no specialisation of production can take place and, accordingly, no benefits will be gained from economies of scale. Therefore, the possibilities for per capita economic growth remain very limited. Yet when a smooth functioning trade network does exist, a far-reaching division of labour can take place, with all its positive effects on the economy.

When talking about trade, it is important to realise that free market trade is not the only possible exchange mechanism. As Polanyi has made clear, produce can also be distributed through non-market modes of exchange.[2] Therefore, it can be helpful to conceptually break down the distribution of goods into different categories. David Mattingly has argued that the Roman economy can be divided into three distinct spheres: an imperial economy, extra-provincial economies, and provincial economies.[3] The imperial economy and the extra-provincial economies operated on the largest geographical scale, as they concerned the dealings on the level of the whole empire (and beyond). The difference between these two spheres is that the imperial economy encompassed all the economic mechanisms that were directly related to the Roman state, such as taxation, costs of government, imperial exploitation, and redistribution by the state. On the other hand, extra-provincial economies operated through the workings of the free market, with production, trade, and consumption being regulated by the general rules of supply and demand. Provincial economies, then, consisted of all economic activities that took place within the provincial borders and thus ranged from the regional to the local level. Like the extra-provincial economies, the provincial economies were largely regulated by the workings of the free market, but these economies also integrated certain aspects of socially embedded economic practices.

---

1 Hopkins, 1983, p. x.

2 Polanyi, 1957. Nevertheless, throughout this work, I often use the term 'trade' for exchange in the broader sense. This does not mean that I automatically assume that all this trade was guided by the free market. In order to avoid confusion, I will make it explicitly clear when I am talking about free market trade or redistribution by the state.

3 Mattingly, 2011, pp. 138–140.

© ERIK TIMMERMAN, 2024 | DOI:10.1163/9789004682214_007

As a conceptual tool, the model is useful as it makes the complicated Roman economy more comprehensible. The model is particularly useful regarding the role of trade because the economic spheres allow different types of economic exchange to be meaningfully assigned to an understandable category. As such, following Mattingly's model, we get three different levels of exchange that may have been of importance for the research area: long-distance redistribution by the state (imperial economy), long-distance free market trade (extra-provincial economies), and shorter distance free market trade (provincial economy). The distinction between redistribution by the state and free market trade is especially relevant for questions about economic growth, because only free market trade can lead *directly* to an increased division of labour. Redistribution by the state, on the other hand, may only lead to increased division of labour *indirectly* by stimulating free market trade.[4] It is therefore important to know whether goods were mainly redistributed by the state or whether they were mostly traded in the free market, as this can both determine and explain the Roman economy's degree of economic development.[5]

At the same time, it needs to be pointed out that such a theoretical model is a simplification and that in reality, the different spheres of the economy, to a certain extent, overlapped and mutually influenced each other.[6] This also means that we should not understand the distinction between redistribution by the state and trade through the free market as being clear-cut. Instead, it seems much better to view both modes of exchange as being 'interlocked' and at times working in concert with each other.[7] For example, it is well conceivable that Roman state officials used tax money to place large orders with private merchants for the supply of the army, while both parties together arranged the means of transportation. Indeed, in such a scenario, both parties would had an interest in the successful delivery of goods. Using too rigid a binary distinction between redistribution by state and free market trade, though important from a theoretical standpoint, might thus obscure the realities of Roman trade.

4 The difference lies in the fact that, in the case of free market trade, a producer receives something in return for his product, which enables him to specialise. In the case of redistribution by the state, the product is claimed by the state, for example, in the form of taxation, without giving the producer anything in return, so that he cannot specialise his production. However, this does not mean that redistribution by the state cannot contribute at all to an increase in the division of labour. Indirectly, redistribution by the state can indeed have a major impact.

5 Morley, 2007a, p. 580.

6 Morley, 2007b, p. 11.

7 Tchernia, 2016, p. 114.

In addition to the subdivision based on different economic spheres, trade can also be categorised according to the different product categories or specific products that were being exchanged. Trade can, for instance, be subdivided between the trade in food, metals, clothing, or ceramics, but also between the trade in grain, fibulae, shoes, or terra sigillata. There is a large variability in the extent to which evidence of different types of trade has survived. This has primarily to do with differences in the preservation of the traded goods (or their containers). The remains of traded products that consisted of non-organic materials are more likely to have survived in the archaeological record than those that consisted of organic materials. In particular, ceramics and stone are good indicators of trade, but some sort of determination is required to know their provenance.[8] Metal and glass are also relatively durable, but the problem with these materials is that they were recyclable and that the determination of their provenance is often very complicated. Organic materials are only preserved in exceptional conditions, for example in a waterlogged context, as is the case with the grain ship from Woerden.[9] However, since organic products were often transported in ceramic containers (amphorae), of which specific types are known to have carried specific products, the trade in some of these products can be reconstructed to a certain extent. Products that were transported in sacks or barrels are, of course, less archaeologically visible. In addition to the evidence about trade from the archaeological remains of the products and their containers themselves, epigraphical, pictorial, and literary sources also convey information about Roman trade. However, although these sources can provide important insights about the organisation of trade, the material is often very fragmentary.

Furthermore, our knowledge of Roman trade networks is significantly biased towards long-distance trade.[10] The reason for this, is that the provenance of products that were produced in a faraway, geographically distinct area, is much more likely to be traced than that of products that are produced much closer to the area in which they are found. For instance, a Dressel 20 amphora that is found in the research area is a clear indication of the importation of olive oil from the province of Baetica. On the other hand, the place of production of a ceramic vessel in the Gallo-Belgic style, which could have been produced in many different parts of the region, is much more difficult to determine. Yet this bias should not lead us to underestimate the importance

8 E.g. recognition of forms or stylistic elements, or geological analysis.
9 Pals and Hakbijl, 1992.
10 Wilson, 2009a, p. 215.

of regional or local trade compared to long-distance trade.[11] In fact, it seems likely that short-distance trade, in terms of the total number of transactions and total volume of traded goods, was much more important than the much better documented trade over longer distances.[12]

It is the aim of this chapter, to find out to what extent the trading sector contributed to the economic growth of the Lower Germanic Limes region and how we should characterise this growth. It needs to be stressed that several important aspects of trade have already been discussed in previous chapters. In chapter 3, the large demand of the military and civilian populations, as well as the Roman system of taxation, have been identified as the most important drivers of an increase in trade in the research area. Moreover, this chapter explains how the Roman institutional framework and the expansion of the infrastructure network in the region must have facilitated the exchange of goods. In chapters 4 and 5, the distribution of the goods that were produced in the region was discussed. Accordingly, much has already been said about internal trade within the province and about the export of regionally produced products to other parts of the empire. What has not received much consideration are the long-distance imports of products to the research area, as well as the general organisation of trade. These topics will therefore be the main foci of the current chapter.

6.1 Amphorae

One of the most important sources of evidence regarding long-distance imports are amphorae. Amphorae are large ceramic containers used for the transportation and storage of a wide range of products and have been found in practically all parts of the Roman Empire and beyond.[13] They were most commonly used for the packaging of olive oil, wine, and fish sauces, but it is known that many other food products, such as beer, juices, vinegar, (pickled) olives, fruits, nuts, and seafood, were also contained in amphorae.[14] Furthermore, amphorae were sometimes used for the transportation of wares that were used by craftsmen, such as colour pigments, alum, pitch, and iron nails. The remains

11 Drexhage, Konen and Ruffing, 2002b, pp. 120–126.

12 Furthermore, long-distance trade is biased towards the typical Mediterranean products, such as amphorae and terra sigillata. Therefore, the trade with the Mediterranean region is much better known than the trade with other regions, such as Britannia or Germania Magna, from where less well documented products came (see below).

13 Peacock and Williams, 1986; Martin-Kilcher, 2006.

14 Höpken, 2018, pp. 374–375.

of amphorae that are found by archaeologists can convey a lot of important information about the flow of goods between, sometimes, very distant, areas. Specialists can analyse the clay from which the amphorae are made, the typological characteristics of the vessels, stamps, *tituli picti*, or graffiti that were inscribed on the amphorae, and, in rare cases, even the remains of the products that were contained. The potential of the amphora material for answering questions about trade is therefore very high, even though it should always be realised that amphorae are only one type of container in which the products were carried. Accordingly, many of the conclusions about trade that can be reached based on amphorae material alone, especially those of a quantitative nature, should be taken cautiously since a significant part of this trade may be archaeologically invisible, as it was carried in barrels or other containers.[15]

Research to date for the Lower Germanic Limes region lags somewhat behind that of nearby regions. For these regions, important studies based on large quantified assemblages of amphora remains, such as those of north-eastern Gaul, Augst and Kaiseraugst, and Mainz and its hinterland, have considerably advanced our knowledge of long distance trade in the north-western provinces.[16] Studies of comparable scope and significance are lacking for the research area, and although more studies based on quantified assemblages from different sites have appeared in the last two decades, a detailed and well-founded overarching synthesis of amphorae finds in the region is still a desideratum.[17] Nevertheless, based on the publications that currently exist, the main outlines of the amphora trade in the region can already be drawn and give us an impression of how this trade developed over time.

As we have already seen, the initial stimulus for the development of the (large-scale) amphora trade came from the large demand of the Roman army.[18] On the one hand, this demand for (mostly food) products from remote areas can be explained by the general inability of local producers to produce sufficient agricultural surpluses to feed the large number of soldiers stationed in the region. On the other hand, the products contained in the amphorae were products that could not be produced at all, or at least not in comparable

---

15 The use of barrels in the research area is known from pictorial evidence and from archaeological remains. Ellmers, 1978; Marlière, 2001.

16 Martin-Kilcher, 1987; 1994; Ehmig, 2003; 2007a; Laubenheimer and Marlière, 2010.

17 A first attempt for the German Lower Rhine region has been made by Heimberg. Heimberg, 1997. For criticism of this attempt, see Ehmig, 2003, pp. 42–44. Franconi also discusses material from the Lower Rhine but focuses more on the data from nearby regions. Franconi, 2014, 194–214.

18 Before the Roman period, amphorae had already found their way to the research area. Fitzpatrick, 1985.

quality, in the research area. For climatic reasons, olives and grapes do not grow in the area, and while local fish sauces may have been produced in the region during the second half of the second century AD (see below), this does not seem to have been the case during the initial phases of the Roman conquest. The imports that came in the amphorae were thus, apart from an absolute nutritional necessity, also the result of the soldiers' taste for typical Roman foodstuffs. Furthermore, in the course of the Roman period, these tastes increasingly spread to the non-military segments of the population.

There has been much debate about the extent to which the amphora trade was directed by the state or guided by the free market. Pointing to the very large number of southern Spanish oil amphorae on sites in the western part of the Empire, José Remesal Rodríguez and his followers claim that the state must have played a crucial role in the supply of the troops along the *limes*.[19] They believe that the supply of the army was considered too important to be left to the vagaries of the market, as the transport and communication infrastructure of the Roman world were inadequate. Therefore, only control, or at least close supervision, by the Roman state could guarantee that steady amounts of goods would reach the soldiers. This does not, however, mean that they deny the existence of free market trade all together. On the contrary, they argue that the state-directed distribution of oil paved the way for the development of private trade and that some traders may even have used the unused transport capacity of the military supply system.[20]

Even though the interpretation of the role of the state in the amphora trade outlined here has had a great influence on the debate about the Roman economy, it has also received much criticism. This is not the place to go into too much detail about this criticism. Nevertheless, the fact of the matter is that the methodology used by Remesal Rodríguez has been seriously questioned.[21] This has led to the conclusion that there is no convincing evidence for the large-scale involvement of the state in the oil trade. At the same time, such an absence of evidence does not automatically allow the conclusion that the state was not at all involved in the supply of the army. It is very well conceivable that the state sometimes operated in concert with private traders, for example, by sharing transport facilities, as it also had an interest in the supply of its soldiers.[22] Nevertheless, it is now generally assumed that most of the supplies

19 Jacobsen, 1995; Remesal Rodríguez, 2002a; 2002b; Funari, 2002; Carreras, 2002.

20 In this context, Jacobsen speaks of *Folge-* and *Nebenhandel*. Jacobsen, 1995.

21 Wierschowski, 2001; Ehmig, 2003, pp. 91–110; Eck, 2006.

22 Tchernia, 2016, pp. 260–261.

were moved by the free market and that the state did not play a particularly dominant role in the trade in amphorae.[23]

The most important transport route for the import of Mediterranean amphorae into the Germanic provinces, was the Rhône-Saône axis.[24] These two rivers, with Lyon at their confluence, connected the Mediterranean coast in southern Gaul with the provinces in the north. From here, the markets in the Lower Germanic Limes region could easily be supplied via the Moselle and the Rhine, or via the Meuse. The only real problem with this route was the lack of a direct waterway connection between the Saône and the Moselle. Therefore, the cargo had to be loaded off the ships in order to be transported over land to the next harbour.[25] This led to high transport costs, and it is thus not surprising that plans to dig a canal existed.[26] Some scholars also argue for the importance of an alternative route.[27] They believe that, at least for imports out of Spain, transport along the Atlantic coast was more economical. Although the absolute distance of both routes was almost the same, it is assumed that much less time was needed for the transportation over the Atlantic.[28] Nevertheless, the limited source material makes it impossible to say which route was the most efficient or important. For the time being, it is therefore best to assume that both routes were used for the Spanish imports.

The amphorae data from the military fortresses in Nijmegen and Neuss are useful to get a good impression of the imports during the earliest phase of the Roman occupation. In the legionary fortress at the Hunerberg in Nijmegen, which dates from circa 19 to 12 BC, a very significant proportion of the amphorae originated from the Iberian Peninsula (Table 5).[29] Most amphorae came from the province of Baetica, in the south, which was an important supplier of olive oil and various kinds of fish sauces for many parts of the Roman Empire and for the Rhineland in particular.[30] Furthermore, amphorae filled with wine came from Hispania Tarraconensis, on the north-eastern coast of the peninsula, where intensive, specialised, and export-oriented wine production took place from at least the last second half of the first century BC until late in the first century AD.[31] Wine also came from other parts of the empire.

23 Lo Cascio, 2007; Tchernia, 2016; Franconi, 2014, pp. 214–215.
24 Martin-Kilcher, 1994, p. 526; Campbell, 2012, pp. 270–271.
25 It is unclear where exactly the goods were loaded on and off. Therefore, it is unknown what distance had to be covered by land transport.
26 Tac. Ann. 13, 53.
27 Remesal Rodríguez, 2002a; Carreras and Morais, 2012.
28 Schäfer, 2017, p. 106.
29 van den Berg, González Cesteros and Niemeijer, 2017.
30 Remesal Rodríguez, 2002a.
31 Remesal Rodríguez and Revilla-Calvo, 1991, pp. 389–392.

TABLE 5 Amphorae from the Hunerberg (19–12 BC), MNI (n=31)[a]

	Olive oil	Wine	Fish sauce	Defr./olives	Other/ unknown	Total
Spain	10%	10%	26%	3%	6%	55%
(Southern) Gaul		6%				6%
Italy		16%				16%
East. Mediter.		23%				23%
Total	10%	55%	26%	3%	6%	

a The percentages in the tables in this section are based on the minimum number of individuals (MNI) or the total number of sherds (sherds). The percentages are rounded off. This means that the value 0% indicates that less than 0.5% of the sherds or individuals fit into a certain category. If a field is blank, this means that this category did not occur at all. The amphorae have been categorised according to amphora type, at least when this was not already done in the original publication. The category '*Defrutum*/Olives' mainly represents Haltern 70 amphorae, which sometimes may also have carried other products (see below).

At the Hunerberg, amphorae from the Italian Peninsula, the Aegean, Gallia Narbonensis, and the region around Lyon have also been found.

The findings from the fort on the Kops Plateau in Nijmegen, which succeeded the fortress on the Hunerberg and existed from around 12 BC until the Batavian Revolt, can provide insights into the supply of amphorae in a somewhat later stage of the early Roman period (Table 6).[32] Broadly speaking, the situation remained the same. Baetica was still the most important region for the importation of olive oil.[33] From the Tiberian period onwards, Baetican oil was increasingly transported in the large globular Dressel 20 amphorae, which are one of the most commonly found amphorae in the north-western provinces from the late first to the early third century AD.[34] Amphorae from other important oil producing regions, such as Italy, North Africa, and Istria, appear much less often in the research area.[35] Baetica also remained an important supplier of fish sauces, even though southern Gaul (Gallia Narbonensis, including the region around Lyon) now also accounted for a large share of the imports.[36] In general, the total import of fish sauces to the Kops Plateau already seems to display the first indications of the decline that took place in the post-Augustan

32 Carreras, 2017.
33 Carreras, 2017, p. 25.
34 Peacock and Williams, 1986, p. 136.
35 Carreras and van den Berg, 2017, p. 356.
36 Carreras, 2017, p. 16.

TABLE 6 Amphorae from the Kops Plateau (12 BC–AD 69), MNI (n=654)

	Olive oil	Wine	Fish sauce	Defr./olives	Other/ unknown	Total
Spain	30%	4%	8%	12%	0%	54%
(Southern) Gaul		10%	8%	2%	0%	20%
Italy		9%				9%
East. Mediter.		17%			0%	17%
North Africa		0%				0%
Total	30%	41%	15%	14%	0%	

period.[37] Furthermore, a rather high proportion of Haltern 70 amphorae has been found on the Kops Plateau.[38] These amphorae appear to have been multi-purpose containers and are believed to have contained mainly syrups (*defrutum/sapa*), sometimes with olives pickled in them, but also wine, fish sauces, or olive oil. Haltern 70 amphorae came primarily from Baetica, but imitations from southern Gaul are also known (Haltern 70 similis). Wine amphorae were, until the middle of the first century AD, still imported from various parts of the empire. However, after this period, wine from southern Gaul, carried in Gauloise 4 amphorae, began to dominate the market in Nijmegen.[39]

Many similarities to the results from Nijmegen can be observed in the amphora data from the fortresses and forts in Neuss that were in existence from 16 BC to AD 43 (Table 7 and Table 8).[40] The dominance of Iberian imports is also very pronounced here.[41] The main share of this consisted of Baetican fish sauce and the multi-purpose Haltern 70. The high number of Haltern 70s and the relative low proportion of olive oil amphorae probably indicate that the Haltern 70s were to a large extent used for the transportation of olive oil during this period.[42] Italian fish sauces, which were still present in the earliest contexts, diminished over time, while the share originating from southern Gaul gradually increased.[43] In general, though, there seems to have been

37 Carreras and van den Berg, 2017, pp. 357–365.
38 Carreras and van den Berg, 2017, pp. 363–365.
39 Carreras and van den Berg, 2017, pp. 360–363.
40 Carreras and Berni Millet, 2015.
41 Carreras and Berni Millet, 2015, pp. 176–177.
42 Wegert, 2011, p. 25.
43 Wegert, 2011, pp. 21–22.

TABLE 7 Amphorae from Neuss, fortifications 1–4 (16 BC–AD 16), sherds (n=936)

	Olive oil	Wine	Fish sauce	Defr./olives	Other/ unknown	Total
Spain	8%	5%	30%	27%	1%	72%
(Southern) Gaul		5%	4%			9%
Italy		4%	4%			8%
East. Mediter.		10%			1%	11%
Germania		0%				0%
Unknown					0%	0%
Total	8%	24%	38%	27%	2%	

TABLE 8 Amphorae from Neuss, fortifications 5–6 (AD 16–43), sherds (n=1608)

	Olive oil	Wine	Fish sauce	Defr./olives	Other/ unknown	Total
Spain	15%	3%	16%	3%	1%	38%
(Southern) Gaul		11%	17%	0%		29%
Italy	2%	5%				7%
East. Mediter.		19%			2%	21%
North Africa					2%	2%
Germania		1%				1%
Total	17%	39%	33%	4%	5%	

a decrease in the total number of imported fish sauce amphorae following the late Augustan period, as was the case in Nijmegen.[44] The provenance of wine amphorae was also very diverse in Neuss. Most of the amphorae came from the eastern Mediterranean (primarily from Rhodes, Crete, and Kos) and from southern Gaul, but Iberian and Italian products have also been found.[45] Considering the long-distances over which the eastern amphorae had to be transported, it is perhaps somewhat remarkable that they turn up in such large numbers in Neuss. It has therefore been suggested that the troops who took

44 Gonzáles Cesteros and Berni Millet, 2018, p. 122.

45 Wegert, 2011, pp. 22–24; Gonzáles Cesteros and Berni Millet, 2018, pp. 120–121.

part in the Germanic campaigns were important enough to be supplied with good quality wines from the east, or that there were perhaps some auxiliaries from the east among them, who organised their own supplies.[46]

The general trends identified in Nijmegen and Neuss probably give a good indication of the situation in other military fortifications along the Lower Germanic Limes during this period. Olive oil amphorae from Baetica dominate practically all the assemblages from the first to the early third century AD. Furthermore, a relatively high proportion of fish sauce amphorae has been found in the military bases with a dating in the Augustan period, such as in Vechten and Xanten (Vetera I).[47] This percentage is much lower in the bases, in which the dating lies more towards the late first century AD and early second century AD, as for example in Alphen aan den Rijn, Woerden, and Alteburg.[48] Moreover, in these later fortifications, the increased dominance of southern Gaul in the wine trade that was observed at the Kops-Plateau is also visible.

The limitations of research to date make it difficult to say much about developments regarding military supply in the period after the early second century AD. The reduction in the total numbers of troops undoubtedly led to a general decrease in imports, but it remains largely unknown whether the composition or provenance of the products also changed. Until future research sheds more light on this, our best guess is to assume that the imports in the military settlements were not so different from those in the civilian settlements, for which we do have some information (see below). In fact, the research in Germania Superior has indicated that the assemblages of military and civilian sites were, at least after the Augustan period, very similar.[49]

In Cologne, the military presence, with two legions and the fleet, also played an important role in the earliest development of trade. However, the importance of this military component was soon surpassed by the enormous attraction of the civilian settlement, which was the most important central place of the research area.[50] A complete and summarizing study of the inventory of amphora finds in Cologne is still awaited.[51] Yet some of the main flows of goods that went to the city are already known.[52] In the period from the earliest phase of Roman occupation until the promotion of the settlement to the status of

46 Wegert, 2011, pp. 23–24.

47 Hanel, 1995; van der Werff, 2004.

48 Hanel, 2003; Polak, Kloosterman and Niemeijer, 2004; van der Linden, 2008.

49 Martin-Kilcher, 1994, p. 564; Ehmig, 2007a, p. 11.

50 Jaschke and Schmitz, 2018, pp. 317–319.

51 Mayer, 2016, p. 311.

52 Unfortunately, no quantified assemblage has yet been published. The following overview is based on Liesen, 2004.

colonia in AD 50, Iberian imports made up a substantial part of the amphorae spectrum. Most amphorae, filled with olive oil, fish sauce, and syrup/olives (Haltern 70) came from Baetica, but amphorae carrying Tarraconensian wine have also been identified. In addition to this, olives from southern Gaul, Italian wine, and fruits and (sweet) wine from the Eastern Mediterranean have also been documented by the amphorae that have been found in Cologne. From the second half of the first century AD to the end of the third century AD, the variety of amphorae seems to have become more limited. The Dressel 20 amphorae from Baetica and the Gauloise 4 amphorae from southern Gaul now dominated the olive oil and wine imports to Cologne. Southern Gaul also supplied the city with fish sauce. Furthermore, amphorae filled with wine came from the eastern Mediterranean and, during the third century AD, from North Africa. From Germania Superior came amphorae that most probably carried beer. From the fourth century AD onwards, North Africa became the most important supplier of wine, while Baetica remained the most important for olive oil imports. Yet, in general, the import of amphorae appears to have dwindled during this period, and it seems that, in contrast to the much more sustained trade in previous periods, trade in this period consisted more of occasional imports of luxury goods destined for a more limited group of consumers.[53]

The *tituli picti* that have been found on some of the amphorae remains from Cologne also convey interesting information about the city's imports. *Tituli picti* are painted inscriptions that, under favourable conditions, have survived on amphorae and can contain information about the weight, content, quality, or the producer of the products, as well as markings related to taxation and tolls, or sometimes a consular dating.[54] As such, they are indicative of the high degree of organisation in the amphora trade, and they can confirm or extend the information that can be gained from a study of the vessel types themselves.

Ehmig has studied the *tituli picti* that have been found on amphorae that were disposed in and filled up the branch of the Rhine to the east of the city.[55] These inscriptions, which date from the late first and early second centuries AD, confirm that products from all over the Mediterranean found their way to Cologne.[56] Although, in general, it is difficult to make quantitative statements based on the *tituli picti*, they clearly indicate that the majority of the imports originated from the Iberian Peninsula. The inscriptions show that olive oil, fish

53 Liesen, 2004, p. 478.
54 Höpken, 2018, p. 378.
55 Ehmig, 2007b; 2009; 2018.
56 Ehmig, 2009, p. 400.

sauce, and wine came from there. Furthermore, the inscriptions confirm that the Haltern 70 amphorae, which came from that area, carried syrups (*defrutum*) with sometimes black olives (*oliva nigra*) pickled in them.[57] That olives were contained in these vessels is also indicated by the round stains that have been observed at regular intervals on sherds of Haltern 70 amphorae that have been found in Cologne.[58] The import of green olives has been demonstrated by amphorae from southern Gaul, which were inscribed with the text: *oliva alba*, or *oliva viridis*.[59] The painted inscriptions also confirm the varied provenances of the wine amphorae. In addition to the Spanish imports, wine came from Italy, the eastern Mediterranean (Kos, Rhodes, Crete, and the coast of Asia Minor), and most importantly, from southern Gaul.[60]

The *tituli picti* also allow interesting observations regarding the import of fish sauces. Although the research on the amphorae types has already shown that fish sauces came from southern Gaul, the inscriptions indicate that not all these sauces were necessarily produced in the region itself. Amphorae with the text *muria hispana*, *garum hispanum*, or *garum pompeianum* suggest that the Gaulish vessels contained sauces that originated in Spain and Italy, respectively.[61] A popular hypothesis is therefore that these products were shipped to Lyon, where they were repackaged into the Gaulish amphorae, which ended up along the Rhine.[62] However, on the basis of the current source material, it is impossible to say anything about the scale on which this happened and what this means for our interpretation of the relative importance of southern Gaulish fish sauce production, in comparison to that from Spain and Italy. Moreover, this might also cast doubt on the southern Gaulish supply of other products, which, after all, could have been repackaged in a similar way. An amphora inscribed with the text *defrutum hispanum* at least shows that fish sauce was not exceptional in this respect.[63] Lastly, the *tituli picti* also make mention of products that do not belong to the standard Mediterranean foodstuffs and are therefore much less likely to be recognised by their containers.

57 Ehmig, 2007b, pp. 223–224.
58 Höpken, 2016b, pp. 104–105.
59 Ehmig, 2007b, pp. 224–226.
60 Ehmig, 2007b, pp. 226–229.
61 Ehmig, 2007b, pp. 234–237.
62 Ehmig, 2009. Gonzáles Cesteros and Berni Millet argue against such an interpretation by explaining the adjectives *hispanum* and *pompeianum* not so much as a reference to the region in which the sauces were produced but as a recipe for the manufactured product. Gonzáles Cesteros and Berni Millet, 2018, pp. 41–47.
63 Ehmig, 2007b, pp. 237–238.

Amphorae with the text *purpuris*(*sum a*) *can*(*usio*) (purple dye from Canosa) and *aerugo* (cupric acetate) indicate that these products, which were probably used in manufacturing or medicine, were also shipped to Cologne.[64]

The amphorae material from the civilian settlement in Xanten is also relatively well known. Since this material consists of assemblages that, together, cover the period from the first to the third centuries AD, it can give us good insights into the general development of imports over time (Table 9, Table 10, Table 11, and Table 12).[65] As practically everywhere in the research area, Spanish imports dominated the amphora trade in Xanten. Most important in this respect, were the Baetican Dressel 20 amphorae, which clearly dominated the market for olive oil for most of the Roman period.[66] Baetica may have begun to lose this leading position only later in the third century AD, as the import of North African oil increased.[67] Remarkable are also the Dressel 20 imitations that were produced in Germania Superior (Dressel 20 similis).[68] These amphorae have also been found in three of the four assemblages and thus seem to have provided a (very) small part of the oil supply.

TABLE 9 Amphorae from Xanten Ostmauer (Augustus–AD 50), sherds (n=2498)

	Olive oil	**Wine**	**Fish sauce**	**Defr./olives**	**Other/ unknown**	**Total**
Spain	27%	7%	22%	13%	1%	69%
(Southern) Gaul		9%	3%	0%	0%	13%
Italy		4%			0%	4%
East. Mediter.		14%			0%	14%
North Africa	0%					0%
Germania		0%				0%
Unknown					0%	0%
Total	27%	34%	25%	13%	1%	

64 Ehmig, 2007b, pp. 239–245. Similarly, the import of red ochre is indicated by the findings of pigment-remains of a vessel that has been found in Cologne. Höpken, 2016b, pp. 105–106.

65 Carreras, 2006.

66 The high percentage of Haltern 70 amphorae in the earliest assemblage (Table 9) suggests that olive oil was initially transported in this vessel as well. Carreras, 2006, p. 35.

67 Höpken, 2018, p. 381.

68 Berni Millet, 2006, p. 23.

TABLE 10 Amphorae from Xanten Hafengrabung (Nero–second century AD), sherds (n=420)

	Olive oil	Wine	Fish sauce	Defr./olives	Other/ unknown	Total
Spain	45%		31%	2%	5%	83%
(Southern)Gaul		7%	2%		0%	9%
Italy		1%				1%
East. Mediter.		4%			0%	4%
Germania	1%	2%				3%
Unknown					1%	1%
Total	46%	14%	33%	2%	6%	

TABLE 11 Amphorae from Xanten Insula 15 (late first–second centuries AD), sherds (n=746)

	Olive oil	Wine	Fish sauce	Defr./olives	Other/ unknown	Total
Spain	72%		1%		0%	73%
(Southern) Gaul		22%				22%
East. Mediter.		0%			4%	5%
Germania	0%					0%
Total	72%	22%	1%		4%	

TABLE 12 Amphorae from Xanten Insula 39 (Trajan–mid third century AD), sherds (n=3794)

	Olive oil	Wine	Fish sauce	Defr./olives	Other/ unknown	Total
Spain	77%	0%	3%	1%	0%	81%
(Southern) Gaul		14%			0%	14%
Italy		2%			0%	2%
East. Mediter.		1%			0%	1%
North Africa	0%					0%
Germania	0%	1%				1%
Unknown					1%	1%
Total	78%	18%	3%	1%	1%	

Baetica was also of great importance for the importation of fish sauces. From the earliest phase, large quantities of Baetican fish sauces were shipped to Xanten. Even though these quantities probably declined significantly over time and some of the imports were also replaced by (perhaps repackaged) Gaulish amphorae from around the middle of the first century AD onwards, Baetica remained the most important supplier of fish sauces.[69] In fact, in the two later assemblages, Baetica appears to have become the only supplier of this product category once again.[70]

With regard to wine, the evidence from Xanten is largely in line with that from the sites already discussed. Up until the middle of the first century AD, Xanten imported wine from various parts of the empire, such as Spain, Gaul, Italy, and the eastern Mediterranean, without any region having a clear predominance.[71] Then from the second half of the first century AD onwards, southern Gaulish wines, mainly transported in Gauloise 4 amphorae, clearly dominated the supply of wine to Xanten. This remained the case throughout the second and third centuries AD, but imitations of Gaulish wine amphorae from Germania Superior also grew in importance during this period.[72]

Furthermore, the so-called Scheldt-Valley amphorae turned up during the second and third centuries AD. According to the latest research, this regional amphora type was produced in Dourges (northern France) and was distributed to sites in western Gallia Belgica and Germania Inferior.[73] What was transported in these amphorae remains unknown. It has been suggested that the amphorae are indicative of the emergence of a local fish sauce industry somewhere in the Scheldt estuary, which was related to a supposed decline in Mediterranean fish sauce imports from around the second century AD (see below).[74] However, there are some (geographical) objections to be made against such an interpretation. Therefore, it is now believed to be more likely that the Scheldt-Valley amphorae were filled with an alcoholic beverage, though it remains difficult to say whether this was wine or beer.[75]

Another large settlement from which the amphorae material is well studied is the secondary agglomeration of Bonn (Table 13). Most of these amphorae date to the second and third centuries AD, so that they can give a good insight into a somewhat later phase of Roman occupation.[76] As might be expected

69 Berni Millet, 2006, p. 22.
70 Carreras, 2006, p. 37.
71 Berni Millet, 2006, p. 21.
72 Berni Millet, 2006, p. 21.
73 Schmidtz, 2014.
74 van der Werff, Thoen and van Dierendonck, 1997, p. 11.
75 van der Werff, Thoen and van Dierendonck, 1997, pp. 11–15.
76 Höpken, 2016a, p. 142.

TABLE 13 Amphorae from Bonn (second–third centuries AD), sherds (n=4075)

	Olive oil	**Wine**	**Fish sauce**	**Defr./olives**	**Other/ unknown**	**Total**
Spain	32%	0%	1%	0%	1%	34%
(Southern) Gaul		25%	1%			26%
Italy		1%			0%	1%
East. Mediter.					1%	1%
North Africa?					1%	1%
Gallia Belgica					8%	8%
Germania Sup.					16%	16%
Germania Inf.					14%	14%
Total	32%	26%	2%	0%	40%	

for this period, Baetican oil and southern Gaulish wine amphorae make up the majority of the finds.[77] For the rest, Mediterranean amphorae are only present to a very limited extent. This is true not only for oil and wine, but also for Mediterranean syrup/olives and fish sauce, which seem to have been imported in limited quantities. On the other hand, a rather large proportion of the amphorae came from more nearby regions. From Gallia Belgica came the already discussed Scheldt-Valley amphorae, while Germania Superior supplied Bonn with amphorae which were probably filled with beer.[78] Furthermore, a significant number of vessels that were locally produced in Soller have been found.[79] By means of an analysis of the content residues found in these amphorae, animal fats and protein compounds have been demonstrated.[80] This indicates that these vessels were used for the containment of (fermented) dairy products.

Interestingly, the lack of Mediterranean fish sauce amphorae in Bonn seems to be part of a more general trend. From the end of the first century AD onwards, the number of fish sauce amphorae in settlements from the Lower Rhine region began to decline, and by the second half of the second century AD, they had disappeared almost completely.[81] It not entirely clear what the

77 Höpken, 2016a, p. 166.
78 Höpken, 2016a, pp. 149–155.
79 Höpken, 2015a, p. 135.
80 Höpken, 2013, pp. 181–182.
81 Heimberg, 1997, p. 307; Carreras and van den Berg, 2017, p. 358.

reason for this decline is. It is possible that the disappearance of these amphorae reflects an actual decline in the consumption of fish sauce in the region. However, it is also possible that fish sauce was still consumed but that it is not as archaeologically visible as before, for example, because it was transported in different containers. In this case, a possible explanation for the decline of Mediterranean imports could be that they were replaced by locally produced fish sauces. Archaeozoological research suggests that such local fish sauces were produced somewhere in the west of present-day Belgium.[82] Still, the evidence for this local production is very thin and more research is needed to clarify the possible relationship between the emergence of local production and the decline of Mediterranean supply.

It is not entirely clear to what extent we can assume that the findings from these well-researched contexts are representative of the situation in the rest of the research area. Firstly, all the sites discussed here are situated on the Rhine (or its distributaries), which was obviously a favourable location with respect to imports from distant regions. It is therefore interesting to see whether sites located more in the hinterland of the Rhine had a similar range of products at their disposal. Unfortunately, there are currently no settlements with sufficiently large amphorae assemblages that can shed light on this question.

An exception to this is the secondary agglomeration of Braives, which was located far away from the Rhine along the *Via Belgica* and is perhaps representative of the situation in the *civitas Tungrorum* (Table 14).[83] The assemblage from Braives, which is dated very broadly in the period between the first and fourth centuries AD, was not radically different from those along the Rhine. Southern Gaulish wine and Baetican oil amphorae clearly dominate the spectrum and together make up more than half of the vessels. The proportion of fish sauce amphorae, which came mostly from Baetica, is somewhat lower but is still relatively well represented. We also see, just as in Bonn, that a rather large number of amphorae came from more nearby regions, namely Gallia Belgica and Germania Superior. However, it is unclear what was transported in these amphorae. In any case, it is clear that even in a settlement far removed from the Rhine, it was possible to acquire the typical Roman food products from both nearby and distant places.

A second point of criticism regarding the representativeness of the well-researched settlements is that these were all sites of significant size and importance. It is therefore questionable whether we can see a similar picture of imports in smaller sites and especially in rural settlements. At the moment,

82 van Neer *et al.*, 2005, pp. 179–180; van Neer, Ervynck and Monsieur, 2010, pp. 187–188.

83 Brulet, Laubenheimer and Vilvorder, 1992.

TABLE 14 Amphorae from Braives (first–fourth centuries AD), MNI (n=146)

	Olive oil	Wine	Fish sauce	Defr./olives	Other/ unknown	Total
Spain	25%		11%	3%	3%	42%
(Southern) Gaul		31%	3%			34%
East. Mediter.		4%				4%
Gallia Belgica					9%	9%
Germania					9%	9%
Unknown					1%	1%
Total	25%	35%	14%	3%	23%	

not much is known about amphorae imports in the rural settlements in the research area. Studies into several rural sites in the *civitas Batavorum*, indicate that these settlements roughly followed the general trends of the larger settlements.[84] In the well-researched settlement of Geldermalsen-Hondsgemet, for example, Baetican olive oil amphorae and southern Gaulish wine amphorae are well represented, while Baetican fish sauce amphorae and Haltern 70s have also been found.[85] Considerable quantities of regional amphorae were also present in the settlement, including some Scheldt-Valley amphorae. Mediterranean amphorae from regions other than Baetica and southern Gaul are completely absent in Geldermalsen-Hondsgemet. It therefore seems that the settlement mainly had access to the amphorae that had already reached the region in large numbers, while the more exclusive products were reserved for other (larger) settlements.

The findings from Geldermalsen-Hondsgemet are likely representative of the rest of the area, though it is clear that there was variation between different settlements and periods.[86] However, the pattern of a large proportion of Baetican, southern Gaulish, and regional amphorae and fewer imports from other Mediterranean regions does seem to be the general picture. It is also interesting to see, that this same pattern was found in a study into the amphorae material from rural settlements in the *civitas Tungrorum*, which perhaps suggests that this pattern applies to rural settlements throughout the

84 An overview is provided in van den Berg, 2016.
85 Van Kerckhove, 2009, pp. 124–128.
86 van den Berg, 2016.

research area.[87] At the same time, an important difficulty with regard to the interpretation of amphorae finds in rural settlements concerns the possibility of secondary use of these amphorae. It is therefore not always clear whether the contents of an amphora were actually consumed in the settlement itself or if the contents were consumed elsewhere and the amphorae only ended up in the settlement as they served a secondary purpose, for instance as storage containers or pissoirs.[88] Hopefully, future research will be able to provide more clarity on this topic and will also provide better insights into the differences between different types of settlements and developments over time.

6.2 Terra sigillata

Another interesting category of material culture that contains important information regarding long-distance trade is terra sigillata. Terra sigillata, which is a modern term, denotes the characteristic red-gloss luxury tableware that was widely distributed throughout the Roman Empire (and beyond) in the period between the first century BC and the third century AD.[89] The high-quality, standardised vessels were mass-produced in a limited number of specialised pottery centres that were primarily located in Italy and Gaul.[90] The high value of the products and their efficient production process meant that, even with the high transportation costs of the ancient world, it was worthwhile to sell the tableware in places far away from the production centres. An important factor in this regard, was also that terra sigillata was normally not transported on its own but piggy-backed on shipments of bulk-goods such as grain, oil, wine, and meat.[91] Although terra sigillata, probably due to its relatively high prevalence on military sites, has also been associated with redistribution by the state, there is no convincing evidence for this, and it seems more likely that it was traded via the free market.[92]

The high-quality and standardisation of the vessels have also made terra sigillata an important source of evidence for modern researchers. The widespread and easily recognizable red sherds were, in contrast to many other categories of Roman material culture, already valued by early archaeologists and,

87 Nicolas, 2011.

88 van der Werff, 1987, pp. 166–169.

89 I follow Van Oyen's definition of terra sigillata by which the so-called Eastern sigillata and the African red slip ware are excluded from the definition. Van Oyen, 2016, pp. 11–17.

90 Wilson, 2008, pp. 396–402.

91 Lewit, 2013, p. 116.

92 Mees, 2018a; 2018b.

accordingly, have been thoroughly studied from the early stages of archaeological research onwards.[93] Furthermore, the terra sigillata vessels were usually stamped with the name of the potter who produced it, or the workshop in which it was produced, so that the place of origin of many of the products can be traced.[94] On the basis of their knowledge of different types, styles, or stamps, specialists are able to extract a wealth of information from the terra sigillata. It is not without reason that terra sigillata can often be used as an important (and very precise) dating tool for archaeological contexts.

However, much of the potential that terra sigillata offers to answer larger historical and archaeological questions, for example about the Roman economy, remains untapped.[95] This is also the case for the research area. Most of the studies discussing the terra sigillata from this region only focus on describing the material from a specific local context (usually a settlement), without placing their results into a larger regional perspective.[96] As a result, a detailed overview of the development of terra sigillata imports in the Lower Germanic Limes region is still largely lacking, perhaps because most specialists assume this development to be well known.[97] This is unfortunate because a good understanding of the development of this trade can give important information about the performance of the economy.[98]

Nevertheless, the general development of terra sigillata imports in the research area, can conveniently be illustrated on the basis of the large 'Samian research' database that has been assembled by the Römisch-Germanisches Zentralmuseum in Mainz.[99] This is a large, open-access internet database that has collected hundreds of thousands of terra sigillata stamps that have been found on (the remains of) vessels from throughout the Roman Empire. The records of many of the stamps in this database, contain important information about these vessels, such as the geographical location where they have been found, their date, and the workshop or area where they were probably produced.[100] From the total number of localised and dated stamps in the database, almost 25,000 have been found in the research area (Figure 19).

---

93 Van Oyen, 2016, p. 3.
94 Eschbaumer, 2001, p. 272.
95 Van Oyen, 2016, pp. 4–5.
96 Still, there are exceptions. E.g. Polak, 2000; D. Visser, 2010.
97 Recently, a brief but good overview of the earliest terra sigillata imports has been published. Rudnick, 2018.
98 Wilson, 2009a, pp. 237–243.
99 Dannell and Mees, 2013; Römisch-Germanische Zentralmuseum, no date.
100 A map with all the production sites referred to in the database can be found in Fulford, 2013, p. 2.

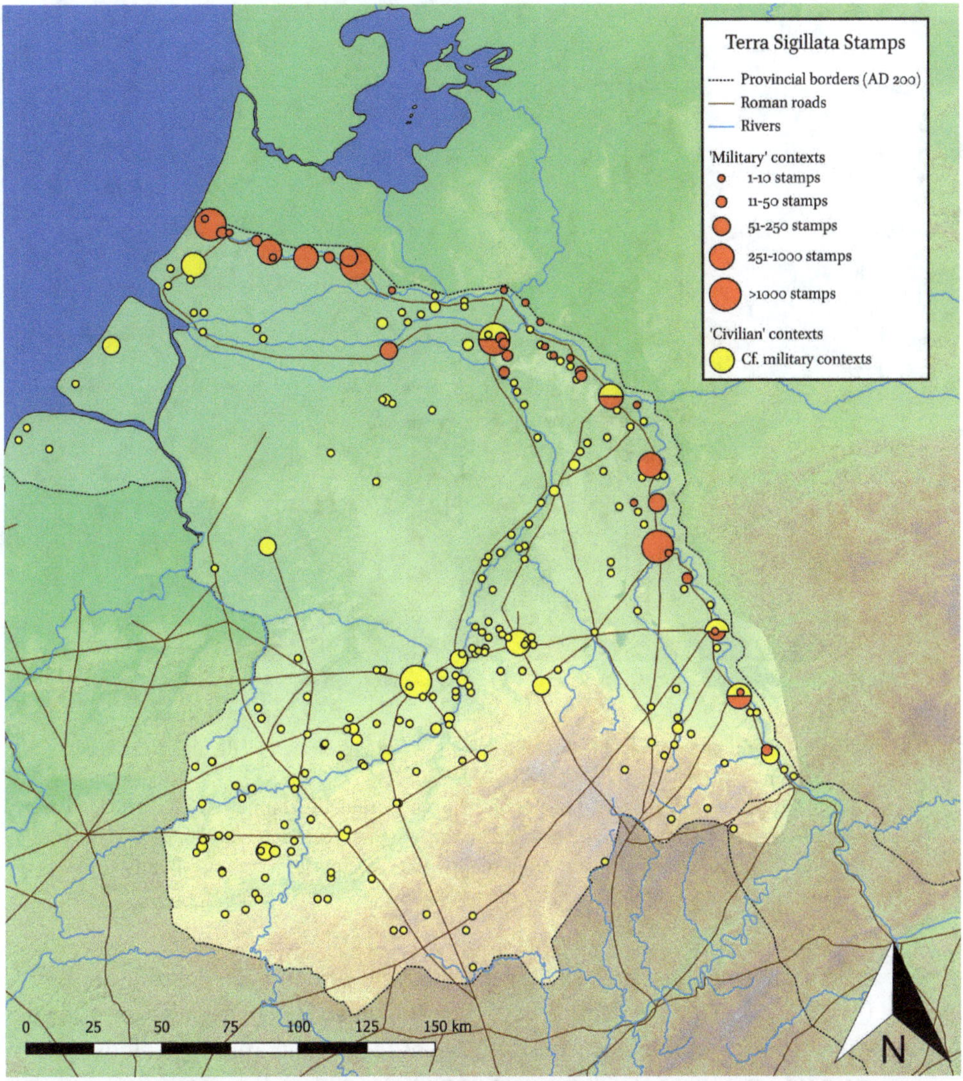

FIGURE 19 The distribution of the dated terra sigillata stamps that have been found in the Lower Germanic Limes region

Based on this large number of dated stamps, it is possible to get a general impression of the development of the terra sigillata imports in the Lower Germanic Limes region (Figure 20). As the graph shows, the import of terra sigillata to the region really commenced during the last quarter of the first century BC. In this period, practically all the terra sigillata that was imported was of the so-called Italian-style (also known as Arretine ware). This style was developed in the late 40s BC in Arezzo (central Italy) but was also produced in

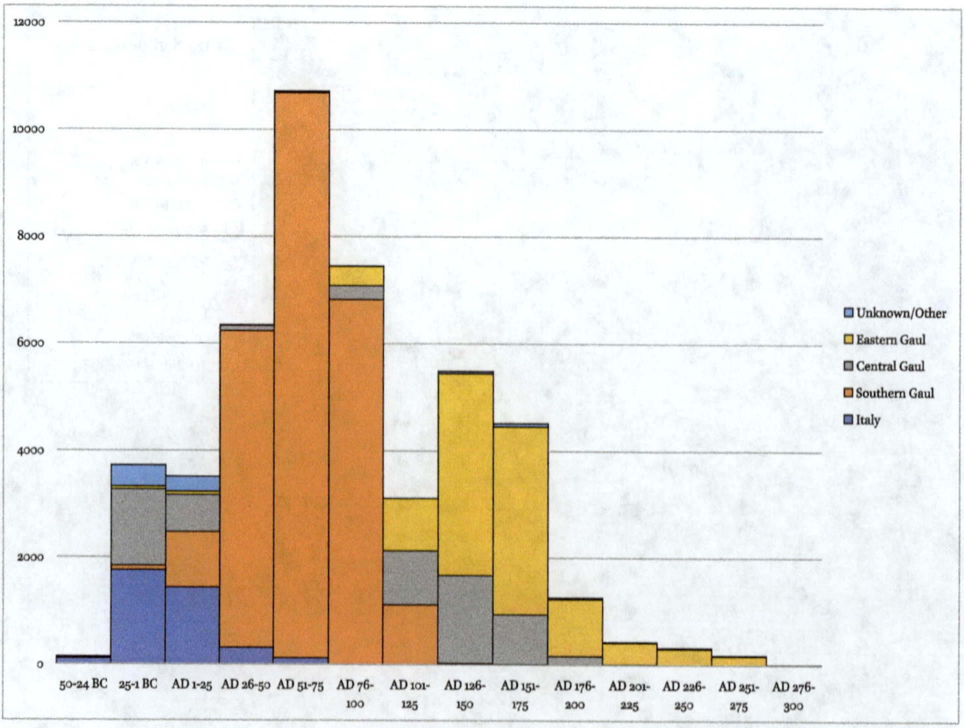

FIGURE 20 The total number of dated terra sigillata stamps per 25-year period, divided by region of origin
Note: Based on the presumed places of their production, the stamps have been divided over one or more production regions. Based on the length of their dating period, the stamps are spread out proportionally over the 25-year periods. Stamps for which the dating period covers two (or more) 25-year periods are therefore somewhat overrepresented.

other Italian centres, such as Pisa and Pozzuoli, and in Lyon (central Gaul).[101] Up until the early first century AD, the Italian-style sigillata was on a large scale exported to the north-western part of the Roman Empire, including the research area. However, from around AD 15/20, large-scale terra sigillata exportation commenced in southern Gaul and soon drove the Italian and Lyonnais producers from the market.[102]

The most important exporter of these southern Gaulish vessels was undoubtedly the production centre in La Graufesenque. In the course of the first century AD, vessels from La Graufesenque flooded the north-western provinces and dominated the market for terra sigillata until the end of the

101 Rudnick, 2018, pp. 344–347. Contrary to amphora studies, in which Lyon usually belongs to southern Gaul, in terra sigillata studies, Lyon is normally classified as central Gaul.

102 Mees, 2011, p. 1.

century.[103] In addition to La Graufesenque, various other centres in southern Gaul set up their production during this period, but of these centres, only Montans and Banassac played a role in extra regional exports.[104] This general development is also clearly reflected in the data from the research area. From the second quarter until the end of the first century AD, southern Gaulish stamps, of which the vast majority originate from La Graufesenque, completely dominate the dataset.

At the beginning of the second century AD, the southern Gaulish producers seem to have lost their dominant position in the north-western provinces, and this trend is also clearly visible in the data from the Lower Germanic Limes region. The exact reasons for the decline of southern Gaulish imports remain unknown. It is generally believed that the production centres came under increasing pressure from producers in central and eastern Gaul, whose products had lower transport costs due to shorter distances to the consumer markets.[105] This is perhaps also why the quality of the southern Gaulish wares deteriorated in this period. This worsening of the quality has been interpreted as the result of a futile attempt to remain competitive by lowering production costs, which made the goods even less desirable. Yet there is perhaps an alternative explanation for the decline of the southern Gaulish terra sigillata industry. Rien Polak argues that the emergence of the central and eastern terra sigillata workshops was more a reaction to the decline of southern Gaulish production, than it was a cause.[106] He explains that since terra sigillata is believed to have often piggybacked on freight of other goods, it is more likely that the decline of the southern imports was the result of the discontinuation of other long-distance trade flows. Thus, as the north-western provinces by the end of the first century AD had become less dependent on external imports, the transportation of terra sigillata may have become more expensive. However, whatever the exact reasons behind the decline of the southern Gaulish terra sigillata imports, it is evident that they had lost practically their entire market share to central and especially eastern Gaulish production centres in the course of the second century AD.

The central Gaulish products in this period no longer came from Lyon but from several centres more to the west. Lezoux was the most important of these centres and dominated the terra sigillata market in most parts of the north-western provinces during the second century AD.[107] From the other

103 Lewit, 2013, p. 111.
104 Polak, 2000, pp. 15–36; Eschbaumer, 2001, p. 280.
105 Eschbaumer, 2001, p. 281.
106 Polak, 2000, pp. 36–37.
107 Van Oyen, 2016, pp. 51–55.

central Gaulish centres, only Les Martres-de-Veyre was a real contender to Lezoux's success and, until the middle of the second century AD, was able to secure another share of this market.[108] Together, stamps from Lezoux and Les Martres-de-Veyre also make up the vast majority of the central Gaulish terra sigillata in the data from the research area, with Lezoux clearly being the most important exporter of the two.

Yet the largest share of the second century AD terra sigillata that found its way to the region seems to have been imported from eastern Gaul.[109] The main production sites in this region were located in the Argonne and in the area between the Mosel and the Rhine. Unlike in southern and central Gaul, there was not one single centre that dominated the market but several centres that together accounted for the supply of terra sigillata.[110] The stamp-data makes clear that the sites along the Mosel were important suppliers for the research area. A large proportion of the terra sigillata probably came from Trier, where production took place from the end of the first century AD until circa AD 260. Another important centre was La Madeleine, which lay more to the south and exported many vessels to the research area in the period between AD 120 and 170. Stamps from other sites in the area between Mosel and Rhine, such as Chémery, Boucheporn, Blickweiler, and Haute-Yutz, have also been recorded in significant numbers, but their share was clearly smaller than that of Trier and La Madeleine. The number of stamps from Rheinzabern is also not so high, even though the site was an important centre of terra sigillata production. It seems that the producers in Rheinzabern concentrated more on the markets to their south and east than those to the north.[111] The most important production centres in the Argonne were Lavoye and Avocourt, where production took place primarily in the period between AD 120 and 200. However, their production was also clearly less substantial than that of the main sites along the Mosel. Of the two sites that were located in the research area itself, Aachen and Sinzig, only Sinzig played a role of any significance. However, compared to the proportion of imports from the more southerly areas, this was also very limited, but it should be remembered that Sinzig only produced for a relatively short period of time (see section 5.2.1.2).

Since Figure 20 is based on a very large number of stamps, it is tempting to assume that it also gives a reliable representation of the development of the total volume of terra sigillata imports that came to the Lower Germanic Limes

---

108 Van Oyen, 2016, pp. 44–47.

109 In the dataset, sites from the provinces of Gallia Belgica, Germania Inferior, and Germania Superior have been comprised under eastern Gaul. Raetia has been categorised under 'unknown/other'.

110 Eschbaumer, 2001, p. 284.

111 Eschbaumer, 2001, p. 287.

region over time. Nevertheless, it should be realised that there are several factors that have to a large extent determined the shape of the graph. Most fundamentally, the dataset only represents terra sigillata that was stamped. Vessels that did not contain a stamp have not been included in the dataset. Although there is no immediate reason to assume that a certain period is underrepresented due to a more limited stamping tradition, this possibility should not be excluded entirely. A more obvious bias in the dataset, though, is the great difference between the number of stamps contributed by different sites. Most of the settlements are only represented by a few stamps. For example, 189 of the 244 sites yielded fewer than 10 stamps, which amounts to less than 2% of the total dataset. Furthermore, 40 of the 244 sites have contributed between 10 and 100 stamps, which is around 5% of the total dataset. A limited number of sites, on the other hand, have contributed vast numbers of stamps. Of the 244 sites, only 16 have yielded 100 or more stamps. Yet these 16 sites together make up circa 93% of the total dataset. Especially the 8 sites that have more than 1,000 stamps (Cologne, Xanten, Valkenburg, Bonn, Tongeren, Nijmegen, Neuss, and Vechten) and together form almost 82% of the total dataset have made a large impact on the shape of the graph. Of these sites, Vechten makes the largest contribution with 7,153 stamps, which comprises around 29% of the total dataset. The impact of Neuss and Nijmegen is also very large, with 3,204 and 3,147 stamps, respectively, which both equal almost 13% of the total dataset. Since there was an (early) Roman military base in all three latter settlements, it is likely that Figure 20 is biased towards (early) military contexts. Nevertheless, it should not be overlooked that it is precisely these specific contexts that have produced the largest number of stamps. Even though the relatively intensive research into military sites might partially explain the large number of stamps, it is also likely that they just reflect the relatively large presence of terra sigillata on such sites.

However, the large differences in the number of stamps per site make it clear that we should be careful not to draw too far-reaching conclusions based on the graph. For instance, it is questionable to what extent the general picture in Figure 20 also applies to civilian settlements. Unfortunately, for most of the stamps, it is not clear whether they were found in a military or in a non-military context. In order to be able to make such a distinction possible, the sites whose location corresponds to that of a known military fortification (cf. Figure 2) or another supposed military context have been considered as military, while the rest of the sites are considered as civilian.[112] For most of the sites, such a subdivision can confidently be made since the sites were clearly, for the most part either military or civilian. However, in Cologne, Bonn, Xanten, and Nijmegen,

112 Cf. Mees, 2018b.

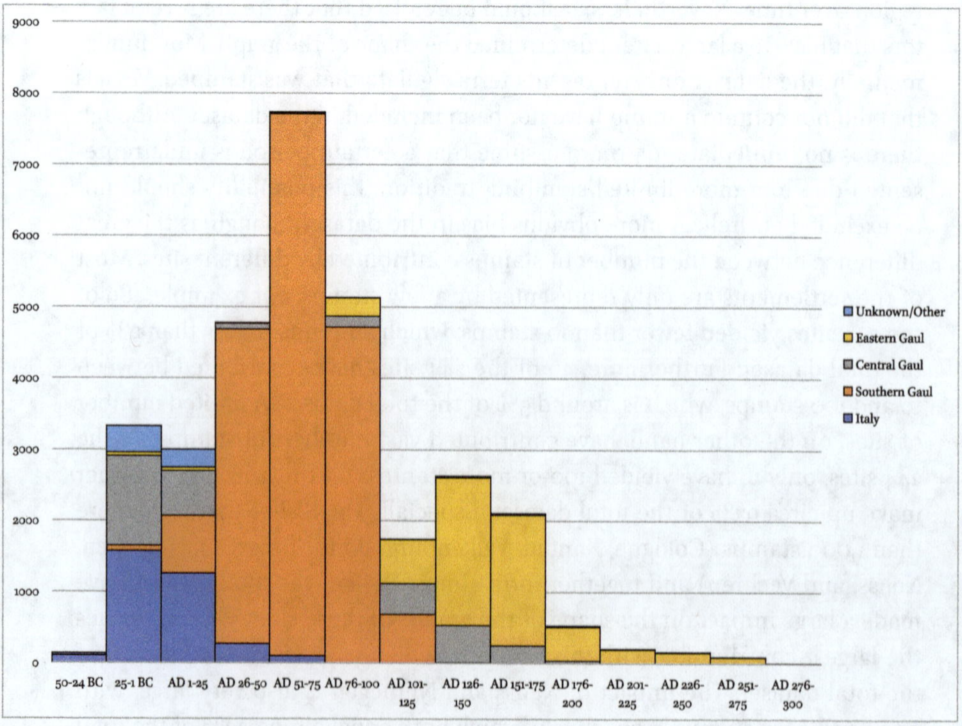

FIGURE 21 The total number of dated terra sigillata stamps from military contexts per 25-year period, divided by region of origin

an important military presence existed along with a significant civilian population.[113] Thus, in order to reflect that, the stamps from these sites have been divided over both categories.[114] Of course, this is a crude method, but it will probably suffice to distinguish the general differences between military and civilian contexts.

Figure 21 and Figure 22 show the results of this subdivision. First, it is important to point out the difference in the total number of stamps used for both graphs. For the civilian graph, only 8,431 stamps are used, while the military

113 An argument for the inclusion of other sites can also be made. However, I believe that this problem is most pressing in these four cases.

114 In Cologne the main military fortress is believed to have been disbanded by the late Tiberian period. Müller, 1987, p. 583. Therefore, the stamps of which the finding place is not explicitly characterised as military and which date after AD 37 have been considered as civilian. Furthermore, the stamps from Cologne from AD 37 and before, of which the finding place is not explicitly characterised as either military or civilian, have a value of 50% in both graphs. The same is the case for all the stamps with non-characterised finding places in Bonn, Xanten, and Nijmegen.

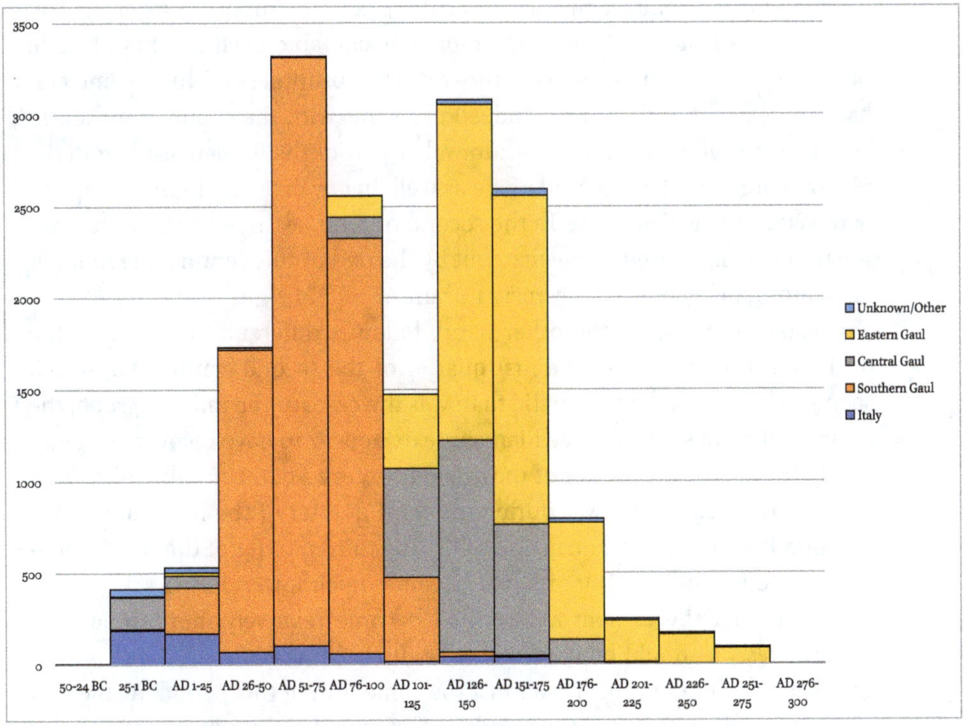

FIGURE 22 The total number of dated terra sigillata stamps from civilian contexts per 25-year period, divided by region of origin

graph makes use of 16,297 stamps. This seems to confirm once more that terra sigillata was much more common in military contexts. Furthermore, the graphs take largely different trajectories.

Whereas the military graph shows an already high volume of stamps in the 50 years around the turn of the century, the number of stamps from this period is very low in the civilian graph. This shows clearly that terra sigillata in this period was mainly imported to account for the needs of the Roman military, while the civilian purchasing power was probably not yet sufficient to create much demand. This seems to have changed in the course of the first century AD. In both graphs, the number of stamps increases from the second quarter of the first century AD onwards, and both graphs reach their peak in the third quarter of this century.[115] Nevertheless, it is clear that most of the imports were

115 According to Polak, this peak may, to a certain extent, be the result of the Batavian Revolt. He explains that in addition to an increase in the loss of vessels as a result of this destructive event itself, it is also quite possible that archaeologists' use of this event as an end or beginning point for dating has also played a role. Polak, 2000, p. 58.

destined for the military market. After the peak, the import of terra sigillata appears to fall slightly. However, a more considerable decline takes place in the first quarter of the second century AD. The abruptness of this decline perhaps indicates that there were indeed problems with the supply from southern Gaul (see above), but the withdrawal of part of the Roman army from the research area may have played a role as well. In any case, the military imports had passed their high point. In the second quarter of the second century AD, the numbers increased somewhat, but by the end of this century, the number of stamps had become largely insignificant.

Civilian imports, on the other hand, follow a different course. After the decline of the imports in the first quarter of the second century AD, which seems to have been less dramatic than was the case for the military graph, the imports of terra sigillata in civilian contexts appear to have recovered significantly. In the second quarter of the second century AD, the number of stamps was almost as high as it was during the third quarter of the first century AD. The number of imports remained high in the third quarter of the second century AD. Since military imports had become much lower during this period, it is clear that the civilian market had become relatively more important. Nevertheless, it should be noted that the distribution between the two categories in absolute numbers is almost the same during this period. At the end of the second century AD, the number of stamps from civilian contexts also decreased considerably, and from the third century AD onwards, the import of terra sigillata was probably largely over.

As for the regions from which the terra sigillata was imported, there are no major differences between the two categories of sites. Therefore, it seems that the general development outlined above, applies to both military and civilian sites. The only thing that stands out is that the percentage of second century AD imports from central Gaul is much higher in the civilian contexts. An explanation for this is that an important part of the stamps originates from the Meuse region. In contrast to the sites from the north and east of the research area, which were located closer to the Rhine and its delta, central Gaulish imports were much more common here. This is most clearly seen in Tongeren, where central Gaulish imports make up the vast majority of second century AD stamps.[116]

116 Cf. Vanvinckenroye, 1989, pp. 55–57.

6.3 Trade with Other Regions

The distribution of amphorae and terra sigillata thus provides us with important insights into the long-distance trade from southern regions to the Lower Germanic Limes region. Still, it should be realised that trade goods did not only come from these southern regions. Trade also took place with Britannia and Germania Magna, but since this trade has left fewer traces, it is much more difficult to assess its significance. Nevertheless, it is good to give a general overview of the (limited) extent of knowledge about trade with these regions, as this trade did play a role in the economy of the research area.

In general, little is known about the trade relations between the research area and Britannia. The rich epigraphical material from Domburg and Colijnsplaat suggests that, at least in the second and third centuries AD, there must have been a flourishing trade between Britannia and the research area (see section 6.4).[117] The archaeological material, however, is very limited and does not in any way allow statements to be made about the nature and extent of the trade.[118] Ceramic finds from Britain, originating from production centres in the Rhineland, such as Cologne and Soller, do make clear that trade in ceramics took place, but the importance of this trade was probably not particularly great.[119] Furthermore, the presence of amphorae and terra sigillata on British sites suggests that goods were also transported through the Lower Germanic Limes region, which may have involved traders from the research area. Still, what proportion of these goods were moved through the region remains unclear since alternative routes, such as the Atlantic route and routes through central Gaul, were also used.[120]

It is equally difficult to grasp the nature and extent of the trade with Germania Magna, even though much more has been written about it by modern authors.[121] What is clear, in any case, is that although the *limes* area was heavily militarised, it did not form an impenetrable barrier.[122] Instead, the fortifications functioned as a way to control the frontier area and as a guarantee

---

117 Hassall, 1978, p. 44.

118 Werner Oenbrink gives the most recent overview of the sparsely documented archaeological record. Oenbrink, 2018. See also the somewhat older contributions in du Plat Taylor and Cleere, 1978.

119 Greene, 1978.

120 Campbell, 2012, p. 275.

121 In this chapter, I do not have the time or space to do real justice to the real complexity of this topic. However, with this brief exposition, I hope to address the main points of discussions on the subject.

122 Whittaker 1994, 7–9.

of a quick response if a threat was to emerge. Therefore, the Rhine was a *fluid* border, where two geographic and cultural spaces met and along which the movement of goods, people, and ideas could take place.[123] That many goods were transported across the border is clear from the large number of finds of Roman goods in Germania Magna.[124] However, the main question with regard to these goods is how they got there. Do these findings indicate real trade, or are they the result of other exchange mechanisms? It is, for example, possible that the goods were lost by Roman troops, or taken as loot by Germanic warrior groups.[125] We also know that Rome recruited soldiers from across the Rhine, who, after their service, may have brought Roman goods back to their homelands.[126] Moreover, Tacitus mentions the paying of gifts and subsidies to Germanic leaders in order to keep the peace.[127]

As the archaeological material is ambiguous, scholarly interpretations of the importance of the trade with Germania Magna vary. Michael Erdrich, for instance, has argued that the extent of trade was probably fairly insignificant.[128] He explains that the chronology of many of the found objects coincides with that of many Roman political and military crises, and he therefore concludes that it is likely that the goods represent gifts that were given to the Germanic people to keep them quiet.[129] At the same time, there are studies that show a more or less continuous flow of goods into Germania Magna and which is thus more in line with a scenario of regular trade contacts.[130] But if these goods are indeed indicative of trade between the Romans and Germans, what did the Romans get in return? Although it is generally believed that the Germanic tribes were only able to produce surpluses to a very limited extent, they are likely to have had at least some sort of merchandise to offer.[131] Based on historical sources, most scholars assume that the range of Germanic products included amber, soap, cow hides, furs, goose feathers, women's hair, and

123 Mirschenz, 2013, pp. 8–10; Kyritz, 2014, pp. 236–238.
124 A large international research project collects all the findings of Roman objects in Germania Magna. Voss, 2017.
125 Frank, 2018, p. 545.
126 A rather large proportion of the finds seem to indicate a military connection. Frank, 2011, p. 94; Karlsen, 2018, pp. 580–581.
127 Tac. Hist. 4, 76.
128 Erdrich, 2001.
129 It is possible that the gifts consisted of money with which the Germanic people bought products at the border. Wolters, 2000.
130 Galestin, 2010; Mirschenz, 2013, pp. 151–153; Frank, 2018.
131 Wolters, 2000, pp. 91–92.

slaves.[132] Yet since these products are all organic and have not been handed down archaeologically, it is impossible to know the scale on which they were traded.

In general, it is assumed that in the areas directly across the border, in the so-called *Vorlimes* region, trade with the Romans was most intense.[133] This means that most of the typical goods that were available on the Roman side of the border were also available here, even though in smaller quantities. It is thus believed that this region was well connected to the Roman economy. Nevertheless, the degree of integration of this region should not be overstated, and it is striking that the inhabitants in many ways clung to their indigenous traditions and did not, for example, adopt the Roman building, agricultural, and production techniques that must have been known to them.[134] This is also indicated by the fact that the Germanic people mainly seem to have imported goods with which they were already familiar but whose Roman variants were of better quality.[135] Both the intensity and the character of the economic exchange appear to have changed between areas depending on their relative proximity to the *limes*.[136] In the more distant areas, the density of Roman finds is much lower, and these finds are primarily to be interpreted as prestige objects that ended up there in non-commercial ways.

Although such a model of exchange with Germania Magna is good to get a general impression of the differences between nearby and remote areas, the reality was much more complex. For instance, the degree of intensity of trade contacts depended not only on geographical distance but also on good infrastructure.[137] In addition, there was a distinction between what the different natural environments had to offer in exchange for Roman goods. Furthermore, the relationship between the Romans and the various Germanic tribes, and their receptiveness to trade, also played an important role. For example, the Frisii seem to have had very close relations with the Romans, which is also reflected in the finds from their area.[138]

---

132 Wolters, 2000, p. 91; Ruffing, 2008; Mirschenz, 2013, p. 33; Karlsen, 2018, pp. 583–586.

133 Whittaker, 1994, pp. 122–131; Karlsen, 2018, pp. 587–590.

134 Bemmann, 2007, p. 105; Frank, 2018, p. 557.

135 Waugh, 1998, p. 296.

136 Karlsen, 2018, pp. 589–590.

137 Traditionally, the so-called Hellweg is believed to have played an important role in the trade with Germania Magna. Reichmann, 2001.

138 Galestin, 2010, pp. 81–82.

6.4 The Traders

Even though archaeological material is of great importance in identifying the main flows of goods, it provides few insights about the people that were involved in this trade. Regarding this topic, epigraphic material is a much better source of information. Compared to many other regions in the Roman Empire, the epigraphic material relating to traders is very extensive in the Lower Germanic Limes region.[139] However, it should be noted that most of these inscriptions originate from a limited number of sites. Apart from a few isolated inscriptions from Vechten, Nijmegen, Düsseldorf, Aachen, and Bonn, the vast majority of the inscriptions come from Cologne or from Domburg and Colijnsplaat.[140] Nevertheless, there is no reason to assume that the inscriptions from these sites are not representative of the region in general. The only real limitation of the epigraphic material seems to be that the inscriptions all date into the second and, to a lesser extent, third centuries AD.[141] Therefore, they are not necessarily representative of the situation in the preceding and following centuries.

The most extensive corpus of inscriptions related to trade comes from Domburg and Colijnsplaat, at the mouth of the Scheldt, where more than 150 votive altars, mainly dedicated to the goddess Nehalennia, have been recovered from the sea.[142] Nehalennia was a local goddess, who was honoured primarily by traders who specialised in trade with Britannia and other regions along the North Sea and Channel coasts.[143] Most of the altars seem to have been dedicated after a successful trade mission, as a fulfilment of a vow that was made with a request for the goddess' protection of the dedicant (and his goods). The inscriptions that have been found on many of these altars provide us with valuable information about the trade with these regions, as well as about the organisation of trade in the research area in general. Four of the inscriptions have a consular dating (AD 188, 193, 223, and 227), which together with a peak in the coin finds from Domburg (from AD 180 to 218), indicates that most of the altars were erected in the period between the second half of the second century AD and the first half of the third century AD.[144]

139 Verboven, 2007, pp. 299–300.

140 Schmidts, 2011, p. 99.

141 This is in line with the general 'epigraphic habit' of the Roman Empire. See MacMullen, 1982; Meyer, 1990.

142 Hondius-Crone, 1955; Stuart and Bogaers, 2001.

143 Spickermann, 2018, pp. 601–605.

144 Hassall, 1978, p. 44; Stuart and Bogaers, 2001, pp. 40–41.

A considerable number of the inscriptions mention the profession of the dedicants. Most of them were so-called *negotiatores*, traders who appear to have specialised in long-distance trade.[145] In several cases, the traders explicitly mention that they specialised in a specific type of goods. Three of the traders describe themselves as *negotiatores allecarii*, which shows that they traded fish sauces.[146] Perhaps they shipped the products that were produced on the North Sea coast during the second century AD (see section 6.1), but it is also possible that they got their products from Britannia. Another person, who dedicated with an identical inscription in both Domburg and Colijnsplaat, was a *negotiator cretariu*[*s*], a term which probably denotes a trader in fine pottery or ceramic figurines.[147] It has been suggested that he was a member of a family that ran a large ceramics business in the provincial capital.[148] Inscriptions mentioning *negotiatores cretarii* have also been found in Cologne and Bonn.[149] It has also been documented that there were four *negotiatores salarii*.[150] They were traders in salt, and it is likely that they were connected to the salt production along the North Sea coast or to that of the eastern British coast. Several other inscriptions do not explicitly mention the *negotiatores'* specialisation in a specific type of good. Even though these traders may still have specialised in certain goods, it is also possible that they traded a variety of different goods and therefore did not add such a specification.[151] However, in the case of two inscriptions, the specialisation of the traders becomes clear from the pictorial evidence on the altars themselves, which display images of grapes and ships loaded with barrels.[152] These traders thus seem to have been wine traders, just like the *negotiator vinarius*, who is known from an inscription from Bonn.[153]

Sometimes the inscriptions also inform us about the regions where the traders conducted their business. The already discussed ceramics trader described himself as a *negotiator cretariu*[*s*] *Britannicianu*[*s*]. This indicates that he specialised in the ceramics trade with Britannia. Furthermore, there are three other dedicants that describe themselves as *negotiatores Britannicianii* but without mention of a specialisation in a specific type of trade good.[154] Another

145 Schmidts, 2011, p. 95.
146 AE 2001, 1460; AE 1973, 365; 375.
147 AE 1973, 370; CIL XIII 8793; Hassall, 1978, pp. 44–45.
148 Stuart and Bogaers, 2001, pp. 53–54.
149 IKöln[2] 426, AE 1931, 0027.
150 AE 1973, 362; 364; 378; AE 2001, 1464.
151 Stuart and Bogaers, 2001, p. 36.
152 AE 1975, 650; AE 1980, 658.
153 *Negotiato*[*ri*] / [*v*]*inari*[*o*]. CIL XIII 8105.
154 AE 1975, 651; AE 1983, 721; 722.

trader seems to have focused on the trade with Kent and Boulogne-sur-Mer.[155] He describes himself as a *negotiator Cantianus et Geserecanus*.[156] There is also an inscription where the word *Gallicanu*[*s*] may have been preceded by *negotiator*.[157] If this is indeed the case, this person must have focused on trade with (the coast of) Gaul.[158] Most traders, thus appear to have focused on Britannia, even though there can be no doubt that trade along the North Sea and Channel coasts was also important.

Apart from the *negotiatores*, there are a few other professions that are mentioned in the inscriptions. One dedicator calls himself a *nauta*, which means sailor, but can probably better be translated as ship-owner.[159] An inscription of a *nauta* has also been found in Vechten, but they are much more widespread in the Rhône-Saône area.[160] These *nautae* are believed to have been well-to-do transport entrepreneurs who also participated in long-distance trade as *negotiatores*. Another dedicant worked as an *actor navis* for a certain Florus Severus. This term is unique for Colijnsplaat and is most often translated as captain.[161] An alternative translation assumes that *actor* can be better understood as an agent who managed the administrative affairs for the owner of the ship.[162] The *actor navis* could, in the latter case, have been responsible for the coordination of the shipment of the cargoes of various traders. This could indicate that ships were also leased out.[163] Lastly, there is an *agens rem adiutor*.[164] This dedicant seems to have worked as an agent and assistant for a certain Caius, possibly his brother.[165]

It is therefore clear that practically all the dedicants with a known profession were, in one way or another, active in long-distance trade. A few other inscriptions also show that the dedicants were traders since they used the phrase *pro mercibus conservandis* (or a similar formulation), which can be translated as: 'for the safekeeping of his goods'.[166] Accordingly, it can be safely assumed that the majority of the altars from Domburg and Colijnsplaats were

155 AE 1983, 720.
156 *Negot*(*iator*) *Can*[*tianus*] / [*et*] *Geserecan*[*us*]. It is possible that Cologne was also mentioned in the inscription. Stuart and Bogaers, 2001, p. 59.
157 AE 1973, 374.
158 Hassall, 1978, p. 44.
159 AE 1973, 372; Stuart and Bogaers, 2001, pp. 36–37.
160 CIL XIII 8815; Schmidts, 2011, p. 45.
161 AE 2001, 1489; Stuart and Bogaers, 2001, p. 37.
162 Aubert, 2020, pp. 204–205; Schmidts, 2011, pp. 8–9.
163 Rothenhöfer, 2014, pp. 17–19.
164 AE 2001, 1458.
165 Stuart and Bogaers, 2001, p. 37.
166 Stuart and Bogaers, 2001, pp. 39–40.

erected by traders. If we also assume that the inscriptions discussed above are representative of all the dedications, it is clear that the traders who were active here were a highly specialised professional group. Although there were three dedicants who were active in the Roman army (two *beneficiarii consularis* and one *sesquip(licarius)*), there seems to be too little evidence to believe that much trade was organised directly by the army.[167] It is therefore more likely that the majority of the traders belonged to a civilian 'business class'.[168] Of course, this does not mean that these civilian traders could not have been hired by the state in order to supply the Roman army. However, based on the available source material, it cannot be determined what role the state played in this trade.[169]

Regarding the origin of the traders, the inscriptions can also provide some clarity. Cologne, Trier, Nijmegen, Dormagen, and Ganuenta (near Colijnsplaat) are mentioned as places of origin or residence of dedicants, and there are also people who state that they come from the lands of the Sequani (near Besançon), Valiocasses (near Rouen), and the Rauraci (near Augst). Furthermore, since some altars were made from a very specific type of stone, it is likely that the dedicants of these altars came from the *civitas Tungrorum*.[170] This makes clear that most of the traders came from north-eastern Gaul and the Germanic provinces and not from Britannia. In particular, many traders seem to have come from Cologne, which probably underlines the importance of this city as a central hub in the trade with Britannia.[171]

In Cologne itself, there have also been found many inscriptions mentioning *negotiatores*. It should be noted, though, that not all these *negotiatores* can be regarded as long-distance traders. For a number of inscriptions, it is more likely that the term *negotiator*, at least in this city, was also used as a synonym for 'professional'.[172] Nevertheless, some other inscriptions were made by *negotiatores* in the regular sense, and they can corroborate and expand the information that we have gained from the sanctuaries at the mouth of the Scheldt. As indicated above, the specifications of some merchants from Cologne correspond to those of Domburg and Colijnsplaat. There are also two other specifications, namely a *negotiator seplasarius* and a *negotiator lignarius*, who,

167 *B(ene)f(iciarius) co(n)s(ularis)*. AE 1975, 0625; AE 2001, 1447; AE 2005, 1073. Stuart and Bogaers, 2001, p. 38.

168 Verboven, 2007.

169 Jacobsen believes that the majority of the trade was directed by the state. He does not, however, offer convincing arguments for this. Jacobsen, 1995, pp. 166–168.

170 Stuart and Bogaers, 2001, pp. 47–48.

171 Jacobsen, 1995, p. 167.

172 Galsterer and Galsterer, 2010, p. 356.

respectively, traded in perfume and ointments and in wood.[173] Moreover, two of the *negotiatores* from Cologne dedicate to the Suebian *Matronae* (female deities), which seems to indicate that these traders originated from the lands east of the Rhine.[174] Of particular interest is also the inscription of a *negotiator Britannicianus moritex*.[175] The person in question is namely the same as one of the *negotiatores Britannicianii* from Colijnsplaats. This confirms once again the important role of Cologne in the trade with Britannia. The addition *moritex* is probably Celtic and means overseas trader or sailor.[176]

Outside of Domburg, Colijnsplaat, and Cologne, the number of inscriptions is thus very limited. Nevertheless, these inscriptions are also informative. The two inscriptions from Bonn have already been mentioned above and confirm the existence of a wine and ceramics dealer. The inscription from Düsseldorf is also interesting as it was made by a *negotiator vestiarius*, that is a trader in clothing.[177] The inscriptions from Nijmegen and Vechten have already been discussed in section 4.2.3 and mention a *negotiator frumentarius* from the Nervian region and *nautae* from the *civitas Tungrorum*. Together with another *negotiator frumentarius*, that is known from an inscription from Aachen, these traders emphasize the importance of the grain trade for the economy of the research area.[178]

6.5 Conclusions

There can be no doubt that the total volume of trade expanded and played a crucial role in the economic development of the region. The main driver of this expansion was the large-scale presence of the Roman army in the fortifications along the *limes*. This created a large demand for various trade goods in the region, a process that was gradually reinforced by the urbanisation and general population growth that took place in the region. In order to facilitate the trade that was needed to meet this demand, the Romans set up a well-organised infrastructure network. In combination with the introduction of an institutional framework that was also beneficial to trade, producers and consumers from within and outside the Lower Germanic Limes region could engage in commercial exchange on an unprecedented scale. This allowed a high degree

173 *Negot(i)ato/ri seplasia/rio* and *nego/tiato(ri) / lign(ario)*. IKöln² 428; 431.
174 IKöln² 144; 157.
175 IKöln² 5.
176 Schmidts, 2011, pp. 11–13.
177 *[N]egotiatori vest(iario)*. CIL XIII 8568.
178 *Nego/[tiator] / frumen/[tarius]*. AE 2005, 1061.

of specialisation and division of labour, which led to significant economic growth both inside and outside of the research area.

Unfortunately, it is not possible to determine the extent of this growth with much precision. The reason for this, is that research is currently not developed enough to give more than a limited insight into the role of trade in the region. Nevertheless, from the evidence that we do have at our disposal, it is clear that a large-scale and well-organised system of long-distance trade existed that connected the research area with the rest of the Roman Empire and beyond. In addition to this, much trade took place within the region itself. This shorter distance trade must have been even more important than the trade over longer distances. Still, since the former has left far fewer traces, it is much more difficult to assess its significance.

The amphora data provides clear evidence for the existence of the system of long-distance trade. This data indicates that the region, from the earliest period on, was supplied with a wide range of Mediterranean products. Although Spanish products, mainly Baetican olive oil and fish sauce, accounted for the majority of imports from the beginning of the Roman period, wine came from several regions, including Spain, southern Gaul, Italy, and the Eastern Mediterranean. This changed after the middle of the first century AD, when wine from southern Gaul began to dominate the market. Meanwhile, Baetica remained the most important supplier of olive oil and fish sauces, even though (perhaps repackaged) southern Gallic fish sauce amphorae had also begun to turn up in considerable numbers.

It is therefore clear that from the second half of the first century AD onwards, the amphora market was dominated by products from Baetica and southern Gaul. This was probably due to the large-scale of production in these regions and the good infrastructure connections they had with the research area. It is also possible that the dominance of the amphorae from these two regions reflects a general increase in the total volume of amphorae imports into the region. This could be explained by the increased demand from the growing civilian population, which added to the already large military demand for products. However, since the amphorae material from the research area is still too limited to reconstruct such general trends over time, this cannot be confirmed.

Another important development took place somewhere in the second century AD. In the assemblages from this and the following century, there seems to be a rather large proportion of non-Mediterranean amphorae that came from the nearby provinces of Gallia Belgica and Germania Superior, as well as from the Lower Germanic Limes region itself. It is unclear whether these regional amphorae should be seen as a replacement for, or as an addition to, the imports from the Mediterranean area. In any case, it is clear these products were, at least in terms of transport costs, more cost-effective. Perhaps, the gradual disappearance of Mediterranean fish sauce amphorae, which had already begun in the first century AD, should also be viewed in this light. Although there are several explanations for this development, it is possible that it was related to the emergence of a local fish sauce industry. The increase in regional amphorae can perhaps be seen as a form of import replacement, with the north-western provinces setting up their own production, making them less dependent on Mediterranean imports.

The terra sigillata finds shed light on the evolution of a luxury product's long-distance trade. The analysis of the number of stamps that have been found in the research area shows that the imports took place in three general phases. After a short initial phase, during which almost all objects came from Italy and Lyon, the terra sigillata market was taken over early in the first century AD by southern Gaulish producers, who dominated this market until the end of the century. Then, during the early part of the second century AD, production centres from central and especially eastern Gaul set up their production and took over the market until the end of the second century AD, after which the imports of terra sigillata seem to have become largely insignificant. Here, too, it is quite possible that the success of the more nearby production centres can be explained by lower transportation costs. However, in the transition from southern Gaulish to central and eastern Gaulish centres, the decline of larger supply networks for bulk goods, on which terra sigillata may have piggy-backed, can also have played a role.

The stamps may also give an indication of the development of the total volume of imports over time, even though we should realise that such a reconstruction is, for several reasons, problematic. Still, in general terms, it can be concluded that the total number of imports was probably the highest during the first century AD and significantly lower in the second century AD. Yet it should be noted that there appears to be a clear difference between military and civilian settlements. In the military contexts, the total number of imports is much higher in the period before the second century AD. In the civilian context, on the other hand, the largest number of imports date to the second century AD. It is thus clear that, after the great importance of the military market in the first century AD, the civilian market for terra sigillata had become increasingly important during the second century AD.

In addition to the trade with the Mediterranean and the research area's neighbouring provinces, it is also clear that trade took place with Britannia and with the free Germanic tribes on the eastern side of the Rhine. We can assume that this trade, too, was important for the economic development of the Lower

Germanic Limes region. However, because of the seemingly organic nature of the traded goods, very little is known about these trade flows. Accordingly, it is practically impossible to say much about the nature and extent of this trade.

It is an interesting question to what extent long-distance trade was organised by the state or by the free market. Especially during the earliest phase of the Roman occupation, it may be difficult to imagine that the sudden large demand of the Roman army could be met directly by trade through the free market alone. However, at least regarding the amphora and terra sigillata trades, there seems to be no evidence for direct state involvement in the supply of the army. Furthermore, there is no convincing evidence in the epigraphic material of large-scale military involvement in long-distance trade. Therefore, it can best be assumed that most of the trade was indeed guided by the free market. Of course, this does not mean that the state was not at all involved in the supply of the army. It is well conceivable that the state worked closely with private merchants, as both parties had an interest in supplying goods to the Roman soldiers.

The rich epigraphic material that was dedicated by traders, clearly shows that this trade was organised by a highly specialised group of professionals. The inscriptions mention a wide variety of specialisations in specific product categories, or geographical areas. In addition, there are quite a few inscriptions in which the dedicant does not mention any specific specialisation, which means that he probably traded several products. This picture also fits in well with the production level of the 'nucleated workshops' discussed in the previous chapter, where specialised producers focused on production, while specialised traders focused on trade. Of course, we cannot assume that the traders who have made themselves known to us by means of these inscriptions are representative of all the people who engaged in trade in the research area during the Roman period. There must also have been, certainly in the case of shorter-distance trade, many traders who were a lot less specialised, as well as many producers who traded their own products. Nevertheless, it remains a good indication of the high degree of organisation of the long-distance trade that we have found so many inscriptions of this specific group of specialised traders.

CHAPTER 7

Living Standards

In the previous chapters, it has become evident that the Lower Germanic Limes region experienced significant economic growth during the Roman period. All sectors of the economy, whether it was agriculture, exploitation of raw materials, manufacturing, or trade, expanded considerably. Even though it remains difficult to characterise this economic growth, it is clear that it was not merely the result of an increase in scale. In all these sectors, there are indications that the economy also grew because it became more efficient. An important question that remains, though, is to what extent the economic growth that took place in the research area, outstripped population growth. In other words, in addition to aggregate economic growth, was there per capita economic growth? Ideally, in order to answer this question, we would like to set the total output of the economy against the total population of the region and see to what extent the relative size of these variables changed over time. However, since both variables are unknown and the best we can get are very imprecise approximates using proxy datasets, the estimation of per capita economic growth with this method very much remains guesswork. Accordingly, we would not be able to decide whether the economic development of the region corresponds better to a Malthusian or a sustainable growth scenario.

Still, there might be, as I hope to demonstrate in this chapter, an alternative way to find out to what extent the research area experienced (sustained) per capita economic growth. As I have already explained in the introduction, there is a direct relationship between per capita incomes and living standards. This means that if it can be shown that the living standards of the population in the region increased during the Roman period, we can be sure that the economic growth also encompassed a certain degree of per capita growth. Of course, regarding the relationship between per capita incomes and living standards, it is important to realise that the distribution of the per capita growth among different parts of the population might have varied.[1] For example, it is quite possible that the growth only improved the standard of living of a certain group, while that of the rest of the population remained the same. Thus, even though per capita economic growth does increase the average standard of living of the population, it does not necessarily improve the standard of living for the whole population, as inequality may also increase. Accordingly, if we want to

1 Cf. Jongman, 2007b, pp. 594–596.

© ERIK TIMMERMAN, 2024 | DOI:10.1163/9789004682214_008

know to what extent the standard of living of the population increased during the Roman period, it is less interesting to look at the elite. This is the case because if we see an increase in the standard of living here, it is also possible that this was the result of increasing inequality. Yet when we see that the standard of living of the lower social classes has risen, we can be sure that this is due to per capita economic growth.[2]

It is therefore the main aim of this chapter to find out to what extent the living standards of the general population in the Lower Germanic Limes region improved. But how is it possible to identify an improvement in living standards in the ancient evidence? First, it is good to recall the definition that was given in the introduction of living standards (or wealth) as 'the total of desirable goods, social and material, possessed by someone or existing in a community'.[3] Thus, in order to find out whether living standards improved, we want to find indications that people had more (or better quality) goods and services available to them than before.

There are several ways in which such indications can be found.[4] With regard to the Roman Empire in general, some scholars have compared documentary evidence of wages with that of the prices of goods, in order to find out to what extent these wages exceeded the estimated costs of subsistence.[5] Though, in principle, this is a good method, the data is so scarce that such calculations contain a very large margin of error. Probably a more reliable way to identify an increased standard of living is to look at changes in the consumption patterns of the (general) population, to see whether people increasingly succeeded in meeting their needs and desires for specific consumer goods. In his theoretical discussion of consumption in the Roman Empire, Greene makes a distinction between 'consumption' and 'consumerism'.[6] He defines consumption as biological needs, such as food, drink, and clothing, needs that are essential for human subsistence, although they are to a certain extent subject to cultural influences. Consumerism, on the other hand, he defines as desires for material goods or foodstuffs that transcend the subsistence level and are to an even larger extent determined by cultural factors. Since an increase in per capita income would allow (at least certain) people to increase

2 In theory, there is also the possibility that inequality decreased in Roman times, which would mean a rising standard of living for the lower classes. However, considering the egalitarian nature of the population in the research area during the Late Iron Age (see section 2.2), this is not really a realistic option.

3 Smith, 2019b, p. 489.

4 Drexhage, Konen and Ruffing, 2002b, pp. 161–191; Jongman, 2007b.

5 E.g. Rathbone, 2009; Allen, 2009.

6 Greene, 2008, pp. 65–66. See also: Ray, 2009, p. 25.

the level of their consumption above subsistence level, it is the consumption of goods with a relatively high income elasticity (luxury goods) in which we are primarily interested when investigating a possible improvement in living standards.[7] Lastly, indications of an improvement in the biological standard of living might be found in skeletal data.[8] Since people's stature can, to a certain extent, reflect their nutritional status, measurements of human bone material can provide insights into the quality of their diets.[9] In general, people who have had a good and varied diet during their (early) life are larger than people who ate less well or were malnourished. As a result, an increase in the average height of a population can be a good indication of an increase in the standard of living.[10]

In theory, there are thus some viable methods to find indications for improvements in living standards. Yet in practice, finding such indications is much more complicated. The reason for this is that the amount of available evidence is very limited and can often be interpreted ambiguously. The debate on a possible increase in the standard of living of the Roman population is therefore still in its infancy. This is certainly the case with regard to the Lower Germanic Limes region, where questions about the standard of living have received virtually no attention at all. Nevertheless, I believe that in this region too, we can find some first indications of an increase in the standard of living of the general population.

As there is neither wage and price data nor a sufficiently large human bone dataset available for the region, these indications are to be found in changing consumption patterns. As I will argue in this chapter, important changes in housebuilding and portable material culture (metal objects and pottery) suggest that part of the population in the region was increasingly able to obtain various luxury products. However, it is important to point out in advance that this argument is to be regarded as very preliminary. As I will make clear in the following pages, the interpretation of the material sources as evidence for an improvement in living standards is far from straightforward. Nevertheless, in combination with the economic developments of the research area that have been discussed in the previous chapters, I believe that they are a good first indication of an increase in living standards.

7 Jongman, 2007b, p. 609.
8 Garnsey, 1999, pp. 51–61; Kron, 2019; Jongman, Jacobs and Klein Goldewijk, 2019.
9 Of course, other factors, such as diseases and genetics, also play an important role.
10 However, there are many methodological issues that make estimations of such averages for the Roman world problematic. Flohr, 2019.

7.1 Housebuilding

Domestic architecture is generally considered to be the best indicator of the wealth of people in pre-industrial societies.[11] Accordingly, improvements in the standard of living of the general population of the Lower Germanic Limes region during the Roman period, seem to be most clearly visible in the archaeological record through changing traditions in rural housebuilding.

These developments have been investigated in great detail by Habermehl in his study of villa development in the northern provinces.[12] He differentiates between four general categories of houses that existed in this area in the Late Iron Age and the Roman period.[13] The first of these categories is the so-called traditional house, which is the only category that existed in the Late Iron Age. These houses were constructed in a native tradition using local, organic materials. Within this category, there is a general differentiation between the houses in the northern and the southern areas of the research area (see section 2.2). In the north, these post-built houses took the form of byre houses, combining living quarters and stables under one roof, while in the southern regions, these houses were constructed as smaller, separate buildings. The second category of houses is the Romanised traditional house. These houses were practically the same as the traditional houses but included certain elements that clearly reflect Mediterranean influences, for example, the addition of a portico (a colonnaded gallery).[14] Furthermore, they were sometimes ornamented with non-traditional building materials, such as tiles, plaster, natural stone, and even window glass.[15] The third category is the timber framework house. These houses were constructed in a novel way, including new architectural techniques and utilizing new materials. They were usually built on a stone foundation, and the walls consisted of a solid wooden framework construction, which allowed for a heavier roof covered with tiles. Sometimes a façade was created through the construction of a risalith (a protruding gallery). The fourth category is the multi-roomed house on stone foundations, which is generally referred to as a villa in the literature. These villas were built on linear stone foundations and consisted of various separate rooms. The foundations were often low stone walls on which wooden framework walls were placed, although sometimes these walls were entirely constructed of stone. A façade

11 Smith, 2019b, p. 3.

12 Habermehl, 2013.

13 Habermehl, 2013, p. 67.

14 For discussion of these so-called porticus houses, see Vos, 2009, pp. 237–251; Heeren, 2009, pp. 155–160.

15 van Enckevort and Hendriks, 2014, p. 237; Brüggler, 2018, p. 299.

was a standard element of these houses and usually took the form of a portico or a portico-risalith façade.

Much variety existed within this last category of houses. There were a few very large monumental complexes with a main house with more than 30 rooms, such as Aldenhoven-Schleiden and Basse-Wavre-L'Hosté, but these were exceptional. The vast majority of the villas in the region were small or medium-sized, which, according to the gradation system used by Habermehl, corresponds to less than 10 and between 10 and 29 rooms, respectively.[16] The already mentioned study by Jeneson confirms this, by showing that in the area between Tongeren and Cologne, small and medium-sized villas, with a practically equal share, make up 96% of the total (usable) villa settlement evidence.[17]

As I have mentioned above, the traditional house was the only type of house that was built in the pre-Roman Iron Age. In the course of the Roman period, an increasing number of people adopted any of the other three housebuilding traditions. Yet there are significant differences, in this respect, between the northern and the southern parts of the research area. In the northern part, the adoption of radically new housebuilding traditions was rare and relatively late.[18] Traditional houses remained the dominant category throughout the Roman period and, in general, it seems that the addition of Romanised elements to some of these houses only occurred from the second century AD onwards. Moreover, the construction of timber framework houses and villas was exceptional and was, generally speaking, similarly late. The story is different in the southern part of the research area, where a radical break with the pre-Roman housebuilding traditions can be observed.[19] During Roman times, a few of the houses discovered in this area were still constructed in the traditional way (sometimes with Romanised elements), or were, from around the second half of the first century AD, constructed as timber framework houses.[20] However, in this same period, the vast majority of houses discovered in this area were built as multi-roomed houses on stone foundations, so that this region increasingly developed into a villa landscape.

The trend towards new housebuilding traditions, especially visible in the southern regions, indicates a clear increase in the level of consumption of

16 Habermehl, 2013, p. 104.

17 Her dataset contains settlement evidence from 51 sites that are detailed enough for this analysis. Jeneson, 2013, p. 90.

18 Habermehl, 2013, pp. 56–59.

19 Habermehl, 2013, pp. 60–65.

20 However, it should be realised that the traditional houses are much less likely to be discovered. Jeneson, 2013, pp. 155–156.

luxury goods by the inhabitants of the research area. The new construction techniques, often requiring professional architects and builders, and especially the use of new building materials, represent a vast increase in the amount of wealth that people invested in their houses.[21] While the traditional houses were built exclusively of relatively cheap organic materials from local sources, the new housebuilding traditions required much more expensive materials, such as stone and ceramic building materials. Since significant costs accompanied the quarrying, production, as well as the transportation of these materials, it is evident that these new houses were vastly more expensive consumer goods than the traditional ones.

It is therefore tempting to interpret these changes in housebuilding traditions as a direct reflection of changes in wealth. However, even though wealth formed a prerequisite for investments in housebuilding, it is important to realise that these changes are essentially the result of the adoption of 'Roman ideas about the house as a medium for self-representation and social distinction.'[22] In the Late Iron Age societies, the house had only played a minor role in demarking differences in social status. In fact, in traditional housebuilding, more emphasis was placed on the expression of ideas of communality and collective identities. In the Roman period, though, this changed, and the house increasingly attained a central role as a platform for the competitive display of status and prestige among higher social groups.[23] Moreover, housebuilding also served as a powerful tool to express social relationships that seem to have become increasingly hierarchised already by the end of the Late Iron Age. This increasing hierarchisation of society is, for instance, visible in the spatial organisation of rural settlements.[24] Already in several Late Iron Age settlements in the southern loess region, a trend is discernible in which certain houses were located in prominent positions within the settlement, which is suggestive of asymmetrical social relationships between a dominant family and dependent families. This trend continued and intensified in the Roman period, and housebuilding, therefore, became increasingly important in demonstrating these social differences.

---

21 Habermehl, 2013, pp. 73–75.

22 Roymans and Derks, 2011, p. 15. As such, this social definition of the house, provides a third definition of the villa, in addition to the morphological and economic definitions of the villa that were already given in section 4.2. For criticism on the interpretation of the villa as an element of conspicuous consumption, see Woolf, 1998, pp. 148–149; Martins, 2004.

23 Roymans and Derks, 2011, pp. 15–16.

24 Habermehl, 2013, pp. 96–99.

There is, of course, an obvious argument to be made against the above interpretation of the changed rural house building traditions as an indication of an increase in the standard of living of the general population. If the new types of houses are believed only to have been the properties of a privileged elite, the increasing investments do not necessarily reflect an increase in general wealth. Instead, they are, then, only indicative of a social divide between small groups of powerful families and a large group of powerless, dependent peasants. Although the construction of several of the large multi-roomed and luxurious villas surely reflects a growing dominance of certain mighty families over part of the rural population, the high density of medium and, especially, small-sized villas in the loess zone indicates that, apart from this small group of large landowners, a broad middle class of landowning farmers existed.[25] Of course, we must bear in mind that this middle class was not a homogenous group and that large differences in social status must have existed between individuals.[26] The farmers who owned most of the middle-sized villas probably belonged to a kind of sub-elite, while some of the owners of the small villas might not even have been too far removed from lower social groups. However, what is clear is that there was a relatively large group of people in the research area who could afford to invest significantly in their homes.

Moreover, the assertion that the inhabitants of these medium and small-sized villas were merely tenant farmers, who leased their property from large landowners, is highly unlikely. After all, it would be strange if a large landowner who owned multiple rural estates would invest his money to develop residences on more than a few of them, or if a tenant would spend large sums on a house that was the property of his landlord.[27] Instead, it is much more likely that the large-scale occurrence of these villas in the archaeological record, indeed, reflects the extension of increased purchasing power to the middle class, who, like the elite, invested their wealth in housebuilding for self-representation and social distinction. The houses of these people could, of course, not compete with those of the elite, which were vastly more expensive. Yet they could imitate the examples set by the elite to a certain extent by building on a smaller scale, with less elaborate construction techniques, and through the use of cheaper building materials. In this way, middle class

25 Roymans and Derks, 2011, p. 20. It is interesting to note that there does not seem to have been a direct relation between the size of villas and the presence of luxurious elements such as hypocausts, baths, and rich building materials. Thus, bigger did not always mean better. Jeneson, 2013, pp. 90–91.

26 Unfortunately, there is not much additional evidence (for example, epigraphical) to confirm or refute assumptions about the social status of the villa inhabitants.

27 Woolf, 1998, pp. 163–164; Roymans and Derks, 2011, pp. 20–21.

farmers could compete with their peers while at the same time distinguishing themselves from groups lower down the social ladder.[28]

These lower social groups are believed to have largely continued the pre-Roman housebuilding traditions. However, since their dwellings were constructed from organic materials, they are much more difficult to identify in the archaeological record. We should therefore, as Jeneson has convincingly argued, allow for the existence of substantially more post-built houses than has previously been assumed (see section 4.2).[29] The detailed excavations in the lignite mining area near Hambach, which perhaps are representative for the rest of the loess region, show that the proportion of stone-built to post-built settlements was roughly equal. Thus, although we should certainly allow for a significantly larger quantity of traditional house types in the region, their number does not seem to have been large enough to erase the dominance of stone-built houses in the landscape. Accordingly, the argument that it was not just the elite that invested their wealth in their houses holds up.

The changes in housebuilding in the southern part of the research area are thus a clear indication that members of the upper and middle classes increased their consumption levels during the Roman period. The question remains, however, whether the money that these people invested in their homes was earned by the selling of agricultural surpluses on the farm itself, or if it was perhaps capital that had been obtained from outside of the agricultural world. For the direct hinterland of Cologne, for example, it has been argued that the villas built there, from the second half of the first century AD onwards, mainly belonged to veterans who had been allocated pieces of land.[30] In this case, the changes in housebuilding would not so much indicate an increase in the prosperity of the general population but only underline the good economic position of the former soldiers.[31] Unfortunately, it is not possible to find out exactly where the money that was invested in villas came from.[32]

Nevertheless, the veteran-scenario is probably not a major obstacle for the interpretation of rising living standards of the general population in the southern regions, as it seems that veterans mainly settled in the immediate vicinity of their old bases or in large urban settlements and not in the rural hinterland.[33] Of course, the number of veterans who settled in rural settlements after their

28 Roymans and Derks, 2011, pp. 29–30.

29 Jeneson, 2013, pp. 155–156.

30 Gaitzsch, 1986, p. 408; Rothenhöfer, 2005a, p. 47.

31 Such a scenario is known, for instance, from Roman Syria. Hoffmann-Salz, 2014, pp. 296–297.

32 Woolf, 1998, p. 48.

33 Lenz, 2006, pp. 89–90; Roymans, 2011, p. 141.

military service must have been higher in areas that supplied large numbers of auxiliary troops, such as the Batavian area. In the southern part of the research area, though, this appears to have been much less common, and the settlement of veterans was most likely limited to a strip of about 20 kilometres west of the Rhine.[34] Furthermore, even in this small area, the large-scale settlement of veterans is far from undisputable, and a (Gallic) civilian background has also been suggested for the settlers.[35]

Therefore, most of the villas in the loess area were probably the property of civilians. Surely, it cannot be said with complete certainty that the invested capital was actually earned on the farm. However, based on the large-scale development that the agricultural sector underwent during the Roman period (see section 4.2), this is by far the most logical explanation. This interpretation is further endorsed by the fact that many of the villa settlements seem to have evolved from native settlements.[36] Moreover, it appears that most of the villas started out small and simple and were gradually expanded with the addition of new rooms, or architectural elements.[37] This also fits better with the image of the farmer experiencing a steady increase in his prosperity than with the image of an external settler who came to the area with a large sum of money to build a villa from scratch.

In the northern regions, the scale of investments in housebuilding was clearly much smaller. There are several possible explanations for this. The first of these is a practical one. Building stone was not as readily available in the northern regions as in the southern regions. The acquisition of building materials, thus, involved significantly higher costs since the material needed to be transported over much longer distances.[38] In the northern regions, a house largely constructed of stone would, therefore, represent a much higher investment than a similar house in the south. This may partly explain the fact that only a wealthy few in the north were willing and able to make such an investment. Related to this is the likely possibility that the increase in purchasing power of the inhabitants of the northern regions was smaller than that of those from the south. It is not hard to believe that the fertile loess soils of the south permitted larger agricultural surpluses than the poorer soils of the northern regions. Combined with the fact that the construction of the new

34 Lenz, 2006, p. 90.

35 Lenz, 1998, p. 69; Heimberg, 2003, pp. 71–77.

36 It should be noted that continuity is often difficult to prove, since the Late Iron Age settlements are usually difficult to identify. Roymans, 2011, p. 155; Habermehl, 2013, pp. 33–39.

37 Habermehl, 2013, pp. 72–73.

38 Even though this will have been less of an issue for sites located along a main waterway.

house types was relatively more expensive, this offers a reasonable explanation for the general lower degree of investment in housebuilding in the north.

However, apart from these economic explanations, the reluctance to adopt radically new housebuilding traditions may also be rooted in the socio-cultural characteristics of society in the northern regions. Roymans asserts that, certainly in the first century AD, the adherence to martial and pastoral values and norms among the native population and, in particular among the native elite, made these people less receptive to the cultural influences that caused the significant changes in housebuilding in the southern regions.[39] Moreover, the trend towards increasing hierarchisation, which in the southern regions originated in the Late Iron Age, seems to have begun later in the north. Only from the mid first century AD onwards, did the spatial structure of northern settlements begin to reflect an increasingly hierarchised society.[40] This may not only be an indication that the development towards an increasingly unequal society was later, but perhaps also that this development was less profound. In a less hierarchised society, expressing status and prestige through housebuilding must have been less relevant.

In any case, the relatively sparse adoption of new housebuilding traditions in the northern regions cannot be taken as an indication of rising living standards for a large part of the general population, as was the case for the south. The few real villas that have been discovered in the northern regions probably only reflect the increased wealth of members of the elite.[41] Furthermore, even though the use of new materials for the construction of the Romanised traditional and timber framework houses may also indicate a somewhat higher degree of investment, these houses are most often interpreted as the dwellings of returned veterans.[42] Accordingly, these changes may not reflect the increased wealth of the general civilian population. It should be noted, though, that the interpretation of these houses as veteran farms is mainly based on the Batavian area, where a large part of the population served in the army. Whether this also applies to the other areas can perhaps be questioned, and the possibility that a part of the non-military population also invested in their homes can certainly not be excluded entirely.[43]

---

39 Roymans, 1996, p. 79.
40 Habermehl, 2013, pp. 96–97.
41 van Enckevort, 2012, p. 280.
42 Vos, 2009, p. 250; Heeren, 2009, p. 160.
43 Cf. de Bruin, 2017, pp. 11–17.

7.2 Portable Material Culture

Thus, for the non-villa landscapes of the research area, changes in house-building provide no convincing evidence for increased living standards of the general population. But what other indications of changes in the level of consumption can be found in the archaeological record? Another type of evidence that has great potential to answer questions about changes in the level of consumption of luxury goods is the category of portable material culture. This broad category includes a wide variety of items for everyday use, of which especially ceramic and metal objects have survived in considerable quantities in the archaeological record. For the Roman Empire in general, several scholars have mentioned a vast increase in the total volume and variety of such products at Roman sites, in comparison to sites from earlier or later periods.[44] It is therefore interesting to see whether there are also indications of such a 'consumer revolution' in the Lower Germanic Limes region.[45]

7.2.1 *Metal Objects*

An increase in the total volume of portable material culture during the Roman period can most clearly be illustrated by data from the Portable Antiquities of the Netherlands (PAN) project.[46] This project has collected an enormous number of small metal finds that have been discovered in the Netherlands.[47] Interestingly, since the dataset is not just limited to the Roman period, it also allows comparisons with other periods. An analysis of the metal finds from the period between 250 BC and AD 750, can give a good overview of how the total number of metal objects in circulation developed over this long period of time (Figure 23).[48] The graph shows that the number of objects that date to the Late Iron Age is very low. Then, in the early Roman period, the number of objects that were lost must have increased dramatically. The graph peaks in the first half of the first century AD, and the number of objects stays high for at least

44 Woolf, 1998, pp. 171–174; Hingley, 2005, p. 107; Ward-Perkins, 2005, pp. 89–90; Pitts, 2019.

45 This term is used by Woolf, 1998, p. 174.

46 *Portable Antiquities of the Netherlands*, no date.

47 The ever-expanding project also aims to collect objects made from other types of material, but, at the moment, the very small amounts of these objects pale in comparison to the 66,350 metal objects that have already been documented. A similar project is being conducted in Belgium. However, since the number of objects in this project is still very small, I have not included it. *MEDEA*, no date.

48 I have excluded coin finds from the dataset, as these have already been discussed in section 3.4.2. The dataset used for this analysis encompassed 20,861 metal objects in total. The vast majority (66%) of these objects have been categorised as jewellery (mainly fibulae).

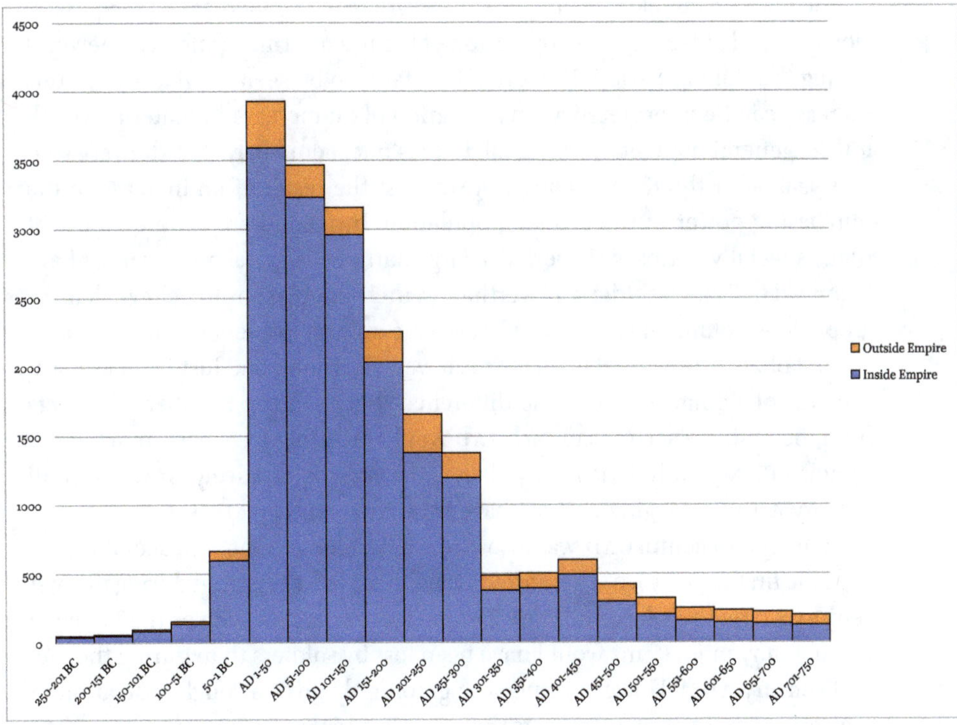

FIGURE 23 The total number of dated metal objects that have been collected in the PAN-database in 50-year periods

the first half of the second century AD.[49] In the second half of this century, the numbers seem to have been significantly lower, and this downward trend continued during the third century AD. By the fourth and fifth centuries AD, the number of objects in circulation was again very low, but it is only after the fifth century AD, that the number of finds, at least in the part that falls within the (former) Roman Empire, is roughly reduced to pre-Roman levels.

49 Regarding the peak in the first half of the first century AD, it should be mentioned that this peak is probably to a certain extent inflated by the fact that a relatively large proportion of the objects that date to this period have been dated very precisely. Of all the objects from inside the Empire that are dated within a period of 50 or fewer years, 83% of the objects are dated within this specific period. The reason for the inflation is that many of these precisely dated objects contribute their entire weight in a single period, whereas the weight of more broadly dated objects is distributed proportionally across several periods. Accordingly, it seems more likely that the number of metal finds from the first half of the first century AD should be more along the lines of those from the following two 50-year periods, or even below that.

The graph, thus, clearly shows the magnitude of the increase in the possession of metal objects by the population of the research area (and even beyond) during the Roman period. However, it remains to be seen to what extent this increase can be interpreted as an indication of an increase in material wealth for the general population. After all, it does not seem likely that the very sudden peak after the Roman conquest was just the result of an increase in the purchasing power of the civilian population. Instead, there can be no doubt that, especially in this early period, a large part of the metal objects must have belonged to Roman soldiers. Nevertheless, there are reasons to believe that the graph does not merely reflect the large-scale military presence in the region.

First of all, if the metal objects that have been found had just been the possessions of Roman soldiers, the differences between the number of objects from the first and second centuries AD would probably have been much more significant. Not only is it believed that the size of the army in the second century AD was roughly half of that of the first century AD (see section 3.1), but the second century AD was also a much quieter and more peaceful period than the first century AD. Therefore, it is not hard to believe that during the first century AD, with its large military campaigns and events such as the Batavian revolt, many more items would have been lost by soldiers than during the second century AD.[50] However, since the graph only gives a rough indication of the development of metal objects that were in circulation, it is risky to base too precise conclusions on it.

A more important reason why we should probably not just explain the metal objects as items lost by military personnel is the fact that the objects were not just found at former military sites or in their immediate surroundings. Figure 24 shows the distribution of the metal finds that date from the Roman period.[51] What is most striking, is that the vast majority of the finds are concentrated in the central and eastern parts of the river area. The reason for this is that metal finds are very well conserved in the river clay, in contrast to, for example, the more southerly sandy soils. Moreover, compared to the rest of the country, the archaeological remains in the river area are fairly close to the surface. This largely explains the much larger density of sites with finds and the number of finds per site in this area.[52] Furthermore, the distribution of the finds that exclusively date to the pre-Roman period, a period when there was no Roman

50 Even though we can be sure that during periods of great turmoil, many metal objects were really lost by people, it should be realised that the objects that were found could also have been deposited ritualistically or simply thrown away. Furthermore, it is known that metal objects were re-used or recycled. Heeren and van der Feijst, 2017, pp. 255–258.

51 I have concentrated the finds according to the modern places where they were found, in order to keep the map clearer.

52 Heeren and van der Feijst, 2017, p. 2.

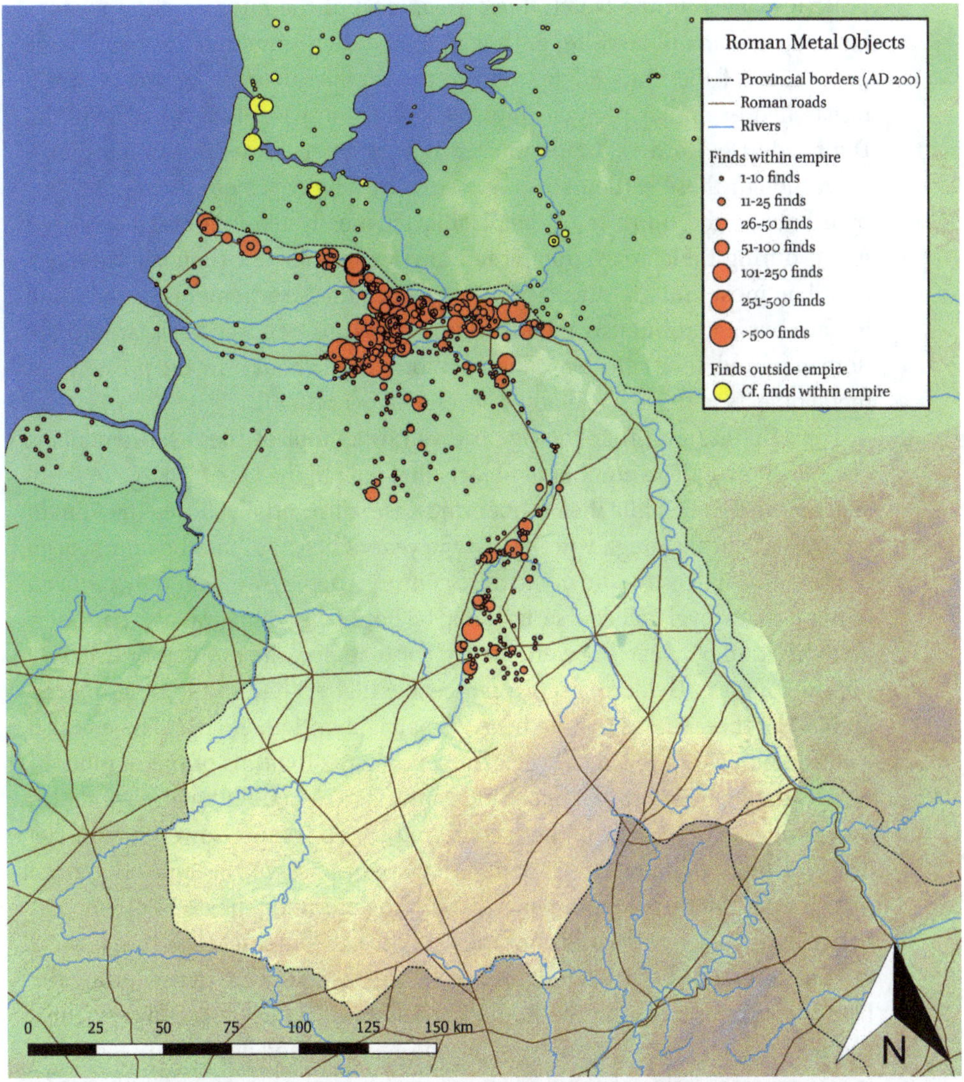

FIGURE 24 The distribution of the metal objects collected in the PAN-database and dated within the Roman period

military presence, also largely corresponds to the general distribution pattern (though with a much lower number of total finds). This seems to confirm that the presence of the army was not the deciding factor for the spread of the objects during the Roman period. Accordingly, we can safely assume that if the level of recovery in the other parts of the country had been comparable to that in the Dutch River Area, there would also have been found many more metal objects in areas that were further removed from the *limes*.

Besides, even in the Dutch River Area, most of the finds do not appear to have come from military sites or their immediate surroundings. Instead, a large proportion of the finds originate from the rural settlement landscape. Well-researched examples of such rural settlements are Tiel-Passewaaij, Wijk bij Duurstede-De Horden, Geldermalsen-Hondsgemet, and Elst-Brienenshof.[53] Even though these settlements were small rural villages consisting of a few byre houses, the number of metal objects (mostly fibulae) that have been found during their excavation, is not any less significant than the numbers found on most military sites.[54] Moreover, since these settlements are believed to have been continuously inhabited from the Late Iron Age until far into the Roman period, they can give valuable information about how the presence of metal objects in these settlements developed over time.

The general trend that can be observed in all four of these settlements is clear (Figure 25). The number of objects that date to the Late Iron Age in these settlements is low, while the numbers increase substantially during the Roman period, with peaks roughly in the first 150 years AD. After that, the numbers go down again, and by the end of the third century AD, they are, generally, reduced to pre-Roman levels. Of course, it should be noted that there was also considerable variation between the settlements. For instance, the number of Iron Age objects found in Geldermalsen is noticeably higher than in the other places, and in Elst there seems to have been a small late-antique revival. There is also a considerable difference between the settlements in terms of the number of objects dating from the first or second centuries AD. In Geldermalsen and Elst, the number of objects from the second century AD is much lower than in Tiel and Wijk bij Duurstede. This variation can also be observed in some other rural settlements.[55] It therefore remains difficult to determine the exact differences between the first and second centuries. What is, in any case, clear is that there is a big difference between the number of objects that were in use during the Late Iron Age and during the Roman period (at least until roughly the third century AD). As a result, it appears that the general trend depicted in Figure 23 is also representative of the development of the number of metal objects in the majority of rural settlements.

53 van der Roest, 1988; Heeren, 2009, pp. 118–153; van Renswoude, 2009; Heeren and van der Feijst, 2017, pp. 262–267.

54 The largest collection of fibulae from the Netherlands, for instance, comes from Tiel-Passewaaij. Heeren and van der Feijst, 2017, p. 302.

55 Heeren and van der Feijst, 2017, pp. 303–308.

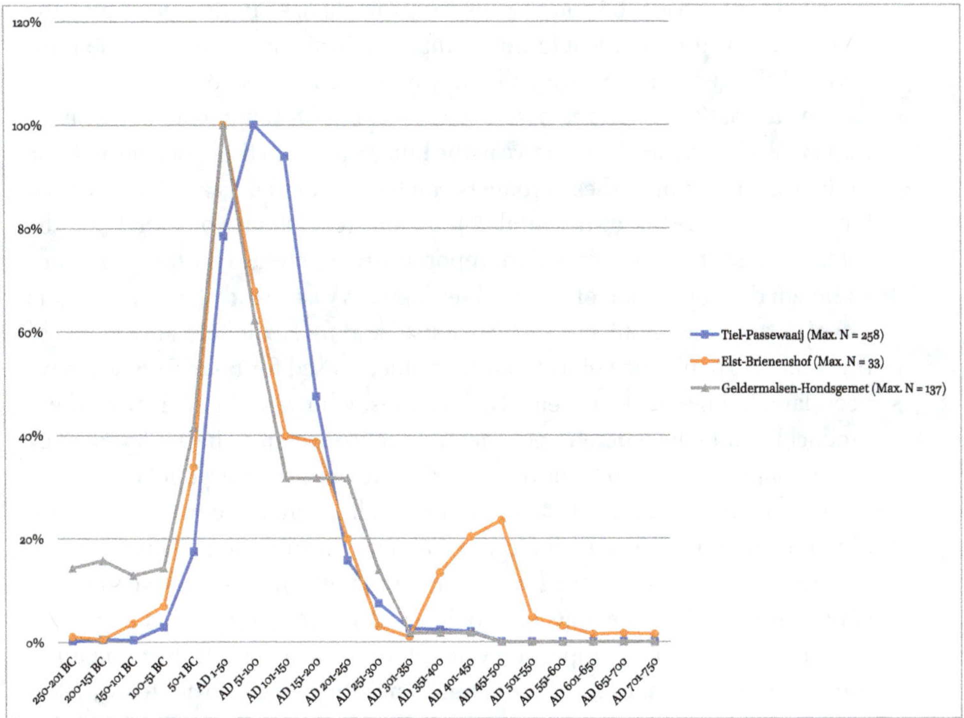

FIGURE 25 The development of the number of metal objects in specific rural settlements
Note: The data is presented as a percentage of the maximum (the period in which the number of objects is highest). Wijk bij Duurstede-De Horden could not be added, since the data in the original publication was not organised in a usable manner.

Of course, the question remains how these objects ended up in these settlements. Generally, there seem to be two ways in which this could have happened.[56] First, it is possible that the objects were brought in by veterans who returned to their hometown after their military service.[57] This is probably the case for most of the militaria and horse gear found in the rural settlements.[58] Furthermore, this may apply to the other objects that have been found, as veterans could have bought them with their pay during, or after,

56 Surely, one can think of several other ways in which the objects came to the settlements, but I believe these two will have been the most important.

57 It seems unlikely that many veterans from other areas settled in the (native) rural settlements in this part of the research area.

58 It should, however, be realised that weaponry and horse gear were also used by civilians. Nicolay, 2007, pp. 211–217.

their military service. In this case, as with the changes in housebuilding, the increased consumption would not so much indicate an increase in the prosperity of the general population but only of the (former) soldiers.

The alternative is that the objects were acquired through market exchange by people who had not been active in the Roman army. In this case, the increase in the consumption of these products can be interpreted as a reflection of an increase in the wealth of the rural population. Yet it should be noted that the veterans may still have played an important role here as cultural mediators. Although the population of the rural settlements was already familiar with the use of certain metal objects, such as fibulae and tools, the Roman variants of these and certainly new objects, such as objects used for body care, will have been largely unknown to them. The veterans, who were familiar with these products and knew where to get them, therefore, seem to have played a key role in making these products known among the indigenous population.[59]

Thus, in order to find out the extent to which the increase in the consumption of metal objects can be interpreted as an indication of an increase in the material wealth of the general rural population, it is important to determine which proportion of the objects were brought home or purchased by returning veterans and which proportion was obtained by the rest of the population through market exchange. Unfortunately, since the objects do not tell whether they were bought by a regular native inhabitant or by a (former) soldier, this question is practically impossible to answer.[60]

Much depends on the extent to which veterans actually returned to their native villages. It has already been indicated above that many veterans probably settled in the immediate vicinity of their old bases, or in large urban settlements. Settlement in the rural hinterland, at least in the southern areas, seems to have been much less common. However, it is unclear whether this was also the case for the northern areas. Particularly in the *civitas Batavorum*, where the majority of metal objects have been found, returning veterans may have played a much more important role.[61] The main reason for this is the intensive military recruitment among the Batavians, about which we are informed by Tacitus.[62] According to demographic calculations, this must mean that every Batavian household had, on average, at least one son serving in the

59 Derks and Roymans, 2006, pp. 133–134; Heeren, 2014, pp. 167–169.

60 A partial solution would be to characterise the database finds as either (typical) 'military' or 'civilian', but this has a number of implementation flaws.

61 Vos, 2009, pp. 260–265; Roymans, 2011.

62 Tac. Germ. 29; Tac. Hist. 4,12.

Roman army.[63] Even though it should be noted that these calculations assume that all the Batavian cohorts mentioned by Tacitus consisted entirely of ethnic Batavians, something that is not certain, it is clear that a very significant proportion of the Batavian men served in the Roman army.[64] Of course, not all soldiers will have completed their 25 years of service, but there can be no doubt that many Batavian soldiers successfully reached retirement and could return to their homelands.[65] In fact, there is sufficient archaeological evidence that demonstrates that Batavian veterans did indeed return to their hometowns.[66] However, it is unknown on what scale this happened and what impact this had on the native societies. Jasper de Bruin has argued that the significance of returning veterans for their native societies has often been overemphasised.[67] He points out that the evidence for the large-scale return of Batavian veterans to rural settlements is meagre and that it is not even certain that many veterans wanted to return. He also indicates that the role of the veterans is often presented as too positivistic. Instead of just seeing the veterans as the successful bearers of Roman culture, he points out that some of them may have suffered from severe physical and mental discomforts.

In sum, much uncertainty exists regarding the role of returning veterans in rural societies. We can be sure that in the Batavian area, returning veterans played a more important role than elsewhere. Still, this cannot be taken as the sole explanation for the much larger density of finds in this area, since metal finds are, because of the soils, also much more likely to be found here. Nevertheless, we should certainly realise that a large proportion of the metal objects from the Roman period that were found in the Dutch part of the research area were imported by veterans. Yet it seems unlikely that this was the only reason for the enormous increase in the number of metal finds. I therefore believe that it is best to assume that consumption by the non-military population also increased. This could indicate that the standard of living of this part of the population increased in Roman times, even though it needs to be stressed that this last conclusion must remain very tentative.

63 Willem Willems assumes an average of 1.2 men per household every 20 years. Willems, 1986; Vossen, 2003.

64 van Driel-Murray, 2003; van Rossum, 2004.

65 It is likely that more than half of the soldiers did not survive until their retirement. Willems, 1986.

66 Roymans, 2011.

67 de Bruin, 2017, pp. 11–17.

7.2.2 *Pottery*

Another category of portable material culture finds that may provide insights into changes in the level of consumption is pottery. However, in contrast to metal objects, it is practically impossible to get a reliable indication of the development of the total volume of pottery in the research area. Although, in principle, archaeologists have collected more than enough quantified material for such a reconstruction, for the time being, this material has not been aggregated in a usable way. Moreover, the quality of the material itself is not all the same, and there is a (large) difference in the extent to which the remains of different types of pottery have survived in the archaeological record and the accuracy with which these types can be dated. For example, the hard and noticeable shards of terra sigillata have been well preserved and can be dated rather accurately. The remains of the more porous handmade pots, on the other hand, are less likely to be found and, without an archaeological context, they can often only be dated in very broad time periods, covering several hundred, or even thousands, of years. All in all, this means that a reliable reconstruction of the development of the total volume of pottery in the Lower Germanic Limes region is still impossible at this moment.

Nevertheless, there is an important development that can be observed in the pottery evidence from the research area, which, in my opinion, suggests that the population had become more prosperous. In many rural settlements, there seems to have been a general shift from handmade to wheel-thrown pottery during the Roman period. This is an important development because it indicates that the inhabitants of these settlements increasingly obtained their pottery through market exchange, instead of producing it themselves. Even though this does not necessarily reflect an increase in aggregate consumption levels, I believe that this general trend is at least suggestive of an increase in consumption levels, since the presence of market exchanged goods is an indication of mutually beneficial trading links between transacting parties. Not only was the market exchanged pottery probably of better quality than the locally produced pottery, as it was made by specialised producers, but it could also be acquired at a relatively lower (labour) cost. Through the acquisition of goods through market exchange, people were thus able to obtain better and more diverse types of pottery, without necessarily paying a higher price for these goods.

Of course, the equation of handmade with locally produced and wheel-thrown with market exchanged pottery is not absolute. There were certainly also handmade vessels that were exchanged through the market. Handmade dolia, corkware, and salt containers are a case in point.[68] Furthermore, it is

68 Heeren, 2007, p. 146; Collins, van Enckevort and Hendriks, 2009, p. 192.

not impossible that some rural households produced wheel-thrown pottery without commercial intentions.[69] However, in general, the distinction does seem to apply to most of the pottery that is found in rural settlements.[70] At the same time, we must realise that it was not just economic reasons that led to the adoption of new pottery types or the adherence to native traditions. As was the case with the adoption of new housebuilding traditions, socio-cultural considerations also played an important role here. For example, adherence to native handmade pottery traditions could have been a deliberate cultural choice and need not necessarily reflect a community's inability to obtain goods through the market.[71] On the other hand, if people, for socio-cultural reasons, decided to obtain (part of) their pottery from the market, then they must have been economically capable of this. Therefore, we can be sure that if people obtained an increasing part of their pottery through the market, they must have produced sufficient surpluses in order to do so.

The general development can be illustrated on the basis of several well-researched rural settlements from the northern part of the research area (Figure 27).[72] Figure 26 gives a good overview of this general trend. In the last fifty years BC, Late Iron Age traditions still dominated, and practically all the pottery was handmade. This did not change much during the first half of the first century AD, but by the second half of this century, wheel-thrown pottery already made up a third of the total in the average assemblage. This continued in the second century AD, and in the first half of this century, just over half of the pottery was wheel-thrown. By the second half of the second and during the third centuries AD, wheel-thrown pottery clearly dominated the average assemblage and made up around 70% of the totals. In the fourth century AD, there may have been a shift back to handmade pottery, with the proportion of wheel-thrown pottery falling back to less than a fourth of the total.

It is important to realise that the general development, as is shown in Figure 26, obscures the variation that existed between the different settlements. Table 15 gives a more detailed insight into the individual development trajectories. It shows that there are differences in the timing of the development as well as in the degree of how dramatic the changes were. In Tiel-Passewaaij, for instance, the trend started very early and already in the first half of the second century AD, handmade pottery was almost entirely replaced by wheel-thrown

69 Even though it seems unlikely that the economic benefits will have outweighed the costs.

70 van den Broeke, 2012, pp. 232–233; Heeren, 2014, p. 163.

71 De Clercq, 2005.

72 These sites have been selected because they are well-researched and provide data from different assemblages over long periods of time. The dataset can be expanded with many less well-researched sites, but I believe that the general trend is already very clear.

vessels. In Rijswijk de Bult and Den Haag-Wateringseveld, on the other hand, the vast majority of the vessels that date to this period were still handmade. There are also settlements, such as Oss-Westerveld and Kesteren-De Woerd, where the decline of handmade pots, with percentages around 40, was a lot less than elsewhere. Finally, it should be noted that only two settlements have assemblages that date into the fourth century AD. Accordingly, the revival of handmade ceramics that is shown in Figure 26 is not very well founded.

Of course, data from only ten different settlements is rather limited. Nevertheless, it seems that the general trend as illustrated by Figure 26 is largely representative of the northern part of the research area. Many different studies have documented the gradual disappearance of handmade pottery in rural settlements. An important turning point must have been the Batavian Revolt. Even though in many settlements, the changes were already underway before this event, the process appears to have accelerated in the period thereafter. In the Dutch River Area and the northern part of the MDS region, for example,

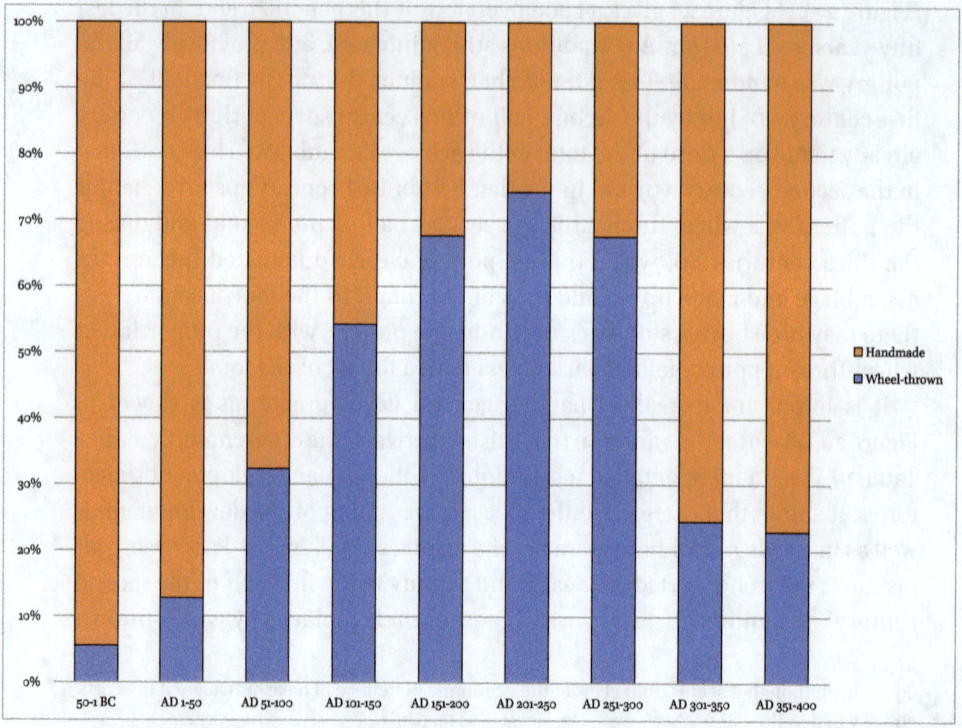

FIGURE 26 The development of average proportions of handmade and wheel-thrown pottery in 10 rural settlements
Note: Data in Table 15

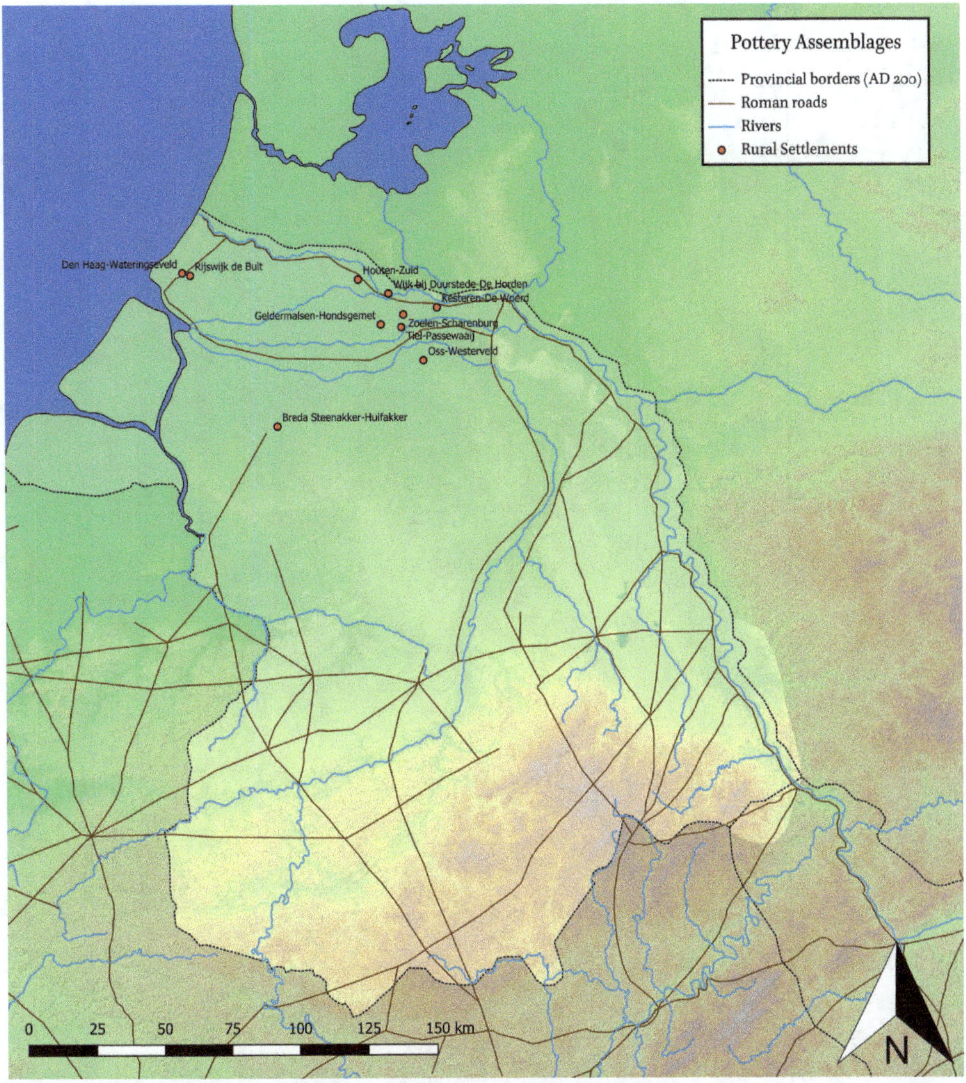

FIGURE 27 The sites that were used for Figure 26 and Table 15

TABLE 15 The percentages of handmade vessels in pottery assemblages from 10 different rural settlements[a]

	50–1 BC	AD 1–50	AD 51–100	AD 101–150	AD 151–200	AD 201–250	AD 251–300	AD 301–350	AD 351–400
Tiel-Passewaaij	100%	75%	17%	2%	x	x	x	x	x
Breda-Steenakker/ Huifakker	x	86%	86%	x	x	45%	10%	77%	77%
Geldermalsen-Hondsgemet	100%	96%	59%	40%	2%	2%	38%	74%	x
Oss-Westerveld	89%	82%	73%	45%	47%	37%	40%	x	x
Zoelen-Scharenburg	x	69%	62%	27%	16%	17%	x	x	x
Wijk bij Duurstede-De Horden	89%	92%	51%	54%	22%	13%	x	x	x
Houten-Zuid	x	94%	74%	42%	25%	x	x	x	x
Rijswijk de Bult	x	96%	86%	69%	69%	30%	30%	x	x
Den Haag-Wateringseveld	x	x	90%	77%	32%	18%	x	x	x
Kesteren-De Woerd	x	95%	79%	57%	45%	44%	44%	x	x

a Bloemers, 1978, p. 73; Wesselingh, 2000, pp. 237–241; Wiepking, 2000, p. 105; 2001, pp. 161–162; Heeren, 2009, p. 105; Van Kerckhove, 2009, p. 158; van der Linden, 2009, pp. 245–246; van Enckevort, 2012, p. 42; Reigersman-van Lidth de Jeude and Vanderhoeven, 2017, p. 123.

there is hardly any handmade material left in the contexts that date to the second century AD.[73] A similar change probably took place in the German Lower Rhine Plain, although the handmade ceramics there may not have disappeared completely in the second and third centuries AD.[74] In the western part of the Dutch river delta, the use of handmade pottery began to decline in the second century AD, and during the second half of this century, the production of handmade vessels seems to have ended altogether.[75] Interestingly, the reversal of the general trend in the Late Antique period has also been documented by several scholars.[76] This may suggest that around the end of the third century AD, the interactions between the inhabitants of the rural settlements and regional producers had become much less intensive. The causes of the revival in the use of handmade pottery remain largely unknown, but it is likely that it originated to a large extent in the disruptions of the trading networks as a result of the Germanic invasions.

7.3 Conclusions

The central question in this chapter is to what extent the general population in the Lower Germanic Limes region experienced an increase in living standards in the course of the Roman period. Even though it remains very difficult to answer this question with certainty or precision, I hope to have shown that there are at least some indications that may suggest that a significant part of the population became more prosperous during Roman times.

The strongest indication of increased prosperity comes from the southern loess zone. From around the second half of the first century AD, the rural population in this region invested large amounts of wealth in the construction of their houses, which were built according to new architectural traditions and with new materials. Although it should be realised that the adoption of these new housebuilding traditions was rooted in changed socio-cultural ideas about the house, there can be no doubt that sufficient purchasing power formed an important pre-requisite for the construction of these houses. Because these

73 In addition, it is possible that many of the hand-shaped sherds that have been found are the result of post depositional processes (*'opspit'*). Vos, 2009, p. 88; Heeren, 2009, pp. 236–237; Hiddink, 2011, pp. 5–6; van Enckevort, 2012, pp. 265–266.

74 Brüggler *et al.*, 2017, pp. 48–52.

75 Again, handmade sherds that have been found in contexts after this period may date to an earlier period. Van Kerckhove, 2011, pp. 143–145; de Bruin, 2017, pp. 271–272.

76 Hiddink, 2011, p. 6; van Enckevort, 2012, p. 41; Ball and van Heeringen, 2016, p. 254; van Lanen *et al.*, 2016, pp. 126–132.

new house types (the villa being the most common) were so widespread in the loess area, they cannot be viewed solely as the possessions of the elite. It also seems that, with the possible exception of the direct hinterland of Cologne, not many of the houses belonged to veterans. Accordingly, it is fair to conclude that most of the new types of houses in the southern loess zone belonged to a middle class of free, landowning farmers, who had been able to gradually expand and embellish their houses with the earnings from the agricultural surpluses that they produced on their lands.

Unlike in the south, the new house building traditions had much less of an impact in the northern parts of the research area. This is primarily due to the fact that the natural stone required for the houses was virtually absent in these areas, which made construction much more expensive. In combination with possibly lower yields from agriculture, this meant that only the wealthier families in this area could afford to build such houses. Furthermore, it is possible that socio-cultural differences played a role in the much less widespread adoption of the new housebuilding traditions in these regions.

Thus, while house building does not provide evidence for an increase in the prosperity of the general population in the northern regions, important changes relating to portable material culture may suggest that a larger part of the population became wealthier. The clearest evidence of a 'consumer revolution' during the Roman period is the large number of metal finds that were made in the Netherlands. There is an enormous difference between the number of finds dating from the Roman period and those dating from the Late Iron Age or Early Middle Ages. Although it remains difficult to determine the extent to which these metal finds were the property of active or former Roman soldiers, it is likely that at least a large proportion of the objects were acquired by the rural population through market exchange. This seems to imply that during the Roman period, the rural population had a greater number and, most likely, a greater variety of metal objects at their disposal.

Unfortunately, it is not yet possible to obtain a reliable indication of the development of the total volume of pottery consumed in the region. However, a very interesting development can be observed in the ratio between handmade and wheel-thrown pottery found in rural settlements from throughout the northern parts of the research area. In the course of the Roman period, handmade pottery was gradually replaced by wheel-thrown pottery. Although this development does not necessarily mean that the population had more pottery than before, I believe that it may still indicate an increase in prosperity. This is the case because it can reasonably be assumed that, in general, handmade pottery was produced more often at the household level, whereas wheel-thrown pottery was made by more specialised producers. Accordingly, the increasing presence of wheel-thrown pottery in the rural settlements indicates that the inhabitants of these settlements, through market exchange, had been able to obtain better and more diverse types of pottery. Moreover, they did not necessarily pay a higher price for this pottery since the specialised potters could produce the pottery a lot more efficiently than the rural population could do themselves. Therefore, both parties could benefit from the exchange. Still, from the end of the third century AD, the relative proportion of handmade pottery appears to have increased again, perhaps as a result of the disruption caused by the Germanic invasions.

In sum, the discussions in this chapter suggest that the inhabitants of the Lower Germanic Limes region experienced an increase in the level of luxury goods they consumed. This increase seems to have been particularly large in the southern loess region, where large agricultural surpluses were also produced. The increases in the less fertile northern areas were probably smaller but should not be underestimated. Even though the observed increase in material welfare in these regions may appear largely insignificant in comparison to the large investments made in housebuilding in the south, for people who lived close to the subsistence level, this increase must have been quite important. Yet it needs to be stressed that the conclusions from this chapter must remain tentative. The argument is only based on three different types of consumer goods, and even for these goods, the interpretation of the data is not unambiguous, as the discussions in this chapter have made clear. Undoubtedly, people will also have consumed a broad range of other items, of which many have not left any traces in the archaeological record. It can only be hoped that these very preliminary conclusions can in the future be tested with more and better data.

CHAPTER 8

Final Conclusions

In this book I have studied the Roman impact on the economy of the Lower Germanic Limes region. The central question has been to what extent the Roman conquest and occupation led to economic growth in the region and how we can characterise and explain this growth. Of crucial importance here is the distinction between aggregate economic growth, which indicates an increase in the total output of the economy without taking its population into account, and per capita economic growth, which indicates an increase in economic output relative to the size of the population. Although both types of economic growth are important, per capita growth is particularly interesting, as it might have caused part of the population to experience an increase in their standard of living.

8.1 Synthesis

In order to find an answer to this central question, it was first of all necessary to determine what the situation was like in the region before the arrival of the Romans. Therefore, in the second chapter, an overview of the historical geography of the research area in the pre-Roman Iron Age was given. This overview has demonstrated that the area consisted of several distinct subregions, which differed considerably in terms of the availability of raw materials, soil fertility, and natural infrastructure. These regions were inhabited by several native tribes, whose rural economies were aimed at local self-sufficiency and the spread of risk. Accordingly, the scale of commercial exchange was very limited, and the production of non-agricultural goods took place, primarily, at the household level, without much technological sophistication.

To properly understand the impact of the Roman domination, I discussed the most important general developments that followed in the wake of the Roman conquest in the third chapter. First of all, I have stressed the importance of the large-scale presence of the Roman army in the region. Not only did the military presence guarantee a long period of relatively peaceful conditions, which was beneficial for economic life, but it also created a large demand for regional and inter-regional produced goods and services. Moreover, this process was reinforced by the fact that the military market attracted many

© ERIK TIMMERMAN, 2024 | DOI:10.1163/9789004682214_009

civilians, who settled in the vicinity of the military fortifications. Apart from these extramural settlements, important changes also took place in the civilian settlement landscape in general: throughout almost the entire region, there developed a large number of more independent urban settlements. These settlements often seem to have been centres of production and trade, acting as central nodes between their rural hinterlands and larger exchange networks. Furthermore, this urbanisation was part of a more general demographic trend. As rural settlement data indicates, the population in the countryside also grew noticeably. Taken together, this increase in military, urban, and rural populations had a large impact on economic life in the Lower Germanic Limes region. It gradually transformed the subsistence oriented Late Iron Age economy into an economic system in which commercial exchange began to play an increasingly large role.

Importantly, this development was further stimulated and facilitated by other features of the Roman occupation. The introduction of Roman taxation into the region, for example, forced the farmers (as well as the rest of the population), to produce at least enough surpluses to pay their taxes with. However, if their surpluses exceeded the tax requirements, they could sell the rest for profits that they could pocket themselves. Besides, the development of the infrastructure network, the introduction of Roman coinage (which was to a large extent spread by the soldiers), Roman law, and a common language and metrological system must have reduced the transaction and transportation costs associated with commercial exchanges. Since the reduction of these costs made exchange more attractive, the total volume of trade in the research area is likely to have increased significantly during the Roman period.

These general developments made a large impact on the agricultural economy, which forms the topic of the fourth chapter. The large population increase posed a major challenge for agricultural producers, who now had to produce enough food not only for themselves, but also for a large non-rural population that did not produce their own food. Furthermore, since the rural population itself had also grown, the land-to-labour ratio was reduced, which, if everything else remained the same, would have lowered agricultural productivity. But it seems that not everything remained the same. Instead, there are good indications that suggest that per capita production increased through a combination of more intensive and more efficient cultivation of agricultural land. Crucially, an important prerequisite for this development to take place was that a well-functioning and reliable market system was in place, which could guarantee the livelihood of the farmers who specialised in one or more specific agricultural products.

This development was most profound in the southern loess zone. From the second half of the first century AD onwards, this region increasingly developed into a villa landscape, where the focus was on the production of cereal surpluses. Even though it remains impossible to determine the size of these surpluses with much certainty, quantitative models suggest that they must have been large enough to cover the demand for cereal of a substantial part of the non-rural population in the research area. This was different in the more northerly non-villa landscapes. In these regions, there are few indications of an increase in productivity in arable farming. Although we might, perhaps, allow for the production of some small cereal surpluses, it appears that crop growing largely continued in the way it had been practiced in the Late Iron Age. However, there are strong indications that farmers in the Dutch River Area specialised in the production of animal products for the (military) market. Still, it remains difficult to determine how large these surpluses were. Moreover, it is unclear to what extent a similar development took place in other sub-regions. In any case, model-based calculations for the western part of the Dutch river delta and the Lower Rhine Plain have concluded that the landscape was probably not much of a constraint for the production of quite significant agricultural surpluses in these regions.

The agricultural population's ability to feed, at least, a large proportion of the non-agricultural population, meant that the latter could specialise in other types of production. This was an important development because increased division of labour leads to economies of scale. As I have argued in the fifth chapter, this was, together with certain organisational and technological improvements, one of the main drivers of a large increase in the total output and per capita production in non-agricultural production.

First of all, this was the case for the exploitation of raw materials. There are strong indications that suggest that the total production of wood, stone, and metal increased dramatically during the Roman period. Importantly, this increase was not just the result of an increase in labour input; the production process also became more efficient. The main driver of this development was, without doubt, the large-scale involvement of the Roman state and army in the exploitation of the resources. The Romans initiated new industries in the region, and military workforces were directly involved in the exploitation of many of the materials. In addition, the technological and organisational know-how of Roman specialists ensured that operations were structured according to the highest available standards. This high level of expertise must also have had an impact on civilian exploitation, which often seems to have been overseen and organised by Roman specialists. Sometimes, the state also leased out the exploitation of a mine or quarry to private individuals. It is thus clear that output and productivity increased in both the military and civilian industries.

Secondly, the degree of economic complexity and the size of total production both increased considerably in the manufacturing sector. Whereas manufacturing, or more precisely, craftworking, in the Late Iron Age was mainly conducted as a secondary activity by subsistence farmers, in the course of the Roman period, this was increasingly taken over by specialised manufacturers who made use of more advanced techniques and produced on a completely different scale. This is most clearly illustrated by the gradual replacement of handmade pottery by wheel-thrown pottery in rural settlements. This development suggests that the rural inhabitants did no longer produce all their pottery, ineffectively, themselves but could also rely on the market to obtain pottery that was produced by skilled artisans in the urban settlements. Furthermore, in many of these settlements, there seems to have been a large increase in the production of metal and glass objects in Roman times. In contrast to the exploitation of raw materials, the role of state and military production appears to have been much less important regarding manufacturing. Although in the initial phase of the Roman occupation, the army still produced many of its manufactured goods themselves, from around the second half of the first century AD, civilian manufacturers were able to take over a large part of this production. Moreover, in addition to producing for the military market, they also produced sufficient goods to supply the large civilian market that had developed in the region and consisted of both urban and rural settlements.

In order to enable the large-scale specialisation and division of labour between and within the agricultural and non-agricultural production sectors, a well-functioning trade system was crucial. There can therefore be no doubt that the above developments went hand in hand with a large increase in the volume and efficiency of trade in the research area. In the first place, this will have been the case for regional and local trade, but it is also clear that the region was integrated into trade networks that went beyond the provincial borders, as I demonstrated in the sixth chapter. This was important since long-distance trade stimulated economic growth both in the region itself as well as in the areas with which the trade was conducted. Although our knowledge of long-distance trade is relatively good, at least in comparison to shorter distance trade, the picture is rather one-sided. We have a pretty good understanding of Mediterranean imports into the research area, but we do not know much about regional exports. Furthermore, our knowledge of trade with Britannia and Germania Magna is very limited, even though this trade must also have been important.

Nevertheless, despite the somewhat limited evidence, it is clear that the degree to which the Lower Germanic Limes region was involved in long-distance trade increased significantly during the Roman period. The initial driver was the large demand of the Roman soldiers in the region, who desired typical Mediterranean products such as wine, fish sauce, olive oil, and terra sigillata. However, demand for these products also soon arose in many of the urban settlements and, perhaps, later, even in the rural countryside. Although initially the products came mainly from the Mediterranean area itself, in the second century AD there seems to have been a relative increase in products from more nearby regions. This development could possibly be interpreted as a form of import replacement. Interestingly, there is not much convincing evidence for the large-scale involvement of the Roman state in the imports. Instead, it appears that long-distance trade was guided largely by the market and was organised by highly specialised groups of professional traders.

To see to what extent the economic growth in the region also led to an increase in the standard of living of the general population, in the seventh chapter, I looked at changes in the rural population's consumption of portable and non-portable material culture. Even though this conclusion is still very preliminary, I have argued that there are good indications that suggest that a significant part of the population became more prosperous during Roman times.

This increase in prosperity is most evident in the villa landscape in the south of the research area. From around the second half of the first century AD, the people in this region invested large amounts of wealth in the construction of their houses. This development is so widespread in the area that it cannot just reflect an increase in the wealth of the elite. Moreover, there are no indications that many of the villas were built by veterans. Therefore, it seems most likely that they belonged to a middleclass of free, landowning farmers, who had been able to gradually expand and embellish their houses with the earnings from the agricultural surpluses that they produced on their lands.

In the northerly regions, however, these developments in housebuilding are much less widespread. Accordingly, it appears that the few villas that were built in these regions can only be interpreted as signs of the prosperity of a wealthy few. Nonetheless, here too, there are indications that a larger share of the population, albeit on a somewhat more modest scale than in the south, had become somewhat more prosperous. For example, it is clear that the number of metal objects in rural settlements in the Dutch part of the research area, increased significantly in the Roman period. Although part of this increase can be attributed exclusively to the large numbers of Roman soldiers and veterans in the region, it seems that at least a part of it reflects an increase in purchasing power by the general rural population. Similarly, in many rural settlements, a general shift from handmade to wheel-thrown pottery was observable during the Roman period. Of course, this trend is not necessarily a reflection of an increase in the aggregate consumption of pottery, but it is indicative of mutually beneficial trading links between producers and consumers. Furthermore, the wheel-thrown pottery was probably of better quality and included a wider range of products. It is thus likely that by obtaining their pottery through the market, rural consumers got more value for their labour than before.

8.2 Interpretation

So, where does all that leave us? To what extent did the region experience economic growth and how can we characterise and explain this growth? First of all, it is important to realise that part of the growth that took place in the Lower Germanic Limes region can be attributed exclusively to the productive activities of the Roman state and military. Since this production had no other purpose than to provide for the needs of the army and state, it was entirely separate from the civilian economy in the region. Therefore, although technically they were both part of the general growth of the regional economy, it is vital not to confuse the performance of the state and military economy with that of the civilian economy. This does not, however, mean that all production that was destined for the state or army, was separate from the civilian economy. Civilians, who worked for the state or army, or provided or sold goods and services to them, did still contribute to the performance of the civilian economy.

Despite the fact that part of the regional economic growth was thus due to the state and military production, I do not think that anyone will deny that the Roman conquest and occupation led to a significant amount of aggregate economic growth in the research area. After all, we can be confident that the total civilian population increased substantially during the first circa 250 years of Roman occupation. In addition to this, practically all the available source material indicates a large increase in economic activity for about the same period. There can also be no doubt that the economy became increasingly complex during Roman times. The largely undifferentiated subsistence economy of the Late Iron Age was gradually changed into a market-oriented economic system, within which a large degree of division of labour took place. This division of labour led to increased specialisation, which, together with certain organisational and technological improvements, made possible production on a completely different scale.

However, it is less clear whether the regional economy, in addition to the aggregate growth, also experienced per capita growth. Unfortunately, the proxy data that we have for the development of population numbers and the total output of the economy are too imprecise to compare with each other. It is thus very difficult to find out whether there was per capita growth in the region, let alone attempt to determine the scope of this growth. Nevertheless, I believe that a case for per capita growth can still be made, even though it needs to be stressed that this argument is based on a lot of uncertain assumptions.

In any case, it is clear that the existence of a certain degree of per capita economic growth is not an unrealistic scenario. As I have demonstrated in this study, there are strong indications that in all major sectors of the economy (agricultural production, non-agricultural production, and trade), not only total economic output, but also per capita production, had increased. If this was indeed the case, there can be little doubt that there was per capita economic growth in these sectors during the Roman period. This is because, if the people who worked in these sectors, on average, had been able to increase their productivity, their per capita output must also have increased. Yet when determining whether per capita economic growth took place in the region at large, it is not sufficient to only take into account the people who were active in these sectors of the economy. After all, per capita growth concerns the regional population as a whole. Therefore, the question is whether there were large groups of people in the region that were not active in these sectors of the economy. For if the number of such people was large enough, it could, perhaps, cancel out the increase in per capita production of those who did work in these sectors.

The first large group of people that might perhaps spring to mind is the Roman army, for this was indeed a large group that was not active in one of the main sectors of the economy. Still, since the army cannot be considered part of the civilian economy, this group should be omitted as part of the total population when discussing the scope for per capita economic growth in the region. Otherwise, we could also consider their production, which, in addition to the production of material goods, consisted primarily of the security they provided to the empire, as part of the total output of the regional economy. This would, of course, make little sense, especially since the security offered by the army benefited, and was paid for, by the entire empire.

Apart from the Roman army, there were essentially two other groups that lived in the Lower Germanic Limes region that could afford not to be directly involved in one of the major sectors of the economy. Members of the (landowning) elite were not necessarily productive themselves but could live off their wealth or from the agricultural products that they exacted from the rural population through rents. In a similar way, veterans who had earned enough money from their service were also able to support themselves without having to be productive anymore. The question remains whether these two groups were large enough to bring down the average per capita production of the rest of the population. Unfortunately, it is impossible to accurately estimate the size of these groups, and even if we could do this, it would be of little use if we did not also have reliable figures on the size and aggregate economic output of the rest of the population.

Nonetheless, I believe that there are two developments that indicate that the increase in productivity that was realised by the productive part of the population was also large enough to lead to per capita economic growth for the region as a whole. First, the fact that the civilian population had to pay taxes to the Roman state means that they must have produced enough goods to sustain themselves and pay these taxes. Although taxes are believed to have been rather low, they are likely to have necessitated a small amount of output growth per capita. However, since these taxes were collected by the Roman state, the benefits of this per capita production growth did not (directly) benefit the consumption of the civilian population in the research area. This was different from the second development that can be observed in the region. As I have argued in this study, there are indications that at least a part of the rural population, despite the increased tax burden, experienced an improvement in material wellbeing during the Roman period. Nevertheless, it should be noted that this is a very tentative conclusion and that this increase was probably not equally strong in all parts of the research area. However, if this was indeed the case, then it must have been caused by an increase in per capita production, as the increased consumption had to come from somewhere.

It thus seems that the Lower Germanic Limes region, in addition to a large degree of aggregate economic growth, also experienced a certain degree of per capita economic growth during the Roman period. Even though this per capita growth was partly absorbed by the Roman state through the taxation system, there are also indications that a part of the general population may have become somewhat wealthier. Accordingly, this suggests that the development in this part of the empire is more in line with the sustainable growth scenario than with the Malthusian scenario. After all, the large population growth that the region experienced does not appear to have lowered the per capita production and living standards of the regional population. Instead, for part of the population, the Roman period, at least until somewhere in the late third century AD, might have been a time of increased prosperity. Of course, we should not make too much of this. There will also have been a significant proportion of the population who were not able to profit from the possibilities that market exchange offered. For these people, the situation might even have worsened, as they now had to work harder to earn a living than before. Furthermore, it has to be borne in mind that the pathway to growth in this region was very specific because of the large military presence. As we have seen throughout this book, the army was an important economic stimulus in the area, and it remains to be seen to what extent growth would have taken place without it.

8.3 Future Research

It is clear that many of the conclusions in this study are still tentative and that more research is needed to test and refine them. Moreover, it is important to compare these conclusions with the results of other studies to place them in larger historiographical contexts. Therefore, I would like to end this book with a few recommendations for future research that I believe deserve particular attention:

1. More research into per capita growth and living standards in the region.
In order to better connect local and regional studies to the general debate about the Roman economy, it is important that these studies integrate questions from this larger debate into their research. For example, it is interesting to see whether more accurate estimates of population growth can be made for certain areas, so that we have a better baseline for questions about per capita growth. In addition, more research into living standards is important because it can provide clear evidence of per capita growth and can also show to what extent this growth reached different parts of the population. In this study I have only been able to discuss a few preliminary indications of an increase in the standard of living in the research area. However, it is interesting to see whether more detailed and focused research in this area can provide us with more and better insights. Therefore, I hope that my research will help to generate more interest in this topic among scholars working with the material from this area, as they have the opportunity to provide much more clarity on the subject in the future.

2. Investigate the decline of the economy in the late Roman period.
The central theme of this research has been the impact of the Roman occupation on the economy of the Lower Germanic Limes region, in which the main focus was on the transition from the Late Iron Age to the Roman period. Detailed research into another important transitional phase, namely that of

the late Roman period to the early medieval period, has been beyond the scope of this study. Nevertheless, many of the datasets discussed have shown that this period is also certainly worth investigating. After all, it is clear that the economy in the research area experienced a significant decline during this period and, in many respects, returned to the level of the pre-Roman period, or even below it. What developments lay at the root of this decline, and from when did it commence? Indeed, many of the datasets show that the decline already started in the first half of the third century AD, which makes it difficult to blame everything on the Germanic invasions that only began at the end of that century. Did climate change or empire-wide plagues perhaps play a role? Or could an argument still be made for a Malthusian scenario? These are interesting questions to answer.

3. Draw comparisons with other parts of the Roman Empire.
Lastly, it is crucial to find out how the developments in the Lower Germanic Limes region compare to those in other parts of the Roman Empire. As we have seen in this study, the large military presence played a very important role in this part of the empire. If we want to better understand how this very specific situation determined the economic development in this region, it is interesting to investigate to what extent similarities and differences can be observed between other regions. First of all, one can think of areas where a similar situation existed. There was also a large military presence along the neighbouring Upper Germanic-Rhaetian Limes and in Britannia, which must have made an impact on the economy. Do we see a similar development in those regions, or are there important differences? And how can these be explained? Furthermore, it is important to look at areas where no large-scale military presence existed. The adjacent Gallia Belgica lends itself well to this, but other parts of Gaul also seem very suitable. And if the general picture of the northwestern provinces of the empire is further specified, it is also interesting to compare these findings with other parts of the empire. In sum, there is plenty of work to be done and many more areas to be explored. Only together can they lead to a better understanding of the Roman economy as a whole. With this book, I hope to have made a contribution to this.

Appendix 1

This appendix and the corresponding map (Figure 2) and graph (Figure 4) give an overview of the military and civilian central places that existed in the research area during the Roman period. Extramural settlements are not indicated. However, these will have been present in the vicinity of almost all fortresses and forts. The appendix is the result of an extensive literature search. Initially, I based myself primarily on existing overviews, but where necessary, I also consulted more detailed publications. Although I have tried to be as complete and accurate as possible, it is possible that I have missed (or perhaps mistakenly included) some central places. Overall, though, I believe that the dataset is a good reflection of the current state of research. The following abbreviations have been used in the 'Production' column: P(ottery), M(etal), G(lass), C(eramic building material), S(tone), O(ther). The different types of settlement are: Leg(ionary) fortress, Aux(iliary fort), Fle(etbase), Col(onia), Mun(icipium), Sec(ondary agglomeration), San(ctuary). A question mark indicates that the existence or dating of a central place (or production activity) is uncertain.

© ERIK TIMMERMAN, 2024 | DOI:10.1163/9789004682214_010

No.	Name	Production	50–1 BC	AD 1–50	AD 51–100	AD 101–150
1	Aachen	P/M/G/S/O	Sec	Sec	Sec	Sec
2	Alpen-Drüpt		Aux?	Aux?	Aux?	Aux?
3	Alphen aan den Rijn		–	Aux	Aux	Aux
4	Alteburg		–	–	Fle	Fle
5	Altkalkar		–	Aux	Aux	Aux
6	Amay	P/M/C	–	Sec	Sec	Sec
7	Arnhem		–	Aux	Aux	Aux
8	Bad Neuenahr-Ahrweiler	M	–	–	–	Sec
9	Baesweiler		–	Sec	Sec	Sec
10	Bedburg-Hau		–	–	Aux	Aux
11	Billig	M	–	–	Sec	Sec
12	Blatzheim		San?	San?	San?	San?
13	Blerick		Sec?	Sec?	Sec?	Sec?
14	Bodegraven		–	Aux	Aux	Aux
15	Bonn	P/M/G/C/S/O	Aux	Leg	Leg/Sec	Leg/Sec
16	Braives	P/M/S	Sec	Sec	Sec	Sec

AD 151–200	AD 201–250	AD 251–300	AD 301–350	AD 351–400	AD 401–450	Reference
Sec	Sec	Sec	Sec	Sec	Sec	Heimberg 2000; Rothenhöfer 2005; Schaub 2013; Ulbert 2013.
Aux?	Aux?	Aux?	Aux?	Aux?	Aux?	Graafstal *et al.* 2018.
Aux	Aux	Aux	–	–	–	Fischer 2012; Graafstal *et al.* 2018; Polak/Kooistra 2013; Vici.org/Livius.org.
Fle	Fle	Fle	–	–	–	Fischer 2012; Graafstal *et al.* 2018; Polak/Kooistra 2013; Vici.org/Livius.org.
Aux	Aux	Aux	Aux	Aux	–	Fischer 2012; Graafstal *et al.* 2018; Polak/Kooistra 2013; Vici.org/Livius.org.
Sec	Sec	Sec	Sec	Sec	–	Brulet 2008; Petit *et al.* 1994; Van Thienen *et al.* 2019.
Aux	Aux	Aux	–	–	–	Fischer 2012; Graafstal *et al.* 2018; Polak/Kooistra 2013; Vici.org/Livius.org.
Sec	Sec	Sec	Sec	Sec	–	Heimberg 2000; Rothenhöfer 2005.
Sec	Sec	Sec	–	–	–	Ulbert 2013.
–	–	–	–	–	–	Burandt 2017.
Sec	Sec	Sec	Sec	Sec	Sec	Petit *et al.* 1994; Rothenhöfer 2005; Ulbert 2013.
San?	San?	San?	San?	San?	San?	Rothenhöfer 2005.
Sec?	Sec?	Sec?	Sec?	Sec?	Sec?	Petit *et al.* 1994.
Aux	Aux	Aux	–	–	–	Fischer 2012; Graafstal *et al.* 2018; Polak/Kooistra 2013; Vici.org/Livius.org.
Leg/Sec	Leg/Sec	Leg/Sec	Leg	Leg	Leg	Polak/Kooistra 2013; Rothenhöfer 2005; Ulbert 2013; Vici.org/Livius.org.
Sec	Sec	Sec	Sec	Sec	–	Brulet 2008; Petit *et al.* 1994; Van Thienen *et al.* 2019.

(*cont.*)

No.	Name	Production	50–1 BC	AD 1–50	AD 51–100	AD 101–150
17	Breinigerberg	P/M/C	–	–	Sec	Sec
18	Büderich-Steinacker		–	–	Aux	Aux
19	Burtscheid		–	San	San	San
20	Colijnsplaat		San?	San?	San?	San?
21	Cologne	P/M/G/C/S/O	Sec	Col/Leg	Col	Col
22	Cuijk		–	Aux	Aux	Sec
23	De Meern		–	Fle	Fle	Fle
24	Dilsen		–	Sec	Sec	Sec
25	Dinant		Sec?	Sec?	Sec?	Sec?
26	Domburg		San?	San?	San?	San?
27	Dormagen		–	–	Aux	Aux
28	Driel		Aux?	Aux?	Aux?	Aux?
29	Elfrath		–	San	San	San
30	Elsdorf		–	San	San	San
31	Elst		–	–	Sec	Sec
32	Empel		San	San	San	San
33	Flerzheim		–	Sec	Sec	Sec
34	Fontaine-Valmont	M	–	–	Sec	Sec
35	Friesheim	P	–	Sec	Sec	Sec
36	Fronhoven		San?	San?	San?	San?
37	Goedereede		–	Sec	Sec	Sec
38	Gressenich	M	–	Sec	Sec	Sec
39	Gripswald		San?	San?	San?	San?
40	Grobbendonk		–	–	Sec	Sec
41	Halder	P	–	Sec	Sec	Sec

AD 151–200	AD 201–250	AD 251–300	AD 301–350	AD 351–400	AD 401–450	Reference
Sec	Sec	Sec	–	–	–	Petit *et al.* 1994; Rothenhöfer 2005; Ulbert 2013.
Aux	–	–	–	–	–	Graafstal *et al.* 2018; Vici.org/Livius.org.
San	San	San	–	–	–	Rothenhöfer 2005; Ulbert 2013.
San?	San?	San?	San?	San?	San?	Heimberg 2000.
Col	Col	Col	Col	Col	Col	Eck 2004; Fischer 2012, Hanel 2020; Vici.org/ Livius.org.
Sec	Sec	Sec	Sec	Sec	–	Fischer 2012; Graafstal *et al.* 2018; Heimberg 2000; Vici.org/Livius.org.
Fle	Fle	Fle	–	–	–	Graafstal *et al.* 2018; Vici.org/Livius.org.
Sec	–	–	–	–	–	Van Thienen 2019; Vici.org/Livius.org.
Sec?	Sec?	Sec?	Sec?	Sec?	Sec?	Brulet 2008; Van Thienen *et al.* 2019.
San?	San?	San?	San?	San?	San?	Heimberg 2000.
Aux	Sec	Sec	Sec	Sec	–	Polak/Kooistra 2013; Rothenhöfer 2005; Vici.org/Livius.org.
Aux?	Aux?	Aux?	Aux?	Aux?	Aux?	Fischer 2012; Vici.org/ Livius.org.
San	San	San	–	–	–	Reichmann 1991.
San	San	San	San	San	–	Rothenhöfer 2005; Ulbert 2013.
Sec	Sec	Sec	–	–	–	Stillwell *et al.* 2017.
San	San	San	–	–	–	Vici.org/Livius.org.
Sec	Sec	Sec	Sec	Sec	–	Rothenhöfer 2005.
Sec	Sec	Sec	–	–	–	Van Thienen *et al.* 2019.
–	–	–	–	–	–	Rothenhöfer 2005; Ulbert 2013.
San?	San?	San?	San?	San?	San?	Rothenhöfer 2005.
Sec	Sec	–	–	–	–	Vici.org/Livius.org.
Sec	Sec	Sec	Sec	–	–	Rothenhöfer 2005; Ulbert 2013.
San?	San?	San?	San?	San?	San?	Heimberg 2000.
Sec	Sec	Sec	–	–	–	Stillwell *et al.* 2017; Van Thienen *et al.* 2019.
Sec	Sec	–	–	–	–	Borgers *et al.* 2017.

(*cont.*)

No.	Name	Production	50–1 BC	AD 1–50	AD 51–100	AD 101–150
42	Heerlen	P/M	Sec	Sec	Sec	Sec
43	Herwen		–	Aux	Aux	Aux
44	Hoven		San?	San?	San?	San?
45	Huy	P	–	–	–	–
46	Jülich	P/M/G/C/S/O	Sec	Sec	Sec	Sec
47	Jünkerath	M/S	–	–	Sec	Sec
48	Jupille-sur-Meuse	P	–	–	Sec	Sec
49	Katwijk		–	Fle	Fle?	Fle?
50	Keldenich	M	Sec	Sec	Sec	Sec
51	Kessel-Lith		–	–	–	–
52	Kesteren		Aux?	Aux?	Aux?	Aux?
53	Kontich		–	Sec	Sec	Sec
54	Kornelimünster		–	San	San	San
55	Krefeld-Gellep	M/C	Sec	Sec	Aux/Sec	Aux
56	Leiden		–	Aux	Aux	Aux
57	Liberchies	P/M/G	Sec	Sec	Sec	Sec
58	Loowaard		–	Aux	Aux	Aux

AD 151–200	AD 201–250	AD 251–300	AD 301–350	AD 351–400	AD 401–450	Reference
Sec	Sec	Sec	Sec	Sec	–	Heimberg 2000; Rothenhöfer 2005.
Aux	Aux	Aux	–	–	–	Fischer 2012; Graafstal *et al.* 2018; Polak/Kooistra 2013; Vici.org/Livius.org.
San?	San?	San?	San?	San?	San?	Rothenhöfer 2005; Ulbert 2013.
–	Sec	Sec	Sec	Sec	Sec	Brulet 2008; Petit *et al.* 1994; Van Thienen *et al.* 2019.
Sec	Sec	Sec	Sec	Sec	Sec	Petit *et al.* 1994; Rothenhöfer 2005; Ulbert 2013.
Sec	Sec	Sec	Sec	Sec	–	Petit *et al.* 1994; Rothenhöfer 2005.
Sec	Sec	Sec	–	–	–	Brulet 2008; Van Thienen *et al.* 2019.
Fle?	Fle?	Fle?	Fle?	Fle?	Fle?	Fischer 2012; Graafstal *et al.* 2018; Polak/Kooistra 2013; Vici.org/Livius.org.
Sec	Sec	Sec	Sec	Sec	Sec	Rothenhöfer 2005.
–	–	–	Aux	Aux	–	Graafstal *et al.* 2018; Vici.org/Livius.org.
Aux?	Aux?	Aux?	Aux?	Aux?	Aux?	Fischer 2012; Graafstal *et al.* 2018; Polak/Kooistra 2013; Vici.org/Livius.org.
Sec	Sec	Sec	–	–	–	Stillwell *et al.* 2017; Van Thienen *et al.* 2019.
San	San	–	–	–	–	Rothenhöfer 2005; Ulbert 2013.
Aux	Aux	Aux	Aux	Aux	Aux	Polak/Kooistra 2013; Rothenhöfer 2005; Vici.org/Livius.org.
Aux	Aux	Aux	–	–	–	Fischer 2012; Graafstal *et al.* 2018; Polak/Kooistra 2013; Vici.org/Livius.org.
Sec	Sec	Sec	Sec	Sec	–	Brulet 2008; Petit *et al.* 1994; Van Thienen *et al.* 2019.
Aux	Aux	Aux	Aux	Aux	–	Fischer 2012; Graafstal *et al.* 2018; Polak/Kooistra 2013; Vici.org/Livius.org.

(*cont.*)

No.	Name	Production	50–1 BC	AD 1–50	AD 51–100	AD 101–150
59	Maastricht	C	–	–	Sec	Sec
60	Mariaweiler	M	–	Sec	Sec	Sec
61	Maurik		–	–	Aux	Aux
62	Melick		–	–	–	Sec
63	Moers-Asberg		Aux	Aux	Aux/Sec	Sec
64	Momalle	P	–	Sec	Sec	Sec
65	Morken	S?	San?	San?	San?	San?
66	Mülfort	P/C/S	–	–	Sec	Sec
67	Namur	M/O	–	–	Sec	Sec
68	Nettersheim	M/S	–	–	Sec	Sec
69	Neubourheim		–	–	Sec	Sec
70	Neuss		Leg	Leg/Sec	Leg/Sec	Aux/Sec
71	Nijmegen	P/M/G/S	Aux/Leg/Sec	Aux/Sec	Aux/Leg/Mun	Leg/Mun
72	Nörvenich	M	Sec	Sec	Sec	Sec
73	Pesch	S?	–	San	San	San
74	Pont		–	–	Sec	Sec
75	Qualburg		–	–	–	–
76	Randwijk		Aux?	Aux?	Aux?	Aux?

AD 151–200	AD 201–250	AD 251–300	AD 301–350	AD 351–400	AD 401–450	Reference
Sec	Sec	Sec	Sec	Sec	–	Rothenhöfer 2005; Van Thienen *et al.* 2019.
Sec	Sec	–	–	–	–	Rothenhöfer 2005; Ulbert 2013.
Aux	Aux	Aux	–	–	–	Graafstal *et al.* 2018; Polak/Kooistra 2013; Vici.org/Livius.org.
Sec	–	–	–	–	–	Rothenhöfer 2005.
Sec	–	–	–	–	–	Heimberg 2000; Polak/Kooistra 2013; Ulbert 2013; Vici.org /Livius.org.
Sec	Sec	Sec	–	–	–	Petit *et al.* 1994.
San?	San?	San?	San?	San?	San?	Rothenhöfer 2005.
Sec	Sec	Sec	–	–	–	Rothenhöfer 2005; Ulbert 2013.
Sec	Sec	Sec	Sec	Sec	Sec	Brulet 2008; Petit *et al.* 1994; Van Thienen *et al.* 2019.
Sec	Sec	Sec	Sec	Sec	Sec	Ortisi 2013; Rothenhöfer 2005; Ulbert 2013.
Sec	Sec	Sec	Sec	Sec	Sec	Ulbert 2013.
Aux/Sec	Aux/Sec	Aux/Sec	Sec	Sec	–	Polak/Kooistra 2013; Rothenhöfer 2005; Ulbert 2013; Vici.org/ Livius.org.
Mun	Mun	Aux/Mun	Aux/Mun	Aux/Mun	Aux/Mun	Fischer 2012; Graafstal *et al.* 2018; Polak 2005; Vici.org/Livius.org.
Sec	Sec	Sec	Sec	Sec	Sec	Rothenhöfer 2005; Ulbert 2013; Vici.org/ Livius.org.
San	San	San	San	San	–	Rothenhöfer 2005.
Sec	Sec	–	–	–	–	Heimberg 2000; Petit *et al.* 1994; Ulbert 2013.
–	–	Aux	–	–	–	Fischer 2012; Graafstal *et al.* 2018; Polak/ Kooistra 2013; Vici.org/ Livius.org.
Aux?	Aux?	Aux?	Aux?	Aux?	Aux?	Fischer 2012; Polak/Kooistra 2013; Vici.org/Livius.org.

(*cont.*)

No.	Name	Production	50–1 BC	AD 1–50	AD 51–100	AD 101–150
77	Remagen		–	Aux	Aux	Aux
78	Rijsbergen		San?	San?	San?	San?
79	Rimburg	P/M/O	–	Sec	Sec	Sec
80	Roermond		San?	San?	San?	San?
81	Rosellen	M	Sec?	Sec?	Sec?	Sec?
82	Rossum		–	–	Aux?	Aux?
83	Schönforst	P/M	–	–	Sec	Sec
84	Sechtem		San?	San?	San?	San?
85	Sinzig	P/C	–	–	–	Sec
86	Soller	P	–	–	–	–
87	Steincheshof		–	–	Aux	Aux
88	Taviers		Sec	Sec	Sec	Sec
89	Theux	P?/M/S	–	–	–	Sec
90	Tienen	P/M/G/O	Sec	Sec	Sec	Sec
91	Tongeren	P/M/G?	Sec	Sec	Sec	Mun
92	Tourinnes-St.-Lambert	P	–	–	–	Sec
93	Tüddern		Sec?	Sec?	Sec?	Sec?
94	Utrecht		–	Aux	Aux	Aux
95	Valkenburg		–	Leg/Aux	Aux	Aux

AD 151–200	AD 201–250	AD 251–300	AD 301–350	AD 351–400	AD 401–450	Reference
Aux	Aux	Aux	Aux	Aux	–	Fischer 2012; Graafstal *et al.* 2018; Polak/Kooistra 2013; Vici.org/Livius.org.
San?	San?	San?	San?	San?	San?	Vici.org/Livius.org.
Sec	Sec	Sec	Sec	Sec	–	Petit *et al.* 1994; Rothenhöfer 2005; Ulbert 2013.
San?	San?	San?	San?	San?	San?	Heimberg 2000.
Sec?	Sec?	Sec?	Sec?	Sec?	Sec?	Heimberg 2000; Rothenhöfer 2005.
Aux?	Aux?	Aux?	Aux?	Aux?	Aux?	Fischer 2012; Graafstal *et al.* 2018; Vici.org/Livius.org.
Sec	–	–	–	–	–	Rothenhöfer 2005; Schaub 2013.
San?	San?	San?	San?	San?	San?	Rothenhöfer 2005; Ulbert 2013.
Sec	Sec	–	–	–	–	Petit *et al.* 1994; Rothenhöfer 2005.
Sec	Sec	Sec	–	–	–	Rothenhöfer 2005; Ulbert 2013.
Aux	Aux	–	–	–	–	Graafstal *et al.* 2018; Polak/Kooistra 2013; Vici.org/Livius.org.
Sec	Sec	Sec	Sec	–	–	Brulet 2008; Petit *et al.* 1994.
Sec	Sec	Sec	Sec	Sec	–	Brulet 2008; Petit *et al.* 1994; Van Thienen *et al.* 2019.
Sec	Sec	Sec	–	–	–	Martens 2012; Van Thienen *et al.* 2019.
Mun	Mun	Mun	Mun	Mun	Mun	Van Thienen 2019; Veldman and Geerts 2014.
Sec	Sec	–	–	–	–	Van Thienen *et al.* 2019; Petit *et al.* 1994
Sec?	Sec?	Sec?	Sec?	Sec?	Sec?	Rothenhöfer 2005; Ulbert 2013.
Aux	Aux	Aux	–	–	–	Fischer 2012; Graafstal *et al.* 2018; Polak/Kooistra 2013; Vici.org/Livius.org.
Aux	Aux	Aux	–	–	–	Fischer 2012; Graafstal *et al.* 2018; Polak/Kooistra 2013; Vos *et al.* 2020.

(*cont.*)

No.	Name	Production	50–1 BC	AD 1–50	AD 51–100	AD 101–150
96	Vechten		–	Aux	Aux	Aux
97	Veldwezelt	M	Sec	Sec	Sec	–
98	Venlo	C?	Sec	Sec	Sec	Sec
99	Vervoz	P	–	–	Sec	Sec
100	Voorburg	M	–	–	Sec	Mun
101	Wenau	M?	Sec?	Sec?	Sec?	Sec?
102	Wesseling		Aux?	Aux?	Aux?	Aux?
103	Wijchen		Sec?	Sec?	Sec?	Sec?
104	Wijk bij Duurstede		–	–	Aux	Aux
105	Woerden		–	Aux	Aux	Aux
106	Worringen		Sec?	Sec?	Sec?	Sec?
107	Xanten	P/M/C/S/O	Leg/Sec	Leg/Sec	Leg/Sec	Col/Leg
108	Zieverich		–	–	Sec	Sec
109	Zülpich	O?	–	Sec	Sec	Sec
110	Zwammerdam		–	Aux	Aux	Aux

AD 151–200	AD 201–250	AD 251–300	AD 301–350	AD 351–400	AD 401–450	Reference
Aux	Aux	Aux	–	–	–	Fischer 2012; Graafstal *et al.* 2018; Polak/Kooistra 2013; Vici.org/Livius.org.
–	–	–	–	–	–	Van Thienen *et al.* 2019.
Sec	Sec	–	–	–	–	Vici.org/Livius.org.
Sec	Sec	Sec	Sec	Sec	–	Borgers 2015; Brulet 2008; Petit *et al.* 1994; Van Thienen *et al.* 2019.
Mun	Mun	Mun	–	–	–	Buijtendorp 2010; Stolk 2014.
Sec?	Sec?	Sec?	Sec?	Sec?	Sec?	Rothenhöfer 2005.
Aux?	Aux?	Aux?	Aux?	Aux?	Aux?	Polak/Kooistra 2013; Vici.org/Livius.org.
Sec?	Sec?	Sec?	Sec?	Sec?	Sec?	Heimberg 2000.
Aux	Aux	Aux	Aux	–	–	Fischer 2012; Graafstal *et al.* 2018; Polak/Kooistra 2013; Vici.org/Livius.org.
Aux	Aux	Aux	–	–	–	Fischer 2012; Graafstal *et al.* 2018; Polak/Kooistra 2013; Vici.org/Livius.org.
Sec?	Sec?	Sec?	Sec?	Sec?	Sec?	Rothenhöfer 2005.
Col/Leg	Col/Leg	Col/Leg	–	–	–	Graafstal *et al.* 2018; Hanel 2020; Reuter 2008; Vici.org/Livius.org.
–	–	–	–	–	–	Rothenhöfer 2005; Ulbert 2013.
Sec	Sec	Sec	Sec	Sec	Sec	Petit *et al.* 1994; Rothenhöfer 2005; Ulbert 2013.
Aux	Aux	Aux	–	–	–	Graafstal *et al.* 2018; Polak/Kooistra 2013; Vici.org/Livius.org.

Appendix 2

This appendix and the corresponding map (Figure 15) and graph (Figure 16) give a rough indication of the development of the total number of pottery kilns that existed in the research area during the Roman period. Kilns that were exclusively used for ceramic building materials have been excluded. The appendix is the result of an extensive literature search. The bibliography of Höpken, Liesen, and Niemeijer and the article by Borgers *et al.* have been most helpful in this regard.[1] Although I have tried to be as complete and accurate as possible, there can be no doubt that I have missed known kilns. Nevertheless, I believe that this dataset provides a representative reflection of the general trend in the number of pottery kilns in the research area. Where possible, I have tried to use an individual dating for each kiln. In doing so, I aimed to avoid too broad a dating per site. Because the dating of the kilns has sometimes been (very) broad, the same kiln sometimes turns up in multiple 50-year periods. The column 'Total kilns' indicates the total number of individual kilns. The extra kilns in parentheses indicate that these kilns have only been dated as 'Roman' and have therefore not been included in the analysis.

1 Höpken, Liesen and Niemeijer, 2014; Borgers *et al.*, 2019.

© ERIK TIMMERMAN, 2024 | DOI:10.1163/9789004682214_011

No.	Name	Category	50–1 BC	AD 1–50	AD 51–100	AD 101–150	AD 151–200
1	Aachen	Urban	0	0	1	2	8
2	Aldenhoven	Rural	0	0	0	1	1
3	Altkalkar	Military	1	2	0	0	0
4	Amay	Urban	0	0	3	3	0
5	Bedburg	Rural	0	0	0	0	0
6	Bergheim	Rural	0	3	2	0	0
7	Bonn (civilian)	Urban	0	0	1	10	24
7	Bonn (military)	Military	1	18	12	0	0
8	Bornheim	Rural	0	2	0	0	0
9	Braives	Urban	0	15	15	0	0
10	Breinigerberg	Urban	0	0	1	1	1
11	Cologne	Cologne	0	41	46	24	14
12	Cuijk	Urban	0	1	1	0	0
13	De Holdeurn	Military	0	0	2	2	4
14	Erftstadt	Urban	0	8	8	8	1
15	Eschweiler	Rural	0	0	0	0	0
16	Euskirchen	Rural	0	0	0	1	1
17	Grobbendonk	Urban	0	0	0	1	1
18	Habscheid-Hollnich	Rural	0	0	0	1	1
19	Halder	Urban	0	0	1	0	0
20	Heerlen	Urban	0	0	16	20	24
21	Huy	Urban	0	0	0	0	0
22	Inden	Rural	0	0	0	1	1
23	Jülich	Urban	0	0	10	16	10
24	Jupille-sur-Meuse	Urban	0	0	0	0	1
25	Kontich	Urban	0	0	1	1	0
26	Krefeld-Gellep	Military	0	0	0	0	0
27	Liberchies	Urban	0	0	0	0	4

AD 201–250	AD 251–300	AD 301–350	AD 351–400	AD 401–450	Total kilns	Reference
8	8	0	0	0	9	Schaub 2013.
0	0	0	0	0	1	Rothenhöfer 2005.
0	0	0	0	0	2	Brüggler 2014.
0	0	0	0	0	3	Brulet 2008.
0	0	3	0	0	3	Piepers 1971.
0	0	0	0	0	3	Smani and Tutlies 2012.
7	5	0	0	0	26(+3)	Andrikopolou-Strack 1996; Holtschneider 2011; Wirtz 1998.
0	1	1	1	1	19(+1)	Frank 2007; Gechter 2007; Wirtz 1998.
0	0	0	0	0	2	Ulbert 2003; Ulbert 2005.
0	0	0	0	0	15	Borgers *et al.* 2019; Brulet 2008.
1	1	0	0	0	1	Rothenhöfer 2005.
2	1	1	0	0	91(+2)	Höpken 2005; Höpken 2015b.
0	0	0	0	0	1	Niemeijer and Thijssen 2014.
2	0	0	0	0	4	van Diepen and Polak 2009; Weiss-König 2014.
1	1	0	0	0	9	Gross and Heimberg 1973; Rothenhöfer 2005.
0	0	1	1	0	1	Bruckner and Piepers 1963; Liesen 2014.
1	1	1	1	0	1	Rothenhöfer 2005; Wohlfarth 1995; Wohlfarth 1996.
0	0	0	0	0	1	Borgers *et al.* 2019.
0	0	0	0	0	1	Polfer 2005; Rothenhöfer 2005.
0	0	0	0	0	1	Borger *et al.* 2017.
18	4	0	0	0	35(+10)	Gielen 1987; Hoevenberg 1996; van der Linden 2007.
0	0	1	1	0	1	Brulet 2008.
1	1	0	0	0	1	Rothenhöfer 2005.
0	0	0	0	0	16	Lenz *et al.* 2007; Perse 2012.
0	0	0	0	0	1	Borgers *et al.* 2019; Brulet 2008.
0	0	0	0	0	1	Borgers *et al.* 2019; Clerbaut 2010.
0	0	1	0	0	1	Brulet 2010; Liesen and Pirling 1998; Pirling and Siepen 2006.
4	4	0	0	0	4	Brulet 2008.

(*cont.*)

No.	Name	Category	50–1 BC	AD 1–50	AD 51–100	AD 101–150	AD 151–200
28	Meerbusch	Rural	0	0	0	0	0
29	Moers-Asberg	Military	0	3	3	0	0
30	Momalle	Urban	0	2	0	0	0
31	Mönchengladbach	Urban	0	0	0	10	10
32	Neuss (civilian)	Urban	0	1	1	1	1
32	Neuss (military)	Military	0	19	13	0	0
33	Nideggen	Rural	0	0	0	0	0
34	Nijmegen (civilian)	Urban	0	0	15	9	3
34	Nijmegen (military)	Military	3	2	2	2	0
35	Remagen	Military	0	6	7	0	0
36	Rimburg	Urban	0	0	0	0	5
37	Rumst	Urban	0	0	0	1	1
38	Schönforst	Urban	0	0	2	2	0
39	Sinzig	Urban	0	0	0	4	4
40	Soller	Urban	0	0	0	0	12
41	Tienen	Urban	0	0	4	6	6
42	Tongeren	Urban	0	0	5	1	1
43	Tourinnes-St.-Lambert	Urban	0	0	0	1	1
44	Venlo	Urban	0	0	1	1	0
45	Vervoz	Urban	0	0	14	0	1
46	Wegberg	Rural	0	0	0	1	1
47	Weilerswist	Rural	0	0	1	0	0
48	Wesel	Urban	0	1	1	0	0
49	Xanten (civilian)	Urban	0	3	3	4	7
49	Xanten (military)	Military	2	0	0	0	0
			7	127	192	135	149

AD 201–250	AD 251–300	AD 301–350	AD 351–400	AD 401–450	Total kilns	Reference
0	0	0	0	0	0(+1)	Klaus and Rech 1985.
0	0	0	0	0	3	Bechert 1989; Filtzinger 1972.
0	0	0	0	0	2	Brulet 2008.
10	0	0	0	0	10	Hupka 2011.
1	1	1	1	0	1	Rothenhöfer 2005.
0	0	0	0	0	19	Filtzinger 1972.
0	0	0	0	0	0(+1)	Haupt 1984.
0	0	0	0	0	17	Hendriks 2014; Willems and van Enckevort 2009.
0	0	0	0	0	5	Hendriks 2014; Stoffels 2014.
0	0	0	0	0	7(+1)	Friedrich 2014.
5	0	0	0	0	5	Höpken and Liesen 2005.
0	0	0	0	0	1	Borgers *et al.* 2019.
0	0	0	0	0	2	Kaszab-Olschewski 2011.
0	0	0	0	0	4	Rothenhöfer 2005; Vilvorder 2010.
12	12	0	0	0	12	Haupt 1984.
3	3	0	0	0	7	Borgers *et al.* 2014; Martens 2007.
1	1	0	0	0	4(+3)	De Winter 2019; Veldman and Geerts 2014.
1	0	0	0	0	1	Brulet 2008.
0	0	0	0	0	1	Hupperetz 1993.
0	0	0	0	0	15	Borgers 2015.
1	1	0	0	0	1	Janssen and Goebel 1977.
0	0	0	0	0	1	Höpken 2011.
0	0	0	0	0	1	von Detten and Weber 1990.
6	2	0	0	0	11	Boelick 1995; Liesen 2001; Wirtz 1998.
0	0	0	0	0	2	Wirtz 1998.
85	47	10	5	1	387	

Appendix 3

This appendix and the corresponding map (Figure 18) show the sites where metal manufacturing has been documented. I have relied in particular on the overviews of Gralfs, Rothenhöfer, and Brulet.[1]

No.	Name	Furnaces	Category	Type	Dating	Reference
1	Aachen	?	Urban	Iron, non-ferrous	Roman	Schaub 2013.
2	Aldenhoven	?	Rural	Unknown	1b–1c	Rothenhöfer 2005a.
3	Alteburg	?	Military	Unknown	Roman	Höpken 2009.
4	Amay	3?	Urban	Iron	1c–3c	Brulet 2008.
5	Anthée	?	Rural	Iron, non-ferrous	2a–3d	Gralfs 1994.
6	Baudecet	?	Urban	Unknown	Roman	Polfer 2000.
7	Billig	?	Urban	Iron, non-ferrous	Roman	Rothenhöfer 2005b.
8	Bonn (civilian)	?	Urban	Non-ferrous	Roman	Andrikopolou-Strack 1996.
8	Bonn (military)	7?	Military	Iron, non-ferrous	1a–3d	Gralfs 1994; Rothenhöfer 2005b.
9	Braives	?	Urban	Iron, non-ferrous	2a–3d	Brulet 2008.
10	Breinigerberg	1	Urban	Iron, non-ferrous	1a–1a	Gralfs 1994.
11	Cologne	4	Urban	Iron, non-ferrous	1a–3d	Gralfs 1994; Rothenhöfer 2005b.
12	Erp	?	Rural	Unknown	2a–2d	Rothenhöfer 2005a.
13	Flerzheim	?	Rural	Unknown	4a–4d	Rothenhöfer 2005a.
14	Froitzheim	?	Rural	Unknown	Roman	Rothenhöfer 2005a.
15	Garsdorf	1?	Rural	Iron	4a–4d	Gralfs 1994.
16	Geldermalsen	?	Rural	Unknown	Roman	van Renswoude 2009.
17	Gressenich	?	Urban	Iron, non-ferrous	1a–4b	Rothenhöfer 2005b.
18	Hambach	4	Rural	Iron	3a–3d	Gralfs 1994.
19	Heerlen	?	Urban	Iron, non-ferrous	3a–3d	Rothenhöfer 2005b.
20	Huy	?	Urban	Iron	4a–5d	Brulet 2008.

1 Gralfs, 1994; Rothenhöfer, 2005a; 2005b; Brulet, 2008.

© ERIK TIMMERMAN, 2024 | DOI:10.1163/9789004682214_012

(*cont.*)

No.	Name	Furnaces	Category	Type	Dating	Reference
21	Inden	?	Rural	Unknown	4a–4b	Rothenhöfer 2005a.
22	Jülich	2?	Urban	Iron, non-ferrous	1a–3d	Gralfs 1994; Rothenhöfer 2005b.
23	Jünkerath	1?	Urban	Iron	4a–4d	Gralfs 1994; Rothenhöfer 2005b.
24	Kirchberg	?	Rural	Unknown	4a–5a	Rothenhöfer 2005a.
25	Kontich	?	Urban	Unknown	1a–3d	Gralfs 1994.
26	Krefeld-Gellep	?	Military	Unknown	Roman	Rothenhöfer 2005b.
27	Lanaye	4	Rural	Iron, non-ferrous	1d–3d	Brulet 2008.
28	Liberchies	8	Urban	Iron, non-ferrous	1a–3d	Brulet 2008; Gralfs 1994.
29	Mariaweiler	?	Urban	Iron, non-ferrous, precious	1a–3c	Rothenhöfer 2005b.
30	Müngersdorf	2?	Rural	Iron, non-ferrous	3a–4d	Gralfs 1994.
31	Nettersheim	1	Sanctuary	Iron, non-ferrous	2a–5a	Gralfs 1994.
32	Neuss (civilian)	2	Urban	Iron	1a–3d	Gralfs 1994.
32	Neuss (military)	2?	Military	Iron, non-ferrous	1a–3d	Gralfs 1994.
33	Nijmegen (civilian)	1	Urban	Non-ferrous	1c–1d	Gralfs 1994.
33	Nijmegen (military)	?	Military	Unknown	-1d–1d	Polak 2005; Hendriks 2014.
34	Nörvenich	?	Urban	Iron, non-ferrous	Roman	Rothenhöfer 2005b.
35	Oerle-Zuid	?	Rural	Unknown	2c–3c	Ball and Jansen 2018.
36	Pattern	?	Rural	Unknown	2a–3d	Rothenhöfer 2005a.
37	Remagen	?	Military	Unknown	-1d–4c	Luik 2002.
38	Rimburg	?	Urban	Iron, non-ferrous	1a–4d	Rothenhöfer 2005a.
39	Sauvenière	1	Rural	Unknown	3a–3d	Brulet 2008.
40	Schönforst	?	Urban	Iron	1c–2d	Rothenhöfer 2005b.
41	Theux	?	Urban	Unknown	2a–3d	Polfer 2000.
42	Tienen	?	Urban	Iron, non-ferrous	-1d–3d	Martens 2012.
43	Tongeren	?	Urban	Unknown	Roman	Veldman and Geerts 2014.

(*cont.*)

No.	Name	Furnaces	Category	Type	Dating	Reference
44	Tourinnes-St.-Lambert	?	Urban	Unknown	2a–3a	Brulet 2008.
45	Valkenburg	?	Military	Unknown	1b–3c	van Daele 1999.
46	Venlo	?	Urban	Iron, non-ferrous	1a–2b	Hupperetz 1993.
47	Vervoz	?	Urban	Iron	1b–3d	Petit *et al.* 1994.
48	Vodecée	?	Sanctuary	Iron, non-ferrous	1a–4a	Brulet 2008.
49	Voorburg	?	Urban	Unknown	Roman	Stolk 2014.
50	Xanten	3	Urban	Iron, non-ferrous	1a–3d	Gralfs 1994; Luik 2002.
51	Zwammerdam	?	Military	Unknown	Roman	van Daele 1999.

Sources and Bibliography

Shapefiles

Ancient World Mapping Center (no date) "Background_16; carte_hillshade; openwater; ba-rivers; ba_roads." *University of North Carolina*. Available at: http://awmc.unc.edu/wordpress/map-files (Accessed: 18 June 2020).

Websites

Archis (no date) *Rijksdienst voor het Cultureel Erfgoed*. Available at: https://archis.cultureelerfgoed.nl/ (Accessed: 14 December 2022).

Livius.org (no date) *Jona Lendering*. Available at: http://livius.org (Accessed: 18 June 2020).

MEDEA (no date). *Histories*. Available at: https://www.vondsten.be/ (Accessed: 29 September 2022).

NUMIS (no date) *De Nederlandsche Bank*. Available at: https://nnc.dnb.nl/dnb-nnc-ontsluiting-frontend/#/numis/ (Accessed: 5 February 2019).

Portable Antiquities of the Netherlands (no date). *Vrije Universiteit Amsterdam* Available at: https://www.portable-antiquities.nl (Accessed: 29 September 2022).

Samian research (no date) *Römisch-Germanische Zentralmuseum*. Available at: http://www.rgzm.de/samian (Accessed: 7 May 2020).

Vici.org (no date) *René Voorburg*. Available at: https://vici.org (Accessed: 18 June 2020).

Literary sources

Amm. Marc. = Ammianus Marcellinus (2014) *History. Books 14–19*. Translated by J. C. Rolfe. (Loeb Classical Library 300) Cambridge, MA: Cambridge, MA.

App. Hist. Rom. = Appian of Alexandria (2019) *Roman history*. Edited and translated by B. C. McGing. (Loeb Classical Library 2) Cambridge, MA: Harvard University Press.

Caes. Gall. = Gaius Julius Caesar (2014) *The Gallic war*. Translated by H. J. Edwards. (Loeb Classical Library 72) Cambridge, MA: Harvard University Press.

Cass. Dio = Lucius Cassius Dio (2014) *Roman history. Books 56–60*. Translated by E. Cary. (Loeb Classical Library 175) Cambridge, MA: Harvard University Press; Lucius Cassius Dio (2014) *Roman history. Books 61–70*. Translated by E. Cary. (Loeb Classical Library 176) Cambridge, MA: Harvard University Press.

Colum. Rust. = Lucius Junius Moderatus Columella (2001) *On agriculture. Book 1–4*. Edited and translated by H. B. Ash. (Loeb Classical Library 361) Cambridge, MA: Harvard University Press.

Not. dign. occ. = Anon. (1900) *Extracts from the Notitia dignitatum*. Edited by W. Fairley. (Translations and Reprints from the Original Sources of European history 6.4) Philadelphia: University of Pennsylvania Press.

Pall. Agric. = Rutilius Taurus Aemilianus Palladius (2013) *The work of farming*. Translated by J. G. Fitch. London: Prospect Books.

Plin. Nat. = Pliny the Elder (2014) *Natural history. Books 3–7*. Translated by H. Rackham. (Loeb Classical Library 352) Cambridge, MA: Harvard University Press; Pliny the Elder (2014) *Natural history. Books 12–16*. Translated by H. Rackham. (Loeb Classical Library 370) Cambridge, MA: Harvard University Press; Pliny the Elder (2014) *Natural history. Books 17–19*. Translated by H. Rackham. (Loeb Classical Library 371) Cambridge, MA: Harvard University Press.

Strab. = Strabo (2014) *Geography. Books 3–5*. Translated by H. L. Jones. (Loeb Classical Library 50) Cambridge, MA: Harvard University Press.

Suet. Claud. = Gaius Suetonius Tranquillus (2014) *Lives of the Caesars*. Translated by J. C. Rolfe. (Loeb Classical Library 38) Cambridge, MA: Harvard University Press.

Tac. Ann. = Publius Cornelius Tacitus (2008) *The annals. The reigns of Tiberius, Claudius, and Nero*. Edited by A. A. Barrett. Translated by J. C. Yardley. (Oxford World's Classics) Oxford: Oxford University Press.

Tac. Germ. = Publius Cornelius Tacitus (1999) *Germania*. Translated by J. B. Rives. (Clarendon Ancient History Series) Oxford: Clarendon Press.

Tac. Hist. = Publius Cornelius Tacitus (2009) *The histories*. Edited by R. Ash. Translated by K. Wellesley. (Penguin Classics) London: Penguin Group.

Epigraphic sources

AE = L'Année épigraphique (1888-) Paris: Presses Universitaires Françaises.

CIL = Corpus Inscriptionum Latinarum (1863-) Berlin: Berlin-Brandenburgischen Akademie der Wissenschaften.

IKöln^2 = Galsterer, B. and Galsterer, H. (2010) *Die römischen Steininschriften aus Köln*. (Kölner Forschungen 10) Mainz: Philipp von Zabern.

RSO = Castritius, H., Clauss, M. and Hefner, L. (1977) 'Die römischen Steininschriften des Odenwaldes (RSO)', in Wackerfuß, W. (ed.) *Beiträge zur Erforschung des Odenwaldes und seiner Randlandschaften II. Festschrift für Hans H. Weber*. Breuberg-Neustadt: Breuberg-Bund, pp. 237–308.

Bibliography

Aarts, J. G. (2000) *Coins or money? Exploring the monetization and functions of Roman coinage in Belgic Gaul and Lower Germany 50 BC–AD 450*. PhD thesis, Vrije Universiteit Amsterdam.

Aarts, J. G. (2005) 'Coins, money and exchange in the Roman world. A cultural-economic perspective', *Archaeological Dialogues*, 12(1), pp. 1–28.

Aarts, J. G. (2015a) 'A frog's eye view of the Roman market: the Batavian case', in van der Spek, R. J., van Leeuwen, B., and van Zanden, J. L. (eds) *A history of market performance. From ancient Babylonia to the modern world*. London: Routledge, pp. 396–411.

Aarts, J. G. (2015b) 'Marginal money. The circulation of Roman money in the rural world of the Meuse-Demer-Scheldt area', in Roymans, N., Derks, T., and Hiddink, H. (eds) *The Roman villa of Hoogeloon and the archaeology of the periphery*. (Amsterdam Archeological Studies 22) Amsterdam: Amsterdam University Press, pp. 207–227.

Acemoglu, D. and Robinson, J. A. (2012) *Why nations fail. The origins of power, prosperity, and poverty*. London: Profile Books.

Agustoni, C. (2018) *Zahlen oder Buchstaben. Zählen, rechnen, messen in Römischer Zeit*. (Musée Romain Vallon 8) Freiburg: Musée Romain Vallon.

Alcock, S. E. (1993) *Graecia capta. The landscapes of Roman Greece*. Cambridge: Cambridge University Press.

Allen, R. C. (2009) 'How prosperous were the Romans? Evidence from Diocletian's price edict (AD 301)', in Bowman, A. K. and Wilson, A. (eds) *Quantifying the Roman economy. Methods and problems*. (Oxford Studies on the Roman Economy) Oxford: Oxford University Press, pp. 327–345.

Alston, R. (1995) *Soldier and society in Roman Egypt. A social history*. London: Routledge.

Andrikopoulou-Strack, J.-N. (1996) 'Der römische vicus von Bonn', *Bonner Jahrbücher*, 196, pp. 421–467.

Andrikopoulou-Strack, J.-N. and Jenter, S. (2018) 'Straßen und Verkehr in der Germania Inferior', in Eger, C. (ed.) *Warenwege – Warenflüsse. Handel, Logistik und Transport am römischen Niederrhein*. (Xantener Berichte 32) Mainz: Nünnerich-Asmus, pp. 201–219.

Andrikopoulou-Strack, J.-N., Ulbert, C. and White, G. (2010) 'Römische vici im Rheinland – Die Grabung im Bonner Regierungsviertel', in Otten, T. (ed.) *Fundgeschichten. Archäologie in Nordrhein-Westfalen*. (Schriften zur Bodendenkmalpflege in Nordrhein-Westfalen 9) Mainz: Philipp von Zabern, pp. 147–152.

Aubert, J.-J. (2020) 'Law and life in Roman harbours', in Arnaud, P. and Keay, S. (eds) *Roman port societies*. Cambridge: Cambridge University Press, pp. 198–215.

Bagnall, R. (2009) 'Response to Elio Lo Cascio', in Bowman, A. K. and Wilson, A. (eds) *Quantifying the Roman economy. Methods and problems*. (Oxford Studies on the Roman Economy) Oxford: Oxford University Press, pp. 107–112.

Bakels, C. C. (1996) 'Growing grain for others or how to detect surplus production?', *Journal of European Archaeology*, 4, pp. 329–336.

Bakels, C. C. (2009) *The Western European loess belt. Agrarian history, 5300 BC–AD 1000*. Dordrecht: Springer.

Ball, E. A. G. and van Heeringen, R. M. (eds) (2016) *Westelijk Noord-Brabant in het Malta-tijdperk. Synthetiserend onderzoek naar de bewoningsgeschiedenis van het westelijk deel van het Brabants zandgebied.* (Nederlandse Archeologische Rapporten 51) Amersfoort: Rijksdienst voor het Cultureel Erfgoed.

Ball, E. A. G. and Jansen, R. (eds) (2018) *Drieduizend jaar bewonings-geschiedenis van oostelijk Noord-Brabant. Synthetiserend onderzoek naar locatiekeuze en bewoningsdynamiek tussen 1500 v.Chr. en 1500 n.Chr. op basis van archeologisch onderzoek in het Malta-tijdperk. Deel 1.* (Nederlandse Archeologische Rapporten 61) Amersfoort: Rijksdienst voor het Cultureel Erfgoed.

Bang, P. F. (2008) *The Roman bazaar. A comparative study of trade and markets in a tributary empire.* (Cambridge Classical Studies) Cambridge: Cambridge University Press.

Bang, P. F. (2009) 'The ancient economy and new institutional economics', *The Journal of Roman Studies*, 99, pp. 194–206.

Bechert, T. (1989) *Die Römer in Asciburgium.* (Duisburger Forschungen 36) Duisburg: Braun.

Bechert, T. (2001) 'Wirtschaft und Gesellschaft in der Provinz Germania Inferior: Zum stand der Forschung', in Grünewald, T. (ed.) *Germania Inferior. Besiedlung, Gesellschaft und Wirtschaft an der Grenze der römisch-germanischen Welt.* (Reallexikon der Germanischen Altertumskunde – Ergänzungsbände 28) Berlin: Walter de Gruyter, pp. 1–18.

Becker, T. (2007) 'Viehwirtschaft bei Kelten, Römern und Germanen im Rheinland', in Uelsberg, G. (ed.) *Krieg und Frieden. Kelten – Römer – Germanen.* Bonn: Rheinische Landesmuseum Bonn, pp. 133–143.

Becker, T. (2009) 'Straßenbau als Grenzetablierung. Neue Erkenntnisse zur Anfangsdatierung der Limesstraße in Niedergermanien', in Morillo, Á., Hanel, N., and Martín, E. (eds) *Limes XX. XXth International Congress of Roman Frontiers Studies. León (España), Septiembre, 2006.* (Anejos de Gladius 13) Madrid: Polifemo, pp. 931–943.

Bemmann, J. (2007) 'Das rechtsrheinische Vorland im 1. Jahrhundert n. Chr.', in Uelsberg, G. (ed.) *Krieg und Frieden. Kelten – Römer – Germanen.* Bonn: Rheinische Landesmuseum Bonn, pp. 97–105.

Bemmann, J. and Mirschenz, M. (2016a) 'Der Rhein als europäische Verkehrsachse – eine Zwischenbilanz', in Bemmann, J. and Mirschenz, M. (eds) *Der Rhein als europäische Verkehrsachse II.* (Bonner Beiträge zur Vor- und Frühgeschichtlichen Archäologie 19) Bonn: Rheinische Friedrich-Wilhelms-Universität Bonn, pp. 9–22.

Bemmann, J. and Mirschenz, M. (eds) (2016b) *Der Rhein als europäische Verkehrsachse II*. (Bonner Beiträge zur Vor- und Frühgeschichtlichen Archäologie 19) Bonn: Rheinische Friedrich-Wilhelms-Universität Bonn.

Berg, J. van den (2016) 'Excurs 1: amforen in rurale context', in Heirbaut, E. N. A. and Koot, C. W. (eds) *Archeologische monumentenzorg in het plangebied van de dijkteruglegging bij Lent. 4. Archeologisch onderzoek naar vindplaats 9/57 en de bewoningsgeschiedenis van de ijzertijd en Romeinse tijd.* (Archeologische Berichten Nijmegen 61) Nijmegen: Gemeente Nijmegen, pp. 179–188.

Berg, J. van den, González Cesteros, H. and Niemeijer, R. A. J. (2017) 'Excursus: amphorae from the early-Augustan legionary camp on the Hunerberg, Nijmegen. Early Augustan amphorae from Nijmegen-Hunerberg (19–16/12 BC): new evidence from selected contexts', in Carreras, C. and van den Berg, J. (eds) *Amphorae from the Kops Plateau (Nijmegen). Trade and supply to the Lower-Rhineland from the Augustan period to AD 69/70*. (Archaeopress Roman Archaeology 20) Oxford: Archaeopress, pp. 345–354.

Berni Millet, P. (2006) 'Einige Aspekte des Handels mit römischen Amphoren in Xanten', in Müller, M. (ed.) *Grabung – Forschung – Präsentation. Sammelband.* (Xantener Berichte 14) Mainz: Philipp von Zabern, pp. 19–24.

Beurden, L. M. van (2002) 'Botanisch onderzoek in het Maas-Demer-Schelde gebied. De Romeinse en de vroegmiddeleeuwse periode', in Fokkens, H. and Jansen, R. (eds) *2000 jaar bewoningsdynamiek. Brons- en ijzertijdbewoning in het Maas-Demer-Scheldegebied.* Leiden: Leiden University, pp. 287–314.

Beyaert, M. *et al.* (2006) *België in kaart. De evolutie van het landschap in drie eeuwen cartografie*. Brussels: Lannoo.

Bloemers, J. H. F. (1978) *Rijswijk (Z.H.), 'De Bult'. Eine Siedlung der Cananefaten. Interpretation.* (Nederlandse Oudheden 8) Amersfoort: ROB.

Bockius, R. (2002) 'Das Wrack von Vechten', in Mees, A. and Pferdehirt, B. (eds) *Römerzeitliche Schiffsfunde, in der Datenbank 'Navis I'.* (Kataloge Vor- und Frühgeschichtlicher Altertümer 29) Bonn: R. Habelt, pp. 60–62.

Bockius, R. (2018) 'Zur Bedeutung von Landtransport und Flussschiffahrt in vorrömischer Zeit am Niederrhein', in Eger, C. (ed.) *Warenwege – Warenflüsse. Handel, Logistik und Transport am römischen Niederrhein.* (Xantener Berichte 32) Mainz: Nünnerich-Asmus, pp. 179–199.

Bode, M. (2008) *Archäometallurgische Untersuchungen zur Blei-/Silbergewinnung im Germanien der frühen Römischen Kaiserzeit.* Phd thesis, Westfälischen Wilhelms-Universität Münster.

Bode, M., Hauptmann, A. and Mezger, K. (2009) 'Tracing Roman lead sources using lead isotope analyses in conjunction with archaeological and epigraphic evidence – a case study from Augustan/Tiberian Germania', *Archaeological and Anthropological Sciences*, 1, pp. 177–194.

Boelicke, U. (1995) 'Abfall einer neu entdeckten römischen Töpferei', in Zelle, M. (ed.) *Tatort CUT. Die Spur führt nach Xanten. Ausstellung im Regionalmuseum Xanten vom 20. August bis 29. Oktober 1995*. (Führer und Schriften des Archäologischen Park Xanten 17) Cologne: Rheinland-Verlag, pp. 51–54.

Bonnie, R. (2010) 'Did cadastres exist in the Roman northwest?', in Moore, A. et al. (eds) *TRAC 2009. Proceedings of the nineteenth annual Theoretical Roman Archaeology Conference, Michigan and Southampton 2009*, pp. 91–104.

Boreel, G. L. and van Renswoude, J. (2014) 'Huisplattegronden uit de late-ijzertijd en de Romeinse Tijd in het Midden-Nederlandse rivierengebied', in Lange, G. et al. (eds) *Huisplattegronden in Nederland. Archeologische sporen van het huis*. Amersfoort: Barkhuis & Rijksdienst voor het Cultureel Erfgoed, pp. 273–295.

Borgers, B. (2015) 'Roman pottery production at the site of Vervoz, Belgium, between the mid-first century AD and the end of the second century AD', *Journal of Roman Pottery Studies*, 16, pp. 54–72.

Borgers, B. *et al.* (2019) 'Roman pottery production in civitas Tungrorum, central Belgium, during the first-third centuries CE', *Archaeometry*, 62(2), pp. 267–284.

Borgers, B., Debruyne, T. and Martens, M. (2014) 'Romeinse aardewerkproductie in de vicus Tienen', in Degryse, H. (ed.) *Archeologie 2014*. (Recent Archeologisch Onderzoek in Vlaams-Brabant) Leuven: Provincie Vlaams-Brabant, pp. 28–31.

Borgers, B., Wijnen-Jackson, R. and Bink, M. (2017) 'The Roman pottery kiln at Halder, North-Brabant (the Netherlands), revisited', in Müller, M. (ed.) *Grabung – Forschung – Präsentation. Sammelband*. (Xantener Berichte 30) Darmstadt: Philipp von Zabern, pp. 169–184.

Bos, V. van den, *et al.* (2014) 'Roman impact on the landscape near castellum Fectio, the Netherlands', *Vegetation History and Archaeobotany*, 23(3), pp. 277–298.

Boserup, E. (1965) *The conditions of agricultural growth. The economic of agrarian change under population pressure*. London: George Allen & Unwin.

Boulakia, J. D. C. (1972) 'Lead in the Roman World', *American Journal of Archaeology*, 76(2), pp. 139–144.

Bowersock, G. W. (1974) '"The social and economic history of the Roman Empire" by Michael Ivanovitch Rostovtzeff', *Daedalus*, 103(1), pp. 15–23.

Bowman, A. K. (2018) 'The state and the economy: fiscality and taxation', in Wilson, A. and Bowman, A. K. (eds) *Trade, commerce, and the state in the Roman world*. (Oxford Studies on the Roman Economy) Oxford: Oxford University Press, pp. 27–52.

Bowman, A. K. and Thomas, J. D. (1994) *The Vindolanda writing-tablets (Tabulae Vindolandenses II)*. London: British Museum Press.

Bowman, A. K. and Wilson, A. (2009a) 'Quantifying the Roman economy: integration, growth, decline?', in Bowman, A. K. and Wilson, A. (eds) *Quantifying the Roman economy. Methods and problems*. (Oxford Studies on the Roman Economy) Oxford: Oxford University Press, pp. 3–84.

Bowman, A. K. and Wilson, A. (eds) (2009b) *Quantifying the Roman economy. Methods and problems.* (Oxford Studies on the Roman Economy) Oxford: Oxford University Press.

Breeze, D. J. *et al.* (2018) *Frontiers of the Roman Empire. The Lower German Limes.* Leiden: Sidestone Press.

Broeke, P. W. van den (2012) *Het handgevormde aardewerk uit de ijzertijd en de Romeinse tijd van Oss-Ussen. Studies naar typochronologie, technologie en herkomst.* PhD thesis, Universiteit Leiden.

Bruckner, A. and Piepers, W. (1963) 'Lohn. Jahresbericht des staatlichen Vertrauensmannes für kulturgeschichtliche Bodenaltertümer vom 1. Januar bis 31. Dezember 1961', *Bonner Jahrbücher*, 163, p. 545.

Brue, H. De, *et al.* (2017) 'The Hesbaye and Condroz Regions (Belgium). Analysis of archaeological site patterns from Roman to Merovingian times through logistic regression modelling', in Reddé, M. (ed.) *Gallia rustica 1. Les campagnes du nord-est de la Gaule, de la fin de l'âge du Fer à l'Antiquité tardive.* Bordeaux: Ausonius, pp. 153–178.

Brüggler, M. (2006) 'Spätrömische Glasherstellung im Hambacher Forst', in Creemers, G., Demarsin, B., and Cosyns, P. (eds) *Roman glass in Germania Inferior. Interregional comparisons and recent results. Tongeren, May 13th, 2005.* Tongeren: Gallo-Romeins Museum (Atuatuca), pp. 68–71.

Brüggler, M. (2010) 'HA 132 – villa rustica and spätantike Glashütte', in Aufleger, M. (ed.) *Braunkohlenarchäologie im Rheinland. Entwicklung von Kultur, Umwelt und Landschaft. Kolloquium der Stiftung zur Förderung der Archäologie im rheinischen Braunkohlenrevier in Brauweiler vom 5.–6. Oktober 2006.* Weilerswist: Ralf Liebe, pp. 91–94.

Brüggler, M. (2014) 'Eine frühkaiserzeitlicher Töpferei in Burginatium, Kalkar, Kreis Kleve', in Liesen, B. (ed.) *Römische Keramik in Niedergermanien. Produktion – Handel – Gebrauch. Beiträge zur Tagung der Rei Cretariae Romanae Fautores. 21.–26. September 2014, LVR-RömerMuseum im Archäologischen Park Xanten.* (Xantener Berichte 27) Darmstadt: Philipp von Zabern, pp. 37–60.

Brüggler, M. *et al.* (2017) 'The Roman Rhineland. Farming and consumption in different landscapes', in Reddé, M. (ed.) *Gallia rustica 1. Les campagnes du nord-est de la Gaule, de la fin de l'âge du Fer à l'Antiquité tardive.* (Mémoires 49) Bordeaux: Ausonius Éditions, pp. 19–96.

Brüggler, M. (2018) 'Landwirtschaft und Güterversorgung im Hinterland der Colonia Ulpia Traiana bei Xanten', in Eger, C. (ed.) *Warenwege – Warenflüsse. Handel, Logistik und Transport am römischen Niederrhein.* (Xantener Berichte 32) Mainz: Nünnerich-Asmus, pp. 289–303.

Bruin, J. de (2017) *Rurale gemeenschappen in de civitas Cananefatium 50–300 na Christus.* PhD thesis, Universiteit Leiden.

Brulet, R. (1983) 'Les structures', in Brulet, R. (ed.) *Braives Gallo-Romain II. Le quartier des potiers*. (Publications d'Histoire de l'Art et d'Archéologie de l'Université Catholique de Louvain) Louvain-la-Neuve: Institute Supérieur d'Archéologie et d'Histoire de l'Art, pp. 11–54.

Brulet, R. (2008) *Les Romains en Wallonie*. Brussels: Racine.

Brulet, R. (2010) 'La céramique à glaçure plombifère du Bas-Empire, vallèe Rhénane', in Brulet, R. et al. (eds) *La céramique romaine en Gaule du Nord. Dictionnaire des céramiques. La vaisselle à large diffusion*. Turnhout: Brepols, pp. 297–299.

Brulet, R. (2017) 'The Roman army and military defence in northern Gaul and the Germanic provinces during the late Empire', in Roymans, N., Heeren, S., and De Clercq, W. (eds) *Social dynamics in the northwest frontiers of the late Roman Empire. Beyond decline or transformation*. (Amsterdam Archaeological Studies 26) Amsterdam: Amsterdam University Press, pp. 39–56.

Brulet, R., Laubenheimer, F. and Vilvorder, F. (1992) 'Les amphores de Braives, un vicus de Gaule Belgique', in Laubenheimer, F. (ed.) *Les amphores en Gaule. Production et circulation. Table ronde internationale. Metz 4–6 octobre 1990. CNRS, Ministère de la Culture et de la Communication, Service Régional de l'Archéologie de Lorraine*. (Annales Littéraires de l'Université de Besançon 474) Besançon: Université de Franche-Comté, pp. 171–178.

Brun, J.-P. (2003) *Le vin et l'huile dans la Méditerranée antique. Viticulture, oléiculture et procédés de transformation*. (Collection des Hespérides) Paris: Errance.

Brun, J.-P. (2013) 'Techniques et économies de la Méditerranée antique', in Corvol, P. (ed.) *Annuaire du Collège de France 2011–2012. Résumé des cours et travaux 112e année*. Paris: Collège de France, pp. 465–490.

Brun, J.-P. (2016) 'The archaeology of Roman urban workshops: a French approach?', in Wilson, A. and Flohr, M. (eds) *Urban craftsmen and traders in the Roman world*. (Oxford Studies on the Roman Economy) Oxford: Oxford University Press, pp. 77–94.

Buijtendorp, T. M. (2010) *Forum Hadriani. De vergeten stad van Hadrianus. Ontwikkeling, uiterlijk en betekenis van het 'Nederlands Pompeji'*. PhD thesis, Vrije Universiteit Amsterdam.

Bunnik, F. P. M. *et al.* (1995) 'Archäopalynologische Betrachtungen zum Kulturwandel in den Jahrhunderten um Christi Geburt', *Archäologische Informationen*, 18(2), pp. 169–185.

Büntgen, U. *et al.* (2011) '2500 years of European climate variability and human susceptibility', *Science*, 331, pp. 578–583.

Burandt, B. (2017) 'Neue Grabungsergebnisse zu den römischen Lagern bei Till, Kapitelshof', *Archäologie im Rheinland*, 2016, pp. 107–109.

Buringh, E., van Zanden, J. L. and Bosker, M. (2012) *Soldiers and booze: the rise and decline of a Roman market economy in north-western Europe, CGEH Working Paper Series*. 32.

Burmeister, S. (2018) 'Die drei großen W: Waren – Wagen – Wege. Überlegungen zum Überlandverkehr in prähistorischer Zeit, mit besonderem Blick auf Nordwestdeutschland', in Nessel, B., Neumann, D., and Bartelheim, M. (eds) *Bronzezeitlicher Transport. Akteure, Mittel und Wege.* (Ressourcenkulturen 8) Tübingen: Tübingen University Press, pp. 119–138.

Bursche, A. (2008) 'Function of Roman coins in Barbaricum of later antiquity. An anthropological essay.', in Bursche, A., Ciolek, R., and Wolters, R. (eds) *Roman coins outside the empire. Ways and phases, contexts and functions. Proceedings of the ESF/SCH exploratory workshop, Radziwiłł Palace, Nieborów (Poland), 3–6 September 2005.* (Collection Moneta 82) Wetteren: Moneta, pp. 395–416.

Campbell, B. (2012) *Rivers & the power of ancient Rome.* (Studies in the History of Greece and Rome) Chapel Hill: The University of North Carolina Press.

Campbell, D. B. (2017) 'Clerks, artisans, and specialists. The immunes', *Ancient Warfare*, pp. 55–57.

Carreras, C. (2002) 'The Roman military supply during the Principate. Transportation and staples', in Erdkamp, P. (ed.) *The Roman army and the economy.* Amsterdam: J.C. Gieben, pp. 70–89.

Carreras, C. (2006) 'A quantitative approach to the amphorae from Xanten: a more comprehensive view of the long distance Roman trade', in Müller, M. (ed.) *Grabung – Forschung – Präsentation. Sammelband.* (Xantener Berichte 14) Mainz: Philipp von Zabern, pp. 25–39.

Carreras, C. (2017) 'Methodology for the study of the amphorae: quantification and mapping', in Carreras, C. and van den Berg, J. (eds) *Amphorae from the Kops Plateau (Nijmegen): trade and supply to the Lower-Rhineland from the Augustan period to AD 69/70.* (Archaeopress Roman Archaeology 20) Oxford: Archaeopress, pp. 13–27.

Carreras, C. and van den Berg, J. (2017) 'Conclusions: Kops Plateau in context', in Carreras, C. and van den Berg, J. (eds) *Amphorae from the Kops Plateau (Nijmegen): trade and supply to the Lower-Rhineland from the Augustan period to AD 69/70.* (Archaeopress Roman Archaeology 20) Oxford: Archaeopress, pp. 355–380.

Carreras, C. and Berni Millet, P. (2015) 'Hispanic imports in the first military camps of Novaesium (Neuss): Lager 1–7 (Augustus-Flavians)', *Marburger Beiträge zur Antiken Handels-, Wirtschafts- und Sozialgeschichte*, 32–2014, pp. 173–207.

Carreras, C. and Morais, R. (2012) 'The Atlantic Roman trade during the Principate: new evidence from the western façade', *Oxford Journal of Archaeology*, 31(4), pp. 419–441.

Carroll, M. (1998) 'Spezialisierung im Töpferbezirk', *Aktuelles aus der Landesarchäologie*, 1, p. 43.

Carroll, M. (2001) *Romans, Celts & Germans. The German provinces of Rome.* Stroud: Tempus.

Carroll, M. (2005) 'The early Roman pottery industry in Cologne, Germany: a new kiln site in the Oppidum Ubiorum', *Journal of Roman Pottery Studies*, 11, pp. 75–88.

Cascio, E. Lo (2006) 'The role of the state in the Roman economy: making use of the new institutional economics', in Bang, P. F., Ikeguchi, M., and Ziche, H. G. (eds) *Ancient economies modern methodologies. Archaeology, comparative history, models and institutions*. Bari: Edipuglia, pp. 215–234.

Cascio, E. Lo (2007) 'The early Roman empire: the state and the economy', in Scheidel, W., Morris, I., and Saller, R. P. (eds) *The Cambridge economic history of the Greco-Roman world*. Cambridge: Cambridge University Press, pp. 619–648.

Cascio, E. Lo (2009) 'Urbanization as a Proxy of Demographic and Economic Growth', in Bowman, A. K. and Wilson, A. (eds) *Quantifying the Roman Economy. Methods and Problems*. (Oxford Studies on the Roman Economy) Oxford: Oxford University Press, pp. 87–106.

Cascio, E. Lo (2017a) *Die neue Wirtschaftsgeschichte des Römischen Reiches. Paradigmen und Ansätze*. (Beiträge zur Wirtschaftsarchäologie 1) Bonn: Habelt.

Cascio, E. Lo (2017b) 'Market regulation and transaction costs in the Roman Empire', in Wilson, A. and Bowman, A. K. (eds) *Trade, commerce, and the state in the Roman world*. (Oxford Studies on the Roman Economy) Oxford: Oxford University Press, pp. 117–132.

Casparie, W. A. (1986) 'The two Iron Age wooden trackways XIV (Bou) and XV (Bou) in the raised bog of southeast Drenthe (the Netherlands)', *Palaeohistoria*, 28, pp. 169–210.

Castree, N., Demeritt, D. and Liverman, D. (2009) 'Introduction: making sense of environmental geography', in Castree, N. et al. (eds) *A companion to environmental geography*. (Blackwell Companions to Geography) Chichester: Wiley-Blackwell, pp. 1–15.

Cavallo, C., Kooistra, L. I. and Dütting, M. K. (2008) 'Food supply to the Roman army in the Rhine delta in the first century A.D.', in Stallibrass, S. and Thomas, R. (eds) *Feeding the Roman army: the archaeology of production and supply in NW Europe*. Oxford: Oxbow Books, pp. 69–82.

Chorus, J. P. (2017) 'Building timber auxiliary forts in the Lower Rhine delta in the Netherlands (AD 40–140)', *Archäologische Berichte*, 27, pp. 19–36.

Clark, G. (2007) *A farewell to alms. A brief economic history of the world*. (The Princeton Economic History of the Western World) Princeton: Princeton University Press.

Cleary, S. E. (2013) *The Roman west, AD 200–500. An archaeological study*. Cambridge: Cambridge University Press.

Clerbaut, T. (2010) *Een inleiding tot de Gallo-Romeinse pottenbakkersovens in Gallia Belgica en Germania Inferior: inventaris, spreiding en morfologie*. MA thesis, Universiteit Gent.

Clerbaut, T. (2015) 'Der Produktion und Verbreitung römischer Baukeramik auf der Spur: Organisation einer neuen Grossindustrie entlang der Rheingrenze', in Grunwald, L. (ed.) *Den Töpfern auf der Spur. Orte der Keramikherstellung im Licht der neuesten Forschung. 46. Internationales Symposium Keramikforschung des Arbeitskreises für Keramikforschung und des Römisch-Germanischen Zentralmuseum*

Mainz vom 16. bis zum 20. September 20. (RGZM – Tagungen 21) Mainz: Verlag des Römisch-Germanisch Zentralmuseum, pp. 85–90.

Clercq, W. De (2005) 'Shaped by tradition. On the persistence of hand-made pottery traditions in northern Gaul, ca. 100 BC–300 AD', *Rei Cretariae Romanae Fautorum*, 39, pp. 201–208.

Clercq, W. De (2009) *Lokale gemeenschappen in het Imperium Romanum. Transformaties in rurale bewoningsstructuur en materiële cultuur in de landschappen van het noordelijk deel van de civitas Menapiorum (provincie Gallia-Belgica, ca. 100 v. Chr.–400 n. Chr.)*. PhD thesis, Universiteit Gent.

Clercq, W. De, Creemers, G. and Hiddink, H. (2015) 'An inventory of Roman habitation in the Meuse-Demer-Scheldt area', in Roymans, N., Derks, T., and Hiddink, H. (eds) *The Roman villa of Hoogeloon and the archaeology of the periphery*. (Amsterdam Archaeological Studies 22) Amsterdam: Amsterdam University Press, pp. 33–44.

Collins, A., van Enckevort, H. and Hendriks, J. (2009) 'A grey area between the Batavians and the Romans. Wheel-thrown domestic pottery in the civitas Batavorum', in van Enckevort, H. (ed.) *Roman material culture. Studies in honour of Jan Thijssen*. Zwolle: Foundation for the Promotion of Archaeology, pp. 171–199.

Corbier, M. (2005) 'Coinage, society and economy', in Bowman, A. K., Cameron, A., and Garnsey, P. (eds) *The crisis of empire, AD 193–337*. (The Cambridge Ancient History 12) Cambridge: Cambridge University Press, pp. 393–439.

Daele, B. Van (1999) 'The military fabricae in Germania Inferior from Augustus to A.D. 260/270', *Journal of Roman Military Equipment Studies*, 10, pp. 125–136.

Dannell, G. and Mees, A. W. (2013) 'The Mainz internet database of names on terra sigillata', in Fulford, M. and Durham, E. (eds) *Seeing red. New economic & social perspectives on Gallo-Roman terra sigillata*. (Bulletin of the Institute of Classical Studies Supplement 102) London: Institute of Classical Studies, School of Advanced Study, University of London, pp. 28–25.

Daszkiewicz, M., Liesen, B. and Schneider, G. (2003) 'Chemische und technische analysen an Terra Sigillata aus Sinzig', in Liesen, B. and Brandl, U. (eds) *Römische Keramik. Herstellung und Handel. Kolloquium Xanten, 15.–17.6.2000*. (Xantener Berichte 13) Mainz: Philipp von Zabern, pp. 29–38.

Denayer, J., Pacyna, D. and Boulavin, F. (2011) *Le minerai de fer en Wallonie. Cartographie, histoire et géologie. L'aventure de la plus grande richesse de la Wallonie*. Namur: Service Public de Wallonie.

Derks, T. and Roymans, N. (2002) 'Seal-boxes and the spread of Latin literacy in the Rhine delta', in Cooley, A. E. (ed.) *Becoming Roman, writing Latin? Literacy and epigraphy in the Roman west*. (Journal of Roman Archaeology Supplementary Series 48) Portsmouth: Journal of Roman Archaeology, pp. 87–134.

Derks, T. and Roymans, N. (2006) 'Returning auxiliary veterans: some methodological considerations', *Journal of Roman Archaeology*, 19(1), pp. 121–135.

Deru, X. (2017) 'Croissance et crise dans le nord de la gaule romaine', *Topoi Orient Occident*, 21(1), pp. 217–232.

Deschler-Erb, E. (2012) 'Das Handwerk in der Antike', in Amrein, H. et al. (eds) *Das römerzeitliche Handwerk in der Schweiz. Bestandsaufnahme und erste Synthesen.* (Monographies Instrumentum 40) Montagnac: Éditions monique mergoil, pp. 13–15.

Detten, D. von, and Weber, C. (1990) 'Archäologischer Fundbericht für den Kreis Wesel 1988', *Heimatkalender Kreis Wesel*, pp. 217–220.

Diepen, L. van, and Polak, M. (2009) *Resten van de steen- en pottenbakkerij van het Romeinse leger op Landgoed Holthurnsche Hof in Berg en Dal (gem. Groesbeek).* (Auxilia 8) Nijmegen: Auxilia.

Dijk, J. van, and Groot, M. (2013) 'The Late Iron Age-Roman transformation from subsistence to surplus production in animal husbandry in the central and western parts of the Netherlands', in Groot, M., Lentjes, D., and Zeiler, J. (eds) *Barely surviving or more than enough? The environmental archaeology of subsistence, specialisation and surplus food of production.* Leiden: Sidestone Press, pp. 175–200.

Dinter, M. van, *et al.* (2014) 'Could the local population of the Lower Rhine delta supply the Roman army? Part 2. Modelling the carrying capacity using archaeological, palaeo-ecological and geomorphological data', *Journal of Archaeology in the Low Countries*, 5, pp. 5–50.

Domínguez-Delmás, M. *et al.* (2014) 'Long-distance oak supply in mid-2nd century AD revealed: the case of a Roman harbour (Voorburg-Arentsburg) in the Netherlands', *Journal of Archaeological Science*, 41, pp. 642–654.

Dommergue, C. *et al.* (2006) 'Mines et métallurgies en Gaule à la fin de l'âge du Fer et à l'epoque Romain', in *Celtes et Gaulois: l'archéologie face à l'histoire -v- La Romanisation et la question de l'héritage celtique, Actes de la table ronde de Lausanne, 17–18 juin 2005.* (Bibracte 12/5) Glux-en-Glenne: Centre archéologique européen, pp. 131–162.

Dreesen, R., De Ceukelaire, M. and Ruppienė, V. (2018) 'On the Roman use of "Belgian marbles" in the civitas Tungrorum and beyond', in Coquelet, C. et al. (eds) *Roman ornamental stones in north-western Europe. Natural resources, manufacturing, supply, life & after-life.* (Études et Documents Archéologie 38) Namur: Wallonie patrimoine AWaP, pp. 25–50.

Drexhage, H.-J. (1991) *Preise, Mieten, Pachten, Kosten und Löhne im römischen Ägypten bis zum Regierungsantritt Diokletians.* (Vorarbeiten zu einer Wirtschaftsgeschichte des Römischen Ägyptens 1) St. Katharinen: Scripta Mercaturae.

Drexhage, H.-J., Konen, H. and Ruffing, K. (2002a) 'Die Wirtschaft der römischen Kaiserzeit in der modernen Deutung: einige Überlegungen', in Strobel, K. (ed.) *Die Ökonomie des Imperium Romanum. Strukturen, Modelle und Wertungen im Spannungsfeld von Modernismus und Neoprimitivismus. Akten des 3. Trierer Symposiums zur Antiken Wirtschaftsgeschichte.* (Pharos 17) St. Katharinen: Scripta Mercaturae, pp. 1–66.

Drexhage, H.-J., Konen, H. and Ruffing, K. (2002b) *Die Wirtschaft des Römischen Reiches (1.–3. Jahrhundert). Eine Einführung.* Berlin: Akademie.

Driel-Murray, C. van (2003) 'Ethnic soldiers: the experience of the Lower Rhine tribes', in Grünewald, T. and Seibel, S. (eds) *Kontinuität und Diskontinuität. Germania Inferior am Beginn und am Ende der römischen Herrschaft. Beiträge des deutsch-niederländischen Kolloquiums in der Katholieke Universiteit Nijmegen (27. bis 30. 06. 2001).* (Ergänzungsbände zum Reallexikon der Germanischen Altertumskunde 35) Berlin: Walter de Gruyter, pp. 200–217.

Dries, F. M. A. van den (2007) *Breekbaar verleden. Romeins glas in de Lage Landen.* Utrecht: Matrijs.

Duncan-Jones, R. P. (1990) *Structure and scale in the Roman economy.* Cambridge: Cambridge University Press.

Dungworth, D. (2016) 'Metals and metalworking', in Millet, M., Revell, L., and Moore, A. (eds) *The Oxford handbook of Roman Britain.* Oxford: Oxford University Press, pp. 532–554.

Durali-Müller, S. *et al.* (2009) 'Roman lead mining in Germany: its origin and development through time deduced from lead isotope provenance studies', in Meyer, J.-W. (ed.) *Zwischen Euphrat und Rhein. Ergebnisse des Graduierten-Kollegs »Archäologi sche Analytik« an der Johann Wolfgang von Goethe-Universität Frankfurt am Main.* (Frankfurter Archäologische Schriften 7) Wiesbaden: Reichert, pp. 139–143.

Eck, W. (2004) *Köln in römischer Zeit. Geschichte einer Stadt im Rahmen des Imperium Romanum.* (Geschichte der Stadt Köln 1) Cologne: Greven Verlag Köln.

Eck, W. (2006) 'Der praefectus annonae: ein Superminister im Imperium Romanum? Heeresversorgung und praefectura annonae: nicht eine Großadministration, sondern zwei getrennte administrative Welten', in *Grabung – Forschung – Präsentation. Sammelband.* (Xantener Berichte 14) Mainz: Philipp von Zabern, pp. 49–57.

Eck, W. (2007) 'Der Rhein als Lebensader der Städte des römischen Germaniens', in Ohlig, C. (ed.) *Von der cura aquarum bis zur EU – Wasserrahmenrichtlinie – Fünf Jahre DWhG.* (Schriften der Deutschen Wasserhistorischen Gesellschaft 11) Siegburg: Deutschen Wasserhistorischen Gesellschaft, pp. 109–126.

Ehmig, U. (2003) *Die römischen Amphoren aus Mainz.* (Frankfurter Archäologische Schriften 4) Möhnesee: Bibliopolis.

Ehmig, U. (2007a) *Die römischen Amphoren im Umland von Mainz.* (Frankfurter Archäologische Schriften 5) Wiesbaden: Reichert.

Ehmig, U. (2007b) 'Tituli Picti auf Amphoren in Köln', *Kölner Jahrbuch*, 40, pp. 215–322.

Ehmig, U. (2009) 'Tituli Picti auf Amphoren in Köln II', *Kölner Jahrbuch*, 42, pp. 393–445.

Ehmig, U. (2012) 'Auf dem Holzweg. Bevölkerungsdichte und natürliche Ressourcen. Überlegungen zum Holzbedarf im römischen Rheinland', *Ancient Society*, 42, pp. 159–218.

Ehmig, U. (2018) 'Tituli Picti auf Amphoren in Köln III', *Kölner Jahrbuch*, 51, pp. 399–405.

Ellmers, D. (1978) 'Shipping on the Rhine during the Roman period: the pictorial evidence', in du Plat Taylor, J. and Cleere, H. (eds) *Roman shipping and trade: Britain and the Rhine provinces*. (CBA Research Report 24) London: The Council for British Archaeology, pp. 1–14.

Enckevort, H. van (2012) *Gebundelde sporen. Enkele kanttekeningen bij aardewerk en nederzettingen uit Romeins Nederland*. PhD thesis, Universiteit Leiden.

Enckevort, H. van, Haalebos, J. K. and Thijssen, J. (2000) *Nijmegen. Legerplaats en stad in het achterland van de Romeinse Limes*. (Archeologische Berichten Nijmegen 3) Nijmegen: Bureau Archeologie van de Gemeente Nijmegen.

Enckevort, H. van, and Hendriks, J. (2014) 'Gebouwplattegronden uit de Romeinse tijd in Zuidoost-Nederland', in Lange, G. et al. (eds) *Huisplattegronden in Nederland. Archeologische sporen van het huis*. Amersfoort: Barkhuis & Rijksdienst voor het Cultureel Erfgoed, pp. 235–271.

Enckevort, H. van, and Thijssen, J. (2002) *Cuijk. Een regionaal centrum in de Romeinse tijd*. (Archeologische Berichten Nijmegen 5) Utrecht: Matrijs.

Epstein, R. A. (2016) 'The economic structure of Roman property law', in du Plessis, P. J., Ando, C., and Tuori, K. (eds) *The Oxford handbook of Roman law and society*. Oxford: Oxford University Press, pp. 513–523.

Erdkamp, P. (2001) 'Beyond the limits of the "consumer city". A model of the urban and rural economy in the Roman world', *Historia: Zeitschrift für Alte Geschichte*, 50(3), pp. 332–356.

Erdkamp, P. (2005) *The grain market in the Roman Empire. A social, political and economic study*. Cambridge: Cambridge University Press.

Erdkamp, P. (2012) 'Urbanism', in Scheidel, W. (ed.) *The Cambridge companion to the Roman economy*. Cambridge: Cambridge University Press, pp. 241–265.

Erdkamp, P. (2016) 'Economic growth in the Roman Mediterranean world: an early good-bye to Malthus?', *Explorations in Economic History*, 60, pp. 1–20.

Erdrich, M. (2001) 'Wirtschaftsbeziehungen zwischen Germania Inferior und dem germanischen Vorland – ein Wunschbild', in Grünewald, T. (ed.) *Germania Inferior. Besiedlung, Gesellschaft und Wirtschaft an der Grenze der römisch-germanischen Welt*. (Reallexikon der Germanischen Altertumskunde – Ergänzungsbände 28) Berlin: Walter de Gruyter, pp. 306–335.

Eschbaumer, P. (2001) 'Terra Sigillata', in Fischer, T. (ed.) *Die römische Provinzen. Ein Einführing in ihre Archäologie*. Stuttgart: Konrad Theiss, pp. 267–290.

Feijst, L. M. B. van der (2011) 'Metaal', in Veldman, H. A. P. (ed.) *Graven in Zoelen. De opgraving van een Romeinse nederzetting en grafveld*. (ADC Rapport 2391) Amersfoort: ADC ArcheoProjecten, pp. 137–155.

Feijst, L. M. B. van der, Langelaar, J. and Kemmers, F. (2014) 'Metalen artefacten', in Veldman, H. A. P. et al. (eds) *Aan de rand van de Romeinse stad Atuatuca*

Tungrorum. Een archeologische opgraving aan de Beukenbergweg in Tongeren. (ADC Monografie 16) Amersfoort: ADC ArcheoProjecten, pp. 257–282.

Fernández-Götz, M. (2014) 'Reassessing the oppida: the role of power and religion', *Oxford Journal of Archaeology*, 33(4), pp. 379–394.

Filtzinger, P. (1972) *Die Römische Keramik aus dem Militärbereich von Novaesium (etwa 25 bis 50. n Chr.)*. Berlin: Gebr. Mann Verlag.

Finley, M. I. (1979) *The Bücher-Meyer controversy*. New York: Arno Press.

Finley, M. I. (1999) *The ancient economy. Updated edition with a foreword by Ian Morris.* Berkeley: University of California Press.

Fischer, T. (2012) *Die Armee der Caesaren. Archäologie und Geschichte.* Regensburg: Verlag Friedrich Pustet.

Fischer, T. (2013) 'Ländliche Siedlungen in den Nordwestprovinzen des Imperium Romanum', in Schörner, G. (ed.) *Leben auf dem Lande. 'Il Monte' bei San Gimignano: ein römischer Fundplatz und sein Kontext.* Vienna: Phoibos, pp. 323–330.

Fitzpatrick, A. (1985) 'The distribution of Dressel 1 amphorae in northwest Europe', *Oxford Journal of Archaeology*, 4, pp. 305–340.

Flohr, M. (2019) 'Skeletons in the cupboard. Femurs and food regimes in the Roman world', in Erdkamp, P. and Holleran, C. (eds) *The Routledge handbook of diet and nutrition in the Roman world.* London: Routledge, pp. 273–280.

Follmann-Schulz, A.-B. (1991) 'Fours de verriers romains dans la provinces de Germanie Inférieure', in Foy, D. and Sennequier, G. (eds) *Ateliers de verriers de l'Antiquité à la période pré-industrielle. Actes des 4èmes Rencontres, Rouen, 24–25 novembre 1989.* Rouen: Association Française pour l'Archéologie du Verre, pp. 35–40.

Franconi, T. V. (2014) *The economic development of the Rhine River basin in the Roman period. 30 BC–AD 406.* PhD thesis, University of Oxford.

Franconi, T. V. (2016) 'Climatic influences on riverine transport on the Roman Rhine', in Schäfer, C. (ed.) *Connecting the ancient world. Mediterranean shipping, maritime networks and their impact.* (Pharos 38) Rahden/Westf.: Marie Leidorf, pp. 27–44.

Frank, K. (2007) 'Zur ‚einheimischen' Bevölkerung Bonns in frührömischer Zeit', in Uelsberg, G. (ed.) *Krieg und Frieden. Kelten – Römer – Germanen.* Bonn: Rheinische Landesmuseum Bonn.

Frank, K. (2011) 'Corpus der römischen Funde im europäischen Barbaricum – das Rheinland', *Archäologie im Rheinland*, 2010, pp. 92–94.

Frank, K. (2018) 'Zwischen Prestigegut, Beute und Import – römische Funde rechts des Rheins', in Eger, C. (ed.) *Warenwege – Warenflüsse. Handel, Logistik und Transport am römischen Niederrhein.* (Xantener Berichte 32) Mainz: Nünnerich-Asmus, pp. 545–560.

Frank, K. and Keller, C. (2007) 'Jüchen-Neuholz. Vom eisenzeitlichen Gehöft zur Villa rustica', in Uelsberg, G. (ed.) *Krieg und Frieden. Kelten – Römer – Germanen.* Bonn: Rheinische Landesmuseum Bonn.

Frank, T., Diethelm, B. and Busch, R. (2013) 'Revision of dendrochronological data in the Rhineland, Germany. An interim report on a generational transfer of dendrodata', in Helle, G. et al. (eds) *TRACE. Tree Rings in Archaeology Climatology and Ecology. Volume 11. Proceedings of the DENDROSYMPOSIUM 2012.* (GFZ series Scientific Technical Report) Potsdam: GFZ Publications, pp. 146–153.

Franzen, P. (2009) 'The Nijmegen canabae legionis (71–102/105 AD). Military and civilian life on the frontier', in Morillo, Á., Hanel, N., and Martín, E. (eds) *Limes XX. XXth International Congress of Roman Frontier Studies. León (Spain), September, 2006.* (Anejos de Gladius 13) Madrid: Polifemo, pp. 1271–1283.

Friedrich, S. (2014) 'Die römischen Töpferein von Remagen/Rigomagus', in Liesen, B. (ed.) *Römische Keramik in Niedergermanien. Produktion – Handel – Gebrauch. Beiträge zur Tagung der Rei Cretariae Romanae Fautores. 21.–26. September 2014, LVR-RömerMuseum im Archäologischen Park Xanten.* (Xantener Berichte 27) Darmstadt: Philipp von Zabern.

Frier, B. W. (2001) 'More is worse: some observations on the population of the Roman Empire', in Scheidel, W. (ed.) *Debating Roman demography.* (Mnemosyne. Supplementum 211) Leiden: Brill, pp. 139–159.

Fulford, M. (2013) 'Gallo-Roman sigillata: fresh approaches, fresh challenges, fresh questions', in Fulford, M. and Durham, E. (eds) *Seeing red. New economic & social perspectives on Gallo-Roman terra sigillata.* (Bulletin of the Institute of Classical Studies. Supplement 102) London: Institute of Classical Studies, School of Advanced Study, University of London, pp. 1–17.

Funari, P. P. A. (2002) 'The consumption of olive oil in Roman Britain and the role of the army', in Erdkamp, P. (ed.) *The Roman army and the economy.* Amsterdam: J.C. Gieben, pp. 235–263.

Gaitzsch, W. (1985) 'Werkzeuge und Geräte in der römischen Kaiserzeit. Eine Übersicht', in Temporini, H. (ed.) *Principat. Zwölfter Band (3. Teilband). Künste (Forts.).* (Aufstieg und Niedergang der Römischen Welt. Geschichte und Kultur Roms im Spiegel der Neueren Forschung 2) Berlin: Walter de Gruyter & Co., pp. 170–204.

Gaitzsch, W. (1986) 'Grundformen römischer Landsiedlungen im Westen der CCAA', *Bonner Jahrbücher*, 186, pp. 397–427.

Gaitzsch, W. *et al.* (2000) 'Spätrömische Glashütten im Hambacher Forst – Produktionsort der ECVA-Fasskrüge. Archäologische und naturwissenschaftliche Untersuchungen', *Bonner Jahrbücher*, 200, pp. 83–241.

Gaitzsch, W. (2011) 'Roman villa landscapes of the lignite mining areas in the hinterland of Cologne', in Roymans, N. and Derks, T. (eds) *Villa landscapes in the Roman north: economy, culture and lifestyles.* (Amsterdam Archaeological Studies 17) Amsterdam: Amsterdam University Press, pp. 285–299.

Galestin, M. C. (2010) 'Roman artefacts beyond the northern frontier: interpreting the evidence from the Netherlands', *European Journal of Archaeology*, 13(1), pp. 64–88.

Galor, O. (2011) *Unified growth theory*. Princeton: Princeton University Press.

Galsterer, B. and Galsterer, H. (2010) *Die römischen Steininschriften aus Köln*. (Kölner Forschungen 10) Mainz: Philipp von Zabern.

Galsterer, H. (2000) 'Local and provincial institutions and government', in Bowman, A. K., Garnsey, P., and Rathbone, D. (eds) *The high empire, A.D. 70–192*. (The Cambridge Ancient History 11) Cambridge: Cambridge University Press, pp. 344–360.

Garnsey, P. (1999) *Food and society in classical antiquity*. (Key Themes in Ancient History) Cambridge: Cambridge University Press.

Garnsey, P. and Saller, R. P. (1987) *The Roman empire. Economy, society and culture*. London: Duckworth.

Gechter, M. (2007) 'Die Militärgeschichte am Niederrhein von Caesar bis Traian', in Uelsberg, G. (ed.) *Krieg und Frieden. Kelten – Römer – Germanen*. Bonn: Rheinische Landesmuseum Bonn, pp. 89–96.

Geerts, R. C. A., Hartoch, E. and Vilvorder, F. (2014) 'Het pottenbakkersatelier aan de Beukenbergweg te Tongeren', *Signa*, 3, pp. 89–96.

Gerritsen, F. (2003) *Local identities. Landscape and community in the Late Prehistoric Meuse-Demer-Scheldt Region*. (Amsterdam Archaeological Studies 9) Amsterdam: Amsterdam University Press.

Gielen, J. . (1987) 'Aardewerk uit Heerlen: productie en datering', in Stuart, P. and de Grooth, M. E. T. (eds) *Langs de weg. De Romeinse weg van Boulogne-sur-Mer naar Keulen, verkeersader voor industrie en handel. Villa Rustica. Het Romeinse boerenbedrijf in het Rijn/Maasgebied*. Heerlen, pp. 90–92.

Giljohann, R., Hunold, A. and Wenzel, S. (2017) 'Rural life and industry between the Eifel and the Rhine', in Reddé, M. (ed.) *Gallia rustica 1. Les campagnes du nord-est de la Gaule, de la fin de l'âge du Fer à l'Antiquité tardive*. (Mémoires 49) Bordeaux: Ausonius Éditions, pp. 125–152.

Gluhak, T. M. and Hofmeister, W. (2011) 'Geochemical provenance analyses of Roman lava millstones north of the Alps: a study of their distribution and implications for the beginning of Roman lava quarrying in the Eifel region (Germany)', *Journal of Archaeological Science*, 38, pp. 1603–1620.

Goldstone, J. A. (2002) 'Efflorescences and economic growth in world history: rethinking the "rise of the West" and the industrial revolution', *Journal of World History*, 13(2), pp. 323–389.

Gonzáles Cesteros, H. and Berni Millet, P. (2018) *Roman amphorae in Neuss. Augustan to Julio-Claudian contexts*. (Roman and Late Antique Mediterranean Pottery 12) Oxford: Archaeopress.

Goodman, P. J. (2016) 'Working together: clusters of artisans in the Roman city', in Wilson, A. and Flohr, M. (eds) *Urban craftsmen and traders in the Roman world*. (Oxford Studies on the Roman Economy) Oxford: Oxford University Press, pp. 301–333.

Graafen, R. (2006) 'Der Naturraum', in Kunow, J. (ed.) *Urgeschichte im Rheinland.* (Jahrbuch des Rheinischen Vereins für Denkmalpflege und Landschaftsschutz 2005) Cologne: Rheinischer Verein für Denkmalpflege und Landschatsschutz, pp. 37–42.

Grabowski, S. (2016) 'Die Trachyt-Steinbrüche vom Drachenfels im Siebengebirge', in Bemmann, J. and Mirschenz, M. (eds) *Der Rhein als europäische Verkehrsachse II.* (Bonner Beiträge zur Vor- und Frühgeschichtlichen Archäologie 19) Bonn: Rheinische Friedrich-Wilhelms-Universität Bonn, pp. 69–135.

Gralfs, B. (1994) *Metallverarbeitende Werkstätten im Nordwesten des Imperium Romanum.* (Schriftenreihe 8) Hamburg: Dr. Kovac.

Greene, K. (1978) 'Roman trade between Britain and the Rhine provinces: the evidence of pottery to c AD 250', in du Plat Taylor, J. and Cleere, H. (eds) *Roman shipping and trade: Britain and the Rhine provinces.* (CBA Research Report 24) London: The Council for British Archaeology, pp. 52–58.

Greene, K. (1986) *The archaeology of the Roman economy.* London: Batsford.

Greene, K. (1992) 'How was technology transferred in the western provinces?', in Wood, M. and Queiroga, F. (eds) *Current research on the Romanization of the western Provinces.* (British Archaeological Reports International Series 575) Oxford: Tempus Reparatum, pp. 101–105.

Greene, K. (2005) 'Roman pottery: models, proxies and economic interpretation', *Journal of Roman Archaeology*, 18, pp. 34–56.

Greene, K. (2008) 'Learning to consume. Consumption and consumerism in the Roman Empire', *Journal of Roman Archaeology*, 21, pp. 64–82.

Groenewoudt, B. J. and van Lanen, R. J. (2018) 'Diverging decline. Reconstructing and validating (post-)Roman population trends (AD 0–1000) in the Rhine-Meuse delta (the Netherlands)', *European Journal of Post-Classical Archaeologies*, 8, pp. 189–218.

Groot, M. (2008a) *Animals in ritual and economy in a frontier community. Excavations in Tiel-Passewaaij.* (Amsterdam Archaeological Studies 12) Amsterdam: Amsterdam University Press.

Groot, M. (2008b) 'Surplus production of animal products for the Roman army in a rural settlement in the Dutch River Area', in Stallibrass, S. and Thomas, R. (eds) *Feeding the Roman army: the archaeology of production and supply in NW Europe.* Oxford: Oxbow Books, pp. 83–98.

Groot, M. *et al.* (2009) 'Surplus production for the market? The agrarian economy in the non-villa landscapes of Germania Inferior', *Journal of Roman Archaeology*, 22, pp. 231–253.

Groot, M. (2011) 'Household specialisation in horse breeding: the role of returning veterans in the Batavian river area', in Moosbauer, G. and Wiegels, R. (eds) *Fines imperii – imperium sine fine? Römische Okkupations- und Grenzpolitik im frühen Principat. Beiträge zum Kongress 'Fines imperii – imperium sine fine?' in Osnabrück vom 14. bis 18. September 2009.* (Osnabrücker Forschungen zum Altertum und Antike-Rezeption 14) Rahden/Westf.: Marie Leidorf, pp. 203–218.

Groot, M. (2016) *Livestock for sale. Animal husbandry in a Roman frontier zone. The case study of the civitas Batavorum.* (Amsterdam Archaeological Studies 24) Amsterdam: Amsterdam University Press.

Groot, M. and Kooistra, L. I. (2009) 'Land use and the agrarian economy in the Roman Dutch river area', *Internet Archaeology*, 27.

Groot, M. and Lentjes, D. (2013) 'Studying subsistence and surplus production', in Groot, M., Lentjes, D., and Zeiler, J. (eds) *Barely surviving or more than enough? The environmental archaeology of subsistence, specialisation and surplus food production.* Leiden: Sidestone Press, pp. 7–27.

Gross, M. and Heimberg, U. (1973) 'Erftstadt. Jahresbericht des Staatlichen Vertrauensmannes für kulturgeschichtliche Bodenaltertümer vom 1. Januar bis 31. Dezember 1971', *Bonner Jahrbücher*, 173, p. 417.

Grünewald, M. and Hartmann, S. (2014) 'Glass workshops in northern Gaul and the Rhineland in the first millennium AD as hints of a changing land use – including some results of the chemical analyses of glass from Mayen', in Keller, D., Price, J., and Jackson, C. (eds) *Neighbours and successors of Rome. Traditions of glass production and use in Europe and the Middle East in the later 1st Millenium AD*. Oxford: Oxbow Books, pp. 43–57.

Haalebos, J. K. (1997) 'Een Romeins graanschip in Woerden', *Jaarboek Oud-Utrecht*, 1997, pp. 67–96.

Habermehl, D. (2013) *Settling in a changing world. Villa development in the northern provinces of the Roman Empire.* (Amsterdam Archaeological Studies 19) Amsterdam: Amsterdam University Press.

Haley, E. W. (2003) *Baetica felix. People and prosperity in southern Spain from Caesar to Septimius Severus.* Austin: University of Texas Press.

Halstead, P. and O'Shea, J. (1989) 'Introduction: cultural response to risk and uncertainty', in Halstead, P. and O'Shea, J. (eds) *Bad year economics: cultural responses to risk and uncertainty.* (New Directions in Archaeology) Cambridge: Cambridge University Press, pp. 1–7.

Hanel, N. (1995) *Vetera I. die Funde aus den römischen Lagern auf dem Fürstenberg bei Xanten.* (Rheinische Ausgrabungen 35) Cologne: Rheinland-Verlag.

Hanel, N. (2003) 'Die Amphoren der Ausgrabungen 1998 im Hauptstützpunkt der Classis Germanica „Alteburg" bei der Colonia Claudia Ara Agrippinensium – Ein Vorbericht', *Rei Cretariae Romanae Fautorum Acta*, 38, pp. 361–364.

Hanel, N. (2006) 'Fabricae, Werkstätten, und Handwerkliche Tätigkeiten des Militärs in den Nordprovinzen des römischen Reichs', in Morillo Cerdán, Á. (ed.) *Arqueología Militar romana en Hispania II. Producción y abastecimiento en el ámbito militar.* Leon: Universidad de Leon Secretariado de Publicaci, pp. 19–32.

Hanel, N. (2007) 'Military camps, canabae, and vici. The archaeological evidence', in Erdkamp, P. (ed.) *A companion to the Roman army.* (Blackwell Companions to the Ancient World) Chichester: Wiley-Blackwell, pp. 395–416.

Hanel, N. (2020) 'Archaeology of Germania Inferior. Urbanization', in James, S. and Krmnicek, S. (eds) *The Oxford handbook of the archaeology of Roman Germany*. Oxford: Oxford University Press, pp. 92–115.

Hanson, J. W. (2016) *An urban geography of the Roman world, 100 BC to AD 300*. Oxford: Archaeopress.

Harl, K. W. (1996) *Coinage in the Roman economy, 300 B.C. to A.D. 700*. London: The John Hopkins University Press.

Harris, W. V. (1993a) 'Concerning this book', in Harris, W. V. (ed.) *The inscribed economy. Production and distribution in the Roman empire in the light of instrumentum domesticum. The proceedings of a conference held at the American Academy in Rome on 10–11 January, 1992*. (Journal of Roman Archaeology. Supplementary Series 6) Ann Arbor: American Academy in Rome, pp. 7–9.

Harris, W. V. (ed.) (1993b) *The inscribed economy. Production and distribution in the Roman empire in the light of instrumentum domesticum. The proceedings of a conference held at The American Academy in Rome on 10–11 January, 1992*. (Journal of Roman Archaeology. Supplementary Series 6) Ann Arbor, MI: American Academy in Rome.

Harris, W. V. (2013) 'Defining and detecting Mediterranean deforestation, 800 BCE to 700 CE', in Harris, W. V. (ed.) *The ancient Mediterranean environment between science and history*. (Columbia Studies in the Classical Tradition 39) Leiden: Brill, pp. 173–194.

Hassall, M. (1978) 'Britain and the Rhine provinces: epigraphic evidence for Roman trade', in du Plat Taylor, J. and Cleere, H. (eds) *Roman shipping and trade: Britain and the Rhine provinces*. (CBA Research Report 24) London: The Council for British Archaeology, pp. 41–48.

Haupt, D. (1984) 'Römischer Töpfereibezirk bei Soller, Kreis Düren. Bericht über eine alte Ausgrabung', in Haupt, D. (ed.) *Beiträge zur Archäologie des römischen Rheinlands 4*. (Rheinische Ausgrabungen 23) Cologne: Rheinland-Verlag, pp. 391–470.

Haynes, I. (2002) 'Britain's first information revolution. The Roman army and the transformation of economic life', in Erdkamp, P. (ed.) *The Roman army and the economy*. Amsterdam: J.C. Gieben, pp. 111–126.

Heeren, S. (2007) 'Romeins importaardewerk en de introductie van nieuwe eetgewoonten', in Roymans, N., Derks, T., and Heeren, S. (eds) *Een Bataafse gemeenschap in de wereld van het Romeinse rijk. Opgravingen te Tiel-Passewaaij*. Utrecht: Matrijs, pp. 145–156.

Heeren, S. (2009) *Romanisering van rurale gemeenschappen in de civitas Batavorum. De casus Tiel-Passewaaij*. PhD thesis, Vrije Universiteit Amsterdam.

Heeren, S. (2014) 'The material culture of small rural settlements in the Batavian area. A case study on discrepant experience, creolisation, Romanisation or globalisation?', in Platts, H. et al. (eds) *TRAC 2013. Proceedings of the twenty-third Theoretical*

Roman Archaeology Conference King's College, London 2013. Oxford: Oxbow Books, pp. 159–173.

Heeren, S. (2017) 'From Germania Inferior to Germania Secunda and beyond. A case study of migrations, transformation and decline', in Roymans, N., Heeren, S., and De Clercq, W. (eds) *Social dynamics in the northwest frontiers of the late Roman Empire. Beyond decline or transformation.* (Amsterdam Archaeological Studies 26) Amsterdam: Amsterdam University Press, pp. 149–178.

Heeren, S. and van der Feijst, L. M. B. (2017) *Prehistorische, Romeinse en middeleeuwse fibulae uit de Lage Landen. Beschrijving, analyse en interpretatie van een archeologische vondstcategorie.* Amersfoort: Stijn Heeren & Lourens van der Feijst.

Heeringen, R. M. van (1989) 'The Iron Age in the western Netherlands V: synthesis', *Berichten van de Rijksdienst voor het Oudheidkundig Bodemonderzoek*, 39, pp. 157–255.

Heesch, J. van (2008) 'On the edge of the market economy: coins used in social transactions, as ornaments and as bullion in the Roman empire', in Bursche, A., Ciołek, R., and Wolters, R. (eds) *Roman coins outside the empire. Ways and phases, contexts and functions. Proceedings of the ESF/SCH exploratory workshop, Radziwiłł Palace, Nieborów (Poland), 3–6 September 2005.* (Collection Moneta 82) Wetteren: Moneta, pp. 49–57.

Heijden, P. van der (2011) 'Romeinse wegen in Nederland', *Archeobrief*, 15(1), pp. 23–35.

Heijden, P. van der (2016a) 'Een onzichtbare weg. De Limesweg in Gelderland', in van der Heijden, P. (ed.) *Romeinse wegen in Nederland.* Utrecht: Matrijs, pp. 57–65.

Heijden, P. van der (2016b) 'Romeinse wegenbouw en bronnen van onderzoek', in van der Heijden, P. (ed.) *Romeinse wegen in Nederland.* Utrecht: Matrijs, pp. 9–19.

Heimberg, U. (1997) 'Zu den römischen Amphoren aus Augst und Kaiseraugst', *Germania*, 75, pp. 298–307.

Heimberg, U. (2000) 'Siedlungsstrukturen in Niedergermanien', in von Büren, G. and Fuchs, E. (eds) *Jülich. Stadt – Territorium – Geschichte. Festschrift zum 75jährigen Jubiläum des Jülicher Geschichtsvereins 1923 e.V.* (Jülicher Geschichtsblätter 67/68) Kleve: B.o.s.s. Druck und Medien GmbH, pp. 189–240.

Heimberg, U. (2003) 'Römische Villen an Rhein und Maas', *Bonner Jahrbücher*, 202–203, pp. 57–148.

Heimberg, U. (2011) *Villa rustica. Leben und Arbeiten auf römischen Landgütern.* Darmstadt: Wissenschaftliche Buchgesellschaft.

Hendriks, J. (2012) 'Aardewerk', in Tichelmans, G. and Janssens, M. (eds) *Wonen langs de Romeinse weg in Coriovallum. Valkenburgerweg 25A, gemeente Heerlen. Een opgraving in de vicus van Heerlen.* (RAAP-Rapport 2210) RAAP Archeologisch Adviesbureau, pp. 60–88.

Hendriks, J. (2014) 'Pottery from Ulpia Noviomagus – Nijmegen. First report on the Maasplein production site: kilns 1–2', in Liesen, B. (ed.) *Römische Keramik in*

Niedergermanien. Produktion – Handel – Gebrauch. Beiträge zur Tagung der Rei Cretariae Romanae Fautores. 21.–26. September 2014, LVR-RömerMuseum im Archäologischen Park Xanten. (Xantener Berichte 27) Darmstadt: Philipp von Zabern, pp. 175–240.

Henrich, P. (2006) *Die römische Besiedlung in der westlichen Vulkaneifel.* (Trierer Zeitschrift. Beiheft 30) Trier: Rheinisches Landesmuseum.

Henrich, P. (2007) 'Leben, Handel und Handwerk im Bonner vicus – die Kleinfunde', *Archäologie im Rheinland*, 2006, pp. 88–91.

Herz, P. (2010) 'Die Versorgung der Römischen Armee mit Waffen und Ausrüstung', in Eich, A. (ed.) *Die Verwaltung der kaiserzeitlichen römischen Armee. Studien für Hartmut Wolff.* (Historia – Einzelschriften 211) Stuttgart: Franz Steiner, pp. 111–132.

Hetzel, E. M. (2022) *Gemeinsam sind wir stark. Eine Analyse und ein umfassender Überblick über die Ballungsräume des Handwerksgewerbes am Wirtschaftsstandort CCAA*. PhD thesis, Universität zu Köln.

Hiddink, H. (2011) *Romeins aardewerk van de Zuid-Nederlandse zandgronden.* (Materiaal en Methoden 2) Amsterdam: Archeologisch Centrum van de Vrije Universiteit en de Hendrik Brunsting Stichting.

Hiddink, H. (2014) *De Romeinse villa-nederzetting op de Kerkakkers bij Hoogeloon (Noord-Brabant).* (Zuidnederlandse Archeologische Rapporten 53) Amsterdam: Archeologisch Centrum Vrije Universiteit – Hendrik Brunsting Stichting.

Hiddink, H. (2015) *De Romeinse bewoning van het Zuid-Nederlandse dekzandgebied in relatie tot het landschap. Een verkenning.* (Zuidnederlandse Archeologische Navorsingen Digitaal 1) Amsterdam: dr. H.A. Hiddink.

Hiddink, H. and Roymans, N. (2015) 'Exploring the rural landscape of a peripheral region', in Roymans, N., Derks, T., and Hiddink, H. (eds) *The Roman villa of Hoogeloon and the archaeology of the periphery.* (Amsterdam Archaeological Studies 22) Amsterdam: Amsterdam University Press, pp. 45–86.

Hingley, R. (2005) *Globalizing Roman culture. Unity, diversity and empire.* London: Routledge.

Hirt, A. M. (2010) *Imperial Mines and Quarries in the Roman World. Organizational Aspects 27 BC–AD 235.* Oxford: Oxford University Press (Oxford Classical Monographs).

Hobson, M. S. (2012) *The African boom? Evaluating economic growth in the Roman province of Africa Proconsularis.* PhD thesis, University of Leicester.

Hobson, M. S. (2014) 'A historiography of the study of the Roman economy: economic growth, development, and neoliberalism', in Platts, H. et al. (eds) *TRAC 2013. Proceedings of the twenty-third Theoretical Roman Archaeology Conference King's College, London 2013.* Oxford: Oxbow Books, pp. 11–26.

Hoevenberg, J. (1996) 'De opgraving en levensgeschiedenis van een opmerkelijke Romeinse pottenbakkersoven in Heerlen-Centrum', *Het Land Van Herle*, 46, pp. 110–115.

Hoffmann-Salz, J. (2011) *Die wirtschaftlichen Auswirkungen der römischen Eroberung. Vergleichende Untersuchungen der Provinzen Hispania Tarraconensis, Africa Proconsularis und Syria*. (Historia Einzelschriften 218) Stuttgart: Franz Steiner.

Hoffmann-Salz, J. (2014) 'Von Räuberhauptmännern zu guten Römern: Die lokalen Eliten des Hauran in der Kaiserzeit', *Zeitschrift für Papyrologie und Epigraphik*, 189, pp. 293–304.

Holleran, C. and Pudsey, A. (2011) 'Introduction. Studies in ancient historical demography', in Holleran, C. and Pudsey, A. (eds) *Demography and the Graeco-Roman world. New insights and approaches*. Cambridge: Cambridge University Press, pp. 1–13.

Holstein, E. (1980) *Mitteleuropäische Eichenchronologie*. Mainz: Philipp von Zabern.

Holtschneider, C. (2011) 'Eine römische Töpferei im Bonner vicus', *Archäologie im Rheinland*, 2010, pp. 113–115.

Hondius-Crone, A. H. (1955) *The temple of Nehalennia at Domburg*. Amsterdam: J.M. Meulenhoff.

Höpken, C. (1999) 'Die Produktion römischer Gefäßkeramik in Köln', *Kölner Jahrbuch*, 32, pp. 759–770.

Höpken, C. (2005) *Das römische Keramikproduktion in Köln*. (Kölner Forschungen 8) Mainz: Von Zabern.

Höpken, C. (2009) 'Metallverarbeitung im römischen Flottenlager Köln Alteburg', *Kölner Jahrbuch*, 42, pp. 787–793.

Höpken, C. (2011) 'Produktions- und Vertriebsstrukturen Römischer Töpfereien in den Nordwestprovinzen', in Bemmann, J. et al. (eds) *Drehscheibentöpferei im Barbaricum. Technologietransfer und Professionalisierung eines Handwerks am Rande des Römischen Imperiums. Akten der Internationalen Tagung in Bonn vom 11. bis 14. Juni 2009*. (Bonner Beiträge zur Vor- und Frühgeschichtlichen Archäologie 13) Bonn: Rheinische Friedrich-Wilhelms-Universität Bonn, pp. 75–84.

Höpken, C. (2013) 'Olivenöl aus Spanien, Wein aus Gallien, Bier und Milchprodukte aus der Region – Amphorenfunde aus dem Bonner vicus', in Kennecke, H. (ed.) *Der Rhein als europäische Verkehrsachse. Die Römerzeit*. (Bonner Beiträge zur Vor- und Frühgeschichtlichen Archäologie 16) Bonn: Rheinische Friedrich-Wilhelms-Universität Bonn, pp. 175–190.

Höpken, C. (2015a) 'Fern-, Regional- und Lokalhandel im römischen Rheinland und der Konsum von Öl, Wein und Bier im Bonner vicus', in Schmidts, T. and Vučetić, M. M. (eds) *Häfen im 1. Millennium AD. Bauliche Konzepte, herrschaftliche und religiöse Einflüsse. Plenartreffen im Rahmen des DFG-Schwerpunktprogramms 1630 »Häfen von der Römischen Kaiserzeit bis zum Mittelalter« im Römisch-Germanischen Zentralmuseum Mainz, 13.–15.* (RGZM – Tagungen 22 = Interdisziplinäre Forschungen zu den Häfen von der Römischen Kaiserzeit bis zum Mittelalter in Europa 1) Mainz: Römisch-Germanischen Zentralmuseums, pp. 133–140.

Höpken, C. (2015b) 'Pottery production in Roman Cologne: A summary of old and new finds', *Journal of Roman Pottery Studies*, 16, pp. 93–104.

Höpken, C. (2016a) 'Amphoren aus dem Zivilen Vicus von Bonn', in Bemmann, J. and Mirschenz, M. (eds) *Der Rhein als europäische Verkehrsachse II.* (Bonner Beiträge zur Vor- und Frühgeschichtlichen Archäologie 19) Bonn: Rheinische Friedrich-Wilhelms-Universität Bonn, pp. 137–211.

Höpken, C. (2016b) 'Entscheidende Wandfragmente: Untersuchungen zum Inhalt von Amphoren aus Köln und Bonn', *Archäologisches Korrespondenzblatt*, 46, pp. 101–112.

Höpken, C. (2018) 'Mediterrane Köstlichkeiten für Xanten – Zu den Amphorenfunden am Niederrhein', in Eger, C. (ed.) *Warenwege – Warenflüsse. Handel, Logistik und Transport am römischen Niederrhein.* (Xantener Berichte 32) Mainz: Nünnerich-Asmus, pp. 373–387.

Höpken, C., Döhner, G. and Fiedler, M. (2009) 'Zur Produktion glasierter Keramik während der mittleren Kaiserzeit in der Provinz Germania Inferior. Zeugnisse aus Köln, Bonn und Soller', *Bonner Jahrbücher*, 209, pp. 129–146.

Höpken, C. and Liesen, B. (2005) 'Die Töpferei bei Schloss Rimburg', *Rei Cretariae Romanae Fautorum Acta*, 39, pp. 61–66.

Höpken, C., Liesen, B. and Niemeijer, R. A. J. (2014) 'Bibliografie zu römischen Töpfereien in Niedergermanien', in Liesen, B. (ed.) *Römische Keramik in Niedergermanien. Produktion – Handel – Gebrauch. Beiträge zur Tagung der Rei Cretariae Romanae Fautores. 21.–26. September 2014, LVR-RömerMuseum im Archäologischen Park Xanten.* (Xantener Berichte 27) Darmstadt: Philipp von Zabern, pp. 403–421.

Höpken, C. and Schäfer, F. (2006) 'Glashütten und Werkstätten in Köln', in Creemers, G., Demarsin, B., and Cosyns, P. (eds) *Roman glass in Germania Inferior. Interregional comparisons and recent results. Tongeren, May 13th, 2005.* (Atuatuca) Tongeren: Gallo-Romeins Museum, pp. 53–63.

Hopkins, K. (1978) *Conquerors and slaves.* (Sociological Studies in Roman History 1) Cambridge: Cambridge University Press.

Hopkins, K. (1980) 'Taxes and trade in the Roman Empire (200 B.C.–A.D. 400)', *The Journal of Roman Studies*, 70, pp. 101–125.

Hopkins, K. (1983) 'Introduction', in Garnsey, P., Hopkins, K., and Whittaker, C. R. (eds) *Trade in the ancient economy.* London: Chatto & Windus, pp. ix–xxv.

Hopkins, K. (2002) 'Rome, taxes, rents and trade', in Scheidel, W. and von Reden, S. (eds) *The ancient economy.* Edinburgh: Edinburgh University Press, pp. 190–230.

Hopkins, K. (2017) 'Conquest by book', in Kelly, C. (ed.) *Sociological studies in Roman history.* (Cambridge Classical Studies) Cambridge: Cambridge University Press, pp. 363–397.

Horn, H. G. (1987) 'Das Leben im römischen Rheinland', in *Die Römer in Nordrhein-Westfalen.* Stuttgart: Konrad Theiss, pp. 139–317.

Hosch, W. L. (2011) *The Britannica guide to numbers and measurement.* (Math Explained) New York: Britannica Educational Publishing.

Howgego, C. (2013) 'The monetization of temperate Europe', *The Journal of Roman Studies*, 103, pp. 16–45.

Hughes, J. D. (2011) 'Ancient deforestation revisited', *Journal of the History of Biology*, 44(1), pp. 43–57.

Huisman, K. (1995) 'De Drususgrachten: een nieuwe hypothese', *Westerheem*, 44, pp. 188–194.

Hunold, A. (2011) *Das Erbe des Vulkans. Eine Reise in die Erd- und Technikgeschichte zwischen Eifel und Rhein*. Regensburg: Schnell + Steiner.

Hupka, D. (2011) *Die römischen Siedlungsfunde, gewerblichen Reste und Straßenbefunde in Mönchengladbach-Mülfort*. PhD thesis, Universität zu Köln.

Hupperetz, W. (1993) 'Een Romeinse pottenbakkersoven te Venlo', in van Pinxteren, A. A. J. J. (ed.) *Pronkstukken. Venlo 650 jaar stad*. Venlo: Goltziusmuseum, pp. 28–31.

Ickler, S. (2007) *Bronze- und Eisenzeitliche Besiedlung im Stadgebiet von Krefeld, Mittlerer Niederrhein*. PhD thesis, Universität zu Köln.

Jacobsen, G. (1995) *Primitiver Austausch oder Freier Markt?. Untersuchungen zum Handel in den gallisch-germanischen Provinzen während der römischen Kaiserzeit*. St. Katharinen: Scripta Mercaturae.

Jansen, R. (2021) *Verleden als leidraad. IJzertijdbewoning en landschapsinrichting in noord-oostelijk Noord-Brabant*. PhD thesis, Universiteit Leiden.

Jansma, E., Haneca, K. and Kosian, M. (2014) 'A dendrochronological reassessment of three Roman boats from Utrecht (the Netherlands): evidence of inland navigation between the lower-Scheldt region in Gallia Belgica and the limes of Germania Inferior', *Journal of Archaeological Science*, 50, pp. 484–496.

Janssen, W. and Goebel, W. (1977) 'Wegberg. Jahresbericht des Staatlichen Vertrauensmannes für kulturgeschichtliche Bodenaltertümer vom 1. Januar bis 31. Dezember 1975', *Bonner Jahrbücher*, 177, p. 721.

Janssens, N. (2015) 'Het verlaten van de regio tussen Maas, Demer en Schelde in de Romeinse periode. Regionale en supra regionale tendensen op lange en korte termijn', *Terra Incognita*, 6, pp. 83–100.

Jaschke, K. and Schmitz, D. (2018) 'Das römische Köln als Handelszentrum im 1. bis 3. Jahrhundert n. Chr.', in Eger, C. (ed.) *Warenwege – Warenflüsse. Handel, Logistik und Transport am römischen Niederrhein*. (Xantener Berichte 32) Mainz: Nünnerich-Asmus, pp. 317–336.

Jeneson, K. (2013) *Exploring the Roman villa world between Tongres and Cologne. A landscape archaeological approach*. PhD thesis, Vrije Universiteit Amsterdam.

Joachim, H.-E. (2007a) 'Die Datierung der jüngerlatènezeitlichen Siedlung von Niederzier-Hambach im Kreis Düren', *Bonner Jahrbücher*, 207, pp. 33–74.

Joachim, H.-E. (2007b) 'Die späte Eisenzeit am Niederrhein', in Uelsberg, G. (ed.) *Krieg und Frieden. Kelten – Römer – Germanen*. Bonn: Rheinische Landesmuseum Bonn, pp. 48–58.

Joachim, H.-E. (2016) *Eisenzeitliche Siedlungen in Pulheim, Rhein-Erft-Kreis.* (Bonner Beiträge zur Vor- und Frühgeschichtlichen Archäologie 18) Bonn: Rheinische Friedrich-Wilhelms-Universität Bonn.

Jongman, W. M. (2006) 'The rise and fall of the Roman economy: population, rents and entitlement', in Bang, P. F., Ikeguchi, M., and Ziche, H. G. (eds) *Ancient economies modern methodologies. Archaeology, comparative history, models and institutions.* Bari: Edipuglia, pp. 237–254.

Jongman, W. M. (2007a) 'Gibbon was right: the decline and fall of the Roman economy', in Hekster, O., de Kleijn, G., and Slootjes, D. (eds) *Crisis and the Roman Empire. Proceedings of the seventh workshop of the international network Impact of Empire (Nijmegen, June 20–24, 2006).* (Impact of Empire 7) Leiden: Brill, pp. 183–199.

Jongman, W. M. (2007b) 'The early Roman empire: consumption', in Scheidel, W., Morris, I., and Saller, R. P. (eds) *The Cambridge economic history of the Greco-Roman world.* Cambridge: Cambridge University Press, pp. 592–618.

Jongman, W. M. (2014a) 'Re-constructing the Roman economy', in Neal, L. and Williamson, J. G. (eds) *The rise of capitalism: from ancient origins to 1848.* (The Cambridge History of Capitalism 1) Cambridge: Cambridge University Press, pp. 75–100.

Jongman, W. M. (2014b) 'Why modern economic theory applies, even to the distant Roman past', in Platts, H. et al. (eds) *TRAC 2013. Proceedings of the twenty-third Theoretical Roman Archaeology Conference King's College, London 2013.* Oxford: Oxbow Books, pp. 27–36.

Jongman, W. M., Jacobs, J. P. A. M. and Klein Goldewijk, G. M. (2019) 'Health and wealth in the Roman Empire', *Economics and Human Biology*, 34, pp. 138–150.

Jursa, M. (2014) 'Babylonia in the first millenium BCE – economic growth in times of empire', in Neal, L. and Williamson, J. G. (eds) *The rise of capitalism: from ancient origins to 1848.* (The Cambridge History of Capitalism 1) Cambridge: Cambridge University Press, pp. 24–42.

Kakoschke, A. (2002) *Ortsfremde in den römischen Provinzen Germania Inferior und Germania superior. Eine Untersuchung zur Mobilität in der germanischen Provinzen anhand der Inschriften des 1. bis 3. Jahrhunderts n. Chr.* Möhnesee: Bibliopolis.

Kalis, A. J. *et al.* (2008) 'Mensch und Vegetation am Unteren Niederrhein während der Eisen- und Römerzeit', in Müller, M., Schalles, H.-J., and Zieling, N. (eds) *Colonia Ulpia Traiana. Xanten und sein Umland in römischer Zeit.* (Geschichte der Stadt Xanten 1 = Xantener Berichte Sonderband) Mainz: Philipp von Zabern, pp. 31–48.

Kalis, A. J. and Meurers-Balke, J. (2007) 'Landnutzung im Niederrheingebiet zwischen Krieg und Frieden', in Uelsberg, G. (ed.) *Krieg und Frieden. Kelten – Römer – Germanen.* Bonn: Rheinische Landesmuseum Bonn, pp. 144–153.

Karlsen, H.-J. (2018) 'Römisch-germanischer Handel zwischen Rhein und Elbe', in Eger, C. (ed.) *Warenwege – Warenflüsse. Handel, Logistik und Transport am römischen Niederrhein.* (Xantener Berichte 32) Mainz: Nünnerich-Asmus, pp. 577–595.

Kaszab-Olschewski, T. (2011) 'Misslungenes Experiment? Über das Scheitern der Aachener Sigillata-Produktion', in Felgenhauer-Schmiedt, S. et al. (eds) *Keramik und Technik. Internationale Fachtagung der Osterreichischen Gesellschaft für Mittelalterarchäologie zugleich 43. Internationales Symposium Keramikforschung des Arbeitskreises für Keramikforschung. Mautern an der Donau, 20 bis 25. September 2010*. (Beiträge zur Mittelalterarchäologie in Österreich 27) Wien: Österreichische Gesellschaft für Mittelalterarchäologie, pp. 19–24.

Kehne, P. (2007) 'War- and peacetime logistics: supplying imperial armies in east and west', in Erdkamp, P. (ed.) *A companion to the Roman army*. (Blackwell Companions to the Ancient World) Chichester: Wiley-Blackwell, pp. 323–338.

Kemmers, F. (2008) 'Interaction or indifference? The Roman coin finds from the Lower Rhine delta', in Bursche, A., Ciołek, R., and Wolters, R. (eds) *Roman coins outside the Empire. Ways and phases, contexts and functions. Proceedings of the ESF/SCH exploratory workshop, Radziwiłł Palace, Nieborów (Poland), 3–6 September 2005*. (Collection Moneta 82) Wetteren: Moneta, pp. 93–103.

Kennecke, H. (ed.) (2014a) *Der Rhein als europäische Verkehrsachse. Die Römerzeit*. (Bonner Beiträge zur Vor- und Frühgeschichtlichen Archäologie 16) Bonn: Rheinische Friedrich-Wilhelms-Universität Bonn.

Kennecke, H. (2014b) 'Der Trachytabbau im Siebengebirge und sein Transfer über den Rhein in römischer Zeit', in Kennecke, H. (ed.) *Der Rhein als europäische Verkehrsachse. Die Römerzeit*. (Bonner Beiträge zur Vor- und Frühgeschichtlichen Archäologie 16) Bonn: Rheinische Friedrich-Wilhelms-Universität Bonn, pp. 93–108.

Kennecke, H. (2016) 'Einrichtungen der Binnenschiffahrt im Bonner Raum. Eine Vergleichende Darstellung von der Antike bis zur Neuzeit', in Bemmann, J. and Mirschenz, M. (eds) *Der Rhein als europäische Verkehrsachse II*. (Bonner Beiträge zur Vor- und Frühgeschichtlichen Archäologie 19) Bonn: Rheinische Friedrich-Wilhelms-Universität Bonn, pp. 23–68.

Kerckhove, J. Van (2009) 'Aardewerk', in van Renswoude, J. and Van Kerckhove, J. (eds) *Opgravingen in Geldermalsen-Hondsgemet. Een inheemse nederzetting uit de Late IJzertijd en Romeinse tijd*. (Zuidnederlandse Archeologische Rapporten 35) Amsterdam: Archeologisch Centrum van de Vrije Universiteit en de Hendrik Brunsting Stichting, pp. 115–192.

Kerckhove, J. Van (2011) 'Aardewerk uit de Romeinse tijd (vindplaats 3)', in Siemons, H. and Kersing, V. L. (eds) *Archeologisch onderzoek aan de Uithofslaan, gemeente Den Haag. Deel 1: Sporen van bewoning uit de ijzertijd (vindplaats 6) en de Romeinse tijd (vindplaats 3)*. (Haagse Archeologische Rapportage 1122) Den Haag: Afdeling Archeologie Dienst Stadsbeheer gemeente Den Haag, pp. 140–231.

Kerckhove, J. Van, *et al.* (2014) 'Understanding consumption patterns in the civitas Tungrorum through the identification of the " NOOR1 " Ware', *Rei Cretariae Romanae Fautorum Acta*, (43), pp. 783–792.

Kerckhove, J. Van, and Boreel, G. L. (2014) 'A characterization of the pottery production in Heerlen (Limburg, the Netherlands): fabric analysis and typo-chronology', in Liesen, B. (ed.) *Römische Keramik in Niedergermanien. Produktion – Handel – Gebrauch. Beiträge zur Tagung der Rei Cretariae Romanae Fautores. 21.–26. September 2014, LVR-RömerMuseum im Archäologischen Park Xanten.* (Xantener Berichte 27) Darmstadt: Philipp von Zabern, pp. 241–285.

Kicken, C. and Mols, S. (2020) 'De infrastructuur in het gebied van de Neder-Germaanse Limes', *Lampas*, 53(2), pp. 146–156.

Klaus, J. and Rech, M. (1987) 'Meerbusch. Ausgrabungen und Funde 1985', *Bonner Jahrbücher*, 187, p. 602.

Kloosterman, R. P. J. (2016) 'Nijmegen-Holdeurn ware from the western canabae legionis at Nijmegen (NL): some remarks on chronological and spatial analysis', *Rei Cretariae Romanae Fautorum Acta*, 44, pp. 381–388.

Klostermann, J. (2001) 'Klima und Landschaft am römischen Niederrhein', in Grünewald, T. (ed.) *Germania Inferior. Besiedlung, Gesellschaft und Wirtschaft an der Grenze der römisch-germanischen Welt.* (Reallexikon der Germanischen Altertumskunde – Ergänzungsbände 28) Berlin: Walter de Gruyter, pp. 36–53.

Komnick, H. (2018) 'Vom Tauschhandel zur Geldwirtschaft? Fragen zur Monetarisierung am römischen Niederrhein', in Eger, C. (ed.) *Warenwege – Warenflüsse. Handel, Logistik und Transport am römischen Niederrhein.* (Xantener Berichte 32) Mainz: Nünnerich-Asmus, pp. 25–67.

Kooistra, L. I. (1996) *Borderland farming. Possibilities and limitations of farming in the Roman period and early Middle Ages between the Rhine and Meuse.* PhD thesis, Universiteit Leiden.

Kooistra, L. I. (2008) 'Vegetation history and agriculture in the cover-sand area west of Breda (province of Noord-Brabant, the Netherlands)', *Vegetation History and Archaeobotany*, 17(1), pp. 113–125.

Kooistra, L. I. (2009a) 'The provenance of cereal for the Roman army in the Rhine delta. Based on archaeobotanical evidence', in *Kelten am Rhein. Akten des dreizehnten Internationalen Keltologiekongresses 23. bis 27. Juli 2007 in Bonn.* (Beihefte der Bonner Jahrbücher 58) Mainz: Philipp von Zabern, pp. 219–237.

Kooistra, L. I. (2009b) 'The provisioning of the Roman army in the Rhine delta between c. AD 40 and 140', *Anejos de Gladius*, 13, pp. 115–122.

Kooistra, L. I. (2012) 'Die pflanzlichen Grundnahrungsmittel der Rheinarmee vor und nach der Gründung der Germania Inferior', in Stobbe, A. and Tegtmeier, U. (eds) *Verzweigungen. Eine Würdigung für A.J. Kalis und J. Meurers-Balke.* (Frankfurter Archäologische Schriften 18) Bonn: Dr. Rudolf Habelt, pp. 171–187.

Kooistra, L. I. *et al.* (2013) 'Could the local population of the Lower Rhine delta supply the Roman army? Part 1: The archaeological and historical framework', *Journal of Archaeology in the Low Countries*, 4(2), pp. 5–23.

Kooistra, L. I. and Groot, M. (2015) 'The agricultural basis of the Hoogeloon villa and the wider region', in Roymans, N., Derks, T., and Hiddink, H. (eds) *The Roman villa of Hoogeloon and the archaeology of the periphery*. (Amsterdam Archaeological Studies 22) Amsterdam: Amsterdam University Press, pp. 141–162.

Kort, J.-W. de (2013) 'Het Kanaal van Corbulo: onderzoek naar een Romeinse waterweg in de gemeente Leidschendam-Voorburg tussen 1989 en 2010', *Westerheem*, 5(62), pp. 233–243.

Kron, G. (2019) 'Comparative perspectives on nutrition and social inequality in the Roman world', in Erdkamp, P. and Holleran, C. (eds) *The Routledge handbook of diet and nutrition in the Roman world*. (Routledge Handbooks) London: Routledge, pp. 259–272.

Kuhnen, H.-P. (2012) 'Die römische Besiedlung der Eifel und die Metallversorgung der germanischen Provinzen des Imperium Romanum', in Olshausen, E. and Sauer, V. (eds) *Die Schätze der Erde – natürliche Ressourcen in der antiken Welt. Stuttgarter Kolloquium zur Historischen Geographie des Altertums 10, 2008*. (Geographica Historica 28) Stuttgart: Franz Steiner, pp. 205–219.

Kunow, J. (1987) 'Die Militärgeschichte Niedergermaniens', in Horn, H. G. (ed.) *Die Römer in Nordrhein-Westfalen*. Stuttgart: Konrad Theiss, pp. 27–109.

Kunow, J. (1988) 'Zentrale Orte in der Germania Inferior', *Archäologisches Korrespondenzblatt*, 18, pp. 55–67.

Kunow, J. and Gechter, M. (1986) 'Zur ländlichen Besiedlung des Rheinlandes in römischer Zeit', *Bonner Jahrbücher*, 186, pp. 377–396.

Kyritz, D. M. (2014) *Haffen-Mehr – Die Kontaktzone am niederrheinischen Limesgebiet Donata Maria Kyritz*. PhD thesis, Rheinischen Friedrich-Wilhelms-Universität Bonn.

Lamprecht, H.-O. (1987) *Opus caementitium. Bautechnik der Römer*. Düsseldorf: Beton.

Lanen, R. J. van, *et al.* (2016) 'Roman and early-medieval long-distance transport routes in north-western Europe: modelling frequent-travel zones using a dendroarchaeological approach', *Journal of Archaeological Science*, 73, pp. 120–137.

Lanen, R. J. van, *et al.* (2018) 'Exploring Roman and early-medieval habitation of the Rhine-Meuse delta: modelling large-scale demographic and land-use changes in the first millennium AD', *Netherlands Journal of Geosciences*, 97(1–2), pp. 45–68.

Lange, S. (2017) *Uit het juiste hout gesneden. Houten gebruiksvoorwerpen uit archeologische context tot 1300 n. Chr.* Amersfoort: Rijksdienst voor het Cultureel Erfgoed.

Laubenheimer, F. and Marlière, É. (2010) *Échanges et vie économique dans le Nord-Ouest des Gaules. (Nord/Pas-de-Calais, Picardie, Haute-Normandie). Le témoignage des amphores du IIe s. av. J.-C. au IVe s. ap. J.-C.* (Collection L'Institut des Sciences et Techniques de l'Antiquité 1161) Besançon: Presses universitaires de Franche-Comté.

Lauwerier, R. C. G. M. (1988) *Animals in Roman times in the Dutch eastern river area*. Amersfoort: ROB.

Lauwerier, R. C. G. M. (1999) 'Eating horsemeat: the evidence in the Roman Netherlands', *Archaeofauna*, 8, pp. 101–113.

Lee, R. D. (1986) 'Malthus and Boserup: a dynamic synthesis', in Coleman, D. and Schofield, R. (eds) *The state of population theory: forward from Malthus*. Oxford: Blackwell, pp. 96–130.

Lenz, K. H. (1998) 'Villae rusticae. Zur Entstehung dieser Siedlungsform in den Nordwestprovinzen des Römischen Reiches', *Kölner Jahrbuch*, 31, pp. 49–70.

Lenz, K. H. (2006) 'Veteranen der römischen Armee im Siedlungsbild einer früh- und mittelkaiserzeitlichen Koloniestadt und deren Hinterland. Das Beispiel der Colonia Claudia Ara Agrippinensium (Köln)', *Germania*, 84(1), pp. 61–91.

Lenz, K. H., Mommsen, H. and Perse, M. (2007) 'Charakterisierung der römischen Keramik aus Jülich durch Neutronenaktivierungsanalyse', *Archäologie im Rheinland*, 2006, pp. 120–123.

Lewit, T. (2013) 'The mysterious case of La Graufesenque? Stimuli to large-scale fine pottery production and trade in the Roman Empire', in Fulford, M. and Durham, E. (eds) *Seeing red. New economic & social perspectives on Gallo-Roman terra sigillata*. (Bulletin of the Institute of Classical Studies. Supplement 102) London: Institute of Classical Studies, School of Advanced Study, University of London, pp. 111–120.

Liesen, B. (2001) 'Neues zur Produktion römischer Keramik in Xanten', *Bonner Jahrbücher*, 201, pp. 203–220.

Liesen, B. (2004) 'Römische Importkeramik in Köln – Eine Bestandsaufnahme', *Kölner Jahrbuch*, 37, pp. 463–487.

Liesen, B. (2006) 'Töpfereiabfall vor der südlichen Stadtmauer der Colonia Ulpia Traiana', in Müller, M. (ed.) *Grabung – Forschung – Präsentation. Sammelband*. (Xantener Berichte 14) Mainz: Philipp von Zabern, pp. 189–191.

Liesen, B. (2008a) 'Soziale und wirtschaftliche Entwicklungstendenzen der Colonia Ulpia Traiana im Spiegel des Fundmaterials. Von den Anfängen bis zum Beginn der Spätantike', in Müller, M., Schalles, H.-J., and Zieling, N. (eds) *Colonia Ulpia Traiana. Xanten und sein Umland in römischer Zeit*. (Geschichte der Stadt Xanten 1 = Xantener Berichte Sonderband) Mainz: Philipp von Zabern, pp. 211–226.

Liesen, B. (2008b) 'Zur zweiten Gruppe verzierter Terra Sigillata aus Sinzig', *Kölner Jahrbuch*, 41, pp. 513–552.

Liesen, B. (2018) 'Der Handel mit Keramik aus Niedergermanien und angrenzenden Gebieten', in Eger, C. (ed.) *Warenwege – Warenflüsse. Handel, Logistik und Transport am römischen Niederrhein*. (Xantener Berichte 32) Mainz: Nünnerich-Asmus, pp. 361–372.

Liesen, B. and Pirling, R. (1998) 'Glasierte spätrömische Keramik aus Krefeld-Gellep', *Germania*, pp. 721–746.

Ligt, L. de (2012) *Peasants, citizens and soldiers. Studies in the demographic history of Roman Italy 225 BC–AD 100*. Cambridge: Cambridge University Press.

Ligt, L. de (2016) 'Roman law, markets and market prices', in du Plessis, P. J., Ando, C., and Tuori, K. (eds) *The Oxford handbook of Roman law and society*. Oxford: Oxford University Press, pp. 660–670.

Ligt, L. de and Bintliff, J. (2020) 'Introduction', in de Ligt, L. and Bintliff, J. (eds) *Regional urban systems in the Roman world, 150 BCE–250 CE*. Leiden: Brill (Mnemosyne Supplements), pp. 1–34.

Linden, E. van der (2007) 'Aardewerk', in Veldman, H. A. P. (ed.) *Romeinse pottenbakkersovens en erven te Heerlen, Dr. Poelsstraat. Een Archeologische Opgraving*. (ADC Rapport 634) Amersfoort: ADC ArcheoProjecten, pp. 29–41.

Linden, E. van der (2008) 'Aardewerk', in Blom, E. and Vos, W. K. (eds) *Woerden-Hoochwoert. De opgravingen 2002–2004 in het Romeinse Castellum Laurium, de vicus en van het schip de 'Woerden 7'*. (ADC Rapport 910) Amersfoort: ADC ArcheoProjecten, pp. 143–188.

Linden, E. van der (2009) 'Handgevormd aardewerk', in Siemons, H. and Lanzing, J. J. (eds) *Bewoningssporen uit de Romeinse tijd in het Wateringse Veld, Den Haag*. (Haagse Oudheidkundige Publicaties 11) Den Haag: Afdeling Archeologie Dienst Stadsbeheer gemeente Den Haag, pp. 225–254.

Linden, M. van der, *et al.* (2016) 'Absolute dating of the Roman road near Bunnik, the Netherlands', in Hevia, A. et al. (eds) *Proceedings of the Dendrosymposium 2015. May 20th–23rd, 2015 in Sevilla, Spain*. (TRACE. Tree Rings in Archaeology, Climatology and Ecology 14) Potsdam: Helmholtz-Zentrum Potsdam, pp. 6–13.

Lith, S. M. E. van, and Randsborg, K. (1985) *Roman glass in the west: a social study*. Amersfoort: Rijksdienst voor het Oudheidkundig Bodemonderzoek.

Love, J. R. (1991) *Antiquity and capitalism: Max Weber and the sociological foundations of Roman civilization*. London: Routledge.

Luik, M. (2002) 'Handwerk in den Vici des Rhein-Maas-Gebietes', in Strobel, K. and Luik, M. (eds) *Die Ökonomie des Imperium Romanum. Strukturen, Modelle und Wertungen im Spannungsfeld von Modernismus und Neoprimitivismus. Akten des 3. Trierer Symposiums zur Antiken Wirtschaftsgeschichte*. (Pharos 17) St. Katharinen: Scripta Mercaturae, pp. 169–208.

MacMullen, R. (1982) 'The epigraphic habit in the Roman Empire', *The American Journal of Philology*, 103(3), pp. 233–246.

Magerman, K. (2006) 'De vici. Een inventarisatie en functionele analyse van enkele zogenaamde vici in Vlaanderen tussen het begin van de 1e eeuw n.Chr. en het einde van de 4e eeuw n.Chr.', *Terra Incognita*, pp. 139–154.

Malthus, T. R. (1966) *First essay on population. A reprint in fascimile of an essay on the princple of population as it affects the future Improvement of society, 1789*. London: Palgrave Macmillan.

Mangartz, F. (2008) *Römischer Basaltlava-Abbau zwischen Eifel und Rhein*. (Monographien des Römisch-Germanischen Zentralmuseums 75 = Vulkanpark-Forschungen 7) Mainz: Römisch-Germanisch Zentralmuseum.

Marlière, É. (2001) 'Le tonneau en Gaule romaine', *Gallia*, 58, pp. 181–201.

Martens, M. (2007) 'Creating order in waste: structured deposits in Roman Tienen', in Hingley, R. and Willis, S. (eds) *Roman finds. Context and theory. Proceedings of a conference held at the University of Durham*. Oxford: Oxbow Books, pp. 150–155.

Martens, M. (2012) *Life and culture in the Roman small town of Tienen. Transformations of cultural behaviour by comparative analysis of material culture assemblages*. PhD thesis, Vrije Universiteit Amsterdam.

Martin-Kilcher, S. (1987) *Die römische Amphoren aus Augst und Kaiseraugst. Ein Beitrag zur römischen Handels- und Kulturgeschichte. 1: Die südspanischen Ölamphoren (Gruppe 1)*. (Forschungen in Augst 7/1) Augst: Römermuseum Augst.

Martin-Kilcher, S. (1994) *Die römische Amphoren aus Augst und Kaiseraugst. Ein Beitrag zur römischen Handels- und Kulturgeschichte. 2: Die Amphoren für Wein, Fischsauce, Südfrüchte (Gruppen 2–24) und Gesamtauswertung*. (Forschungen in Augst 7/2) Augst: Römermuseum Augst.

Martin-Kilcher, S. (2006) 'Amphoren: Archäologische Fragen und Fragestellungen', in Müller, M. (ed.) *Grabung – Forschung – Präsentation. Sammelband*. (Xantener Berichte 14) Mainz: Philipp von Zabern, pp. 11–18.

Martin, S. (ed.) (2019a) *Rural granaries in northern Gaul (6th Century BCE–4th Century CE)*. (Radboud Studies in Humanities 8) Leiden: Brill.

Martin, S. (2019b) 'Storage in a non-villa landscape: the Batavian countryside', in Martin, S. (ed.) *Rural Granaries in northern Gaul (6th century BCE–4th century CE). From archaeology to economic history*. (Radboud Studies in Humanities 8) Leiden: Brill, pp. 106–127.

Matijević, K. (2020) 'Writing and literacy/illiteracy', in James, S. and Krmnicek, S. (eds) *The Oxford handbook of the archaeology of Roman Germany*. Oxford: Oxford University Press, pp. 287–316.

Mattingly, D. J. (2011) *Imperialism, power, and identity. Experiencing the Roman Empire*. (Miriam S. Balmuth Lectures in Ancient History and Archaeology) Princeton: Princeton University Press.

Mayer, D. (2016) 'Stempel auf amphoren aus Köln', *Kölner Jahrbuch*, pp. 309–366.

McCormick, M. *et al.* (2012) 'Climate change during and after the Roman Empire: reconstructing the past from scientific and historical evidence', *Journal of Interdisciplinary History*, 43(2), pp. 169–220.

Mees, A. W. (2011) *Die Verbreitung von Terra Sigillata aus den Manufakturen von Arezzo, Pisa, Lyon und La Graufesenque. Die Transformation der Italischen Sigillata-Herstellung in Gallien*. (Monographien des Römisch-Germanischen Zentralmuseums 93) Mainz: Römisch-Germanischen Zentralmuseums.

Mees, A. W. (2018a) 'Big business in the roman economy. A military or civil affair? Regional and long-distance trading patterns of the Roman Terra-Sigillata (Samian) industry', in Bentz, M. and Helms, T. (eds) *Craft production systems in a cross-cultural perspective*. (Studien zur Wirtschaftsarchäologie 1) Bonn: Dr. Rudolf Habelt, pp. 151–170.

Mees, A. W. (2018b) 'Was there a Difference between Roman "civil" and "military" Samian (terra sigillata) market supply? Finding answers with statistical distribution analysis methods', *Internet Archaeology*, 50.

Meschede, M. (2015) *Geologie Deutschlands. Ein prozessorientierter Ansatz*. Berlin: Springer.

Metzler, J. (1995) 'Kontinuität und Integration in der "Raumplanung" in Gallien im ersten Jahrhundert v. Chr.', in Metzler, J. et al. (eds) *Integration in the Early Roman West. The role of Culture and Ideology. Papers arising from the international conference at the Titelberg (Luxembourg), 12–13 November 1993*. (Dossiers d'Archéologie du Musée National d'Histoire et d'Art 4) Luxembourg: Musée National d'Histoire et d'Art, pp. 153–158.

Meyer, E. A. (1990) 'Explaining the Epigraphic Habit in the Roman Empire: The Evidence of Epitaphs', *Journal of Roman Studies*, 80, pp. 74–96.

Milanovic, B., Lindert, P. H. and Williamson, J. G. (2007) *Measuring ancient inequality*. Policy Research Working Paper 4412.

Millet, M. (1990) *The Romanization of Britain. An essay in archaeological interpretation*. Cambridge: Cambridge University Press.

Mirschenz, M. (2013) *Fließende Grenzen. Studien zur römischen Kaiserzeit im Ruhrgebiet*. (Bochumer Forschungen zur Ur- und Frühgeschichtlichen Archäologie) Rahden/Westf.: Marie Leidorf.

Mirschenz, M. (2016a) 'Der Rhein als europäische Verkehrsachse in römischer Zeit', in *Roman Networks in the West. Approaches and Perspectives in Roman Archaeology between Moselle, Meuse and Rhine. 10./11. März 2016, Pingsdorfer Festsaal, LVR-Freilichtmuseum Kommern*. LVR-Amt für Bodendenkmalpflege im Rheinland, pp. 26–27.

Mirschenz, M. (2016b) 'Römisches Blei im Fokus der Hafenforschung', in Bemmann, J. and Mirschenz, M. (eds) *Der Rhein als europäische Verkehrsachse II*. (Bonner Beiträge zur Vor- und Frühgeschichtlichen Archäologie 19) Bonn: Rheinische Friedrich-Wilhelms-Universität Bonn, pp. 225–248.

Morley, N. (2004) *Theories, models and concepts in ancient history*. (Approaching the Ancient World) London: Routledge.

Morley, N. (2007a) 'The early Roman Empire: distribution', in Scheidel, W., Morris, I., and Saller, R. P. (eds) *The Cambridge economic history of the Greco-Roman world*. Cambridge: Cambridge University Press, pp. 570–591.

Morley, N. (2007b) *Trade in classical antiquity*. (Key Themes in Ancient History) Cambridge: Cambridge University Press.

Morley, N. (2011) 'Cities and economic development in the Roman Empire', in Bowman, A. K. and Wilson, A. (eds) *Settlement, urbanization, and population*. (Oxford Studies on the Roman Economy) Oxford: Oxford University Press, pp. 143–160.

Morris, I. (1999) 'Foreword', in *The ancient economy. Updated edition with a foreword by Ian Morris*. Berkeley: University of California Press, pp. ix–xxvi.

Morris, I. (2004) 'Economic growth in ancient Greece', *Journal of Institutional and Theoretical Economics*, 160(4), pp. 709–742.

Morris, I. and Manning, J. G. (2005) 'The economic sociology of the ancient Mediterranean world', in Smelser, N. J. and Swedberg, R. (eds) *The handbook of economic sociology*. Princeton: Princeton University Press, pp. 131–159.

Morris, I., Saller, R. P. and Scheidel, W. (2007) 'Introduction', in Scheidel, W., Morris, I., and Saller, R. P. (eds) *The Cambridge economic history of the Greco-Roman world*. Cambridge: Cambridge University Press, pp. 1–12.

Müller, G. (1987) 'Novaesium', in Horn, H. G. (ed.) *Die Römer in Nordrhein-Westfalen*. Stuttgart: Konrad Theiss, pp. 580–586.

Murphy, E. A. and Poblome, J. (2011) 'Producing pottery vs. producing models: interpreting workshop organization at the potters' quarter of Sagalassos', in Lawall, M. L. and Lund, J. (eds) *Pottery in the archaeological record: Greece and beyond. Acts of the international colloquium held at the Danish and Canadian Institutes in Athens, June 20–22, 2008*. Aarhus: Aarhus University Press, pp. 29–36.

Neal, L. (2014) 'Introduction', in Neal, L. and Williamson, J. G. (eds) *The rise of capitalism: from ancient origins to 1848*. (The Cambridge History of Capitalism 1) Cambridge: Cambridge University Press, pp. 1–23.

Neer, W. van, *et al.* (2005) 'New evidence from a Roman context in Belgium for fish sauce locally produced in northern Gaul', *Archaeofauna*, 14, pp. 171–182.

Neer, W. van, Ervynck, A. and Monsieur, P. (2010) 'Fish bones and amphorae: evidence for the production and consumption of salted fish products outside the Mediterranean region', *Journal of Roman Archaeology*, 23, pp. 161–194.

Nenninger, M. (2001) *Die Römer und der Wald. Untersuchungen zum Umgang mit einem Naturraum am Beispiel der römischen Nordwestprovinzen*. (Geographica Historica 16) Stuttgart: Franz Steiner.

Nicolas, N. (2011) 'Les amphores dans les milieux ruraux de la Cité des Tongres', *Archéo-Situla*, 31, pp. 51–90.

Nicolay, J. (2007) *Armed Batavians. Use and significance of weaponry and horse gear from non-military contexts in the Rhine delta (50 BC to AD 450)*. (Amsterdam Archaeological Studies 11) Amsterdam: Amsterdam University Press.

Niemeijer, R. A. J. and Thijssen, J. (2014) 'The pottery kilns at Cuijk (North-Brabant, the Netherlands)', in Liesen, B. (ed.) *Römische Keramik in Niedergermanien. Produktion – Handel – Gebrauch. Beiträge zur Tagung der Rei Cretariae Romanae Fautores. 21.–26. September 2014, LVR-RömerMuseum im Archäologischen Park Xanten*. (Xantener Berichte 27) Darmstadt: Philipp von Zabern, pp. 93–111.

Noelke, P. (2001) 'Glasgefäße', in Fischer, T. (ed.) *Die Römische Provinzen. Ein Einführing in ihre Archäologie*. Stuttgart: Konrad Theiss, pp. 308–316.

North, D. C. (1977) 'Markets and other allocation systems in history: the challenge of Karl Polanyi', *Journal of European Economic History*, 6, pp. 703–716.

North, D. C. (1990) *Institutions, institutional change and economic performance.* (Political economy of institutions and decisions) Cambridge: Cambridge University Press.

North, D. C. (1991) 'Institutions', *The Journal of Economic Perspectives*, 5(1), pp. 97–112.

Oenbrink, W. (2018) 'Der Niederrhein und Britannien', in Eger, C. (ed.) *Warenwege – Warenflüsse. Handel, Logistik und Transport am römischen Niederrhein.* (Xantener Berichte 32) Mainz: Nünnerich-Asmus, pp. 507–532.

Ortisi, S. (2013) 'Der römische vicus von Nettersheim', in Heising, A. (ed.) *Neue Forschungen zu zivilen Kleinsiedlungen (vici) in den römischen Nordwest-Provinzen. Akten der Tagung Lahr 21.–23.10.2010.* Bonn, pp. 41–52.

Ortman, S. G. *et al.* (2016) 'Settlement scaling and economic change in the Central Andes', *Journal of Archaeological Science*, 73, pp. 94–106.

Otte, R. (2022) *Monetarisierung und Geldumlauf in ländlichen Siedlungen des niederrheinischen Lössgebietes.* PhD thesis, Goethe-Universität zu Frankfurt am Main.

Oyen, A. Van, (2016) *How things make history. The Roman Empire and its terra sigillata pottery.* (Amsterdam Archaeological Studies 23) Amsterdam: Amsterdam University Press.

Pals, J. P. (1997) 'Introductie van cultuurgewassen in de Romeinse Tijd', in Zeven, A. C. (ed.) *De introductie van onze cultuurplanten en hun begeleiders, van het Neolithicum tot 1500 AD.* Wageningen: Vereniging voor Landbouwgeschiedenis, pp. 25–51.

Pals, J. P. and Hakbijl, T. (1992) 'Weed and insect infestation of a grain cargo in a ship at the Roman fort of Laurium in Woerden (province of Zuid-Holland)', *Review of Palaeobotany and Palynology*, 73(1–4), pp. 287–300.

Pamuk, Şevket (2014) 'Institutional change and economic development in the Middle East, 700–1800', in Neal, L. and Williamson, J. G. (eds) *The rise of capitalism: from ancient origins to 1848.* (The Cambridge History of Capitalism 1) Cambridge: Cambridge University Press, pp. 193–224.

Peacock, D. P. S. (1982) *Pottery in the Roman world: an ethnoarchaeological approach.* (Longman Archaeology Series) London: Longman.

Peacock, D. P. S. and Williams, D. F. (1986) *Amphorae and the Roman economy. An introductory guide.* (Longman archaeology series) London: Longman.

Pellegrino, F. (2018) *The urbanization of the north-western provinces of the Roman Empire. A juridical and functional approach to town life in Roman Gaul, Germania Inferior and Britain.* PhD thesis, Universiteit Leiden.

Perse, M. (2012) 'Der vicus von Jülich', in Rupp, V. and Birley, H. (eds) *Landleben im römischen Deutschland.* Stuttgart: Theiss, pp. 108–109.

Peters, J. (1994) 'Nutztiere in den westlichen Rhein-Donau-Provinzen während der römischen Kaiserzeit', in Bender, H. and Wolff, H. (eds) *Ländliche Besiedlung und Landwirtschaft in den Rhein-Donau-Provinzen des römischen Reiches. Vorträge eines internationalen Kolloquiums vom 16.–21. April 1991 in Passau.* (Passauer Universitätsschriften zur Archöologie 2) Espelkamp: Marie L. Leidorf, pp. 37–63.

Peters, J. (1998) *Römische Tierhaltung und Tierzucht. Eine Synthese aus archäozoologischer Untersuchung und schriftlich-bildlicher Überlieferung.* (Passauer Universitätsschriften zur Archäologie 5) Rahden/Westf.: Marie Leidorf.

Petit, J.-P., Mangin, M. and Philippe, B. (eds) (1994) *Atlas des agglomérations secondaires de la Gaule Belgique et des Germanies.* (Archéologie Aujourd'hui) Paris: Errance.

Pezzolo, L. (2014) 'The via italiana to capitalism', in Neal, L. and Williamson, J. G. (eds) *The rise of capitalism: from ancient origins to 1848.* (The Cambridge History of Capitalism 1) Cambridge: Cambridge University Press, pp. 267–313.

Picavet, P. (2015) 'Production régionale et importation de meules rotatives dans le sud de l'Entre-Sambre-et-Meuse dans l'Antiquité. Les collections du musée du Malgré-Tout (Treignes, Prov. de Namur)', *Archéo-Situla*, 35, pp. 105–119.

Piepers, W. (1971) 'Römische Ziegel- und Töpferöfen bei Bedburg-Garsdorf, Kreis Bergheim/Erft.', in Binding, G. (ed.) *Beiträge zur Archäologie des römischen Rheinlands II.* (Rheinische Ausgrabungen 10) Düsseldorf: Rheinland, pp. 340–349.

Pigière, F. (2015) 'Arable farming and animal husbandry in the core area of the civitas Tungrorum', in Roymans, N., Derks, T., and Hiddink, H. (eds) *The Roman villa of Hoogeloon and the archaeology of the periphery.* (Amsterdam Archaeological Studies 22) Amsterdam: Amsterdam University Press, pp. 163–175.

Pigière, F. (2017) 'The evolution of cattle husbandry practices in the Roman period in Gallia Belgica and western Germania Inferior', *European Journal of Archaeology*, 20(3), pp. 472–493.

Pigière, F. and Lepot, A. (2013) 'Food production and exchanges in the Roman civitas Tungrorum', in Groot, M., Lentjes, D., and Zeiler, J. (eds) *Barely surviving or more than enough? The environmental archaeology of subsistence, specialisation and surplus food production.* Leiden: Sidestone Press, pp. 225–246.

Piketty, T. (2014) *Capital in the twenty-first century.* Translated by A. Goldhammer. Cambridge, MA: The Belknap Press of Harvard University Press.

Pirling, R. and Siepen, M. (2006) *Die Funde aus den römischen Gräbern von Krefeld-Gellep. Katalog der Gräber 6348–6361.* (Germanische Denkmäler der Völkerwanderungszeit 20) Stuttgart: Franz Steiner.

Pitts, M. (2019) *The Roman object revolution. Objectscapes and intra-cultural connectivity in Northwest Europe.* (Amsterdam Archaeological Studies 27) Amsterdam: Amsterdam University Press.

Plat Taylor, J. du, and Cleere, H. (eds) (1978) *Roman shipping and trade: Britain and the Rhine provinces.* (CBA Research Report 24) London: The Council for British Archaeology.

Pleiner, R. (2000) *Iron in archaeology. The European bloomery smelters.* Prague: Archeologický ústav AVČR.

Pleiner, R. (2006) *Iron in archaeology. Early European blacksmiths.* Prague: Archeologický ústav AVČR.

Pleket, H. W. (1990) 'Wirtschaft', in Vittinghoff, F. (ed.) *Europäische Wirtschafts- und Sozialgeschichte in der Römischen Kaiserzeit.* (Handbuch der Europäischen Wirtschafts- und Sozialgeschichte) Stuttgart: Klett-Cotta, pp. 25–160.

Polak, M. (2000) *South Gaulish terra sigillata with potters' stamps from Vechten.* (Rei Cretariae Romanae Fautorum Acta Supplementum 9) Nijmegen: Katholieke Universiteit Nijmegen.

Polak, M. (2005) 'Lokale nijverheid: baksteen, aardewerk, metaal en glas', in Willems, W. et al. (eds) *Nijmegen. Geschiedenis van de oudste stad van Nederland. Prehistorie en Oudheid.* Wormer: Inmerc, pp. 243–249.

Polak, M. (2009) 'The Roman military presence in the Rhine delta in the period c. AD 40–140', in Morillo, Á., Hanel, N., and Martín, E. (eds) *Limes XX. XXth International Congress of Roman Frontiers Studies. León (España), Septiembre, 2006.* (Anejos de Gladius 13) Madrid: Polifemo, pp. 945–953.

Polak, M., Kloosterman, R. P. J. and Niemeijer, R. A. J. (2004) *Alphen aan den Rijn – Albaniana 2001–2002. Opgravingen tussen de Castellumstraat, het Omloopkanaal en de Oude Rijn.* (Libelli Noviomagenses 7) Nijmegen: Radboud Universiteit Nijmegen.

Polak, M. and Kooistra, L. I. (2013) 'A sustainable frontier? The establishment of the Roman frontier in the Rhine delta. Part 1: From the end of the Iron Age to the death of Tiberius (c. 50 BC–AD 37)', *Jahrbuch des Römisch-Germanischen Zentralmuseums Mainz*, 60, pp. 355–458.

Polanyi, K. (1957) 'Aristotle discovers the economy', in Polanyi, K., Arensberg, C. M., and Pearson, H. W. (eds) *Trade and market in the early empires. Economies in history and theory.* New York: Free Press, pp. 64–94.

Polfer, M. (1999) 'Production et travail du fer en Gaule du Nord et en Rhénanie à l'époque romaine: le rôle des établissements ruraux', in Polfer, M. (ed.) *Artisanat et productions artisanales en milieu rural dans les provinces du nord-ouest de l'Empire-romain. Actes du colloque organisé à l'Erpeldange (Luxembourg) les 4 et 5 mars 1999.* (Monographies Instrumentum 9) Montagnac: Mergoil.

Polfer, M. (2000) 'Eisenproduktion und Eisenverarbeitung in Nordgallien und dem Rheinland während der römischen Kaiserzeit', in Feugère, M., Guštin, M., and Serneels, V. (eds) *Iron, blacksmiths and tools. Ancient European crafts. Acts of the Instrumentum Conference at Podsreda (Slovenia) in april 1999.* (Monographies Instrumentum 12) Montagnac: Mergoil, pp. 67–87.

Polfer, M. (2001) 'L'archéologie de l'artisanat et le débat sur la nature de l'économie romaine: quelques réflexions critiques', in Polfer, M. (ed.) *L'artisanat romain: évolutions, continuités et ruptures (Italie et provinces occidentales). Actes du 2e Colloque d'Erpeldange (26–28 octobre 2001), organisé par le Séminaire d'études anciennes du Centre universitaire de Luxembourg et Instrumentum.* (Monographies Instrumentum 20) Montagnac: Monique Mergoil, pp. 7–17.

Polfer, M. (ed.) (2005) *Artisanat et économie romaine. Italie et provinces occidentales de l'Empire. actes du 3e colloque international d'Erpeldange (Luxembourg) 14–16 octobre 2004.* (Monographies Instrumentum 32) Montagnac: Mergoil.

Polfer, M. (2008) 'Zur Rolle des städtischen Handwerks in der Wirtschaft der römischen Provinz "Gallia Belgica" auf der Grundlage der archäologischen, epigraphischen und ikonographischen Quellen', *Zeitschrift für schweizerische Archäologie und Kunstgeschichte*, 65, pp. 37–42.

Pollard, N. (2000) *Soldiers, cities, and civilians in Roman Syria*. Ann Arbor: The University of Michigan Press.

Prior, J. D. (2015) *The impact of glassblowing on the early-Roman glass industry (circa 50 B.C.–A.D. 79)*. PhD thesis, Durham University.

Pucci, G. (2001) 'Inscribed instrumentum and the ancient economy', in Bodel, J. (ed.) *Epigraphic evidence. Ancient history from inscriptions*. (Approaching the Ancient World) London: Routledge, pp. 137–152.

Raepsaet-Charlier, M.-T. and Raepsaet, G. (2013) 'Der in Tongern aufgefundene Bleibarren mit dem Namen des Kaisers Tiberius', in Creemers, G. (ed.) *Archaeological contributions to materials and immateriality*. (Atuatuca 4) Tongeren: Gallo-Romeins Museum, pp. 38–49.

Raepsaet, G. (1995) 'Les prémices de la mécanisation agricole entre Seine et Rhin de l'Antiquité au XIIIe siècle', *Annales. Histoire, Sciences Sociales*, 50(4), pp. 911–942.

Rathbone, D. (2009) 'Earnings and costs: living standards and the Roman economy (first to third centuries AD)', in Bowman, A. K. and Wilson, A. (eds) *Quantifying the Roman economy. Methods and problems*. (Oxford Studies on the Roman Economy) Oxford: Oxford University Press, pp. 299–326.

Rathbone, D. W. (1991) *Economic rationalism and rural society in third century A.D. Egypt. The Heroninos archive and the Appianus estate*. (Cambridge Classical Studies) Cambridge: Cambridge University Press.

Rathbone, D. W. (1996) 'The imperial finances', in Bowman, A. K., Champlin, E., and Lintott, A. (eds) *The Augustan empire, 43 B.C.–A.D. 69*. (The Cambridge Ancient History 10) Cambridge: Cambridge University Press, pp. 309–323.

Rathmann, M. (2004) 'Die Reichsstraßen der Germania Inferior', *Bonner Jahrbücher*, 204, pp. 1–45.

Ray, N. M. (2009) *Household consumption in ancient economies: Pompeii and the wider Roman world*. PhD thesis, University of Leicester.

Reddé, M. (2018) 'The impact of the German frontier on the economic development of the countryside of Roman Gaul', *Journal of Roman Archaeology*, 31, pp. 131–160.

Rehren, T. and Hauptman, A. (1995) 'Silberraffinations-Schlacken aus der CUT (Xanten), Insula 39: Mineralogische Untersuchung und archäometallurgische Interpretation', in Precht, G. (ed.) *Grabung – Forschung – Präsentation*. (Xantener Berichte 6) Cologne: Rheinland, pp. 119–138.

Reichmann, C. (1991) 'Das Heiligtum in Krefeld-Elfrath', *Die Heimat*, 62, pp. 1–30.

Reichmann, C. (2001) 'Gelduba (Krefeld-Gellep) als Fernhandelsplatz', in Grünewald, T. (ed.) *Germania Inferior. Besiedlung, Gesellschaft und Wirtschaft an der Grenze der römisch-germanischen Welt*. (Reallexikon der Germanischen Altertumskunde – Ergänzungsbände 28) Berlin: Walter de Gruyter, pp. 480–516.

Reigersman-van Lidth de Jeude, W. F. and Vanderhoeven, T. (2017) 'Aardewerk uit de nederzetting en het grafveld', in Veldman, H. A. P. (ed.) *Graven in Zoelen. De opgraving van een Romeinse nederzetting en grafveld te Zoelen Scharenburg, gemeente Buren*. (ADC Rapport 2391) Amersfoort: ADC ArcheoProjecten, pp. 97–131.

Remesal Rodríguez, J. (1997) *Heeresversorgung und die wirtschaftlichen Beziehungen zwischen der Baetica und Germanien. Materialien zu einem Corpus der in Deutschland veröffentichten Stempel auf Amphoren der Form Dressel 20*. (Materialhefte zur Archäologie in Baden-Württemberg 42) Stuttgart: Theiss.

Remesal Rodríguez, J. (2001) 'Politik und Landwirtschaft im Imperium Romanum am Beispiel der Baetica', in Herz, P. and Waldherr, G. (eds) *Landwirtschaft im Imperium Romanum*. (Pharos 14) St. Katharinen: Scripta Mercaturae, pp. 235–255.

Remesal Rodríguez, J. (2002a) 'Baetica and Germania. Notes on the concept of "provincial interdependence" in the Roman Empire', in Erdkamp, P. (ed.) *The Roman army and the economy*. Amsterdam: J.C. Gieben, pp. 293–308.

Remesal Rodríguez, J. (2002b) 'Heeresversorgung im frühen Prinzipat. Eine Art, die antike Wirtschaft zu verstehen', *Münstersche Beiträge zur Antiken Handelsgeschichte*, 11(1), pp. 69–84.

Remesal Rodríguez, J. and Revilla-Calvo, V. (1991) 'Weinamphoren aus Hispania Citerior und Gallia Narbonensis in Deutschland und Holland', *Fundberichte aus Baden-Württemberg*, 16, pp. 389–439.

Reniere, S. *et al.* (2016) 'Querns and mills during Roman times at the northern frontier of the Roman Empire (Belgium, northern France, southern Netherlands, western Germany): unravelling geological and geographical provenances, a multidisciplinary research project', *Journal of Lithic Studies*, 3(3), pp. 403–428.

Renson, V. *et al.* (2008) 'Roman road pollution assessed by elemental and lead isotope geochemistry in east Belgium', *Applied Geochemistry*, 23, pp. 3253–3266.

Renswoude, J. van (2009) 'Metaal', in van Renswoude, J. and Van Kerckhove, J. (eds) *Opgravingen in Geldermalsen-Hondsgemet. Een inheemse nederzetting uit de Late IJzertijd en Romeinse tijd*. (Zuidnederlandse Archeologische Rapporten 35) Amsterdam: Archeologisch Centrum Vrije Universiteit Hendrik Brunsting Stichting, pp. 231–286.

Reuter, M. (2008) 'Wirtschaftsstandort Colonia Ulpia Traiana – Handel und Handwerk in der CUT', in Müller, M., Schalles, H.-J., and Zieling, N. (eds) *Colonia Ulpia Traiana. Xanten und sein Umland in römischer Zeit*. (Geschichte der Stadt Xanten 1 = Xantener Berichte Sonderband) Mainz: Philipp von Zabern, pp. 471–493.

Ritzdorf, H. (2003) *Die römerzeitliche Eisenmetallurgie in der Eifel*. PhD thesis, Rheinischen Friedrich-Wilhelms-Universität Bonn.

Röder, J. (1974) 'Römische Steinbruchtätigkeit am Drachenfels', *Bonner Jahrbücher*, 174, pp. 509–544.

Roest, J. van der (1988) 'Die Römischen Fibeln von "De Horden". Fibeln aus einer Zivilsiedlung am Niedergermanischen Limes', *Berichten van de Rijksdienst voor het Oudheidkundig Bodemonderzoek*, 38, pp. 141–202.

Rogge, M. (2004) 'Het wegennet van de Romeinen in Gallië en Germanië', *Vlaanderen*, 53, pp. 174–177.

Roggenkamp, T. and Herget, J. (2014) 'Rekonstruktion römerzeitlicher Wasserstände und Abflüsse an Nieder- und Mittelrhein', in Kennecke, H. (ed.) *Der Rhein als europäische Verkehrsachse. Die Römerzeit.* (Bonner Beiträge zur Vor- und Frühgeschichtlichen Archäologie 16) Bonn: Rheinische Friedrich-Wilhelms-Universität Bonn, pp. 25–61.

Rossum, J. A. van (2004) 'The end of the Batavian auxiliaries as "national" units', in De Ligt, L., Hemelrijk, E. A., and Singor, H. W. (eds) *Roman rule and civic life. Local and regional perspectives. Proceedings of the fourth workshop of the International Network Impact of Empire (Roman Empire, c. 200 B.C.–A.D. 476), Leiden, June 25–28, 2003.* (Impact of Empire 4) Amsterdam: Gieben, pp. 113–131.

Rostovtzeff, M. I. (1926) *The social and economic history of the Roman Empire*. Oxford: Clarendon Press.

Rostovtzeff, M. I. (1941) *The social and economic history of the Hellenistic world*. Oxford: Clarendon Press.

Roth, J. P. (1999) *The logistics of the Roman army at war (264 B.C.–A.D. 235)*. (Columbia Studies in the Classical Tradition 23) Leiden: Brill.

Rothenhöfer, P. (2005a) *Die Wirtschaftsstrukturen im südlichen Niedergermanien. Untersuchungen zur Entwicklung eines Wirtschaftsraumes an der Peripherie des Imperium Romanum.* (Kölner Studien zur Archäologie der Römischen Provinzen 7) Rahden/Westf.: Marie Leidorf.

Rothenhöfer, P. (2005b) 'Strukturen des Handwerks im südlichen Niedergermanien. I. Metallverarbeitendes Handwerk', in *Artisanat et économie romaine. Italie et provinces occidentales de l'empire. Actes du 3e colloque international d'Erpeldange (Luxembourg) sur l'artisanat romain, 14–16 octobre 2004.* (Monographies Instrumentum 32) Montagnac: Monique Mergoil, pp. 65–73.

Rothenhöfer, P. (2013) 'Römische Bleigewinnung in der Nordeifel', in Creemers, G. (ed.) *Archaeological contributions to materials and immateriality.* (Atuatuca 4) Tongeren: Gallo-Romeins Museum, pp. 58–67.

Rothenhöfer, P. (2014) 'Rhenus flumen – Bemerkungen zur Bedeutung des Rheins für die Wirtschaft im römischen Rheinland', in Kennecke, H. (ed.) *Der Rhein als europäische Verkehrsachse. Die Römerzeit.* (Bonner Beiträge zur Vor- und Frühgeschichtlichen Archäologie 16) Bonn: Rheinische Friedrich-Wilhelms-Universität Bonn, pp. 11–23.

Rothenhöfer, P. and Bode, M. (2012) 'Römische Bleigewinnung und Bleihandel im Licht neuer epigraphischer und naturwissenschaftlicher Forschungen. Das Beispiel Germanien', in Olshausen, E. and Sauer, V. (eds) *Die Schätze der Erde – natürliche Ressourcen in der antiken Welt. Stuttgarter Kolloquium zur Historischen Geographie des Altertums 10, 2008*. (Geographica Historica 28) Stuttgart: Franz Steiner, pp. 345–360.

Rothenhöfer, P. and Bode, M. (2015) 'Wirtschaftliche Auswirkungen der römischen Herrschaft im augusteischen Germanien', in Lehmann, G. A. and Wiegels, R. (eds) *„Über die Alpen und über den Rhein ...". Beiträge zu den Anfängen und zum Verlauf der römischen Expansion nach Mitteleuropa*. Berlin: De Gruyter Akademie Forschung, pp. 313–338.

Rothenhöfer, P. and Hanel, N. (2013) 'The Romans and their lead – Tracing innovations in the production, distribution, and secondary processing of an ancient metal', in Burmeister, S. et al. (eds) *Metal matters. Innovative technologies and social change in Prehistory and Antiquity*. (Menschen, Kulturen, Traditionen 12) Rahden/Westf.: Marie Leidorf, pp. 273–282.

Rothenhöfer, P., Hanel, N. and Bode, M. (2013) 'Auf den Spuren des Bleis der Römer: Das Forschungsprojekt Corpus der Römischen Bleibarren', in Creemers, G. (ed.) *Archaeological contributions to materials and immateriality*. (Atuatuca 4) Tongeren: Gallo-Romeins Museum, pp. 68–74.

Roymans, N. (1990) *Tribal societies in northern Gaul. An anthropological perspective*. (Cingula 12) Amsterdam: Najade.

Roymans, N. (1996) 'The sword or the plough. Regional dynamics in the romanisation of Belgic Gaul and the Rhineland area', in Roymans, N. (ed.) *From the sword to the plough. Three studies on the earliest Romanisation of northern Gaul*. (Amsterdam Archaeological Studies 1) Amsterdam: Amsterdam University Press, pp. 9–126.

Roymans, N. (1999) 'Man, cattle and the supernatural in the Northwest European plain', in Fabech, C. and Ringtved, J. (eds) *Settlement and landscape. Proceedings of a conference in Århus, Denmark, May 4–7 1998*. Jutland Archaeological Society, pp. 291–300.

Roymans, N. (2004) *Ethnic identity and imperial power. The Batavians in the early Roman Empire*. (Amsterdam Archaeological Studies 10) Amsterdam: Amsterdam University Press.

Roymans, N. (2011) 'Ethnic recruitment, returning veterans and the diffusion of Roman culture among rural populations in the Rhineland frontier zone', in Roymans, N. and Derks, T. (eds) *Villa landscapes in the Roman north: economy, culture and lifestyles*. (Amsterdam Archaeological Studies 17) Amsterdam: Amsterdam University Press, pp. 139–160.

Roymans, N. *et al.* (2014) 'La Tène glass armrings in Europe. Interregional connectivity and local identity construction', *Archäologisches Korrespondenzblatt*, 44(2), pp. 215–228.

Roymans, N. and Aarts, J. G. (2009) 'Coin use in a dynamic frontier region. Late Iron Age coinages in the Lower Rhine area', *Journal of archaeology in the Low Countries*, (1), pp. 5–26.

Roymans, N. and Derks, T. (2011) 'Studying Roman villa landscapes in the 21st century. A multi-dimensional approach', in Roymans, N. and Derks, T. (eds) *Villa landscapes in the Roman north. economy, culture and lifestyles*. (Amsterdam Archaeological Studies 17) Amsterdam: Amsterdam University Press, pp. 1–44.

Roymans, N. and Derks, T. (2015) 'The archaeology of a peripheral region. Theoretical perspectives and methodology', in Roymans, N., Derks, T., and Hiddink, H. (eds) *The Roman villa of Hoogeloon and the archaeology of the periphery*. (Amsterdam Archaeological Studies 22) Amsterdam: Amsterdam University Press, pp. 1–18.

Roymans, N. and Fernández-Götz, M. (2015) 'Caesar in Gaul: new perspectives on the archaeology of mass violence', in Brindle, T. et al. (eds) *TRAC 2014. Proceedings of the twenty fourth annual Theoretical Roman Archaeology Conference. Which took place at the University of Reading 27–30 March 2014*. Oxford: Oxbow Books, pp. 70–80.

Roymans, N. and Verniers, L. (2010) 'Glass La Tène bracelets in the Lower Rhine region', *Germania*, 88, pp. 195–219.

Rudnick, B. (2018) 'First to the market – Zur Marktorientierung römischer Qualitätsgeschirrproduzenten aus Italien und Südgallien', in Eger, C. (ed.) *Warenwege – Warenflüsse. Handel, Logistik und Transport am römischen Niederrhein*. (Xantener Berichte 32) Mainz: Nünnerich-Asmus, pp. 339–360.

Ruffing, K. (2008) 'Friedliche Beziehungen. Der Handel Zwischen den römischen Provinzen und Germanien', in Schneider, H. (ed.) *Feindliche Nachbarn. Rom und die Germanen*. Cologne: Böhlau, pp. 153–165.

Ruffing, K. (2015) 'Von der primitivistischen Orthodoxie zum römischen Basar. Die Wirtschaft des Römischen Reiches in der Forschung des ausgehenden 20. und des beginnenden 21. Jahrhunderts', in Lafer, R. and Strobel, K. (eds) *Antike Lebenswelten. Althistorische und papyrologische Studien*. Berlin: De Gruyter, pp. 3–27.

Ruffing, K. (2016) 'Neue Institutionenökonomik (NIÖ) und Antike Wirtschaft', in Dross-Krüpe, K., Föllinger, S., and Ruffing, K. (eds) *Antike Wirtschaft und ihre kulturelle Prägung*. (Philippika 98) Wiesbaden: Harrassowitz, pp. 11–22.

Ruffing, K. (2018) 'Wirtschaft und Handel in der Römischen Kaiserzeit', in Eger, C. (ed.) *Warenwege – Warenflüsse. Handel, Logistik und Transport am römischen Niederrhein*. (Xantener Berichte 32) Mainz: Nünnerich-Asmus, pp. 3–23.

Rüger, C. (2000) 'Roman Germany', in Bowman, A. K., Garnsey, P. D. A., and Rathbone, D. W. (eds) *The high empire, AD 70–192*. (The Cambridge Ancient History 11) Cambridge: Cambridge University Press, pp. 496–513.

Russell, B. (2017) *Stone use and the economy: demand, distribution, and the state, trade, commerce, and the state in the Roman world*. Edited by A. Wilson and A. K. Bowman. (Oxford Studies on the Roman Economy) Oxford: Oxford University Press.

Saller, R. P. (2002) 'Framing the debate over growth in the ancient economy', in Scheidel, W. and von Reden, S. (eds) *The ancient economy*. Edinburgh: Edinburgh University Press, pp. 251–269.

Saller, R. P. (2012) 'Human capital and economic growth', in Scheidel, W. (ed.) *The Cambridge companion to the Roman economy.* Cambridge: Cambridge University Press, pp. 71–86.

Salvucci, R. (2014) 'Capitalism and dependency in Latin America', in Neal, L. and Williamson, J. G. (eds) *The rise of capitalism: from ancient origins to 1848.* (The Cambridge History of Capitalism 1) Cambridge: Cambridge University Press, pp. 403–430.

Schaaff, H. (2010) 'Steine für das Römische reich. Zu den anfängen des antiken steinbruch- und bergwerksreviers zwischen Eifel und Rhein', *Archaologisches Korrespondenzblatt*, 40, pp. 265–272.

Schaaff, H. (2015) *Antike Tuffbergwerk am Laacher See-Vulkan.* (Monographien des Römisch-Germanischen Zentralmuseums 107 = Vulkanpark-Forschungen 11) Mainz: Römisch-Germanisches Zentralmuseum.

Schaaff, H. (2018) 'Steine, Städte und Soldaten – Zu den staatlichen Bauprogrammen in der Germania Inferior', in Eger, C. (ed.) *Warenwege – Warenflüsse. Handel, Logistik und Transport am römischen Niederrhein.* (Xantener Berichte 32) Mainz: Nünnerich-Asmus, pp. 157–176.

Schäfer, A. (2014) 'Köln: Römischer Hafen und rheinseitige Stadtbefestigungen. Zur Rolle des römischen Heeres als Bauträger', in Kennecke, H. (ed.) *Der Rhein als europäische Verkehrsachse. Die Römerzeit.* (Bonner Beiträge zur Vor- und Frühgeschichtlichen Archäologie 16) Bonn: Rheinische Friedrich-Wilhelms-Universität Bonn, pp. 117–143.

Schäfer, C. (2017) 'The debate on the ancient economy as a "battlefield" and the question of transport routes to the Rhine region', in Remesal Rodríguez, J. (ed.) *Economía Romana. Nuevas Perspectivas. The Roman Economy New Perspectives.* (Col·lecció Instrumenta 55) Barcelona: Universitat de Barcelona, pp. 89–118.

Schamuhn, S. and Zerl, T. (2009) 'Zur Landwirtschaft der Kelten, Römer und Germanen im Gebiet von Nordrhein-Westfalen. Kontinuität oder Wandel?', in *Kelten am Rhein. Akten des dreizehnten Internationalen Keltologiekongresses 23. bis 27. Juli 2007 in Bonn.* (Beihefte der Bonner Jahrbücher 58) Mainz: Philipp von Zabern, pp. 239–250.

Schaub, A. (2013) 'Aachen in römischer Zeit aus archäologischer Sicht – Versuch einer Neubewertung', in von Haehling, R. and Schaub, A. (eds) *Römisches Aachen. Archäologisch-historische Aspekte zu Aachen und der Euregio.* Regensburg: Schnell + Steiner, pp. 131–205.

Scheidel, W. (2006) 'Stratification, deprivation and quality of life', in Atkins, M. and Osborne, R. (eds) *Poverty in the Roman world.* Cambridge: Cambridge University Press, pp. 40–59.

Scheidel, W. (2007a) 'A model of real income growth in Roman Italy', *Historia: Zeitschrift für Alte Geschichte*, 56(3), pp. 322–346.

Scheidel, W. (2007b) 'Demography', in Scheidel, W., Morris, I., and Saller, R. P. (eds) *The Cambridge economic history of the Greco-Roman world.* Cambridge: Cambridge University Press, pp. 38–86.

Scheidel, W. (2009) 'In search of Roman economic growth', *The Journal of Roman Studies*, 22, pp. 46–70.

Scheidel, W. (2012) 'Approaching the Roman economy', in Scheidel, W. (ed.) *The Cambridge companion to the Roman economy.* Cambridge: Cambridge University Press, pp. 1–21.

Scheidel, W. (2015) 'State revenue and expenditure in the Han and Roman Empires', in Scheidel, W. (ed.) *State power in ancient China & Rome.* (Oxford Studies in Early Empires) Oxford: Oxford University Press, pp. 150–180.

Scheidel, W. (2017) *The great leveler. Violence and the history of inequality from the Stone Age to the twenty-first century.*

Scheidel, W., Morris, I. and Saller, R. P. (eds) (2007) *The Cambridge economic history of the Greco-Roman world.* Cambridge: Cambridge University Press.

Schettler, G. and Romer, R. L. (1998) 'Anthropogenic influences on Pb/Al and lead isotope signature in annually layered Holocene Maar lake sediments', *Applied Geochemistry*, 13(6), pp. 787–797.

Schmidhuber-Aspöck (2018) 'Binnenschifffahrt auf dem Rhein in römischer Zeit', in Eger, C. (ed.) *Warenwege – Warenflüsse. Handel, Logistik und Transport am römischen Niederrhein.* (Xantener Berichte 32) Mainz: Nünnerich-Asmus, pp. 229–243.

Schmidt, B. and Gruhle, W. (2003a) 'Klimaextreme in römischer Zeit. Eine Strukturanalyse dendrochronologischer Daten', *Archäologisches Korrespondenzblatt*, 33, pp. 421–426.

Schmidt, B. and Gruhle, W. (2003b) 'Niederschlagsschwankungen in Westeuropa während der letzten 8000 Jahre. Versuch einer Rekonstruktion mit Hilfe eines neuen dendrochronologischen Verfahrens (Grad der Wuchshomogenität)', *Archäologisches Korrespondenzblatt*, 33, pp. 281–300.

Schmidts, T. (2011) *Akteure und Organisation der Handelsschiffahrt in den nordwestlichen Provinzen des Römischen Reiches.* (Monographien des Römisch-Germanischen Zentralmuseums 97) Mainz: Römisch-Germanisches Zentralmuseums.

Schmidts, T. (2018a) 'Die Legionsziegeleien – Römische Baustoffindustrie am Niederrhein', in Eger, C. (ed.) *Warenwege – Warenflüsse. Handel, Logistik und Transport am römischen Niederrhein.* (Xantener Berichte 32) Mainz: Nünnerich-Asmus, pp. 133–155.

Schmidts, T. (2018b) *Gestempelte Militärziegel ausserhalb der Truppenstandorte. Untersuchungen zur Bautätigkeit der römischen Armee und zur Disposition ihres Baumaterials.* (Studia Archaeologica Palatinal 3) Wiesbaden: Harrassowitz.

Schmidtz, S. D. (2014) 'Scheldt-Valley Amphoren aus der Colonia Ulpia Traiana', in Liesen, B. (ed.) *Römische Keramik in Niedergermanien. Produktion – Handel – Gebrauch. Beiträge zur Tagung der Rei Cretariae Romanae Fautores. 21.–26. September*

2014, LVR-RömerMuseum im Archäologischen Park Xanten. (Xantener Berichte 27) Darmstadt: Philipp von Zabern, pp. 317–363.

Schmitz, D. (2002) 'Militärische Ziegelproduktion in Niedergermanien während der römischen Kaiserzeit', *Kölner Jahrbuch*, 35, pp. 339–374.

Schmitz, D. (2004) 'Die gestempelten Ziegel des Römischen Köln', *Kölner Jahrbuch*, 37, pp. 223–447.

Schneider, H. (1990) 'Die Bücher – Meyer Kontroverse', in Calder, W. M. (ed.) *Eduard Meyer. Leben und Leistung eines Universalhistorikers.* (Mnemosyne. Supplementum 112) Leiden: Brill, pp. 417–445.

Schneider, H. (2007) 'Technology', in Scheidel, W., Morris, I., and Saller, R. P. (eds) *The Cambridge economic history of the Greco-Roman world.* Cambridge: Cambridge University Press, pp. 144–172.

Schubert, T. (2016) *Pars fructuaria. Studie zu Nebengebäuden mit Speicherfunktion auf römerzeitlichen Villae im Tagebaugebiet Hambacher Forst. Mit Vergleichen aus den germanischen und britannischen Provinzen.* PhD- thesis, Universität zu Köln.

Sievers, S. (2020) 'The lands of Germania in the later pre-Roman Iron Age', in James, S. and Krmnicek, S. (eds) *The Oxford handbook of the archaeology of Roman Germany.* Oxford: Oxford University Press, pp. 5–27.

Smani, R. and Tutlies, P. (2012) 'Ein singulärer römischer Töpferofen im Rheinland', in Kunow, J. (ed.) *Archäologie im Rheinland. 25 Jahre Archäologie im Rheinland 1987–2011.* Stuttgart: Theiss, pp. 110–111.

Smith, M. E. (2019a) 'Energized crowding and the generative role of settlement aggregation and urbanization', in Attila, G. (ed.) *Coming together. Comparative approaches to population aggregation and early urbanization.* (The Institute for European and Mediterranean Archaeology Distinguished Monograph Series 8) Albany: State University of New York, pp. 37–58.

Smith, M. E. (2019b) 'Quality of life and prosperity in ancient households and communities', in Isendahl, C. and Stump, D. (eds) *The Oxford handbook of historical ecology and applied archaeology.* Oxford: Oxford University Press, pp. 486–505.

Sölter, W. (1970) *Römische Kalkbrenner im Rheinland.* (Kunst und Altertum am Rhein 31) Cologne: Rheinland.

Sommer, C. S. (1984) *The military vici in Roman Britain.* (BAR British Series 129) Oxford: BAR.

Speidel, M. A. (1996) *Die römischen Schreibtafeln von Vindonissa. Lateinische Texte des militärischen Alltags und ihre geschichtliche Bedeutung.* (Veröffentlichungen der Gesellschaft pro Vindonissa 12) Brugg: Gesellschaft Pro Vindonissa.

Speidel, M. A. (2000) 'Sold und Wirtschaftslage der Römischen Soldaten', in Alföldy, G., Dobson, B., and Eck, W. (eds) *Kaiser, Heer und Gesellschaft in der Römischen Kaiserzeit. Gedenkschrift für Eric Birley.* (Heidelberger Althistorische Beiträge und Epigraphische Studien 31) Stuttgart: Franz Steiner, pp. 65–94.

Spickermann, W. (2018) 'Merkur und Nehalennia – Götter der Kaufleute und Händler', in Eger, C. (ed.) *Warenwege – Warenflüsse. Handel, Logistik und Transport am römischen Niederrhein.* (Xantener Berichte 32) Mainz: Nünnerich-Asmus, pp. 599–614.

Stiglitz, J. E., Sen, A. and Fitoussi, J.-P. (2010) *Mismeasuring our lives. Why GDP doesn't add up.* New York: The New Press.

Stillwell, R., MacDonald, W. L. and McAllister, M. H. (eds) (2017) *The Princeton encyclopedia of classical sites.* (Princeton Legacy Library) Princeton: Princeton University Press.

Stockinger, U. (2018) 'Salzproduktion und Salzhandel in den Nordwestprovinzen', in Eger, C. (ed.) *Warenwege – Warenflüsse. Handel, Logistik und Transport am römischen Niederrhein.* (Xantener Berichte 32) Mainz: Nünnerich-Asmus, pp. 451–468.

Stoffels, E. (2014) 'Two pottery kilns at the Kops Plateau', in Liesen, B. (ed.) *Römische Keramik in Niedergermanien. Produktion – Handel – Gebrauch. Beiträge zur Tagung der Rei Cretariae Romanae Fautores. 21.–26. September 2014, LVR-RömerMuseum im Archäologischen Park Xanten.* (Xantener Berichte 27) Darmstadt: Philipp von Zabern, pp. 15–35.

Stolk, M. (2014) 'Metaalslakken', in Driessen, M. and Besselsen, E. (eds) *Voorburg-Arentsburg. Een Romeinse havenstad tussen Rijn en Maas.* (Themata 7) Amsterdam: Diachron, pp. 697–702.

Strobel, K. (1999) 'Die Vindolanda-Tabletts als wirtschaftsgeschichtliche Quelle', in Polfer, M. (ed.) *Artisanat et productions artisanales en milieu rural dans les provinces du nord-ouest de l'Empire-romain. Actes du colloque organisé à l'Erpeldange (Luxembourg) les 4 et 5 mars 1999.* (Monographies Instrumentum 9) Montagnac: Mergoil, pp. 25–27.

Strobel, K. (ed.) (2000) 'Forschungen zur römischen Keramikindustrie. Produktions-, Rechts- und Distributionsstrukturen. Akten des 1.Trierer Symposiums zur antiken Wirtschaftsgeschichte', in. (Trierer historische Forschungen 42) Mainz: Von Zabern.

Strobel, K. (2007) 'Vom marginalen Grenzraum zum Kernraum Europas. Das Römische Heer als Motor der Neustrukturierung historischer Landschaften und Wirtschaftsräume', in de Blois, L. and Lo Cascio, E. (eds) *The impact of the Roman army (200BC–AD 476). Economic, social, political, religious, and cultural aspects. Proceedings of the sixth workshop of the International Network Impact of Empire (Roman Empire, 200 B.C.–A.D. 476), Capri, March 29–April 2, 2005.* (Impact of Empire 6) Leiden: Brill, pp. 207–237.

Stuart, P. and Bogaers, J. E. (2001) *Nehalennia. Römische Steindenkmäler aus der Oosterschelde bei Colijnsplaat.* (Collection of the National Museum of Antiquities at Leiden 11) Leiden: Rijksmuseum van Oudheden.

Taayke, E. *et al.* (2012) *Ede vol erven. Germaanse bewoning op de rand van een vereldrijk (500 voor Chr. tot 500 na Chr.).* Leiden: Hazenberg Archeologie.

Tarpin, M. (2002) *Vici et Pagi Dans L'Occident Romain.* (Collection de l'École Française de Rome 299) Rome: École Française de Rome.

Tchernia, A. (1986) *Le vin de l'Italie romaine. Essai d'histoire économique d'après les amphores.* (Bibliothèque des écoles françaises d'Athènes et de Rome 261) Rome: Ecole française de Rome.

Tchernia, A. (2016) *The Romans and trade.* (Oxford Studies on the Roman Economy) Oxford: Oxford University Press.

Tegtmeier, U. (2018) 'Holzbedarf und Holzhandel im römischen Rheinland. Beispiele für Funde und Befunde zwischen Köln, Xanten und der rheinischen Lössbörde', in Eger, C. (ed.) *Warenwege – Warenflüsse. Handel, Logistik und Transport am römischen Niederrhein.* (Xantener Berichte 32) Mainz: Nünnerich-Asmus, pp. 469–487.

Temin, P. (2013) *The Roman market economy.* (The Princeton Economic History of the Western World) Princeton: Princeton University Press.

Thienen, V. Van, Creemers, G. and De Clercq, W. (2019) 'Mapping the civitas Tungrorum', *Signa*, 8, pp. 181–185.

Thomas, R. and Stallibrass, S. (2008) 'For starters: producing and supplying food to the army in the Roman north-west provinces', in Stallibrass, S. and Thomas, R. (eds) *Feeding the Roman army: the archaeology of production and supply in NW Europe.* Oxford: Oxbow Books, pp. 1–17.

Trier, M. and Naumann-Steckner, F. (eds) (2016) *Zerbrechlicher Luxus. Köln – ein Zentrum antiker Glaskunst. Begleitbuch zur Sonderausstellung im Römisc-Germanischen Museum der Stadt Köln, 3 Juni bis 13. November 2016.* Regensburg: Schnell + Steiner.

Ulbert, C. (2003) 'Eine gut erhaltene römische villa rustica in Botzdorf', *Archäologie im Rheinland*, 2002, pp. 89–92.

Ulbert, C. (2005) 'Der römische Töpferofen von Bornheim-Botzdorf', in Horn, H. G. (ed.) *Von Anfang an. Archäologie in Nordrhein-Westfalen. Begleitbuch zur Landesausstellung Von Anfang an, Köln, Römisch-Germanisches Museum 13. März bis 28. August 2005, Herne, Westfälisches Museum für Archäologie, Landesmuseum 22. September 2005 bis 5. Februar.* Cologne: Römisch-Germanisches Museum, pp. 376–377.

Ulbert, C. (2013) 'Zivile Kleinsiedlungen im Rheinland', in Heising, A. (ed.) *Neue Forschungen zu zivilen Kleinsiedlungen (vici) in den römischen Nordwest-Provinzen. Akten der Tagung Lahr 21.–23.10.2010.* Bonn: Habelt, pp. 7–40.

Unger, R. W. (2000) 'Jan de Vries and Ad van der Woude, The first modern economy: success, failure, and perseverance of the Dutch economy, 1500–1815', *The Journal of Modern History*, 72(1), pp. 239–241.

Vanvinckenroye, W. (1989) *Terra sigillata uit een Romeinse stortplaats te Tongeren.* (Publicaties van het Provinciaal Gallo-Romeins Museum Tongeren 41) Hasselt: Provincie Limburg.

Veal, R. (2017) 'The politics and economics of ancient forests', *Entretiens sur l'Antiquité classique*, pp. 317–368.

Veldman, H. A. P. and Geerts, R. C. A. (2014) 'Locatie Sporthal', in Veldman, H. A. P. et al. (eds) *Aan de rand van de Romeinse stad Atuatuca Tungrorum. Een archeologische opgraving aan de Beukenbergweg in Tongeren.* (ADC Monografie 16) Amersfoort: ADC ArcheoProjecten, pp. 65–184.

Verboven, K. S. (2007) 'Good for business. The Roman army and the emergence of a "business class" in the northwestern provinces of the Roman Empire (1st Century BCE–3rd Century CE)', in de Blois, L. and Lo Cascio, E. (eds) *The impact of the Roman army (200BC–AD 476). Economic, social, political, religious, and cultural aspects. Proceedings of the sixth workshop of the International Network Impact of Empire (Roman Empire, 200 B.C.–A.D. 476), Capri, March 29–April 2, 2005.* (Impact of Empire 6) Leiden: Brill, pp. 295–313.

Verboven, K. S. (2015) 'The knights who say NIE. Can neo-institutional economics live up to its expectation in ancient history research?', in Erdkamp, P. and Verboven, K. S. (eds) *Structure and performance in the Roman economy. Models, methods and case studies.* (Collection Latomus 350) Brussels: Latomus, pp. 33–58.

Verhagen, J. G. M. *et al.* (2017) 'Geoarchaeological prospection for Roman waterworks near the late Holocene Rhine-Waal delta bifurcation, the Netherlands', *Catena*, 149, pp. 460–473.

Verhagen, J. G. M., Kluiving, S. J. and Kars, H. (2022) 'The option of Roman canal construction by Drusus in the Vecht river area (the Netherlands): a geoarchaeological approach', *Netherlands Journal of Geosciences*, 101, p. e4.

Verhagen, P. *et al.* (2016) 'Now you see them, now you don't: defining and using a flexible chronology of sites for spatial analysis of Roman settlement in the Dutch river area', *Journal of Archaeological Science: Reports*, 10, pp. 309–321.

Vilvorder, F. *et al.* (2010) 'La céramique de Tongres, Quatre Siècles de production d'un caput civitatis', in *Actes du Congrès de Chelles 13–16 Mai 2010*. Marseilles: Société Française d'Étude de la Céramique Antique en Gaule, pp. 241–256.

Visser, D. (2010) 'De gestempelde terra sigillata', in van Enckevort, H. and Heirbaut, E. N. A. (eds) *Terra sigillata uit Oppidum Batavorum. Opgravingen op de St. Josephhof in Nijmegen. 3.* (Archeologische Berichten Nijmegen 18) Nijmegen: Gemeente Nijmegen, pp. 47–250.

Visser, R. M. (2006) 'Behoefte aan bouwhout in de Nederrijnse regio tijdens de Romeinse tijd', *SOJAbundel 2006. Symposium voor Onderzoek door Jonge Archeologen*, pp. 107–114.

Visser, R. M. (2009) 'De Romeinse houtvoorziening in de Germaanse provincies', *Westerheem*, 58, pp. 2–12.

Visser, R. M. (2010) 'Growing and felling? Theory and evidence related to the application of silvicultural systems in the Roman period', in Moore, A. et al. (eds) *TRAC 2009. Proceedings of the nineteenth annual Theoretical Roman Archaeology Conference Michigan and Southampton 2009.* Oxford: Oxbow Books, pp. 11–22.

Visser, R. M. (2015) 'Imperial timber? Dendrochronological evidence for large-scale road building along the Roman Limes in the Netherlands', *Journal of Archaeological Science*, 53, pp. 243–254.

Vleeschouwer, F. De, *et al.* (2007) 'Atmospheric lead and heavy metal pollution records from a Belgian peat bog spanning the last two millenia: human impact on a regional to global scale', *Science of the Total Environment*, 377, pp. 282–295.

Vos, W. K. (2009) *Bataafs platteland. Het Romeinse nederzettingslandschap in het Nederlandse Kromme-Rijngebied.* PhD thesis, Vrije Universiteit Amsterdam.

Vos, W. K. et al. (2020) 'De castra van Valkenburg (Zuid-Holland)', *Archeologie in Nederland*, pp. 2–11.

Vos, W. K. and Graafstal, E. (2016) 'Een kleine muur van Hadrianus. De Limesweg in Zuid-Holland en Utrecht', in van der Heijden, P. (ed.) *Romeinse wegen in Nederland.* Utrecht: Matrijs, pp. 41–55.

Voss, H.-U. (2017) 'Corpus der römischen Funde im europäischen Barbaricum – Rückblick und Ausblick', in Hodgson, N., Bidwell, P. T., and Schachtmann, J. (eds) *Roman frontier studies 2009: proceedings of the XXI International Congress of Roman Frontier Studies (Limes Congress) held at Newcastle-upon-Tyne in August 2009.* (Archaeopress Roman Archaeology 25)Oxford: Archaeopress, pp. 318–326.

Vossen, I. (2003) 'The possibilities and limitations of demographic calculations in the Batavian area', in Grünewald, T. and Seibel, S. (eds) *Kontinuität und Diskontinuität. Germania Inferior am Beginn und am Ende der römischen Herrschaft. Beiträge des deutsch-niederländischen Kolloquiums in der Katholieke Universiteit Nijmegen (27. bis 30. 06. 2001).* (Ergänzungsbände zum Reallexikon der Germanischen Altertumskunde 35) Berlin: Walter de Gruyter, pp. 414–435.

Vries, J. de (1974) *The Dutch rural economy in the Golden Age, 1500–1700.* (Yale series in economic history) New Haven: Yale University Press.

Vries, J. de, and van der Woude, A. (1997) *The first modern economy. Success, failure, and perseverance of the Dutch economy, 1500–1815.* Cambridge: Cambridge University Press.

Waasdorp, A. (2016) 'Mijlpalen langs de kust. De weg tussen Naaldwijk en Leiden', in van der Heijden, P. (ed.) *Romeinse wegen in Nederland.* Utrecht: Matrijs, pp. 21–31.

Wagner, P. (2007) 'Legionen als Industrieunternehmer', *Archäologie im Rheinland*, 2006, pp. 112–114.

Ward-Perkins, B. (2005) *The fall of Rome and the end of civilization.* Oxford: Oxford University Press.

Waugh, K. E. (1998) *Germans beyond the limes: a reassessment of the archaeological evidence in the Limesvorland of southern Germania Inferior/Secunda.* PhD thesis, University of Durham.

Wegert, A. (2011) 'Studien zu den frühen Amphoren aus Neuss', *Kölner Jahrbuch*, 44, pp. 7–99.

Wegner, H.-H. (2007) 'Die Kelten an Mittelrhein und Mosel. Von ihren Anfängen bis zur römischen Eroberung', in Uelsberg, G. (ed.) *Krieg und Frieden. Kelten – Römer – Germanen.* Bonn: Rheinische Landesmuseum Bonn, pp. 59–71.

Weiss-König, S. (2014) 'Neue Untersuchungen zur Feinkeramik von De Holdeurn', in Liesen, B. (ed.) *Römische Keramik in Niedergermanien. Produktion – Handel – Gebrauch. Beiträge zur Tagung der Rei Cretariae Romanae Fautores. 21.–26. September 2014, LVR-RömerMuseum im Archäologischen Park Xanten.* (Xantener Berichte 27) Darmstadt: Philipp von Zabern, pp. 137–174.

Wendt, K. P. and Zimmermann, A. (2009) 'Transforming archaeological data between different geograpical scales – A GIS application for the estimation of population density', in Velho, A. and Kamermans, H. (eds) *Technology and methodology for archaeological practice. Practical applications for the past reconstruction.* (BAR International Series 2029) Oxford: Archaeopress, pp. 49–59.

Wendt, K. P. and Zimmermann, A. (2010) 'Zur Bevölkerungsdichte in den römischen Rheinlanden', in Aufleger, M. (ed.) *Braunkohlenarchäologie im Rheinland. Entwicklung von Kultur, Umwelt und Landschaft. Kolloquium der Stiftung zur Förderung der Archäologie im rheinischen Braunkohlenrevier in Brauweiler vom 5.–6. Oktober 2006.* Weilerswist: Verlag Ralf Liebe, pp. 87–90.

Wenzel, S. (2014) 'Vom Steinbruch zum Fernhafen. Untersuchungen zum Schwerlasttransport auf kleinen Gewässern', in Kennecke, H. (ed.) *Der Rhein als europäische Verkehrsachse. Die Römerzeit.* (Bonner Beiträge zur Vor- und Frühgeschichtlichen Archäologie 16) Bonn: Rheinische Friedrich-Wilhelms-Universität Bonn, pp. 229–257.

Werff, J. H. van der (1987) 'Roman amphoras at "De Horden" (Wijk bij Duurstede)', *Berichten van de Rijksdienst voor het Oudheidkundig Bodemonderzoek*, 37, pp. 153–172.

Werff, J. H. van der (2004) 'Amphoras from Vechten (excavations 1946–1947)', in Vermeulen, F., Kathy, S., and Dhaeze, W. (eds) *Archaeology in confrontation. Aspects of Roman military presence in the northwest. Studies in honour of Prof. em. Hugo Thoen.* (Archaeological Reports Ghent University 2) Ghent: Academia Press, pp. 287–304.

Werff, J. H. van der, Thoen, H. and van Dierendonck, R. M. (1997) 'Scheldevallei-amforen. Belgisch bier voor Bataven en Cananefaten?', *Handelingen der Maatschappij voor Geschiedenis en Oudheidkunde te Gent*, 51, pp. 1–19.

Wesselingh, D. A. (2000) *Native neighbours. Local settlement system and social structure in the Roman period at Oss (the Netherlands).* (Analecta Praehistorica Leidensia 32) Leiden: University of Leiden.

White, K. D. (1967) *Agricultural implements of the Roman world.* Cambridge: Cambridge University Press.

Whittaker, C. R. (1994) *Frontiers of the Roman Empire. A social and economic study.* (Ancient Society and History) Baltimore: The John Hopkins University Press.

Wiepking, C. G. (2000) 'Aardewerk', in Vos, W. K. (ed.) *Archeologisch onderzoek Houten-Zuid op terrein 8A*. (ADC Rapport 30) Bunschoten: Archeologisch Diensten Centrum, pp. 89–111.

Wiepking, C. G. (2001) 'Aardewerk', in Sier, M. and Koot, C. W. (eds) *Kesteren-De Woerd. Bewoningssporen uit de ijzertijd en de Romeinse tijd*. (Archeologie in de Betuweroute 3 = Rapportages Archeologische Monumentenzorg 82) Amersfoort: Rijksdienst voor het Oudheidkundig Bodemonderzoek, pp. 113–170.

Wierschowski, L. (1984) *Heer und Wirtschaft. Das römische Heer der Prinzipatszeit als Wirtschaftsfaktor*. (Habelts Dissertationsdrucke. Reihe Alte Geschichte 20) Bonn: Dr. Rudolf Habelt.

Wierschowski, L. (2001) 'Die römische Heeresversorgung im frühen Prinzipat', *Münstersche Beiträge zur Antiken Handelsgeschichte*, 20(2), pp. 37–61.

Wierschowski, L. (2002) 'Das römische Heer und die ökonomische Entwicklung Germaniens in den ersten Jahrzehnten des 1. Jahrhunderts', in *The Roman army and the economy*. Amsterdam: J.C. Gieben, pp. 264–292.

Wiethold, J. (1998) *Archäobotanische Aspekte der 'Romanisierung' in Südwestdeutschland. Bemerkungen zur Unkrautflora römerzeitlicher Dinkeläcker, Studien zur Archäologie der Kelten, Römer und Germanen in Mittel- und Westeuropa. Alfred Haffner zum 60. Geburtstag gewidmet*. (Studia Honoraria 4) Rahden/Westf.: Verlag Marie Leidorf.

Wiethold, J. (2000) 'Kontinuität und Wandel in der landwirtschaftlichen Produktion und Nahrungsmittelversorgung zwischen Spätlatènezeit und gallo-römischer Epoche. Archäobotanische Analysen in der römischen Großvillenanlage von Borg, Krs. Merzig-Wadern', in Haffner, A. and von Schurbein, S. (eds) *Kelten, Germanen, Römer im Mittelgebirgsraum zwischen Luxemburg und Thüringen. Archäologische und naturwissenschaftliche Forschungen zum Kulturwandel unter der Einwirkung Roms in den Jahrhunderten um Christi Geburt. Akten des Internationalen Kolloquiums*. (Kolloquien zur Vor-und Frühgeschichte 5) Bonn: Dr. Rudolf Habelt, pp. 147–159.

Wiethold, J. and Zech-Matterne, V. (2009) 'Pflanzliche Makroreste aus römischen Axialvillen im Saarland und in Lothringen: Ackerbau und Ernährung als Spiegel wirtschaftlicher Tätigkeiten', in *Die römischen Grossvillen vom Axialtyp. Internationale Tagung vom 26.03.2009 bis 28.03.2009, im Archäologiepark Römische Villa Borg*, pp. 21–22.

Wigg-Wolf, D. (2011) 'The function of Celtic coinages in northern Gaul', in Paz García-Bellido, M., Callegarin, L., and Jiménez Díaz, A. (eds) *Barter, money and coinage in the ancient Mediterranean (10th–1st centuries BC)*. (Anejos del Archivo Español de Arqueología 58) Madrid: Consejo Superior de Investigaciones Cientificas, pp. 301–314.

Willems, W. J. H. (1986) *Romans and Batavians. A regional study in the Dutch eastern river area*. PhD thesis, Universiteit van Amsterdam.

Willems, W. J. H. and van Enckevort, H. (2009) *Ulpia Noviomagus. Roman Nijmegen. The Batavian capital at the imperial frontier*. (Journal of Roman archaeology. Supplementary series 73) Portsmouth: Journal of Roman Archaeology.

Wilson, A. (2002) 'Machines, power and the ancient economy', *The Journal of Roman Studies*, 92, pp. 1–32.

Wilson, A. (2008) 'Large-scale manufacturing, standardization, and trade', in Oleson, J. P. (ed.) *The Oxford handbook of engineering and technology in the classical world*. Oxford: Oxford University Press, pp. 393–417.

Wilson, A. (2009a) 'Approaches to quantifying Roman trade', in Bowman, A. K. and Wilson, A. (eds) *Quantifying the Roman economy. Methods and problems*. (Oxford Studies on the Roman Economy) Oxford: Oxford University Press, pp. 213–249.

Wilson, A. (2009b) 'Indicators for Roman economic growth: a response to Walter Scheidel', *Journal of Roman Archaeology*, 22, pp. 71–82.

Winter, N. De (2019) 'Twee Romeinse pottenbakkersovens en een kuil met pottenbakkersafval aan de Astridlaan te Tongeren', *Signa*, 8, pp. 25–34.

Wirtz, R. (1998) *Die römische Töpferei Bastion Sterntor / St. Maria in Bonn. –Vergleichende Studie zu Töpferöfen für Gebrauchskeramik* -. PhD thesis, Universität zu Köln.

Wohlfarth, C. (1995) 'Römische Besiedlung im Raum Euskirchen am Beispiel der Erdgasstrasse Bonn-Euskirchen', *Archäologie im Rheinland*, 1994, pp. 64–66.

Wohlfarth, C. (1996) 'Euskirchen. Ausgrabungen, Funde und Befunde 1994', *Bonner Jahrbücher*, 196, pp. 586–588.

Wolters, R. (2000) *Die Römer in Germanien*. (C.H. Beck Wissen in der Beck'schen Reihe 2136) München: C.H. Beck.

Wood, J. W. (1998) 'A theory of preindustrial population dynamics, economy, and well-being in Malthusian systems', *Current Anthropology*, 39(1), pp. 99–135.

Woolf, G. (1993) 'Rethinking the Oppida', *Oxford Journal of Archaeology*, 12, pp. 223–234.

Woolf, G. (1998) *Becoming Roman. The origins of provincial civilization in Gaul*. Cambridge: Cambridge University Press.

Zanden, J. L. van (2002) 'The "revolt of the early modernists" and the "first modern economy": an assessment', *Economic History Review*, 55(4), pp. 619–641.

Zieling, N. (1995) 'Metallverarbeitung in der Colonia Ulpia Traiana', in Zelle, M. (ed.) *Tatort CUT. Die Spur führt nach Xanten. Ausstellung im Regionalmuseum Xanten vom 20. August bis 29. Oktober 1995*. (Führer und Schriften des Archäologischen Parks Xanten 17) Cologne: Rheinland-Verlag, pp. 65–70.

Zimmermann, A., Hilpert, J. and Wendt, K. P. (2009) 'Estimations of populations density for selected periods Between the Neolithic and AD 1800', *Human Biology*, 81(3), pp. 357–380.

Zuiderhoek, A. (2017) *The ancient city*. Cambridge: Cambridge Scholars Publishing.

Index of Geographical Names

Aachen 67, 114, 122*n*90, 128, 140–141, 147, 153–154, 160, 188, 196, 200
Ahrweiler 128
Alphen aan den Rijn 174
Alteburg 158, 174
Ardennes 22–24, 41, 87*n*72, 114, 116–117, 123, 127–128

Bad Münstereifel 122
Batavian area. *See Civitas Batavorum*
Bonn 121–122, 135, 141, 147–149, 153–154, 158, 160, 162, 179–181, 189, 196–197, 200
Braives 143–144, 160, 181–182
Brilon 124
Britannia 83, 119, 140, 143, 193–194, 196–200, 202, 233, 239

Civitas Batavorum 57–58, 61, 182, 212–213, 220–221
Civitas Cananefatium 58
Civitas Tungrorum 141*n*182, 143–145, 160, 181–182, 199–200
Colijnsplaat 193, 196–200
Cologne 40–41, 45, 66–67, 79, 85, 115–116, 121, 131, 133, 137–140, 142–144, 146–148, 152, 154–156, 160, 162–163, 174–177, 189, 190*n*114, 193, 196–197, 198*n*156, 199–200, 211, 228
Cuijk 39, 114, 147

De Holdeurn 135–136, 149
Den Haag-Wateringseveld 224
Domburg 193, 196–200
Dormagen 148, 199
Drachenfels 120–121
Düsseldorf 196, 200
Dutch North Sea coast 27, 41, 112–113, 197
Dutch River Area 26, 31, 41, 46, 57, 64, 67, 72*n*2, 76, 81*n*43, 82, 87–91, 95, 97, 99, 112–113, 151, 216–218, 224, 232

Eifel 22–24, 41, 76, 87*n*72, 112, 116–119, 122–128, 160
Elst 31, 218–219
Empel 31
Erftstadt 140

Ganuenta 199
Geldermalsen-Hondsgemet 182, 218–219
Gennep 114
German Rhineland 39, 43–44, 46, 70, 109, 112, 193
Germania Magna 167*n*12, 193–195, 233
Goch-Asperden 154

Halder 147
Hambach 68, 78, 83–85, 151, 154–156, 163, 211
Heerlen 67, 85, 140–141, 160, 162
High Fens 24, 123–125, 127, 160
Hoogeloon 94
Hürtgen forest 128
Huy 145

Iversheim. *See* Bad Münstereifel

Jülich 67, 76, 140–141, 154, 160, 162

Katwijk 66
Kessel 31
Kesteren-De Woerd 224
Königswinter-Oberpleis 124
Krefeld-Gellep 154–155, 158

Leiden 67
Leudersdorf 154
Liberchies 145, 154, 160
Lignite mining region 68, 78, 112, 155, 211
Limes road 66–67, 109
Loess region 24–25, 29–32, 41, 47–48, 59, 69, 76–78, 80–84, 98–99, 160, 208–212, 227–229, 232
Lommersdorf-Freilingen 128
Lower Rhine Plain 25–26, 59, 88, 93–94, 96, 100, 227, 232
Lüderich 124, 126, 127

Mariaweiler 160
Mayen 117–120
MDS region 25–26, 31, 41, 43–45, 48, 58, 67–68, 70, 76, 88, 93–94, 97, 224
Mechernich 124
Meuse 24, 26, 64, 143, 170, 192
Moers-Asberg 39, 135

Momalle 143
Mönchengladbach 142

Nettersheim 160
Neuss 116*n*56, 135, 148, 154, 158, 170, 172–173, 189
Nijmegen 39*n*21, 40–41, 66–67, 82, 91, 134*n*150, 135, 145–148, 150*n*252, 152*n*269, 153, 158–159, 162, 170–172, 189, 196, 199–200
North Sea 22, 63–66, 142, 196–198

Oss-Westerveld 224

Remagen 121, 135, 158
Rhine 1, 22, 24, 26, 32–33, 63–64, 99, 117, 119, 121, 139, 142–143, 146, 154–155, 162, 170, 176, 181, 192, 194
Rijswijk de Bult 224
Rimburg 142

Sambre 143
Sinzig 142, 148, 162, 188
Soller 140, 142–143, 162–163, 180, 193
Stolberg 124, 160

Theux 160
Tiel-Passewaaij 91–93, 95, 218–219, 223
Tienen 67, 144, 154, 160, 162
Tongeren 40–41, 66–67, 79, 81, 94, 144–145, 160, 162, 189, 192

Valkenburg 158, 189
Vechten 66, 76, 82–83, 112, 121, 174, 189, 196, 198, 200
Venlo 66, 147, 149
Verviers 124
Vervoz 143–144, 160, 163
Via Agrippa 66–67
Via Belgica 66–68, 139–140, 143–144, 154, 162, 181
Voorburg 40, 58, 64, 67, 112, 147, 160

Western Dutch River delta 26, 41, 58, 88, 93, 96–97, 100, 114, 227, 232
Wijk bij Duurstede-De Horden 95, 218–219
Woerden 83, 148, 166, 174

Xanten 40, 41, 66–67, 112, 121–122, 135, 145–149, 154, 159, 162, 174, 177–179, 189

Zülpich 66–67
Zwammerdam 158

Index of Subjects

Aggregate economic growth 5*n*24, 13–14, 17–19, 43, 73, 204, 230, 235–237
Agriculture 11–12, 24–25, 27–28, 30–32, 72–101, 155, 195, 212, 231–233, 236
Amphorae 60, 62, 135, 144, 146, 166–183, 193, 201–203
Animal husbandry 26, 28–32, 77, 80–82, 87–94, 97–100, 232
Animal size 81–82, 90–91, 99–100
Arable farming 18, 24–32, 74–81, 86–87, 90, 94, 98–100, 232
Army supply. *See* Military and state demand

Building material 24, 29, 77*n*17, 86, 108–109, 112–116, 117*n*63, 119–121, 124, 157, 207, 209–212, 227–228. *See also* Ceramic building material

Central places 29, 31–32, 34, 40–41, 57, 58*n*91, 69, 100, 155, 160–161, 174
Ceramic building material 62, 132, 147–150, 161, 207, 209
Ceramics 105–107, 131–147, 161–163, 166, 193, 197, 200, 222–229, 233, 235
Civilian production 115, 118, 120, 122, 126, 129–131, 136–147, 150, 152, 154–156, 158–162, 232–233, 235
Climate 18, 27, 37, 74–75, 98, 155, 169, 239
Clustering 106, 128, 139, 144, 163
Coinage. *See* Monetisation
Crop growing. *See* Arable farming
Craftworking. *See* Household production

Diminishing marginal returns 10, 12, 17–18, 73
Division of labour 12, 18–19, 31, 40, 118–119, 131, 164–165, 201, 232–233, 235
Draught animals 80–81, 88, 90, 94

Economies of scale 12, 18, 103–104, 163–164, 232
Exchange. *See* Trade
Extensification 73–74, 98
Extramural settlements 38–39, 40*n*31, 41, 231

Factors of production 10, 11*n*59, 17–18, 73–74
Fortifications. *See* Military settlements
Free market trade 4, 164–165, 169–170, 183, 199, 203

Glass 151–156, 162–163, 166, 233
Granaries 83–85, 95–96, 99–100

Handmade pottery 106, 131, 133–134, 222–229, 233, 235
Harbours 64, 112–113, 147
Housebuilding 29–30, 77*n*17, 86, 89, 94, 150, 206–213, 227–228, 234
Household production 29, 105, 130–131, 133, 161

Import replacement 19, 181, 202, 234
Industry. *See* Civilian production and Military production
Inequality 14–15, 204–205, 210, 213
Infrastructure 24, 41, 58, 62–69, 71, 109, 137, 162, 195, 200–201, 230–231
Institutions 8, 18–19, 33, 50–62, 69–70, 200
Intensification 11–12, 73–75, 87, 90–91, 98–99, 104, 123, 125, 231

Local trade. *See* Regional trade
Long-distance trade 31, 83, 112–113, 116–117, 119, 125, 126, 130, 134–135, 140, 143, 146, 149, 151–152, 155, 165–195, 197–198, 201–203, 233–234
Living standards 11, 14–15, 19, 204–229, 230, 234, 237–238

Malthus 10–14, 204, 237, 239
Manufacturing. *See* Civilian production and Military production
Metal 24, 31, 107, 123–130, 157–161, 163, 166, 232–233
Metal objects 57, 157–158, 206, 214–221, 228, 234
Military and state demand 36–39, 62, 69, 71, 80, 83, 89, 91, 100, 109, 115–116, 123, 127–129, 131, 134–135, 147, 154, 168–169, 174, 191–192, 201–203, 230, 232, 234

Military presence 33–36, 39, 69, 216, 230
Military production 72*n*2, 106–107, 115, 118, 120–122, 126–127, 129–131, 134–136, 147–150, 153, 158, 161–162, 232–233, 235–236
Military settlements 33–36, 38–39, 41, 57, 59, 69, 82, 109, 114, 116, 119, 133, 135, 147–149, 154, 158, 174, 189, 193, 200
Millstones 116–119
Modes of production 105–107, 129–130, 162–163, 203
Monetisation 29, 38, 52–59, 70, 89

Negotiatores 82, 115, 197–200

Per capita economic growth 5, 11–14, 17–19, 39, 73–74, 102–103, 164, 204–205, 230–232, 236–238
Pollen 28, 72*n*2, 73, 75–76, 98, 112
Population growth 5*n*24, 9*n*50, 10–14, 18–19, 41–49, 69–70, 200–201, 231, 235, 237
Portable material culture 82, 94, 100, 104, 206, 214–229, 234
Pottery. *See* Ceramics

Redistribution 164–165, 169–170, 183, 199, 203
Regional trade 59, 82–83, 94, 100, 114–115, 116, 121, 125–126, 141, 145–146, 154–155, 167, 220, 222, 228, 233
Roads 63, 66–68, 71, 109, 114, 143
Rural settlements 29–30, 32, 46–49, 57–59, 70, 82, 86, 90, 94, 100, 104, 109, 116, 133, 137, 154, 160–161, 163, 181–183, 209, 211, 218–220, 222–229, 231, 233–235

Secondary agglomerations 34, 40–41, 59, 109, 116, 128, 159
Ships 65–66, 71, 83, 99, 113, 166, 197–198
Soldiers pay 37–38
Specialisation 12, 18, 40, 74, 78, 80, 81*n*43, 90–92, 98–100, 102–106, 115, 119, 131, 137, 144, 154, 157, 161–162, 165*n*4, 196, 197, 199, 201, 203, 228, 232–235
Spelt 78–80, 98
Stone 24, 31, 107, 115–122, 129, 232
Subsistence farming 28, 32–33, 37, 59, 69, 72–73, 77, 80, 87, 98, 230–231, 233, 235
Surplus production 12, 30, 51–52, 59, 70, 77–78, 82–85, 87, 89, 92, 94–101, 104, 106, 194, 211–212, 223, 228–229, 231–232

Taxation 5, 37, 50–52, 70, 103–104, 164, 165*n*4, 231, 237
Technical progress 11–12, 74
Technological innovation 5, 11, 17–19, 74, 79, 87, 98, 105–106, 108, 118–119, 123, 127, 129, 144, 157, 161, 163, 232, 235
Terra sigillata 141–142, 183–193, 202–203, 234
Total factor productivity. *See* Technical progress
Trade 4–5, 18–19, 29, 32, 35–36, 39, 50–54, 60, 63, 69–71, 102, 230–231, 233–234, 236, 238. *See also* Long-distance trade and Regional trade
Traders 82–83, 106, 115, 129, 196–200, 203, 234
Transaction costs 8, 18, 52, 60, 63, 71, 139, 163, 231
Transport 24, 36, 63–66, 68, 83, 99, 113–117, 121, 143, 165, 169–170, 193, 198
Transport costs 37, 62–63, 71, 115, 116*n*53, 119, 137, 147, 152, 157*n*295, 170, 183, 187, 202, 209, 212, 231

Urban settlements 39–43, 57, 59, 69, 82, 109, 115–116, 119–120, 129, 131, 133, 136–137, 150, 154, 158, 160, 162, 211, 220, 231, 233–234
Urbanisation 19, 39–43, 69–70, 73, 102*n*1, 200, 231

Vallus 79–80, 98
Veterans 38–39, 79, 82*n*48, 91, 94*n*108, 211–213, 219–221, 228, 234, 237
Vexillationes 115, 120–122, 148
Villas 77–78, 82, 84–86, 94, 98–99, 119, 128, 150, 161, 207–213, 228, 232, 234

Wheel-thrown pottery 106, 131*n*140, 133, 222–229, 233, 235
Wood 24, 31, 76, 108–115, 129–130, 155, 199–200, 232